AF519266

Elections
in
Jammu and Kashmir

Elections in Jammu and Kashmir

G.N. Gauhar
Former District & Session Judge

Manas Publications
New Delhi-110 002 (INDIA)

MANAS PUBLICATIONS
(Publishers, Distributors, Importers & Exporters)
4819,Varun House, Mathur Lane,
24, Ansari Road, Darya Ganj,
New Delhi - 110 002 (INDIA)
Ph.: 3260783, 3265523, 7131660
Fax: 011 - 3272766
E-mail: manaspublications@vsnl.com

First Published 2002

ISBN 81-7049-105-3

Typeset at
Manas Publications

Printed in India at
R.K. Offset, Delhi
and Published by Mrs. Suman Lata for
Manas Publications, 4819/XI, Varun House,
Mathur Lane, 24, Ansari Road, Daryaganj
New Delhi 110002 (INDIA)

Dedication

To my grandchildren
Rahique-um-Makhtoom,
Saleh Fayaz, Malik Amir
with the sincere hope that they are able to realise the dream which my father Haji M.A. Muquiem saw in his mid thirties on13 July 1931; which I nourished for six decades and which led my son Shahwar to wander from despair to hope, from confrontration to compromise.

Contents

Part II

Elections to Six Parliamentary Seats from J&K 1967-1999

Preface

This book on the contemporary political history of Jammu and Kashmir bears continuity with my earlier two books. I had little inclination for history, but remained consciously involved with political developments from my childhood. Therefore, my novels, essays and poetry reflect my leanings. As a teenager I took to Kashmiri poetry, but recognition was conferred upon me as a novelist. In view of the very limited existence of fiction in my mother tongue, I decided to achieve distinction as a pioneer novelist, so, curbed the poet within me. But due to my family environment I had to cultivate a commitment to edit with authenticity, the vast stock of verse of the 14th Century saint and patriotic poet Sheikh Noor-Ud-Din Wali, Nund Rishi. This ambition was nourished by the fact that my grandfather G.M. Muqiem had left a stock of manuscripts, mainly in Persian and Kashmiri languages relating to the life and teachings of the saint. My father Haji M.A. Muqiem Sahib preserved the stock and added to it. He encouraged me to work on it and himself introduced me to the intricacies of the mystic Rishi cult. On the basis of two decades of research I wrote a monograph for the Sahitya Akademi, New Delhi on the saint under the title 'Makers of Indian Literature'. Subsequently, this academy assigned me to write another monograph under the same series on Abdul Ahad Azad the revolutionary poet, researcher and critic of Kashmir. Both these books cultivated within me the urge to dedicate myself to literary history, mystic thought and literary criticism.

Literary history holds a connection with social, political and cultural history and all these streams owe their origin to the history of a nation. Simultaneously, the two books written earlier for Sahitya Akademi provided me with confidence that I could express myself in English. I found that the contemporary history of Kashmir had been written with biased views or in a propagandist manner which mainly served the purpose of lobbying for the two contenders for Kashmir viz. India and Pakistan. Even foreign scholars were under the influence of one or the other. Local writers kept record of events, but did not dare to publish for political reasons and due to fear of administrative vindictiveness. There are some works which can be called 'daring' contributions but those authors have also subjected themselves to restraints. Their narration is greatly marred by a sort of self censor or by transparent carerist ambitions.

In October (1993) I was nominated a Truste of J&K Muslim Auqaf Trust which manages affairs of Hazratbal. In the same week Hazratbal mosque housing the Holy Relic was occupied by militants and hence military siege. I was involved in the settlement process created by this imbroglio. During 1958-60, as a lawyer, I was engaged as a defense counsel of the famous Hazratbal murder case. In both these positions I gathered much knowledge about this holy place and so wrote a book entitled *Hazratbal—The Central Stage of Kashmir Politics*" (New Delhi: Virgo Publishers). Before that book went to the press, my home town Charar-i-Sharief fell under insurgency and military siege. A chapter under the heading 'Aasar-e-Sharif (Hazratbal) to Charar-i-Sharief' became relevant, but the siege of Charar-i-Sharief finally resulted in the complete destruction of the town and so I wrote another book *Military Operation in Kashmir and Insurgency* in Charar-i-Sharief"(New Delhi: Manas Publishers). During the siege and after this destruction the Indian Government, the media and national parties all expressed the view that the insurgency at Charar-i-Sharief was meant to sabotage the overdue election process in Jammu and Kashmir so a discussion on the nature of elections became not only relevant but essential too.The three books, therefore, bear a common link whilst analysing the socio-political life of Jammu and Kashmir.

The reader will feel paucity of details, but if I discuss all the facets of every election then the history of elections in Jammu and Kashmir shall cover at least 12 volumes; 9 volumes for assembly elections, 2 volumes for parliamentary elections and 1 volume on discussions on Indo-Kashmir consittutional relationship. Recently Prof. Bhim Singh has come with a volume on his election covering only one constituency and that too confining to a single election.

I have said earlier that it is very daring to embark upon contemporary history—that too about Kashmir where truth has been the first casualty. A writer is unprotected and becomes a victim of various types of displeasure which result in annoyance and where 'those annoyed' are powerful enough to eliminate a person physically; it is an adventure which I am knowingly embarking upon thereby inviting risks. Readers will find that there is objective assessment of matters in these three books which can invite any reaction from concerned quarters. If one becomes too sensitive to consequences which might follow then reality will be buried in the debris of confusion. As victims of this history, hence, the woeful narration of a people who for a full century remained sandwiched inbetween hope and despair, trust and alienation, compromises and confrontations and who urged to be led properly, but found themselves treacherously misled. A verse by Persian poet Urfi Shirazi depicts the intensity of my thirst and ultimate deception created by mirages. It was neither the successful wisdom of those who deceived nor defect in the wisdom of the deceived. I quote the verse, as translated into English by the great poet of the subcontinent, Dr. Sir Iqbal:

> *"It is thine imperfect thirst, nor Thy wisdom*
> *If thee are not deceived by mirages."*

We had perfect thirst, so could not distinguish between a spring of pure and sweet water and a mirage which, in the wilderness of a desert looked more attractive than a spring.

This book introduces the reader to the genuine urge of the people of this unfortunate region misruled for centuries, to have responsible governance accountable to the people. The volcano did burst in 1931 which forced the autocracy to make compromises in this regard so, from 1934 to the end of 1946, several exercises in the name of elections were conducted which though limited yet amounted to a process of surrender before the will of the people. Partition of the subcontinent and its independence threw this region into worse confusion which had both the elements of victory and defeat.

It is in the context of whether its urge for responsible governance met encouragement or frustration that this book gives importance to the first ever exercise in the name of elections conducted for a feudal type of rural office- the Zaildar in 1949, two years after the installation of the rule qualified as 'rule by popular leadership'. It is followed by discussions on the election of the first ever Constituent Assembly and then the topic of drafting of the J&K Constitution became a relevant part of our discussions. The so called 'popularity' of the leadership is described in relation to these three hustings: the election of the Praja Sabha in 1946, the Zaildar election and 'selection' of constitution givers. The first part covers all the elections held to J&K Legislative Assembly from 1957 to 1996.

The second part deals with the representation from Jammu and Kashmir in the Indian Constituent Assembly and for the first three Indian Parliaments. We cannot proceed without an expression of J.K. people's contention about topics such as: the nature of interference by Pakistan aided Pathans in the state in 1947; how they view the declaration of Azad Jammu & Kashmir; and how they view the nature of accession entered into by the Maharaja of Kashmir with India. The statements of the only two witnesses of the event have been sifted after comparative study of the two depositions as contained in the autobiographies of Meharchand Mahajan and Sheikh Abdulla. This topic involved this treatise with a precise discussion on the paramounty of the state and about the nature of the drama of accession which Lt. Gen. Chibber refers to in *Pakistan's Criminal Folly in J&K.* In the light of the Cabinet Mission Memorandum and the decisions arrived at between the

Chamber of Princes and Concerned Committee of Constituent Assembly this book, for the first time, brings under its purview of discussion, the patent disabilities in the representation given to Jammu and Kashmir in constitution making of India and so its consequences are also discussed. The first three Indian Parliaments were not represented directly or indirectly by elected representatives of Jammu and Kashmir. This topic has a bearing upon the legislation made centrally for this state which could not be by-passed; the Presidential (Constitutional) Application Orders have also come within the purview of the book. Delimitation of six parliamentary constituencies in 1966 and elections of these six seats from 1967 to 1999 have been discussed as have been the Autonomy Resolution of J&K Assembly June 2000, its summary dismissal by the Indian Government followed by enthusiasm showed by Indian Government circles on unilateral cease-fire offer of the Hizb-ul-Mujahidin and the lessons learnt from these two successive events. In the Epilogue, I have touched the representative nature of all political parties in Jammu and Kashmir to be or not to be involved with any tripartite proposed deliberations. We should be sensitive enough to feel the admonishments of history in that context. It is suggested that no representation in the final settlement be imposed; democratically chosen representation can prove a more convenient exercise of self determination ushering in an era of peace, tranquility and prosperity in the entire subcontinent including Jammu & Kashmir. This method can serve both purposes - peace for the subcontinent and respect for the Kashmiri ego.

Special references made to Charar-e-Sharief electoral segment in this book provides an appropriate illustration. Further, as destruction of Charar-e-Sharief has formed the background so a special mention of that town or that constituency has become unavoidable.

Last, I am thankful to all authors, editors or contributors to newsapers, journals and magazines whom I have referred to or quoted in the book. I am equally thankful to all personalities who have come under discussion in this book. Publishers also deserve my thanks.

G.N. Gauhar

Abbreviations

ANC	Awami National Conference (J&K)
APHC	All Parties Hurriyat Conference
BJP	Bhartiya Janata Party
BSF	Border Security Force
CJ	Chief Justice
CEC	Chief Election Commissioner
DNC	Democratic National Conference (J&K)
Cong (I)	Congress Indira
Cong (T)	All India National Congress (Tiwari Group)
CM	Chief Minister
CRPF	Central Reserve Police Force.
HM	Hizb-ul Mujahideen.
HA	Harkatul Ansar
IB	Intelligence Bureau
IAS	Indian Administrative Service
IPS	Indian Police Service
JK	Jammu & Kashmir
JKLF	Jammu and Kashmir Liberation Front
LoC	Line of Control
MLA	Member Legislative Assembly
MC	Muslim Conference (J&K)
MUF	Muslim United Front
NC	National Conference (J&K)
NC(K)	National Conference (Khalida)
PAK	Pakistan Administered Kashmir
PSP	Praja Socialist Party
PM	Prime Minister
PMO	Pdrime Minister Office
RO	Returning Officer

Part I

Praja Sabha, Constituent and Legislative Assemblies

Chapter 1

Introduction

A comparative study of the history of various nations and sub-nations who fought for basic human rights during this century, will reveal that the war fought by the people of Jammu and Kashmir to achieve the goal of self-respect proved a long drawn battle and has so far been futile.

In 1934 (the year of birth of this author) this right was conceded, but so far remains only a mirage.

The word 'rigging' hardly conveys the type of gimmicks played in Jammu and Kashmir in the name of elections. In the subcontinent and elsewhere in the democratic world this word conveys the erosion of norms, irregularities committed during the hustings or may even include the capturing of the polling booths; attacks on counting centres; snatching of ballot boxes; fatal attacks on candidates, proposers or sympathisers of candidates; abduction of candidates or even arson and plunder of localities sympathetically inclined towards the opposition candidates. But 'rigging' is not an appropriate term which can to a lesser extent, encompass within its ambit the 'conduct of elections' in Jammu and Kashmir Therefore, we consciously avoid use of this word in reference to the frauds perpetuated in the name of elections in Jammu and Kashmir. Our contention is fortified by the statement of Krishnamurthy, Election Commissioner of India, who stated in Srinagar after the 1996 poll "We did not receive so far any complaint explaining rigging". He was correct in so far as the games played in Jammu and Kashmir in the name of elections can hardly be described in the phraseology which is known to Representation Of the Peoples Acts of India and Jammu and Kashmir and which can be conveyed by prevalent lexicon.

We are basing our discussions mainly on the assessment of the general public. This author acknowledges with gratitude the advice which was given to him in 1954 (then a teenaged boy) by Ashoka Mehta one of the mature politicians of the socialist movement in India. As a result of his advice instead of collecting material from libraries and reading rooms, I collected it from discussions in passenger buses, compounds of shrines or the gossip which takes place in our social functions. One such incident forms part of my personal diary recorded on 12 April 1996. Passengers of a bus in which this author travelled during the journey were busy discussing the impending elections in Jammu and Kashmir. One of the travellers, a witty and humorous villager summed up the discussion, but in rustic and rough phraseology.

The moral of that pornographic folk tale which the villager narrated is quoted in minute detail: A bewildered bride after returning from her honeymoon enquired as to "when her marriage was to be performed?" When told that the honeymoon which she had just had meant that the marriage had really taken place, she retorted in surprise

"Why did we celebrate a lengthy *hangama* in our house for a full year, I am used to it." Nabir Bhat, the traveller in the rural bus concluded, "What for this *hangama*? we are used to it."

The humorous villager indirectly conveyed that 'we have been experiencing such frauds to which we are being subjected once again'. The passengers did not smile as they should have done, but their pensive long faces spoke volumes about the collective agony of this nation. With this background in mind let us describe elections in Jammu and Kashmir.

Chapter 2

Selection to Introduce Election

The blood of martyrs who laid down their lives for the holy cause of Quran consolidated the foundation of the people's movement for a welfare society. These sacrifices and the mood of the Muslims of Kashmir provided cause for the English rulers of India to persuade and even pressurise the state monarch to concede to the genuine demand for a rule which would possess at least a semblance of representative character. Hence, the appointment of the Constitutional Reforms Commission was initiated in 1932. It approved a report drafted by Bertland J Glancy which recommended the establishment of an assembly, representative in nature and free in its legislative powers. Further, it was proposed that such an assembly, would exercise fiscal control. The report recommended creation of a Legislative Assembly which would consist of 60 non-official members of whom only 33 would be elected and others would be nominees of the ruler.

According to this report only 10 per cent of the total population constituted the electoral college which was privileged to exercise right of vote. They included persons:

1. Who were levied land revenue amounting to Rs 20 per year.
2. Who possessed immovable property worth not less than Rs 1000 in value.
3. Members of the legal and medical professions.
4. Who received government pension of not less than Rs 20 per month.
5. Who paid municipal taxes upto not less than Rs 20 per month.
6. Zaildars, Namberdars and Safeed Poshes.
7. Who were assignees of jagirs and pattas not less than Rs 50 per year.
8. Who had received standard education.

In consequence, an act came into being which is called 'J&K Constitution Act 1934'. It provided an Assembly which according to section 14 of this document was constituted of both nominated and elected members. The total number of non-elected members was 42 including ministers, officially nominated and 16 state councillors summoned by name by His Highness for the constituencies and communities specified in Schedule II. The number of ministers and officers nominated by the Maharaja did not exceed 12. The number of elected members was confined to the figure 33. Thus the total strength of the house consisted in all of 75 members.

Schedule II

(see Section 14)

Constituencies for which members shall be nominated

No. of Members	Constituency	Community
1	to be nominated by His Highness	
2	Ladakh Wazarat	Buddhist
1	Skardu Tehsil	Muslim
1	Kargil Tehsil	Muslim
1	Gilgit Wazarat	Muslim
1	North Kashmir Wazarat	Muslim
1	South Kashmir Wazarat	Muslim
1	Muzaffarabad Wazarat	Muslim
1	Jammu Wazarat	Hindu (Megh)
1	Udhampur Wazarat	Hindu (Megh)
1	Srinagar City	Hindu other than Kashmiri Pandit
1	i) Wazarat: Jammu, Udhampur, Reasi Kashmir South and Sri Pratap Singh Pora Tehsil	Sikh
1	(ii) to be nominated by His Highness on the recommendation of Ilaqadar of Poonch	Hindu
1	iii) to be nominated by His Highness on the recommendation of Ilaqadar of Chanani	Hindu

These nominations were intended to guarantee an indirect representation for such sections of the population which could not, ordinarily, be otherwise represented. It is also manifest that the majority consisted of unelected members who were nominated by His Highness, the Maharaja and owed their loyalty to him. A limited number of less than half was elected by only ten per cent of the total population and so its importance and impact can well be imagined. To quote from Alistair Lamb's *Kashmir—A Disputed Legacy:*

> "In 1934 franchise was restricted to village and district headmen, priests, managers of religious property, holders of titles, those who paid Rs 20 either as land revenue or municipal tax or Rs 60 as rent, those who owned a house worth Rs 600 or more, medical practitioners, pensioned officers and those who had passed the middle school examination or equivalent. Women in general were excluded except those with required educational qualifications. It was intended to enfranchise about 10 percent of the adult population but, in practice it gave vote to 3 percent or less."

Those 3 per cent voters mainly belonged to the section which by its nature owed allegiance to the Maharaja and his officers and so were more loyal than the king. Nonetheless, this exercise in the name of elections introduced the concept of franchise and made people conscious of their right to vote. Hence, the election can well be qualified as 'introduction for Election of Representatives.'

It is pertinent to reproduce the reaction of the president of the Muslim Conference Sheikh Mohammad Abdulla. This organisation had agitated for the cause of responsible government so his comments made on January 29, 1934 conveyed the sentiment of the elite. He said:

> "The people of this country did not shed their blood for such a mock-show."

But, for common people this concession amounted to the process of erosion of autocracy which was the theme of the common whispers.

Chapter 3

Election for Limited Participation

The ineffective Praja Sabha (Assembly) constituted under the Constitution Act 1934 created awareness among the ruled that they should be associated with moulding of their own destiny and should have the right to participate as loyal subjects of the Maharaja with his administration. Hence, under the increasing internal and external pressures on the monarch the lame constitution of 1934 was abrogated and based on the model of Government of India Act 1935, the Maharaja promulgated a new constitution for J&K. In reality all such powers enshrined therein were meant to strengthen the authority of the ruler, however, limited participation was allowed. The legislature was not made accountable to the electorate, but to the ruler who in a strict sense retained for himself the right to nominate half of the members of the legislative body. Out of a total membership of 75 only 40 were elected. Though the formation of constituencies was considered a step towards communalisation of Kashmir politics, but in view of utter backwardness of certain sections of the population the measure proved a necessary evil. Inspite of the limited character of this assembly its constitution created, at least, within cities and bigger towns a sort of aspiration for an accountable administration and allowed nourishing of the thinking (contrary to the age old belief that kings are part of His Divine Being) that the people share the 'absolute' authority to mould their destiny.

In my native town Charar-i-Sharief the most politically conscious in the whole tehsil of Sri Pratap Singh Pora (as Budgam tehsil was then called) there was not even a limited section of people who had witnessed electoral activity.

It is pertinent here to give the gist of Section 14 of Act No. I of 1991 (Bik) which had come into force on 7th of Baisakh 1991 corresponding to 19 April 1934. In previous chapter salient features of this Act have been discussed, but the summary of Section 14 will explain to our readers the inferences we have drawn. The section reads:

> "Sec 14: Total number of non-elected members shall include the ministers for the time being and by virtue of their office and 16 state council members appointed by name by his highness for a period of 4 1/2 years. Members nominated by his highness for the communities specified in the attached Schedule. The number of officials nominated shall not exceed 12 including ministers. The elected members shall be elected from the communities specified in Jammu and Kashmir Assembly Electoral Regulators issued by endorsement No: P.B. 157 of 5 March.........

References about the Constitution Act of 1934 and discussions on the elections held under the said act show that such initial exercises of democratisation churned the public opinion, eroded the deep rooted overawing threats of autocracy and created an urge to have maximum involvement with the governance as loyal subjects of the monarch.

Chapter 4

Election: The Game of Hide and Seek

At the dawn of India's independence (end 1946) the Maharaja of Kashmir envisaged fresh elections to the Praja Sabha. This was the time when the ill advised and ill managed Quit Kashmir Movement had faded not due to the pressure exerted by autocratic tyranny, but due to the changed political scenario in the subcontinent. The champions of this movement were either convicted and punished or some of them were busy in the market of the subcontinent to pawn their future loyalties, or were hiding sometimes in decorated drawing rooms of local Khawajas or in poor huts in and around the areas of Dal and Anchar Lakes or were busy repenting for the follies their leadership had committed by subjecting the nation to an unnecessary chain of vissicitudes and so they had disassociated themselves both from the movement and organisation.

The revived Muslim Conference was initially led by the mass response which the slogan of Quit Kashmir gathered and so some cadres of that organisation did 'energetically participate in demonstrations'. R.C. Kak, the then Prime Minister of Jammu and Kashmir had by his 'clear understanding' made some sections in both these organisations realise the futility of the Quit Kashmir agitation at the time when the sun of the British Raj in the subcontinent was setting. He sold the idea that Sheikh Abdulla had defied the unanimous decision of his working committee to raise the slogan only to 'placate' external interests, which in his estimation was established by subsequent events in and around Jammu and Kashmir. But the National Conference propaganda against R.C. Kak had swayed public opinion.

The J&K National Conference had four distinctions and so threw other organisations and more so, the J&K Muslim Conference in the background. These include:

1. it had attracted to its ranks both highly qualified and highly rustic people
2. it had enunciated a radical programme, wrapped in religions slogans
3. it had overawed the masses and opponents with muscle power
4. it possessed the unique craft of whisper campaigns which had the effect of immediate character assassination

R.C. Kak was painted as a demon, who, even if he behaved like an angel would hardly be believed. In this competition of contradictory policies R.C. Kak had a scheme to attribute to himself the future decisive role and so needed to keep the National Conference out of the mainstream. In doing so, he had to carry a section of the populace with him; had to play such gimmicks which would provide a cover to his policies; and had to act in a specific manner to derive such benefits from the election. Hence, the manipulation by him of the hustings provided a reasonable pretext to the National Conference to boycott those elections. These policies of the administration justified the boycott decision of J&K National Conference. It came like a heaven sent blessing for the Conference which had created 'goodwill' mainly through manpower, propaganda and by enticing slogans that it was the 'only political force' in J&K. The support which the Quit Kashmir Movement gathered upto the end of August 1946 and the spontaneous response which the people gave to this adventurous slogan had faded rather vanished by the end of 1946. The changing scenario in the subcontinent and drastic changes at the international level had convinced the majority about the futility of the sacrifices which the nation had made for those eighteen months. The common rural population was neither moved by the 'charisma' of this slogan nor were they conscious of its failures. However, among the urban populace even a large section of the fans of Sheikh (who call themselves 'sheres' and are nicknamed by opponents as 'gadas') too had become fed up with this movement which they dubbed as an aimless adventure (*fazool hungama*). Hence, the National Conference found a pretext in the detention of its leadership and so boycotted the election. Had they participated it would have emerged only as the 'majority party' in the Valley and only a bigger group at the state level. The reasons are:

1. in Kashmir the people whose kith and kin had died or suffered imprisonment would naturally challenge the wisdom to fight elections for a house which protected the authority of a 'leasee' against whom the organisation had fought
2. both among Kashmiri and Jammu Muslims the active involvement of the National Conference with the Indian National Congress was bound to go against its electoral interest
3. elections had no relevance except to a limited group of 'emancipated' lovers of democracy
4. Kashmiri Pandits had both historical and other reasons to go against such an organisation which inspite of its secular pretensions appeared to them to be an organisation of the majority and for the interest of the majority. For Jammu Dogras, this organisation had spread only venom against 'Dogra Rule' and so they hated it
5. in Poonch, Mirpur and Rajouri the ex-servicemen and their families were all pro Pakistan and so were opposed to an organisation which had sworn enmity with the All India Muslim League—the champion for the cause of Pakistan
6. in frontier Wazarats, i.e., Ladhakh, Kargil, Baltistan, Askardo and Gilgit the National Conference had no influence at all.

The J&K Muslim Conference too had its limitations. It had no cadre based organisation; leadership in the Valley was dominated by sycophants of the Molvi dynasty of whom the dominant feature was to remain committed to the interest of Mirwaiz's office rather than to political principles. It had no economic programme even to the limited extent of countering the image which the document of 'Naya Kashmir', the manifesto for National Conference had created. It lacked both propaganda machinery and muscle power. It was a house divided into two distinct and distinguishable compartments—the Kashmir leadership and Jammu leadership. The former had intentions to impose the grip of traditional 'waaz' which modern rhetoric had thrown into the background. In the estimation of modern Muslim intellectuals the waaz (professional sermons) overburdened with fables and anecdotes had severed Muslims from their history and so had made them inactive. The fans of waaz and 'waiz' (preacher) had made this organisation subservient to the politics of waaz.

The Jammu Muslim Conference was also divided into two sections. One had a clear cut pro-Pak policy, but the other approved the idea of an independent Kashmir.

Hence, the Muslim Conference too had its game plan, to see the National Conference out of the hustings. The Mirwaiz group in Srinagar too contributed later on to the boycott policy as papers of its nominees were rejected.

These three contributory factors eroded the sanctity of elections. In this game of hide and seek the budding faith in the system of elections got a fatal jolt. It nipped in the bud the aspirations to mould the destiny with collective but free will. However, the boycott policy of the National Conference did not affect the participation of the conscious voters though it affected results to some extent.

The government had no compulsion to announce the holding of elections at a time when its very authority was challenged and when such elements which constituted a political force were imprisoned. Such a decision could be a welcome step had it been preceded by parleys between the available leadership of the National Conference and the representatives of the state. Similarly, the J&K Muslim Conference would have emerged stronger (in the estimation of posterity) had it forced conditions for the state to persuade the available leadership of the National Conference to participate, at least, in the parleys with the government. Similarly, the National Conference could have emerged stronger had it boycotted the elections on a different ground—that the organisation was not ready to yield on principles as they had challenged the authority of the ruler. On the other hand, they got themselves belittled by adopting the untenable pretext of the detention and imprisonment of their leadership. It appeared that under the pretext of non-participation in elections they avoided the logical consequences of their ill advised and ill devised agitation and adopted tactics to influence the authorities for release of their leaders and workers.

Whatever the pulls and counter pulls which worked with all the three parties, it came to the surface that the advisors of the Maharaja who came from outside facilitated participation of people in these elections. On the other hand, the local advisors created a tradition of erosion before the fairness in elections could become transparent.

One aspect is clear, that inspite of the tainted system the state had an assembly established under the Constitution of which the majority consisted of elected members. Secondly, it was also clear that there existed no way to measure the popularity of a leader or a party except by its role in elections and by the performance it made during the hustings.

The division of opinion which this limited election reflected shows that no party or leader had overall popularity in the state. Had voters on the other hand, boycotted the election, that decision would have amounted to approval of the National Conference policy and simultaneously, would have provided support to the Mirwaiz faction of the Muslim Conference.[1]

Notes

1. The list of elected members is given in part II, Chapter 19, titled: "Representation From J & K in Indian Consituent Assembly".

Chapter 5

The Crude Rehearsal

Certain offices had, during Dogra rule, become symbols of repression and one such notorious position vested in the Zaildar. The village officers included one or two menials as 'dooms,' one among them was designated as chowkidar who could be deemed as an inferior police constable of the village. He was provided a uniform of a turban, shirt and trousers and was paid and controlled by officers of the land department and mainly assisted in collection of land revenue. He was notoriously powerful in the village and would, particularly at marriage celebrations, work as a spy and inform if cows were slaughtered. On occasions he would level false accusations of cow slaughter, hoarding of illicit timber or other criminal allegations against innocent and ignorant peasants. This office had an overpowering impact upon the rural population for its notoriety. A bigger village had a Namberdar (or a Maqdam) over the head of the chowkidar or upon two or three smaller villages one Namberdar would administer authority of collection of land revenue, would administer and execute orders of Begar (forced labour) and would force horse owners to go on forced labour with the forces to the difficult terrains of Gilgit or had to accompany the Hindu pilgrims to Amarnath. The season of the Amarnath Yatra coincided with torrential rain so I remember the pathetic scenes in my town and in the villages around when Namberdar and Chowkidar would force the horse owners from this distant part in central Kashmir to proceed towards the extreme south. The weeping mothers, sisters and wives would bid them farewell in the belief that their men and animals could hardly return safely. The Namberdar and Chowkidar would physically force these horse owners out of their village territory and they would actually drag the wailing womenfolk back to the village from highways and pathways. They would abuse them, curse them and even molest them.

A Patwar Halqa consisting of several such Namberdari's would be, as presently manned, by a Patwari or Halqadar. This office is the lowest in the hierarchy of land officers who has to maintain the land record at the basic level. A few Patwar Halqas constituted a 'Zail' and the head of the Zail was the 'Zaildar'. Present tehsil Chadoora had in all, four 'Zails' and these four Zaildars were the real rulers of this tehsil. Later on Nagam Zail was amalgamated with Charar-i-Sharief Zail and so about half of the present tehsil fell under the territorial jurisdictions of that Zaildar. This office was hereditary and *coincided with the leading Jagirdar (estate holder) Maufidar or the estate grantee. Whereas the Patwari and the Chowkidar were paid employees, the Namberdar was officially paid one-fifth from the land revenue which he collected and extorted by his efforts. On the other hand, the 'Zaildar' was a sort of honorary office, but had an unwritten license to exploit and extort. This parasite lived on the blood and sweat of the peasantry. Hence the Zaildar generally worked as a tyrant agent of autocracy. Though there were some exceptions like Haji Akbar Dar of Drabagam, Pulwama who actively aligned himself with freedom fighters, but the majority of them left no stone unturned to persecute the lovers of freedom. Thus, this office had become a great impediment in the process of revolution and so was an irritant for the new administration. It also needs mention that immediately before partition of the subcontinent some influential Zaildars had thrown their weight with the All J&K Muslim Conference, Some had aligned with Public Minister Mian Ahmad Yar in dyarchy and through him with Prime Minister Pandit. R.C. Kak and a good number of Zaildars in Jammu region worked actively for promoting the interests of the Maharaja. Against this background the National Conference had a genuine grudge against the office, so, they would have got public appreciation if they had abolished this office. Initially they dismissed the existing Zaildars and appointed their own men from their organisational ranks. There was thus, no change in the situation, it remained a symbol of terror even after this change.

It was politically and administratively advisable to abolish this unnecessary office which could hardly be cleared of the stigma it had acquired for a full century. But the National Conference government took the wrong action to convert this office of tyranny into a basic institution of democracy. It was only a gimmick to hoodwink the people and conveyed in clear terms a definite message that the people should actively desist from participation in the political process and on the other hand should, as silent spectators, appreciate what the government of the National Conference would do in the name of democratisation. They further wished to convey to the forces and individuals who wished to put themselves up as a constructive opposition that they should desist from such action otherwise they would face trouble. Hence, the office of the Zaildar was declared an elected office. Without framing any electoral college, defining the methods for franchise and without preparation of an electoral roll the Zaildar election was scheduled some time in 1949-50. No record has been maintained publicly or privately or even at government level which can throw definite light on the events which took place in each constituency. As a sample I will narrate my personal experiences which I witnessed as a fifteen year old boy at Nagam where the Charar-i-Sharief Zail election was to be conducted by the government, but under the supervision of late Ghulam Mohi-ud-din Kara, the district president of the All J&K National Conference, Srinagar.

A student of matriculation I read posters and pamphlets in Urdu containing appeals that a 'peasant' Ismail Yatoo of Nagam be elected to the office of Zaildar and Mohammed Yousuf Baba of Charar-i-Sharief, 'a symbol of treachery and terror be rejected'. The contents of that poster issued by the district president of the National Conference evoked much interest and curiosity in me.

Haji Mohammed Yousuf Baba was post master in charge of the branch post office of Charar-i-Sharief, an unassuming, neatly dressed, non-controversial gentleman, but belonged to the same family of Zaildars and big landed estate holders. The big landed estate, unirrigated and totally dependent on rainfall had an insufficient yield not commensurate with their standard of living. But, the family for its pro-autocracy leanings had assumed the reputation of exploiters. The dismissed Zaildar had recently been released on parole after a two year illegal detention as a pro-Pakistan activist. Thus, Haji Jalal-ud-din had acquired a halo around his personality for his political consistency and the valour with which he had faced persecution by third degree methods of interrogation. His detention in a cell in the Lal Qila, Delhi had enhanced his stature throughout the state and fables and folk anecdotes were coined about his suffering in jail. During this Zaildar election Haji Jalal-ud-din himself made a round of the Charar-i-Sharief market and requested the people of the town to forge unity so that the 'honour of his town' was not snatched. He even requested the people to forget and forgive what had been done in the past to the inhabitants of the villages around Charar-i-Sharief. He made an appeal in the name of the patron saint Sheikh Noor-ud-din and specifically stated that their vote would be treated as Niaz (tribute of offering) at this shrine. The voting was to be held by raising hands in a congregation of hundreds of villagers at Nagam—a village 18 kms away from Srinagar on the Charar-i-Sharief road.

From curiosity and interest to know the realities for myself I tried to persuade my revered father to allow me to be away from school and join the first ever experience of the democratic process in our history. On being refused, I slipped away from school.

The congregation had swelled beyond the assessment of the ruling party, yet the district president Khwaja Ghulam Mohi-ud-din felt annoyed that the voters were not in a mood to receive his dictat and were determined to exercise their right according to their conscience. He uprooted a three year old poplar tree from the bank of a stream and used it indiscriminately against the mob, beating villagers, injuring old and young. The late Abdul Rehman Mir Rahat, tehsil president of the ruling National Conference followed him and within a few minutes the voters from our town and adjoining villages scattered into smaller groups and ran away. Armed with sticks organised 'goondas' of the National Conference chased them. I was just about to receive a blow when an old Imam of Trajibal Amir Mir Mosque a saintly and scholarly figure wrapped me under his loose gown 'pheren'. Due to his age and appearance he was spared and I was saved. However, next day I was admonished and beaten in school.

The 'goondas' chased the voters of Charar-i-Sharief upto the Karewa of Nagam, i.e., a distance of two kilometres. Similarly, voters who had come from other routes met the same fate though many of them had openly expressed support for the National Conference candidate.

The same type of torture was used at every stage in every constituency in which someone had shown courage to contest, otherwise the majority was 'elected' uncontested. Within a year after this fraud in the name of elections was enacted the very institution of Zaildars was scrapped and now even my juniors do not know what 'Zaildar' meant except that we have a locality in Nandpora area of Phykh Pargana known as Zaildar Mohalla. The abolition of this institution was under active consideration of the new rulers from the day they received power from the Maharaja under the aegis of the Indian Army. Why should they go in for the game of elections which tarnished the image of the National Conference and its leaders? This was a puzzling question posed by our elders in the discussion in the office of our headmaster Ghulam Hassan Inqilab, in the market place and at other social functions.

Events which took place a year later showed that the 'benevolent' leader who had made the suppressed 'Hato'[1] Kashmiri search and express his identity; who claimed to have made people conscious of the sight of franchise—the same Sher-i-Kashmir conveyed two lessons through the melodrama of 'Zaildar Election'. In the first place he conveyed to the voter that he should not be under illusions of exercising the right of vote, at least in the coming hustings which were to be held for the first ever Constituent Assembly. Secondly, he conveyed to the opposition candidates, who might have nourished thoughts to enter into the fray that they should not risk their lives unnecessarily. Both lessons were strictly taught and diligently learnt.

It is pertinent to delve into circumstances which were prevalent at the time of the Zaildar elections. Immediately after taking control of the emergency administration in Jammu and Kashmir Sheikh Mohd. Abdulla and his administration either threw pro-Pakistan Muslim Conference activists into jails, or to the other side of the ceasefire line. In Jammu the massacre of Muslims had completely finished most of the pockets of Muslim influence. The Hindus there too had fallen into disarray. The abdication of Maharaja Hari Singh had spread waves of frustration both among the privileged and the communal Hindus. The landless harijan and low caste had seen in the new development a ray of hope and so did the Hindu chauvinist who found himself in the lap of Hindu majority India and out of Muslim Pakistan—which he hardly expected in the given schemes of partition of India. Against this background there were no immediate chances for an organised opposition party to emerge. The majority of voters would hardly vote for the disarrayed groups who had no progressive pretensions like that of the National Conference. So, the National Conference ostensibly had clear chances of sweeping the polls, but why did it send different signals? This question will tax the mind of the reader, but it will be premature to record the conclusion or moral of the story unless the whole story is narrated. The complete narration will portray the edifice for which Sheikh Mohd. Abdulla under the patronage of the great democrat of India, Jawahar Lal Nehru laid an invisible foundation through this 'rehearsal'.

Notes

1. In informal chats with each other Kashmiri villagers would call their addressee, to divert his attention with a suffix of 'Hato'. It means Oh Comrade! In the Punjab where Kashmiri labourers would go for employment during winters the Punjabis would also address them as Hato and in due course of time it became a contemptuous stigma for Kashmiri identity and was frequently used to look down upon people. With the start of his career Sheikh Abdulla would claim to raising his nation from a nadir of degradation and restoring the pride which was the essence of being a Kashmiri.

Chapter 6

Selection without Discretion

While the rehearsal was being played in Jammu and Kashmir, in South Block, New Delhi experts on foreign affairs were busy (advised by the Prime Minister cum Foreign Minister of India Jawaharlal Nehru) to prepare, a draft for a caveat. Jawaharlal Nehru had a clear assessment that any drastic changes he might precipitate in regard to the Jammu and Kashmir dispute, Pakistan would, at the best, dispatch a protest note—a paper missile and its able Foreign Minister, Sir Mohammad Zafarulla Khan might engage the members of the Security Council, in heated argumentation. Hence, to blunt that axe, he engaged his experts in the Ministry of Foreign Affairs to prepare a draft which he could get passed unanimously by the General Council of J&K National Conference in Srinagar. In September 1950 Mirza Mohd. Afzal Beg got this draft from New Delhi directly from the Prime Minister who had studied and then approved it. The meeting of the General Council held on October 27, 1950, wherein this draft was read and the majority without knowing what the contents meant cried, as usual to Kashmiri political culture, "Manzoor" (we accept it). The resolution was in the English language overburdened with phraseology which was aimed for use at international fora so was unintelligible to the gathering. It expressed 'great concern' over the repeated failures of the UN to redress the wrongs of aggression'. It lamented upon the 'continued concessions given to Pakistan by placing a premium on her intransigence' and considered that such 'indecision and unrealistic procedures had condemned the people of the state to a life of agonising uncertainty'. After this lengthy preamble the Supreme National Executive of the people was requested to take immediate steps for convening a Constituent Assembly. What meant the phrase "Supreme National Executive Of The People"? The use of this phrase was a cunning device of political pundits in Delhi aimed to hoodwink and confuse the world public opinion, to feed it with wrong assumption (as India did and continues to do) that some representative body existed which exercised the 'Sovereignty' vested in the people after the abdication of the Maharaja. It was big bluff wraping a frog in the tigers skin. The reality was exposed to all. "The Supreme National Executive Of The People" was a teenaged son of the abdicated Maharaja who had under pressure of the Quit Kashmir Movement, Gilgit Scouts Agitation, Poonch Insurgency and Pathan Action (Qabali war) run away from his kingdom and settled in Bombay. His term of lease—authority to rule the state had come to an end in 1946 and he had no moral authority to rule Kashmir. Did he exercise the sovereign powers on the small country after British Raj upto the end of October 1947 when he left his country in a huff is debatable. Discussions will follow in Part II. Had the Sovereignty, in such circum-stances transferred to his ruled subjects, i.e., the people of Jammu and Kashmir? On June 9, 1949 the rulers managed a 'Firman' from the abdicated Maharaja after 19 months of his abdication. The 'firman', in reality was issued from Bombay under which he directed his son 'Yuvraj Karan Singh" to exercise all 'powers which vested in him. It is this arrangement which was accepted by Sheikh Abdulla, the architect of Quit Kashmir Movement. He made his organisation, the J&K National Conference request the same Supreme National Executive to constitute a Constituent Assembly. As tutored, the representative of the abdicated authority and the ruler imposed by Indian Govt upon its occupied portion of the state, issued a proclamation on 1 May 1950 directing the constitution of a Constituent Assembly. It provided in para (3)

'Elections to the Constituent Assembly shall be on the basis of adult franchise, that is to say, every person who is a state subject of any class, is not less than twenty one years of age on the first day of March, has been a resident in the constituency for such period as may be prescribed by the rules shall be entitled to register in the electoral rolls of that constituency, provided that any person who is of...'

Para 1 provided for 'direct and secret ballot'.

In para 2 of this proclamation it was provided that the "State shall be divided into a number of territorial constituencies, each containing a population of 40,000 or as near thereto as possible and each electing one member. A delimitation committee shall be set up by the government..."

Thus, like other democratic societies the election in Jammu and Kashmir had also to go through a process and that systematic process would mould the 'constructive thinking' and 'political activity'. Both received a death blow through various measures of repression let loose during the so called 'emergency' created by Qabalee (Tribal) war. It was qualified as the Armed Struggle For Independency by pro-Pak elements. We will discuss the measures which the state had to adopt before the people could go to polls, but it is most pertinent to describe, at the outset, the political situation at the time of the issuance of this proclamation.

It is widely known that the two belligerent forces were poised to strike upon each other and both had divided this state in two parts; the dividing lines were unrealistic, uneven, unreasonable and unmanageable. This cease fire line was so undefined that in reality Jammu and Kashmir state was (as it continues to be) a battlefield where any minor incident could escalate into a full-fledged war. Exchange of fire, abduction on unrealistic borders, armed infiltration, spying and counter spying, suspicions, vindictiveness and all other allied and auxiliary incidents had put the state on a time bomb. At any moment a devastation would take place. The National Conference resolution of October 27, 1950 also admitted, it, though in twisted manner. The people of the state have been 'condemned to an agonising uncertainty'. It attributed the responsibility for this situation to U.N.O., but the phraseology used made it quite transparent that the 'agonising uncertainty' had created a situation throughout the state which resulted in political suffocation. Let us summarise the constituents of this suffocation inherent in the situation:

1. The emergency laws were draconian in nature and indiscriminately implemented. The entire population was treated like the worst criminals and so prosecuted and persecuted. In this persecution even the most condemnable Nazi methods were adopted which are hinted about, in these sub paras:
    a. Involvement in false and baseless criminal litigation under ordinary penal laws and Special Acts like the Enemy Agents

Ordinance, Defence of India Act and Rules, Indian Arms Act. etc.

b. To protract the trial of these false criminal cases, evidence was created both by force and fraud. Thus, on the one hand members of families of repute were forced to depose as dictated to and on the other a 'professional class' was encouraged to emerge, especially in the areas contiguous to the cease fire line as ready made witnesses against innocent people.

c. Every police station, was converted into a Nazi camp and a notorious force viz. 'special staff' was created and established in Kothi Bagh police Station, Sringar under the most tyrannical police officer Sheikh Ghulam Qadir Ganderbali. He used such third degree methods of terror which had not even been adopted in our primitive society. Chilli powder would be thrown in the eyes, a hot iron was applied on naked thighs and protesting minor students were even subjected to sodomy. Women folk of many respectable families were molested.

d. In areas contiguous to the ceasefire line people were subjected to much severer terror.

e. The prayer sermons were pre-censored. To quote from Charar-i-Sharief where the preachers of Khanqah and Bud Talaw Mosques Mir Waiz Alik Shah and Mir Waiz Jalal-ud-din were ordered not to pray for victory of the forces of virtue against the forces of vice as is ordained by the Quran to pray.

f. The chairs of both these two preachers were removed from these mosques and thrown in the two adjacent water ponds. Further they were, alongwith others, prohibited to wear the green turban, the colour which the Pakistan national flag bears. This type, rather with much severity, was prevelant in the city and other towns.

g. A notorious gang under the pseudo name of Peace Brigade was constituted ostensibly to defend the localities from infiltration, but the same force would persecute the respectable, people of the locality for ordinary pretexts. In view of the closure of Kashmir Jehlum Valley Road scarcity of salt created a situation of famine. Local stocks were exhausted, but under the pretext of recovery of 'hoarded salt' this Peace Brigade used to raid houses of the honoured trader community and harass their families. In a similar raid one kilogram of salt (sufficient for a week's consumption for the family) became the cause of suffering for an honourable trader of Charar-i-Sharief who was flogged in public.

h. Under the pretext of harbouring tribal raiders or their sympathisers many honourable families were subjected to misery. Besides perpetuating physical torture they were turned bankrupt.

i. Many families were put to untold misery. The cadres of special staff would itself dump some arms in a house, godown, cow-shed or farm house of a respectable family, would conduct raids and after the stage managed recoveries they would be involved in criminal cases and adult members, sometimes even minors and women would be thrown in lock-ups and jails.

j. Authority of law courts had since been eroded and so it had become an uphill task for such victims even to get themselves released on bail. The situation was further compounded by the fact that the city Bar was totally manned by Kashmiri Pandit lawyers who did not even choose to defend their own favourite Ram Chand Kak ex-Prime Minister who was made the first victim of vengeance by the Sheikh Abdulla Government. A distinguished Muslim lawyer Hafeez was forced to run away to Azad Kashmir. Another lawyer G.M. Wani was imprisoned and the whole burden fell upon M.L. Qureshi advocate who singlehandedly defended everyone from R.C. Kak to Dr. Sheikh Abdul Majeed, (even Sheikh Abdulla later on) and all such victims of political vendetta.

k. Even suspected political workers were imprisoned or thrown in jails or the externed towards the territories under Azad Kashmir.

l. In every mohalla of the city or a Patwar Halqa or in bigger village in rural areas the 'Halqa Offices' of National Conference were established and fitted with local radio sets. The Halqa president of that particular locality was a terror for the area—a law unto himself, who combined within his powers executive, judicial and police functions. It was the Halqa president who was the complainant, it was he who would issue warrants of arrest against the so called defaulter and it was he who would record punishment which he would get executed in his own presence. A similar Halqa President of Ompora (Budgam) issued contempt notice against a sitting judge of the J&K High Court of Judicature. During autocracy a notorious community of 'Galwans' was socially condemned because they would lift the horses of the people from one area and sell them in another area. The Halqa President of the National Conference went few steps ahead and would patronise, shield and protect the abduction of women and they would be tipped of in different areas.

m. The ministers, office bearers of the National Conference, civil servants, police officers, the kith and kin of politicians in power all were busy in creating assets by extortion.

2. During World War II and thereafter the Kashmir tourist industry and Kashmiri crafts had received world attention and so almost all the sections of the Valley except the landless tenant had experienced an era of prosperity which had, within a couple of years, changed their life standard. After the tribal war closure of Jehlum Valley Road and for the most feeble means of communication, Kashmir was almost severed from the world. The tourist industry was totally smashed, the artists, traders, hawkers, all connected with Kashmiri art again descended below the poverty line. The famine of salt created a psychological situation which gave rise to various diseases. Kashmir was for ages, used to rock salt and so could not, for a year or more, consume any substitute which too due to failure of Communication could not be imported in sufficient quantity.

3. The devastation caused by the war and the situation, thereafter, destroyed the agrarian economy too. Natural calamities compounded the situation. The floods of 1950 had inundated the ripe crops in the fields. So after 1947, Kashmir virtually faced a continued situation of famines. In view of the complete disturbances caused in the means of communication, trade links which went through Rawalpandi and Sialkot were shattered. It caused rampant unemployment. The contradictions in the approach added insult to these oozing wounds. On the one hand each event which took shape exposed the National Conference leadership and particularly affected Sheikh Abdulla's popularity. The graph of his personality cult was continuously coming down. But on the other hand, like a benevolent and popular leader Sheikh Abdulla would request his nation to change its food habits, preached austerity, advised his people to remain content with hunger 'for maintaining individual and national honour'. Such sermons had no relevance in the situation when people believed that they had been cheated and betrayed. Hence their general resentment

could explode any moment.

4. The city people were still privileged as they got 20 kilograms of unhusked 'shali' which could be, after husking and separating grain from chaff, reduced to 12 kgs of rice for an individual for a period of 30/31 days. This quantity would suffice the daily need of two meals only for 12/15 days. The import of rice into the city was also banned, hence the hungry citizen had no alternate source of supply. The smugglers would provide rice in the black market, but at exorbitant rates. Due to unemployment the people had no purchasing power. Hence, a revolt was simmering.

But Sher-i-Kashmir accorded one more epitaph 'Nune Roes Padshah' (salt-less king as he was nicknamed) would advise change in food habits and replace rice with potatoes. Hence, he was accorded one more title of 'Aaloo Bub' the father of potatoes. In villages there were no state supply centres nor could the local produce even cope with the personal demands of the peasantry with the result that the small landholders, landless tenants, village artisans and other professionals went hungry.

Inspite of this famine-like situation repression of Halqa Presidents and the other treacheries of the leadership, the two revolutionary measures had kept the graph from declining. Though all measures had caused widespread hatred, yet the establishment of Debt Cancellation Boards under J&K Debt Cancellation Law and Big Landed Estates Abolition Act, revolutionised the Agrarian Society. The same peasant who had to cultivate the land for generations got ownership rights on that land. The agriculturist got rid of the 'wad system' (which kept the debtor always under the burden of debt). The encumbrances on mortgaged lands were to a great extent made much easier which made it possible for the distressed owner to redeem the mortgaged properties. These revolutionary measures were of great consequence. Even after half a century such drastic measures have not been taken in many parts of the subcontinent. But these measures were taken in an unplanned manner which left certain scars on the economy. On the one hand, the primitive money lender was finished, but on the other an alternate banking system was neither introduced nor encouraged; so, the distressed though relieved of the debt, could not obtain advances from any quarter to rebuild his living standard, to feed himself and his live stock. Consequently he had to sell his oxen and even his plough.

In this economic and political setup inherent with contradictions proclamation to constitute a Constituent Assembly was published in the State Gazette, and in the official organ of the National Conference the Urdu daily *Khidmat* . The proclamation hardly reached the common city people. The remote village people probably heard about the proclamation after two years, i.e., after the coup of 1953. The pre-poll electoral process could have churned public opinion. But there was no activity allowed before, during or after the so-called elections. Let us examine how these stages of process took place.

Delimitation of Constituencies

For the first time the people had to elect their representatives under universal suffrage and so the electoral constituencies needed to be delimited and defined with proper co-operation of the voters so as to avoid gerrymandering of the constituencies. Though a Delimitation Committee was formed but its activities were confined within the limits of officialdom and it is not known whether even the maps were consulted and studied at all. No visits were paid to any area, no representatives were invited, no groups of individuals were ever heard.

Even the cadre of the ruling party were not made conscious associates nor any candidate had any idea of his or her prospects as a candidate from any constituency so that such a prospective candidate, would associate with the said committee. The ruling party high command was sure of the game they had to play and so behaved with utter indifference. They knew that any activity might send signals to conscious quarters of the impending elections so avoided any electoral exercises even within the ruling party.

Preparation of Voter List

Against the background of autocratic repressive rule of centuries it was by the end of 1947 that Kashmiris witnessed celebration of independence in the subcontinent. They had come out of the rule of repression. But Kashmiris felt that the situation for them was no better than before. They had seen a few runners, informers and spies in a locality in the village such as the Chowkidar, Namberdar, Safeed Posh or Zaildar during autocracy but now experienced that like a mouse they were surrounded by cats. Charar-i-Sharief area, the previous pargana of Nagam, (consisting of three blocks presently) was then under a police post headed by a head constable and assisted by five to six constables. In changed circumstances every member of Halqa Committee of the ruling party was a spy, every volunteer of Peace Brigade was an informer—besides, the other government employees. Hence, the people were frightened and under that psychology apprehended dangers to co-operate with census enumerators. In the situation it was incumbent upon the leadership, which was at the helm of affairs, to educate the masses about the purpose of the preparation of lists and involve them with the process actively. It was to be impressed upon them that such lists were not to be prepared for any forced labour as was the age old practice. It was, therefore, necessary to involve the school teachers for preparation of voter lists rather than the revenue officials who were part of the defamed institutions. Had the preparation of voter lists been made in progressive measure involving the voter with it, the atmosphere for an election would have logically been created. Such a situation would have encouraged a contest. On the other hand, preparation of voter lists was assigned to the same outdated and defamed personnel who performed the duty with contempt for people, disregard for human identity and disgraced the right to vote. Hence, these lists were mainly prepared in Patwar Khanasa or in the house of Namberdar or at Tehsil headquarters. After they were prepared, no steps were taken to paste copies thereof on conspicuous places in the villages, nor were objections invited, nor did anyone try to object, even if he somehow came to know of any defects). Even if any one conscious of these proceedings dared to object his claim was never enquired into.

No publicity was made about the nomination of Returning or Assistant Returning Officers or of other members of the poll staff.

In these circumstances the process of election passed in such mystifying circumstances that instead of easing the suffocation the frightened masses felt more terrified even to talk about any election.

It was thus that all the 75 constituencies 'returned' all the 75 members to Constituent Assembly 'unopposed'. It is after the results were declared without conducting any contest that a special number of the official organ of the National Conference—*Khidmat* published names and photographs of so-elected members that we in Charar-i-Sharief saw, from the picture on third page of the daily the 'paper face' of Bakshi Abdul Rashid, a voter of the city who was conferred the honour to represent the people of Charar-i-Sharief constituency spreading over half of the Tehsil of Chadora.

The above discussions have shown that, firstly, without creating an atmosphere at least for a show of contest, and secondly, without allowing even a stage managed contest for a single constituency 75 members were declared elected. Hence, no more details or comments are required to expose this selection of the assembly which had to draft the constitution of Jammu and Kashmir and had to determine (as proclaimed) the nature of states relationship with India. Even some Indian dailies have exposed the uncontested drama, some leaders too did not hide their reaction, but it will make this chapter too lengthy to quote such comments and statements. We confine ourselves to quote the immediate reaction expressed by the first local head of the Indian dominion C. Rajgopalacharya. J.N. Zutshi was one of the members of Emergency Administration headed by Sheikh Abdulla who was in charge of Information and Broadcasting departments. On the completion of this 'selection without discretion' of the75 member assembly J.N. Zutshi was deputed to place before the Governor General of India the list of 'elected' candidates. C. Rajgopalacharya commented, "it is accepted that the organisation of Sheikh Abdulla and he himself (both) enjoy undisputed popularity but could not you, Mr. Zutshi, rig elections in a few constituencies to accommodate a few opposition members so as to make it appear as an election?"[1]

It should not be construed that had a contest been allowed the ruling party would have failed. No, not at all. It would have won not two-thrids but simple majority. The reasons are:

1. Even if a process for churning of the public opinion would have been allowed to go through the stages of delimitation, preparation of electoral rolls, filing of nomination papers and a free campaign for contesting candidates; it too would not create a united, disciplined and cadre based alternate organisation within five or six months. There was no trace of parallel leadership or political organisation in the state as the Muslim Conference had completely disintegrated. Its leadership was either in jails or pushed to the other side of the ceasefire line or killed. Even before, it was not a cadre based organisation. It was represented by the feudal lords and big traders so it could not contain the mechanism of the National Conference and nor could it provide any help or assistance to the tribals who had come to execute the manifesto of the Muslim League. Though there was an exception in men like Abdul Salam Dalal but the Mirwaiz dynasty had not allowed recruitment in it out of the limited group of its fans. So it was confined to a group of the population who had no tradition for struggle and sacrifice. This leadership after Indian occupation was so disarrayed that Haji Jalal-ud-din of Charar-i-Sharief had no liaison with Dr. Abdul Majeed of Islamabad. The style of functioning of the Charar-i-Sharief Muslim Conference leader Jalal-ud-din remained, even after his release from jails, the same which was the style of his 'Zaildari' days. He would summon the sympathisers to his well furnished Dewan Khana (drawing room). Hence, under such a leadership an alternate would not emerge, even if people wanted to reject the National Conference and its leadership.
2. The National Conference had earned resentment for its minus points. People had developed the belief that this organisation had betrayed and cheated them. Late Abdul Ahad Azad a humanist and revolutionary poet (who was even dubbed an atheist for his progressive ideas) had in 1945 warned his nation 'not to follow' like sheep in a herd 'lest they may find themselves floundering in a deeper ditch—in the aspiration of reaching a pasture ground'. The prophecy in this verse of his gazal was deeply appreciated in our area and this

gazal had become a favourite song. It made clear the reaction of the people. Secondly, terror let loose had created hatred against the leadership. But inspite of such a dark side the National Conference government had brought about an agrarian revolution. In these circumstances only such a force would pose a formidable challenge to it which had not minus points, but positive pro-people achievements.

Such leadership would not emerge from a vacuum. The National Conference too was conscious of it, so why did it allow a permanent disability—both morally and politically (even legally) to its created Constituent Assembly? This was due to the following reasons:

1. Sheikh Abdulla was a despot and the mass popularity had made him a dictator. Even as President of the National Conference he ignored the unanimous decision of his working committee taken on May 19, 1946 when he issued the call for Quit Kashmir on May 20, 1946. Now as the ruler he was working under the illusion of becoming King of Kashmir and so he got the title of 'Paadshah' coined for himself.
2. Nehru understood well the psychology of Kashmir. He apprehended that though there was no alternate leadership but the simmering anti-India feeling and suppressed pro-Pak emotion, might sway the people. Let us hear his reaction through Balraj Puri—a veteran freedom fighter and committed human rights activist. He had, during the preparations of these elections organised a small show of anguish to agitate for fairplay, but Jawaharlal Nehru advised him to help Sheikh Abdulla as the 'luxury of democracy' could not be allowed in Jammu and Kashmir.

   'In the Constituent Assembly in 1951 the National Conference won all the 75 seats. Nobody dared to file a nomination paper. The nomination papers of the opposition, mainly candidates of Praja Parishad in Jammu were rejected outright on flimsy grounds.'[2]
3. Inspite of the despot lurking within the tall and robust frame of Sheikh Abdulla he would have been persuaded by the known democrat of the world Jawahar Lal Nehru to conduct the elections, at least, in a manner which

'would not expose Indian case to a ridicule', but he did not wish to do so. He had plans to get this work done by Abdulla, change the agency, install a government which would facilitate Constitutional Application Orders from the President, so as to fulfil a formality contained in the Instrument of Accession to reduce that vital document (which they had themselves devised and drafted) into an ineffective treaty. Hence, encouraged the imposition of selections in the name of elections.

A digression may not be amiss in these discussions. Had the Communist Party of India (CPI) risen from national chauvinism and exploited Kashmir psychology at this important turn of events and acted in the interest of the world communist movement and for the benefit of the working class it could have filled the political vacuum in Jammu and Kashmir. Though the party had no mass base here, but it had a considerable cadre base. It may not have won more than a few seats that time, but could have emerged as a great pro-Indian and pro-people force. Jawaharlal Nehru was omnipresent in every Indian party and so influenced the C.P.I. through Dange and his comrades. Similar folly was committed by it in 1953 which we will discuss later on.

To our contention that it was merely a selection, but, why a selection without discretion? The selection was made by the tallest leader Sheikh Mohammad Abdulla who had personal rapport only with important persons of the two cities or from main towns, he had no personal contacts with the cadre of his organisation in the vastness of the state nor did the National Conference had a cadre in various constituencies. Hence, he had no personal knowledge as to whom to select for which constituency. Secondly, this organisation too like other political organisations had not a nucleus or organised cadre in every region of Jammu and Kashmir or in every part of a region. Thirdly, he had developed a temperament to decide each and every matter himself and so had no accommodation for a collective decision, and did not consult others. Fourthly, he was aware of the simmering self-aggrandisement among his comrades and would plug every loophole. In the pre-1953 era he would not even subject himself to the frequent consultations of his family and honestly desired to keep his son-in-law also (who was Controller Civil Supplies then) out of politics.[3]

In this situation he obtained names of workers or sympathisers from each Tehsil and chose without even knowing the merit and integrity of each. He accommodated Bakshi and Beg's men only due to their sycophancy. He nominated a cousin of Bakshi, Abdul Rasid (Bakshi) for Charar-i-Sharief constituency which then extended from Ram Bagh to Yousmarg. This whole area partly rural and partly urban did not provide him a suitable candidate and Rashid was not even a voter of that constituency. The situation was similar in at least 30 to 36 constituencies. Therefore, in 1953 many of those hand picked non-entities committed treacheries with their patron and mentor. Had Sheikh Abdulla applied discretion only relevant to his own interest he would not have found himself in trouble in August 1953. Before we conclude let us quote from some distinguished personalities and authors:

As narrated above there was no organised opposition party in the State, however, the Jammu based Hindu organisation had some influence among high caste Hindus, but had no organisational network. What the position of this party was is described in the book *Kashmir-Article 370* by Dr. Mohan Kishen Taing. The learned author has made a deep contribution to Kashmiriology and is presently a leader of the migrant Pandit community and so an office bearer of their organisation 'Panun Kashmir'. The readers may peruse his work *Supra*.

To quote a paragraph from my book *Hazratbal—The Central stage of Kashmir Politics,* n. 4.

In his interview to an Urdu daily from Jammu, *Jammu Sandesh*, Sh. P.N. Dogra said, "If we narrate factual history of these elections fascists like Mussolini and Hitler will feel ashamed."

Alistair Lamb has not taken the trouble to make an analytical study on this subject with the same strain with which he has dealt upon other facets of the Kashmir problem yet the extract from his book, *A Disputed Legacy* (Karachi: Oxford University Press, 1993, p. 192) is relevant and helpful.[5]

Had the Indian press been conscious to its long-term interest in Jammu and Kashmir it would have exposed this game of fraud and thereby the erosion in democratic institutions (which was the only basis of the relationship between the two peoples of Jammu and Kashmir and India) would have been arrested. On the other hand, the Indian mass media hailed this imposed selection as confirmation of accession with India "by every single adult voter of Kashmir". In this regard *The Hindu* in its November 1, 1951 issue hailed this election as "ratification of the programme of accession by every single voter." Had the writer or the agency behind this write-up not sacrificed larger interests for the sake of winning a feeble point of argument before the world body and had on the other hand, given vent to the suffocation in Jammu and Kashmir caused in the name of hustings, the fourth domain of democracy would have consolidated the Indo-Kashmir fraternity in a positive direction.

It is for the benefit that note 6 is added regarding the Firman appointing the "Regent".[6]

Notes

1. Ref: Hajni Number Kashmiri Journal 'Sheeraza' literary journal of J&K Academy of Art, Culture and Language contributor Padam Shri Akhtar Mohi-ud-din.
2. Balraj Puri, ' Kashmir Insurgency'.
3. A close confidant of Sheikh Abdulla and co-accused with him in the Kashmir Conspiracy case said that once in the Sub Jail Jammu the late Sheikh had remarked that had not Bakshi Ghulam Mohammad committed the mistake of arresting four of his namesakes: Gh. Mohammad Shah, Gh. Mohammad Bhat (Reda) Gh. Mohammad Chicken and Gh Mohammad Beig (Zaildar) all these four would have joined with Bakshi and gone against Sheikh Abdulla.
4: *Hazratbal—The Central stage of Kashmir Politics,* it is pertinent here to quote from the book: *Kashmir—Article 370* by Dr. Mohan Kishan Taing:

   "Right from the time the preparations for elections began, the parties and candidates in opposition to the NC complained of intimidation and interference. The allegations were largely true. For 41 out of the 43 constituencies in Kashmir province, not a single nomination paper was filed by opposition candidates. In the two remaining constituencies of Haba Kadal and Baramulla, papers were filled by S.N.Fotedar and Sant Singh Teg. But these two leaders too did not remain in the fray. In Jammu province P.N.Dogra nominated candidates for 27 constituencies of the province, generally filing nomination papers for more than one candidate but 41 out of 46 were rejected, leaving only three for the contest."

   On 6 October 1951, P.N.Dogra issued a press statement from New Delhi boycotting the election. It needs to be mentioned that neither S.N.Fotedar nor Sardar Sant Singh Teg posed any formidable challenge from their constituencies of Haba Kadal and Baramulla, and there was very little likelihood of their winning. Both Sheikh Abdulla and Jawahar Lal Nehru had begun to hear the vociferous need for change which had swept public opinion by 1951. Shiv Narain Fotedar was summoned to Delhi, assured a berth in the Upper House of the Indian Parliament and so was persuaded to desist from participating in the hustings. He was not in the good books of the Muslims as he had, in the early thirties, allegedly indulged in certain sacrilegious activities. Thus, he was not likely to get a single Muslim vote. The Hindu vote of Haba Kadal constituency would get divided and the ruling party candidate would certainly win. But Sheikh Abdulla and Jawahar Lal Nehru were both too weak to face the electorate.

5: Alistair Lamb, *Kashmir—A Disputed Legacy*, p. 192. The fairness of the election was certainly open to challenge. While based, unlike the old 1939 Jammu and Kashmir state constitution, on universal adult suffrage, both the compilation of the electoral rolls (which had already begun in 1949) and the registration of nominations were supervised with great care and efficiency by Sheikh Abdulla's partisans. Under 5 per cent of the potential electorate actually voted. No less than 73 delegates were returned unopposed; and the whole process was boycotted by the only other tolerably organized party in the State, the Praja Parishad (associated with Jana Sangh in India) which represented the Hindus of Jammu (with a measure of Sikh support), after the nominations for all 27 of its candidates had been rejected.

6. Mr. Raja Jaswant Singh (Ex CJ of J&K and retired Judge Supreme Court of India) has edited Government Notifications and various constitution Acts of J&K under the name "Political And Constitutional Developments". On Page 201 it carries the "Proclamation" appointing Mr Karan Singh as Regent. It bears no date of its issue. However, was published in J&K extra ordinary gazzet of June 9, 1949. It is contained herein.

"PROCLAMATION"

Whereas I have decided for reasons of health to leave the State for a temporary period and to entrust to the Yuvaraj Shri Karan Singh Ji Bahadur for that period all my powers and functions in regard to the Government of the State.

Now, therefore. I hereby direct and declare that all powers and functions, whether Legislative, Excutive or Judicial, which are exercisable by me in relation to the State and its Government, including in particular my power and prerogative of making laws, of issuing proclamations, orders ordinances, of remitting, commiting or reducing sentence, and of pardoning offenders, shall during the period of my absence from the State, be exercisable by Yuvaraj Sh. Karan Sing Ji Bahadur"

Sd/- Harisingh

Maharajadhiraj

7. Among the living members of this assembly few are yet amongst us. One of them Mr. K.D.Sethi is a living legend. He has authored an autobiography which contains revealing facts about this imposed consembly of which he was a member and about the manner in which it passed a Consitution. He has thereafter fought a few elections and discribes nature of the all. The relevant excepts could not be contained.

Chapter 7

Framing of J&K Constitution Act of 1956

In close succession Pandit Jawahar Lal Nehru made Sheikh Abdulla take two decisions of such far reaching consequences which no other personality was bold and competent enough to take. Sheikh Abdulla was introduced by the Indian Government and the Indian media throughout the world as the moulder of the destiny of Kashmir; so it was he alone who could, with unscrupulous means impose a selected assembly. People would not immediately react unless some severe shock was applied to their benumbed sensitivity as they themselves had built up Sheikh Abdulla. Conscious of the situation Jawahar Lal Nehru used him to select the assembly in consonance with the resolution which Jawahar Lal Nehru's Foreign Ministry had drafted, Jawahar Lal Nehru had vetted and the National Conference had moved and passed in Srinagar. No other personality could so successfully impose the selected assembly nor would India cash in upon the controversy of the establishment of this assembly. Had it been imposed by any other government in Srinagar headed either by Bakshi or by Sadiq or by any other leader it would neither have been created, nor would such an adventure have left any impact.

Within a year Sheikh Abdulla was forced to surrender basic character of autonomy at deliberations with Delhi authorities in the Indian capital which gave birth to a truce called the 'Delhi Agreement'.

However this Agreement of 1952 defined the respective ambits, purviews and provinces within which the applications of the provisions of Indian Constitution will confine and prescribed the broader borders within which the State Constituent Assembly will extend its legislative functions. With particular Stress the Soverignity which after the abdication had vested in the people of J&K was agreed to continue to vest in them. It is in exercise of that Soverign frame work that the J&K Constitution Act 1956 was passed. But in spite of these admissions, the India Govt" did undo with those guarantees which Accession Document had guaranteed.

With the earlier act Sheikh's 'arrogance' had become excessive, but the Delhi Agreement made him feel that he was entangled in a spider's web. The injured lion showed signs of anger, but whatever his strength it could not transgress the iron bars of the cage in which he found himself. His utility for Delhi had ceased. The value of neo-colonist policy lies in 'valuelessness' and so it was decided that the agent must be shown his place in a dustbin. A new agency was created with directions to use the platform created by Sheikh Abdulla and prepare a document to be named as a separate constituent of Jammu and Kashmir, but within the prescribed limits imposed on Sheikh through the Delhi Agreement. The slogan of 'one constitution' was patronised by the other side and under these pulls and counter pulls a photostat copy of the Indian Constitution was adopted with its patent mistakes and deliberate ommissions.

Before his arrest and after he signed the Delhi Agreement Sheikh Abdulla had obtained through his old friend and comrade G.A. Ashai the booklet of *gazals* of the Kashmiri poet G.A. Mehjoor—who had very recently been laid to rest with state honours. During his discussions with his confidants Sheikh Abdulla recited this verse of Mehjoor:

- Oh, Nightingale!
- Thy nest situates on delicate rose branch.
- They shall destroy it,
- Burn it, reduce it into ashes,
- Thee has to vacate the garden, helplessly,
- (*Poshi Lanji Peth aale hin chey walnay Ath zalnay; Kail Trawon Baag Aasee wan tsi kyah inkar chhoi*)

It was during October 1956 that a marathon session of the Constituent Assembly was held in Srinagar in the absence of its creator who was then in jail in Kud. However, a few of his associate members were temporarily released so as to take part in the deliberations on the draft of the constitution. But while coming out from the Ramgarh Palace (state assembly hall) Mirza Mohd Afzal Beg was abused and even attacked by hired ruffians of Bakshi. While going towards the nearby head office of the Plebiscite Front at Shaheed Gunj he received a few blows and his colleagues were physically manhandled. It was due to the courageous intervention of the magistrate (Munsiff) Mirza Saif-ud-din Ahmad who stood like a rock and bolted the door of the front office that Afzal Beg and MLAs of his group were saved. After some time Azad Kashmir Radio for a week continuously aired an announcement that on a particular date at 6.00 p.m. explosions would take place in every part of the city of Srinagar. The government in Srinagar had to spend lakhs of rupees to tighten security, many people were apprehended but at the fixed time and date recording of the firebrand speech of Mirza Afzal Beg made at the floor of house was relayed. It was metaphorically an explosion creating a devastating effect in the corridors of power. It remained a mystery even after deep investigation and enquiries as to how the tape recording of the speech was made and how it was smuggled out from the house to Azad Kashmir.[1]

After the Constituent Assembly was constituted certain tasks were assigned to it. We will not go into the details whether Yuvraj Karan Singh had the authority to call people of Jammu and Kashmir to elect a Constituent Assembly or not, because the very act is pro-people so though we may doubt the motives we should not criticise this act. It is not necessary to discuss whether in the situation which prevailed then it was the right step or not as the territory and people both were divided unevenly and the state overall had become a war field. The act in itself, as claimed by the authorities could have changed the course of history had it been implemented with honesty and with the sincere purpose to consolidate democratic traditions. But later history proved that in spite of his greatness as a man of vision Jawahar Lal Nehru acted with short-sightedness. If he had lived to see the trauma of post-1989 Jammu and Kashmir, he would have openly confessed having committed blunders in understanding the Kashmiri psyche. The action in itself, inspite of all odds could have created a laboratory of democracy in Jammu and Kashmir which could even have influenced the political history in Pakistan.

The notification issued in this behalf conveyed that the

sovereignty had passed to the people of Jammu and Kashmir, but this theoretical transfer was never put into practice as has been discussed. Sheikh Abdulla the creator of this assembly defined its task 'to shape the future of the people which it represented'. A constitution drafting committee was appointed immediately after this assembly was inaugurated on 5 November 1951. The parleys between New Delhi and Srinagar/Jammu also started.

Notes

1. This taped speech of Mirza Afsal Beg was relayed from Azad Kashmir Radio exactly at 6 pm. The author's personal diary containing the dates of delivery of the speech and of this relay was destroyed in his ancestral house in the devastation of Charar-i-Sharief in May 1995.

Chapter 8

Selection with Discretion

In the 1957 Elections, Bakshi wanted to convey a message with full force to New Delhi and to critics within his own party that like a sprawling chinar he had deepened his roots over the last few years and whosoever wished to enjoy its shade should remain docile. He had developed illusions, so to shatter such fancies aides of Nehru drafted plans to uproot him. Unaware of that hidden process he chose the center of the city of Srinagar, Khanyar constituency to convey his might. He officially nominated G.R. Renzo as the candidate for election to the Legislative Assembly who received felicitations from his friends and relations, but within days found himself like a gentle lamb in an abattoir waiting to be sacrificed. The knife belonged to the same butcher. Gazi Abdul Rehman was an independent candidate, thrown in the field by the general secretary of the ruling party (later nicknamed the 'Khruschev of Kashmir'). Other family members of the prime minister had openly come out in support of Gazi Abdul Rehman against their official candidate Renzo.

Boycott Policy

The popular J&K Plebiscite Front established two years earlier and the pro-Pakistan J&K Political Conference established in June 1953 had directed the nation to boycott the elections as in their view the constitution and the assembly both were created fraudulently; no fair elections could be held in J&K in the circumstances and the only solution lay in holding a plebiscite in the state and till then elections were irrelevant.

The Jammu Praja Parishad decided to enter the fray. But both in the Kashmir Valley and in three districts of Jammu the call for boycott met with popular response though some political activists considered the boycott a negative approach. They were conscious that boycott or no boycott the administration would not allow a contest however fake it might have been. Jawahar Lal Nehru, inspite of his might and high claims of democracy, was conscious of the psyche of Kashmiris who can go to the extreme when the situation demands it. Hence, he felt safety lay in letting barking dog lie lest they bit, under his command the local administration had sufficient sanctions behind him to repeat 1950. In the bargain he used Bakshi for a particular purpose. He had used Sheikh Abdulla for imposing a Constituent Assembly and for the Delhi Agreement; now he made Bakshi accommodate his 'progressive' group under G.M. Sadiq and get them selected unopposed to the legislature. Bakshi had also grasped the point, but had no way to overcome this and in his limited sphere he made Renzo a scapegoat.

The people did not approve the exercise of elections and considered it a futile gimmick in which the rulers had a gameplan to sabotage the process of elections. The tempo for elections was not allowed to emerge. People were utterly indifferent. In all, out of 75 seats only in 32 seats was a fake contest allowed. In Kashmir Khanyar contest was one between the Bakshi government and the Bakshi dynasty. Through this election Bakshi conveyed that his dynasty was more powerful than his government. A few candidates were made to remain in the fray so as to work as a pull and they were 'paid' for the campaign and were even compensated beforehand for the disgrace of failure.

After his return from the Aligarh Muslim University the author had revived his contacts with the Jammu and Kashmir unit of Praja Socialist Party of which he was one of the founder members. The party high command decided to field this author against the king-maker of Kashmir, viz., Bakshi Abdul Rashid from Charar-i-Sharief constituency, but to his utter dismay he was not entitled to contest. The author is an eye-witness of that hide and seek game in which the organisation made efforts to mark its presence in the legislature, but was unable to do so. It was caught in its own contradictions and could not exploit the internal rifts within the ruling party. There was no chance for the Praja Socialist Party—for that matter any other party to muster even limited support from the people. However, a small number could be made to participate for a few reasons. Firstly, had the Praja

Socialist Party convinced the pro-plebiscite and pro-Pak leadership of its main designs to highlight genuine difficulties of the masses on the safe platform of the legislature, they would have through a whisper campaign, allowed a limited participation of voters in some constituencies. Secondly, the Praja Socialist Party had an anti-communist manifesto in India and in Jammu and Kashmir so Khawaja Umar Bhat, general secretary state unit argued, "the communist element in the National Conference is weak, we should break the weaker wall to enter into." On the other hand, P.L. Kaul argued that the Bakshi group was corrupt, but the Sadiq group of the ruling party in his view represented progressive politics so the party should remain careful to dislodge that group. Both projected tutored viewpoints.

From a deep study of the happenings to which this author is a witness, it can be inferred that it was New Delhi which patronised Bakshi to cow down the Sadiq group so as to throw it in a situation which would make Sadiq agitate for extension of the jurisdiction of the Indian Election Commission in Jammu and Kashmir and for other steps of complete integration including the induction of the central services. Sadiq came out of the National Conference in 1957 after elections, established the Democratic National Conference (DNC) and again merged with the parent party in 1960 after Bakshi was made to walk some steps ahead in the process of integration. Hereafter, the complete erosion of J&K autonomy and the spirit of the Instrument of Accession got accelerated.

Let us hear from P.L. Kaul, who besides being a PSP candidate in 1957 was an active play-back. He enquired from close associates of G.M. Sadiq as to why they could not know beforehand the designs of Bakshi who had specifically chosen their group for total liquidation. The reply he received contained in his book *Kashmir Key Shab-O-Roz* (daily diary of Kashmir, Srinagar: Suman Publications, 1972) is quoted:

> "...We diverted the attention of Indian government to this situation and the Home Minister of India Govind Vallabh Bhai Pant said:
>
> You must know that we have paid huge sums for the purpose of elections and specially it was paid for the state unit

of PSP. But you have stood within National Conference against each other..."[1]

P.L. Kaul has expressed surprise that neither the chairman, O.P. Saraf nor himself was taken into confidence either by Bakshi or by the secretary of the state unit of PSP Umar Bhat. Kaul has quoted the 'reply' of Govind Vallabh Pant in somewhat ambiguous terms but my enquiries revealed that Umar Bhat (with his connivance or without) was used to provide a mock contest at the behest of the Government of India so that it could blunt criticism within the country and hoodwink the democratic world. Bakshi usurped the lion's share of those huge funds and allowed a small portion to be spent to engage his personal enemies in contests. It cannot be imagined that D.P. Dhar could have been ignorant about this and would not have informed Jawaharlal Nehru to whom he conveyed daily diaries from October 1947. It is believed that Jawaharlal Nehru too derived vicarious pleasure to make the group revengeful towards Bakshi.

Now let us hear what the most respectable figure of Jammu P.N. Dogra of Jammu Praja Parishad tells us about the 1957 elections. It is for the respect he commanded within the Hindu leadership of India that Bakshi, to avoid their annoyance, conceded his entry into the first Legislative Assembly. On July 30, 1957, on the floor of the assembly he said

> "This election had created traditions of such irregularities and multiplicity of bungling which defy description. Being short of time I cannot detail them out herein and defer the discussion to some other opportune time. The party in power has not swept the ballot (papers) but ballot boxes. If the facts are narrated even the fascist dictators like Mussolini and Hitler would stand frightened. I reiterate the demand of my party here on the floor of the house that judicial probe be conducted into the measures of persecution and goondism which the government allowed to reign in these elections. If such commission is established its inevitable verdict will precisely follow that: 'this government is not a government established by law but is established by terror.'" *Jammu Sandesh Weekly*, 11 August 1957.

The moral of the story narrated here is that the 1957 election, the first ever held for a legislative assembly was similar to the elections held for the first ever Constituent Assembly 1955 and can be qualified as merely a selection, distinguishable however from the earlier one to the extent that the selector had used discretion and conveyed a signal of danger through the defeat inflicted upon his official nominee G.R. Renzo from Khanyar constituency. By leaving the trio of 'Sadiq, Saraf, Dhar' in a process of liquidation by hobnobbing with the PSP in Kashmir and by conceding a seat for the Praja Parishad in Jammu he had conveyed that he was the 'Mughle Azam' of Jammu and Kashmir and it was through his benevolence that courtiers would be chosen for his bigger durbar labelled as the Legislative Assembly. But in his arrogance he did not realise that he played a game for Jawaharlal Nehru and the ultimate result was his own liquidation.

The bye-election to the Charar-i-Sharief constituency held in 1957 has great importance in the history of elections in Jammu and Kashmir and deserves a brief mention. It was the first ever battle of strength between the two committed agencies of Teen Murti Bhavan—the official residence of the Indian prime minister. Sadiq was made to part company with Bakshi and alongwith his comrades, D. P. Dhar, Syed Mir Qasim, G.L. Dogra, Ram Piara Saraf and Krishan Dev Sethi (all MLAs) Sadiq founded the All J&K Democratic National Conference (DNC) after the 1957 elections.

The defeat of the ruling party candidate G. R. Renzo at the hands of the 'ruling family' candidate had focussed grievances against Bakshi Rashid who had himself been selected unopposed for the J&K Assembly for the second time from Charar-i-Sharief. The leadership in Delhi also expressed their anguish against the 'anti party' activities of i Rashid. In the battle which Bakshi fought within his party 'Rashid' emerged victorious which also was a cause of apprehension for elder Bakshi. He had further experienced that Sheikh's fall was precipitated by various factors, but could have been delayed had he posted his trusted friend or relation as a watchdog near the corridors of power in Delhi. For these reasons both positive and negative Rashid was nominated to the Indian Parliament (Lok Sabha). Jammu and Kashmir had no direct representation in the Indian house of representatives, but the state government would select six parliament members from the state.[2] By this indirect nomination a vacancy was created in the state assembly from this constituency. At this time DNC took upon itself the role of the opposition. The workers cadre from district Budgam had joined Sheikh Abdulla in 1953, the remaining cadre joined DNC and for Bakshi there was a complete lack of men. Syed Ali Safvi the MLA from Budgam was considered too weak and humble to lead the tehsil Budgam National Conference and was himself reluctant to shoulder the burden. In this situation a 'Namberdar' from Kralpora Rehman Rather was nominated as tehsil president; after his failure G.M. Wani Kanihama was inducted, but the situation taxed the mind of Bakshi. The majority of degree holders in the National Conference had crossed the floor so he wanted at least a degree holder of Charar-i-Sharief town, but a hereditary loyalist for Bakshi and his dynasty.

Since 1951 Bakshi devoted himself to the renovation of the shrine of Sheikh Noor-ud-din Wali at Charar-i-Sharief. During his frequent visits he would usually stay for the night in a house adjacent to the shrine complex which belonged to Abdul Aziz Haji who was Halqa president of the local unit of the National Conference. During the trial period of the Quit Kashmir movement Abdul Aziz had severed all his connections with the National Conference and had taken over as a retail dealer of sugar and kerosene supplies from the state. Immediately after Sheikh Abdulla took over the reins of the emergency administration Abdul Aziz alongwith three other comrades opened the local civil secretariat cum interrogation centre in a room on the western end of the main market. But at the time of the Zaildar election when his cousin Mohd. Yousuf Haji stood against the National Conference candidate, Abdul Aziz worked alongwith his other cousin ex-Zaildar Jalal-ud-din veteran leader of the Muslim Conference, against his own organisation.

Bakshi suffered a complex on account of his socio-economic background and so developed renewed contacts, both on political and social levels with the bourgeoisie and petty bourgeoisie families. He knew that intimacy with *khadims* of shrines had in the circumstances immediate if not long term dividends. For these reasons Bakshi reposed his choice in Abdul Qayoom son of Abdul Aziz, the first post graduate from this town who had in 1955 taken up a job of his choice as a college lecturer. At that time he was posted as the Urdu lecturer at the Degree College Sopore and had cultivated both the taste and aspiration to contribute to Urdu literature. Yet in search of a line in which he could specialise, he had shown signs of becoming a literary critic or an essayist. By nature he was very shy, avoided mixing with people, had no taste even for lively political discussions, but had developed a taste for academics. He had neither the inclination nor any association with politics and so was not personally interested, but the petty feudal background where the *patwari* or forest guard is considered a higher officer than a college principal, his family brought this gentle lamb with 'tied legs' to the election office of the National Conference in Gawkadal. In the office Abdul Gani Goni made him write a resignation letter from government service which was accepted. Simultaneously, he was registered as a basic member of the National Conference. At times the dialogue spoken in dramas or mock plays becomes the reality of life though years later. In a drama at school in Charar-i-Sharief Abdul Qayoom, a student of fourth class had played the role of a magistrate and as such had acquitted the accused, his class mate. This author as second primary student remembers that Mohd. Sidiq Dar Nadaf; the mock accused left the 'court room' and while praying for the prosperity and progress of the judge said,

"May God make you Patwari or Rakha." Inspite of ministerial comforts and his political status which provided him ample chances to build up the future of his children and other relations the 'intellectual' Qayoom was dumped in the position of an ineffective political Patwari or Rakha.

Hence politics was imposed upon Abdul Qayoom and he was imposed as the National Conference candidate. Abdul Gani Namathali was his rival candidate from the defected camp (DNC) and P.L. Handoo was named his chief election agent P.L. Handoo was mercilessly beaten at Wathora and received severe skull injuries. Thus the pro-Indian rather pro-Nehru opposition party had to follow the same path on which Indian democracy had forced the ex-Plebiscite Front and other parties to go.[3] This bye-election made the progressive agents of India have a rethink and before they could be emasculated politically they found safety in their return to the bandwagon of goondas and corrupt people as they themselves called Bakshi's conference. With assurances from New Delhi that their legislative and ministerial berths would remain reserved for them they rejoined the old party two years before the next hustings which were to take place in 1962. However, the Jammu leadership except Girdari Lal Dogra did not desert the Democratic Conference, but could not play any role to correct the views of Indian rulers regarding their Kashmir policy. Even they were not able to create such conscience among Indian communists with whom DNC was aligned.

Reader might feel from these discussions that this Chapter particularly treats history of Charar-e-Sharief. The reasons are patent. Firstly, as explained in the Preface the necessity to write, this tratise arose due to May 1995 devastation of 'Charar' so particular refrences to that place. Secondly it is the Central place geographically, politically volatile and spiritually sensitive hence choosen for specimen study. Thirdly it is the Constituency which saw a straight contest for the first time in our history between two political out fits both with allegiance to one origin.

Chapter 9

Selection by Abduction

The number of opposition contestants rose to 41 in 1962, but they were mostly scattered and confined to the Jammu region where elections were stage managed so as to counter the impact of the boycott policy. Out of 42 constituencies only about 12 constituencies in Kashmir region were situationally ready for a contest, therefore, 30 National Conference candidates were returned uncontested. In political circles it was felt that the Plebiscite Front and Political Conference should remain out of the fray as parties but should not strictly impose boycott so that some genuine democrats or persons committed to the cause of human rights might get a chance to squeak into the legislature and give vent to their frustration. Molvi Masoodi openly preached this idea and I met him alongwith advocate G.M. Malik representing DNC.[1] I filed papers from two constituencies Charar-i-Sharief and Budgam as an independent candidate. Rashid Bakshi MP was again the ruling party candidate from Charar-i-Sharief and Aga Syed Ali Safvi was the National Conference candidate from Budgam. This author had an electoral alignment with the DNC, but before the scrutiny of papers could be done the proposers, seconders and even the candidates were abducted. Consequently, on the fixed day of scrutiny their papers were rejected either for absence of candidates or for the absence of their proposers. However, only those independent candidates were allowed to remain in the fray who had filed nomination papers against such National Conference nominees who were on the hit list of Bakshi Rashid. They included Gh Qadir Masala from Langet Handware, Mir Lasjan from Khan Sahib (Budgam), G.M. Mir from Rajpura Pulwama, D.P. Dhar from Habakadal, S.L. Saraf from Amirakadal. The papers of their opponents Ab. Gani Mir, G.N. Wani Budgami, Ab. Sattar Ranjoor, G.M. Malik, P.N. Kaul and O.P. Saraf were found in order. The author had not cared to be politically wise as to make an entrance through the back door, so he struck his head against an iron wall. Such was the case with Baha-ud-din who had posed a challenge against strong man Gazi who after defeating Renzo in 1957 had become the most influential terror within the National Conference. Bakshi had sent signals for the success of Malik and Ranjoor, but wanted me and Baha-ud-din to withdraw, which despite the dismay of our colleagues both of us resisted. Hence, a plan to physically eliminate the author was directly carried out by the Deputy Commissioner of Srinagar Mir Nasurullah (I.A.S) son-in-law of Bakshi, the prime minister.

This author alongwith his sympathisers Prof. G.M. Sheikh, Prof. G.N. Siddiqui, Prof. M.S. Kuchey, Prof. Abdul Ahad Malik and Prof. Nazir A. Rathore were together at a dinner party at the residence of Prof. Abdul Ahad in Gojwara. As we left the residence the jeep of the deputy commissioner tried to run over me near Malartta aiming to break my legs (state garages jeep— registration no. JK 111A) but I clung to the nearby electricity pole and could save my legs. Earlier he had declared, "We will break his legs so he would be unable to contest". Next day Prof. Siddiqui accompanied by Peer Mohd Yehya Siddiqui president Labour Union and Prof. Sheikh, took me late in the evening in a jeep to a destination not known to anyone except Yehya Peer.

Paper Tiger

In downtown Nawakadal in a centrally heated well-furnished ground floor house this author felt certain about the imminence of instant death. In the corridor leaders like Peer Gyas-ud-din were present, but this author was taken to the special hall. A lady entertained the author with *qahwa* and so his apprehensions were cleared and some intuitions provided strength. He got to know through the lady that the house belonged to the king maker Bakshi Abdul Rashid known as the 'Krushchev' of Kashmir. After some time he came into the hall and to his utter surprise this author did not stand humbly to receive him. He was soon exposed before me, I came to know that the most powerful dictator of Kashmir was so frightened of the contest that he was ready to accept any conditions. He openly said that he could kill the author, could physically disable him but that might 'belittle him' with his puppets. A truce was reached that the papers of this author would be 'accepted' from both the constituencies, but the author would have to withdraw from Charar-i-Sharief to assure the unopposed return of Rashid. Further, assurances were given to me that no bungling would be allowed from Budgam constituency, but warned that I should take care of the local goondas which Safvi, the National Conference candidate had hired.

5 February 1962

It was the day of scrutiny of the nomination papers filed in the state by all the candidates from the ruling party and their opponents. This day has been the blackest day of the 60s in so far as it saw the highest number of abductions, probably unrecorded so far in any country. During the night intervening 4\5 February 1962, candidates, proposers or those who had seconded the nominations were whisked away from their homes. They were detained in hidden places. Though the most 'powerful' man had entered into a truce with this author, but had cautioned that he was not able to undo the plans already approved, so, this author needed to take care. Hence, during this fateful night all the known 'hideouts' of this author in Budgam, Charar-i-Sharief and Mohalla Rehbab Sahib, Srinagar were raided but the raiders failed in their aim. In the morning of 5 February this author hired a taxi driven by Ghulam Mohd. (the same taxi which was usually hired by advocate Lateef Qureshi for his professional visits). The vehicle first took the candidate and his group to Magharmal Bagh Srinagar to the residence of Saif-ud-din Ganai, DIG police where I informed him that this author was voluntarily going to an abattoir to be butchered. He laughed at this statement, but on his return from Budgam he reported to Bakshi, "Sir, the young boy told me that he was going to an abattoir, initially I dismissed the statement as cheap politics but am surprised that how he has returned safe from that butchery."

After we left from Magharmal Bagh our vehicle took a curve near panchayat ghar Humhama (on Srinagar Budgam Road at the 14th km) when from the opposite direction came another taxi in which four village level workers who were known 'goondas' were seated. They tried to collide their vehicle with ours, but our driver Gh. Mohd intelligently saved the situation and increased the speed. It took ten minutes for the 'goondas' to reverse their vehicle and within that time our vehicle was at the door of the official residence of Mohammad Sadiq Bhat Munsiff Magistrate Budgam, the Returning Officer Budgam constituency. Within minutes a batch of 100 goondas attacked this author and his proposers Gh. Ahmad Shakir and Noor-ud-din Garandi. We took refuge in the house of the judge, but 'goondas' made this house a target too, ransacked it and broke its windows and doors. Mrs. Bhat fell unconscious and the munsiff could not restrain himself, he took a rifle in his hand and restored order. Till then the police acted as spectators and after the personal intervention of the magistrate they also started taking action. In the meanwhile the DIG also arrived and under police escort we were taken to the munsiff's court where the returning officer (Munsiff) started examination of papers, but in his presence attempts were made to whisk away the two proposers who resisted. In the meanwhile, a mock funeral procession was arranged which halted near the court building and Shakir was informed that his mother had died of shock. He said, "take her to the graveyard, I am coming". He was heard by the returning officer who immediately started examination of nomination papers which were accepted. Shakir wept mourning his mother's death but within moments he started laughing. A.R. Mir Rahat, the veteran leader of the National Conference and a terror in the area cried, "Oh judge! the proposer has turned mad, allow him to leave".

"No I am not mad, you are mad. Sir, (addressing the judge) my mother is dead for last ten years". Under the impact of continued threat he was so frightened that it took him at least half an hour to recollect that his mother was since dead. After our papers were accepted from Budgam we went to the office of Ujjagar Singh tehsildar Reconstruction of Records Budgam who as R.O. Charar-i-Sharief constituency, had to scrutinise our papers. The National Conference candidate Bakshi Rashid along with his proposers and associates were inside the office conversing with thereturning officer. The door was bolted from inside.

The notorious gang of 'goondas' from the city of Srinagar headed by Mam Gul (Gul Majeed Khan) Ama Kuchloo, Khalil Kachroo and others were on guard outside with *dandas* and sticks. We were not allowed even to knock at the door and were forced to retreat. Outside the campus the president of Budgam Bar Association Damodhar Bhat, a veteran leftist and freedom fighter was waiting. A feeble, dwarf like man, who nevertheless had a lion's courage led us again to the returning officer's office and struck his own head against the door. Goondas loudly cried "Dama Kak don't break your head"which was heard by Bakshi Rashid who 'ordered' the returning officer to open the door. So we managed our entry, but only to hear that due to our absence our papers had already been rejected.

In the tehsil campus territorial tehsildar Akbar Khan scrutinised the papers of the National Conference candidate Mir Lasjan and of independent candidate Gh. Nabi Wani for the Draigam constituency. The Bakshi camp had decided to eliminate Mir Lasjan a fellow traveller of G.M. Sadiq so it was a foregone conclusion that papers of both were to be accepted and this happened inspite of the fact that hired goondas of Lasjan did not lag behind. But Gh.Nabi Wani had also brought along his sympathisers. He had recently defected from the Plebiscite Front to take part in elections but with a clear understanding with Bakshi. He had gone along in 1953 with Sheikh but originally had the patronage of Bakshi. Tehsildar Akbar Khan did 'everything' with tact. He kept Mir Lasjan (who later became his close relation) satisfied. Simultaneously, he assured the prime minister and general secretary, (both the Bakshis) of the liquidation of Mir Lasjan', a task which he tactfully completed.

In Beerwah constituency our candidate was Sheikh Mohd. Qasim of Iskandarpora, whereas Ab. Qadoos Azad by nature meak and humble, represented the National Conference. But with all his humility he too did not lag behind in meanness like his comrade Safvi. Qasim also found his proposers abducted and forms rejected.

Khan was also the returning officer for Khan Sahib constituency for which again the National Conference candidate Sofi G. Ahmad, a notorious figure for his muscle power, but a sound political worker was imported from

Srinagar. He too was relieved unopposed in the same manner.

Tehsil Budgam (now a district) consisted of five electoral constituencies; as a sample we have contained herein the drama that was played in this district as the personal testimony of this author who 'posed contest' in two out of the five constituencies and had arranged a sort of united front with the other three independent candidates. Ultimately, out of five, the contest was allowed in only two, Budgam and Draigam constituencies. In Draigam the contest was in reality between the formal candidate of the ruling party and personal candidate of the prime minister with clear directions given both to the organisation and the government machinery to 'seal' the political career of Mir Lasjan. In the Sadiq group only Mir Lasjan had claims of a political base in Budgam district but he too was mistaken. Therefore, Bakshi wished to put an end to those phantasies. The second contest was from Budgam where this author was in the fray. The papers of this author would also meet the fate of rejection, but because the returning officer a munsiff magistrate from judiciary hailed from Jammu city and was recently posted in Kashmir so he had a comparatively sensitive conscience. Sadiq Bhat now an advocate of J&K High Court and a veteran and respected citizen of Jammu was then more annoyed with the blunders which Safvi's 'goondas' committed by attacking his house which resulted in chaos in his family.

The situation in Srinagar and other parts of the state was more serious as was later known to us. The dance of death was played at Budgam from where members of the National Conference Safvi and Qadoos Azad faced opposition candidates.

The situation there was compared to 'Kerbala' by no less an authority than Alhaj Agha Syed Yousuful Musavi Alsafvi the head of the Shia community—a veteran scholar. On 12 February fell the anniversary of martyrdom of the fourth Calipha Hazrat Ali (K.W.) corresponding to 21 Siyam (21st of the 7th Month Hijri). Agha Sahib, while addressing a lakh of mourners in the Grand Mosque of Budgam hinted in his sermon:

"...On that very soil where every year mourners of martyrs of Kerballa do shed tears and bleed while beating their breasts the same soil was turned into a contemporary Kerballa by those who call themselves condemnors of Yazid...."

On the one hand, those remarks expressed the terror which has become the destiny of Kashmir, on the other hand, the particular tone of Agha Sahib's sermon conveyed to his community that he was not happy with Safvi the National Conference candidate himself a relation of the Agha dynasty. Hence, the propaganda was dashed to the ground which projected Safvi as a 'Shia' candidate and thirdly, a wave of sympathy swept the electorate in favour of this author. Sunnis were already full of emotion for 'Gauher Sahib' the candidate from sacred Charar-i-Sharief. Simultaneously, reaction expressed by Agha Sahib consolidated Shia support behind this author. Hence, the J&K Plebiscite Front and Political Conference were rejected *en masse.*

All that is described about Budgam district was the preface of the book consisting of various chapters of abductions, kidnapping, fatal attacks, corrupt practices which Bakshi wrote during hustings authenticated by Jawahar Lal Nehru.

For various reasons this author had tied himself with the forces represented by the DNC and P.S.P for democratic values to carry Jammu&Kashmir along with the movement in the evolution of democracy in India, hence he remained committed to the collective discipline. The polling in Jammu province proceeded on the polling days fixed in the Valley. In Jammu the worst type of repression was let loose during polling and immediately thereafter. Even the ballot boxes were burnt as accurately described by K.D. Sethi in his autobiography in Urdu. Sethi a veteran progressive leader and freedom fighter is a symbol of principles of courage, confidence and integrity. He was himself a candidate alongwith his close comrade R.P. Saraf.

This mid-day rape of values committed on the highways had exposed not only Bakshi, but invited criticism against Jawaharlal Nehru within and outside the Congress Party. So, Bakshi was used to make some attempts to cover the excesses which were bound to put Jawaharlal Nehru to widespread shame in his own country. Though Bakshi had decided to get Masala and Lasjan defeated from Langat and

Draigam respectively, but right thinking people already knew that these two concessions were a foregone conclusion to suit Bakshi's own interests. They knew that these two concessions were to weed out unwanted elements rather than concede to people the right to vote. Hence, he had to make many more concessions. He had plans to get D.P. Dhar and G.M. Rajpuri defeated. But, the DNC leadership insisted on concession of the third seat from Khanyar where Bakshi's trusted man Gazi Abdul Rehman was the official candidate. At this point of bargaining the Sadiq— group acted in frustration, but tactfully through Gh. Nabi Sheikh Darzi and Peer Abdul Aziz, two leaders of the DNC, they persuaded Malik for boycott. Hence, Malik and his group remained intransigent about the Khanyar seat which Rashid was not going to yield easily. As regards Budgam constituency Bakshi was informed by Rashid that a wave existed against Safvi and even workers of the P.F. were not able to carry the writ of boycott call. Rashid had successfully convinced Bakshi that it was Safvi himself who had fanned the flames. Secondly, Bakshi was conscious that a judicial officer and that too a Jammu man might not be able to commit irregularities which a returning officer, in the circumstances in Jammu&Kashmir, has to commit. Safvi had in his explanations directly accused Rashid and his men especially A.R. Rahat for his own lapses. In these circumstances Budgam constituency was left as a free zone where 'honest' and fair election was decided to be allowed.

This author was certain that against the flood of sympathy and massive support no bungling could deter the defeat of the National Conference candidate, but was deeply tied with the destiny of the DNC as all his polling agents were political workers of that party.

The Jammu leadership though themselves shattered conveyed their resentment against boycott and desired that some of the democrats should make their presence felt in the house. But the local leadership was with Malik whose conscience keepers were Peer Aziz and G. Nabi Sheikh. Our later assessment made it clear that the former was guided by Sadiq and the latter by D.P. Dhar. The Praja Socialist candidate against D.P. Dhar - the third in the fray also joined us in a press conference held at a hotel in Lal Chowk where we declared our boycott 'for the acts of bungling which authorities have made in J&K in these elections'. We highlighted accurately a hundred instances in the boycott document which later on formed an annexure to a memorandum submitted by the permanent representative of Pakistan at UNO to the Security Council.

These intriguing developments in our political history will be discussed in detail in the autobiography of this author entitled *Anthology of Shade* as they are not strictly relevant here. But the precise reasons which made this author be a party to the boycott decisions are:

1. As stated the polling agents were borrowed by this author from the DNC so apprehended that they might be guided by a party directive to abstain. But later their annoyance of our boycott belied the apprehensions.
2. This author had a purpose with which he wished to join the legislature, but singlehanded he could not contribute anything so apprehended that he might fall in the lap of the ruling party and do in Rome what the Romans do.
3. This author was so trapped in the DNC cage that he was not allowed even to go to Budgam to consult his voters and more so seek guidance from Agha Sahib who later expressed his dislike for the decision of boycott.
4. That this author had developed an aversion and hatred against all political parties which had developed a culture of intrigue so as a reaction adopted escapism. That the miseries which had befallen this author from the day he had filed his papers and the sword hanging over the head of his parent had caused apprehensions about his safety in the minds of his parents, so, he had no option but to see at least, a temporary smile on their faces.

Inspite of the boycott, on the day of counting the returning officer Bhat sent three messages from the counting hall advising this author to join the counting of votes as on final count this author was leading his rival by 1,600 votes. Later, before declaration of results some unpolled votes numbering 3,000 were added to the votes polled by Safvi and he was declared successful.

The happenings in Budgam form a specimen of the nature of elections held in Jammu&Kashmir more so the one held in 1962. Let us again quote from the book *Kashmir Key Shab-O-Raz* by P.L. Kaul who was in the fray himself and has participated in almost every election:

> "In the general election of 1962 a few independents, few candidates from PSP provided a colour of contest to it. But again for reasons of the continuation of the policy of denial for holding public meetings, denial of civil liberties etc. the candidates had no alternative but to go for boycott hence a statement to that extent was issued jointly signed by me, Malik Gh. Mohmmad leader of Democratic Conference and Independent candidate Shri Gh. Nabi Gauhar. It contained the grounds of our boycott and was highlighted in media. The government circles felt disturbed but Balraj Puri PSP leader from Jammu contradicted, and stated that O.P. Saraf had remained in fray from Amirakadal".

In subsequent lines Kaul narrated the incidents which occurred and said that directly through S.N. Fotedar Chairman Legislative Council he was persuaded to withdraw the boycott statement in the larger interest of the 'national cause'. It is a unique characteristic that butchering of democracy in J&K has become a distinguishable trait of 'Indian national interest' and whenever the butchered man moans or cries with pain he is dubbed to have been treacherous to the national interest.

Notes

1. In 1957 the so-called progressive group defected from N.C. and formed Democratic National Conference. The leader of the group Mr. G.M. Sadiq addressed the first Convention of his defected Caders in Gandhi Park (on which presently situates JK High Court Building) opening with a famous verse of Faiz Ahmad Faiz.

   I was approached by its second line of leadership late Pandit damodhar Bhat and G.M.Malik Advocates to enter the 'democratic fold'. In 1958 I was again insisted to which I replied: "I will surely, if the outfit Survives upto next elections to be held in 1962". The condition put by me appeared but a lame excuse. But in 1960 when Sadiq and his comrades returned back to the fold (which had created tradition that none should raise his head) Late Mr. Bhel praised my assessment which I had made as a 24 year old youth. Latter the situation established that defection in 1957 and unification in 1960 both were engineered, abetted and instigated moves from Teen Maurti Bhavan, New Delhi, the official residence of Prime Minister Mr. Nehru. The secret will be unfolded in the discussion on the extension of the Indian Election Commission and Supreme Court of India Jurisdiction upon J&K.

Chapter 10

Selection by Rejection

The disillusioned, deceived and dejected Kashmiris had a faint hope that G.M. Sadiq, the new prime minister of Kashmir would make at least minor deviations from the totally undemocratic and rather fascist policies of his predecessor Bakshi. The people knew that Sadiq was a prisoner of duplicity. They were conscious that both as a communist and as a committed pro-Indian he worked as a theoretician for the National Conference at all times, helped to craft the dictatorial policies of Sheikh Abdulla and shared the authorship of fascist treacheries with Bakshi. So they had no illusions about his rule, but young people who had heard him Gandhi Park in 1957 had some expectations from him. Introducing his splinter group of D.N.C he opened his speech in the park with these verses of the Urdu poet Faiz Ahmad Faiz. The verse read:

"Nisar Teri Galiyoon pa Ay Watan Ki Jehan,
Ye Rasam Chal Aayi Hai Ki Koyee Sar Utha key Na Chaley"

"Let me sacrifice myself for thy each inch, oh! My wonderful motherland—The land where tradition has been evolved that no one should possess sense of self respect."

The youth, therefore, expected that under his directions his government might provide a process of reversal in such traditions. But the 1967 election proved beyond doubt that his pretensions were mischievously deceptive and within a refined and civilised frame dwelt a dangerous despot with totalitarian strains in his policies.

Bakshi would at least try to provide grounds for rejection of papers of the opposition candidates which would deceptively appear normal like disposal. So he would stage manage the abductions, (as was done upto 1962) so that the returning officer would dismiss the nominations. On the other hand, Sadiq was a realist and as such considered such pretexts as hypocricy. He believed in transparency and unmindful of what the people might say, he wrote a history of complete rejection of papers of the opposition candidates. He did not feel ashamed when his bandwagon of MLAs was collectively and openly at all levels, qualified as 'Khaliq' made. His government was also called Khaliq- made government. Khaliq is an Arabic word meaning the creator, so like every item, legislature too was a creation of the Absolute Creator (Khaliq-i-Matlaq).The phrase is not used in that sense, but one of the most unscrupulous officers, Khaliq was at that time the deputy commissioner of Anantnag. He was an ordinary official in the Land Revenue Department Jammu, but was selected by Bakshi and made a powerful authority for south Kashmir. Sadiq and his progressive colleagues always used to condemn Khaliq as Bakshi's hand-picked tyrant, but Sadiq made the same hand-picked tyrant a tool for reorientation of democracy.

At that time this author was posted as Munsiff Magistrate First Class at Pulwama district Anantnag and as such had attended one or two meetings called by Khaliq as district magistrate. Before the declaration from the Election Commission for the date of filing of nominations, Sadiq had taken Khaliq into confidence and all the returning officers were selected on his advice. Rajpura is an important electoral segment within Pulwama tehsil which then fell under the jurisdiction of this author. Till then it was represented by G.M. Rajpuri, Speaker of the Legislative Assembly.

Ashok Kumar member All India Service was appointed returning officer Rajpura. One of the lawyers of Pulwama court Omkar Nath Koul Trichal (now a Congress leader) filed papers from the same constituency as an independent candidate. Simnani, a journalist was the nominee of Bakshi's National Conference and a veteran freedom fighter and dedicated political worker Gh. Qadir Mir Muran too filed papers as an independent. The scrutiny of papers was conducted by the returning officer and assisting returning officer Safaya. Papers of all the candidates were found correct, but the returning officer himself tampered with the papers of the three opposition candidates by overwriting, rejected the papers of all the three candidates and declared the Congress candidate Rajpuri elected unopposed.

Later on, while disposing off the election petition challenging this election a retired Indian judge from Patna High Court, as adhoc judge of J&K High Court passed severe and serious strictures against Ashok Kumar, IAS and Safaya, a state officer and ordered that both be prosecuted for "indulging in fabricating and tampering evidence...for committing forgeries."

The extract of this judgment alongwith facts shall be given while we discuss elections held for six parliamentary seats from Jammu and Kashmir and the state legislature in 1996 held under the administration governed and controlled by the same Ashok Kumar who was the chief secretary at that time.

This author was named presiding officer for Pulwama town, but neither was any poll held nor did this author acquire experience to supervise any polling:

> "In the elections of 1967, the rejection of 118 nomination papers of the opposition candidate (including covering candidates) materially affected 39 out of 75 assembly constituencies, and ensured the unopposed return of Congress candidates in 22 out of 42 constituencies in the valley."[1]

The farce in these elections was even exposed by Prime Minister Indira Gandhi who rebuked the majority group of members of this house who called on her to activate for the dismissal of Sadiq. Let us hear from P.L. Kaul, what Indira. Gandhi said to them:

> "You have no locus standi to speak for people because you are not elected representatives of the people. The officials of the state government and the Election Commission had to commit countless irregularities to get you elected."[2]

In a booklet the dignitaries of Kashmir including Sheikh Abdulla, Molvi Farooq (founder president Awami Action Committee), Mirza Mohammad Afzal Beig (founder president of Plebiscite Front), Mohammad Yaseen Hamdani (head of Jamaiti Hamdani), Gh. Mohi-ud-din Kara (founder president of J&K Political Conference, cousin and brother-in-law of Sadiq), Mohammad Abbas Ansari (J&K Itihaadul Muslimeen), Molvi Iftikhar Ansari (President J&K Shia Association, presently a member of Farooq government in J&K), Syed Qasim Shah Bukhari (President Tabligul Islam

J&K) gave their signed statement. The extract is quoted here,

> "Kashmir valley consists of 42 electoral constituencies out of which in 1967, 22 returned to congress candidates of the ruling party unopposed as the papers of opposition candidates were totally rejected."

The Indian national press also condemned these elections in strong words as was done by the jurists, scholars, intellectuals and journalists of India. On February 16, 1967, C.D. Deshmukh, M.C. Stelward, Meharchand Mahajan,[3] K.G. Syedeen, Frank Moraes and others issued a joint statement to the Indian press condemning the en masse rejection of nomination papers of opposition candidates. The extract is as follows,

> "In an assembly of 75 members in J&K in 39 constituencies 118 opposition papers were rejected, they include 22 constituencies which saw unopposed selection. Thus, there are strong suspicions about any fairness in these elections."

These dignitaries demanded establishment of an "enquiry commission and pressed to defer the declaration of results till the commission declared its findings."

But never in the history of 50 years of Indian occupation was any demand to constitute a commission of enquiry to probe into the acts of massacre of values, men and property ever conceded to. However, high powered commissions were constituted even during Sadiq Wazarat to satisfy the demands of the microscopic minority of Pandits which followed the conversion of a Pandit girl Parmeshvari into Parveen Akhtar. The demands too were for restoration of privileges to the privileged community.

It is relevant here to state that such a demand was made even in the Indian Parliament to probe the lapses which resulted in the devastation of the town of Charar-i-Sharief, but it met the same fate which the demand of these Indian dignitaries had met.

Balraj Puri in an article published in the *Indian Express*, 3 June 1967 writes:

> "The ruling party polled only 12% votes whereas the bulk boycotted and others went to opposition candidates."

Based on his own knowledge this author states that those 12 per cent too were due to impersonation, cheating and result of fraud.

The national executive of an Indian opposition party the P.S.P. in its session held on March 12, 1967 demanded that in view of the happenings in J&K holding of fresh elections might create faith in the viability of democracy. But it is not in our destiny due to our folly of showering love on such leadership which had an ingrained mentality of treachery and for the reason that we are occupied by the 'biggest democratic neo-colonial power'.

Notes

1. *Balraj Puri.*
2. Pirey Lal Kaul, *"Kashmir Key Shab... Roz"*, Suman Publishers, p. 97. It needs mention that in 1969-70 the deep rift among two groups of the ruling party left the majority with Syed Mir Qasim the defector and the majority could, of its own, move and pass a no-confidence motion against their leader . Sadiq and could have, in his place elected Mir Qasim. But due to the 'Special Status' of J&K they could not do so and therefore, the majority moved to the Indian capital New Delhi, paraded before Prime Minister Indira Gandh, and insisted for the change of leadership. They argued on the basis of pure arithmetic to which Indira Gandhi replied in a realistic manner as P. L. Kaul has quoted in Supra
3. Meharchand Mahajan is the main broker whom the Indian Home Minister Sardar Patel got imposed as the Maharaja's prime minister and who wrote the script of the fiction of accession.

Chapter 11

Selection by Concessions

In an earlier book *Hazratbal Central Stage of Kashmir Politics* this author has highlighted the pivotal role of such selections in Kashmiri politics before, during and after the Indo-Pak war of 1971. In these discussions references about the 1972 elections have been made, but not in detail. It is not also desirable to ask the reader to wander from book to book and hence repetition of facts cannot be avoided.[1]

The Parliament Election of 1971 also did not invite any involvement of voters, however, the politics of boycott was under serious consideration of the leaders. The Sadiq government had treacherously eroded all the semblances of internal autonomy. The apprehensions lurking in the minds of aware elements was that with one stroke of the pen, the Indian government might get laws regarding 'permanent residentship' status abolished and consequently demographic changes might follow. They further apprehended that in such a political eventuality, Pakistan would, as usual, lodge only a protest with the Security Council.

Against this background Sheikh Abdulla, Molvi Mohd. Syed Masoodi and the leadership of J&K Political Conference and J&K Plebiscite Front were all involved in political rethinking. Activity to undo the boycott politics was in the offing. The leadership had no direct interest in parliament elections yet made overtures to assess public feelings on the subject whether to participate in the coming elections due in 1972 or not.

Though Bakshi was at that time a spent force and G.M. Sadiq was the main political adversary of Sheikh and the Plebiscite Front, yet Sheikh, Syed Masoodi and Mirza Afzal Beig all joined together with Sadiq to finish Bakshi and got him defeated in the 1971 Parliament Election. Mohi-ud-din Karra leader of the pro-Pakistan Political Conference, cousin and brother-in-law of Sadiq, had made an assessment that Bakshi acquiring a base in Delhi might create trouble for the

Sadiq ministry. So, his joining hands with Sadiq was understandable, but the actions of Sheikh and the leadership of the Plebiscite Front was tactically erroneous. They helped their own powerful enemy who was ineffective then, yet all joined hands with Sadiq to emasculate Bakshi, who was the official candidate for the parliamentary constituency of Srinagar. In the words of Molvi Masoodi a 'khamba' (wooden pole) was given life. Shamim Ahmad Shamim was thus supported on one side by the Sadiq government and on the other by the 'popular' leadership and so trounced G.M. Bakshi who had been the kingmaker of the state.

This mini-election made the leadership assess the public mood which was positive for elections, but with reservations. Pro-election psychology held sway, but apprehensions regarding fairness were equally alarming. Sheikh Abdulla was at the crossroads of his long political career. On the one hand, circumstances and public opinion made him approve the participation of his associates in hustings and on the other hand, he was certain that by traditional electoral malpractices he would be cut to size and the tall claims of his leadership would get exposed to the whole world. Hence, he wanted nothing more than a guarantee about free and fair elections.

By the end of 1971, the balance of power in the subcontinent was drastically disturbed. The defeat of Pakistan, its disintegration, the emergence of Bangladesh, the large number of POWs all these factors constituted a serious blow to the expectations of Kashmiris, enveloped them in gloom and created a pessimistic defeatism. It should not be construed that all Kashmiris were politically inclined and aligned with Pakistan, but all were emotionally disturbed for several reasons. Even the limited group of pro-Indian Muslims felt mentally shocked. An instance is reported about G.M. Sadiq who was almost on his deathbed when one of his sycophants informed him with happiness that Pakistan was limping towards defeat as Lahore had fallen (though it was mere propaganda). Sadiq rebuked him and warned him that the situation was bound to open a floodgate of uncertainties and conspiracies for disintegration in the entire subcontinent.

Another pro-Indian political group expressed the view that only a strong Pakistan provided guarantee of safety for Indian Muslims. But the gloom in Kashmir was more severe than was probably expressed and seen in wounded Pakistan. As soon as President Yehya Khan of Pakistan shamefully declared the surrender of his country—every house irrespective of political affiliations, turned into a mourning cell; ignorant women beat their breasts; the youth and children who could not bear the defeat of the Pakistani cricket team at the hands of Indian cricketers fell into deep gloom. From the slurred accent of General Yehya Khan all Kashmiris inferred that he was drunk even at the time that he addressed his nation, resulting in a wave of hatred against the Pakistani leadership.

People were more disturbed at the victory of India which had occupied Kashmir as a neo-colonist power and could harden its attitude against the freedom loving people of Kashmir.

Though the reiteration of the two prime ministers of India and Pakistan at Simla for peaceful settlement of Indo-Pak problems including the Kashmir tangle kept hope alive, but generally it was felt that Pakistan had to face very difficult times to resurrect its shattered image and would hardly be able to provide moral, material and political sustenance to the freedom movement in J&K. Hence, the necessity for change in policy and stance was deeply felt in the leadership ranks which had grown grey in the struggle and felt exhausted. On the other hand, the youth had provided zealous sustenance to the struggle against occupation. 'Al-fatah' a semi militant organisation was committed to overthrow the yoke of Indian occupation. It is also pertinent to mention the activities of such forces which advocated armed struggle.

On January 30, 1971 a Fokker Friendship Indian airliner named 'Ganga' en route from Srinagar to Jammu was hijacked and made to land at Lahore airport. The hijackers received a warm ovation at Lahore airport and it was from the demands of hijackers that Kashmiris came to know about an organisation called the Kashmir National Liberation Front. This hijacking provided one of the reasons for the 1971 war.

Mohammad Maqbool Bhat, with his dashing actions caused a mixed reaction in the mass thinking. On the one hand, the youth was inclined towards his policy that only 'the terror' can undo the occupation. On the other hand, the traditional leadership was terribly shaken by the newly emerging groups. The old leadership was exhausted and dejected. The families of Sheikh Abdulla and Mirza Afzal Beig had felt lured when they compared their lot with these novices of Kashmir politics. Men who could not stand comparison with the stature of Sheikh Abdulla and Mirza Afzal Beig had reached the zenith of prosperity. They included Syed Mir Qasim, Mohammad Shafi Qureshi, D.P. Dhar and other 'political pygmies' as they were nicknamed. The traditional leadership kept in view the rising stature of Shamim Ahmad Shamim who was merely a 'khamba' according to them, but had became an effective pillar through their influence. Why they should create others and themselves die in oblivion? This was the question which dominated all the families concerned. So, Sheikh Abdulla came under pressure; Begum Abdulla and Mirza Afsal Beig would persuade Sheikh Abdulla daily to make a drastic shift in his policies. On the other hand, Sofi Akbar and Haji Mohammad Ishaq, the two veteran leaders of the Plebiscite Front argued that the struggle was a continuing process and as the old guard of leadership faded away the successor leadership was bound to emerge. Hence, they pleaded that the traditional leadership should tacitly retire and allow the new leadership to grow. Mirza Afsal Beig, Molvi Syed, Begum Abdulla and Mohi-ud-din Karra argued that only the mature leadership could pull out the nation from its manifold problems.

Mohi-ud-din Karra the cousin and brother-in-law of Sadiq had seen absolute power pivoting around the Karra building at Batmaloo where these two first cousins had exploited, in their own interests, the genuine progressive cadres. After the death of Sadiq and the installation of the Qasim ministry Karra found his dynasty and the Sadiq group in the ruling party in immediate danger, so was more active about involving Sheikh Abdulla and other politicians in pro-India activity. Finally, Sheikh Abdulla consented to take part in elections but, was genuinely apprehensive that the decision in favour of elections had two edges each sharper than the other. Sheikh Abdulla was certain that the traditional bungling could cut him down in size on an international level. He was aware that the frauds which had become a trait of Kashmiri elections were so devised that it would be very difficult, rather impossible, to convince the outside world about the realities. Furthermore, the Indian media chauvinistically transgressed all norms of professional ethics and have always surreptitiously converted these frauds into fair play. It is for these reasons that the Indian press has eroded its relevance in Jammu and Kashmir. Had it, in the larger national interest preferred professional values to prevail upon what it wrote for foreign consumption it could have played a constructive role in cementing the relations of people of Jammu and Kashmir with the people of India. Sheikh Abdulla knew that even if he got massive support, yet by the jugglery of rulers, he would hardly be able to save his own deposit and thereafter, the world at large would be told lies with confidence and conviction. Sheikh Abdulla had no media rapport and would in the bargain lose his image, hence, without expressing himself either in favour or against elections he sought assurances of fairness from those who advocated participation in elections. Finally, it was decided to depute two vocal advocates from that camp to Delhi so as to elicit, at least, an indirect guarantee from the real rulers in Delhi. Hence, Kh. Gulam Mohi-ud-din Karra and Molvi Syed were assigned the job. They were arrested at Lakhanpur and detained. Sheikh Abdulla, his wife, son-in-law G.M. Shah and his life long associate Afzal Beig all were in Delhi under orders of externment.

The situation was very favourable to India at this time and several alternatives were available. It could have annexed Jammu and Kashmir to India by completely abrogating Article 370 of its Constitution which for practical purposes has no force. Such a decision may have caused a chain reaction throughout the world, but defeated Pakistan and dejected Kashmiris were not in a position to encash the worldwide resentment such a move may have led to.

The second alternative was to satisfy the people of J&K, reverse the process initiated in 1952 by forcing the Delhi Agreement and restore the status of Jammu and Kashmir to that position which the Instrument of Accession (on which India relied) had defined. Such a position would have created some internal problems for victorious Indira Gandhi and her government, but she could have solved them easily. The third alternative was very practicable and beneficial in the long term. It was simply to involve the people of Jammu and Kashmir with the democratic process of India and the situation was ripe for that as all the forces were craving for involvement in the process.

But the policy makers of India either did not think about these alternatives or rejected all of them and preferred a status-quo—a continuation of the policy of imposing her blue-eyed boys, a policy of her dynastic rule and perpetuation of undemocratic traditions. She did not agree to guarantee a free election, which the Indian Constitution guarantees for its citizens. But are Kashmiris citizens of India? The very man who threw Kashmir in the lap of India would not as an exiled man, call emissaries from Kashmir to plead for free elections from Delhi Darbar. The guarantee was offered but with stringent conditions to accommodate the favourites of the prime minister. Sheikh Abdulla was not ready to share power with those that he disparagingly called 'these insects of street gutters'.

The conditions attached to a verbal guarantee for fair elections were not even acceptable to Molvi Masoodi, who from 1954 was actively involved in burying the Plebiscite Front. The conditions were not acceptable even for Karra who was working actively to dislodge Mir Qasim so that the privileged Karra dynasty was not uprooted, as did happen a bit later.

Indira Gandhi was not inclined to grant the largesse of comparatively fair elections for her family's colony. There were some elements within the country who unsuccessfully tried persuading the circles around Indira Gandhi, but the Kashmiri Pandit lobby which was deeply rooted around her sabotaged their attempts. After the1971 war the friendly USSR was also actually pleading to channelise Kashmiri public opinion favourably, but to satisfy all these friendly persuations she advised her local agents and the lobby around to give the 'selection' in Jammu and Kashmir the colour of an election by conceding some seats to contradictory splinter groups. Hence, five seats from the Valley were conceded to All J&K Jamait-i-Islami and an equal number of seats from Jammu went to the Praja Parishad—the predecessor of the state Bhartiya Janata Party.

We have summed up the effects of the1971 Indo-Pak war on Kashmiri politics. It has been said that had the Indian rulers, at this historic juncture acted with vision and foresight they could have subtly involved Kashmiris in the democratic process of India. That involvement would have undone the past bitterness which had caused complete alienation.

But, Kashmir has remained somewhat a family domain of the Nehru dynasty for several reasons, an important one being the personal role of Jawahar Lal Nehru which he played even against the wishes of many Congress leaders. His daughter Indira Gandhi had written the first chapter of victory in Indian history though against the integral part of its own history.

Sycophants had made her believe that it was only she who had courage and wisdom. In the particular diction of the political upstarts of Kashmir Shamim Ahmad Shamim, had said in the Indian Parliament at the fall of Dacca that in the whole of India 'there was only one man and that was Mrs. Indira Gandhi'. With such flattery and sycophancy she had become extremely arrogant and so deliberately lost the opportunity. It has also been said that her friends outside and genuine democrats inside persuaded her to allow Kashmiris to volunteer their participation in moulding the destiny of the country, she followed her own dictates.

With known and tested methods the Congress government under Mir Qasim was installed in Jammu and Kashmir. However, to pacify the friendly elements inside and outside, nearly one dozen seats were 'conceded' for two opposition groups both inimical to each other.[2]

The Government of India had conceded 'some seats' in favour of Jamait-i-Islami which all political parties in India have considered untouchable. Through the trick a message was conveyed to Sheikh Abdulla's friends and family that their continued disobedience and non-participation had created a vacuum. By this signal they were made to feel that in case Sheikh did not 'obey', this vacuum could be filled in by others. Afzal Beig, Molvi Syed and Sheikh's wife would plead almost daily with Sheikh, that the tallest leader would be thrown into oblivion and upstarts would play the power game. On the other hand, a group led by Sofi Mohammad Akbar and Haji Mohammad Ishaq exercised counter pulls upon Sheikh so as to make him stick to his stand. In this conflicting situation Sheikh's lieutenant Mirza Afzal Beig was involved in parleys with the representative of the Indian government G. Parthasarthy. In spite of his reluctance until the end, Sheikh Abdulla had to yield to the pressure, hence, under the face saving device of the '1975 Accord' Sheikh Abdulla was to head the ruling party of the Indian National Congress of which he was not even an ordinary member. This was a unique marriage of convenience in which the Delhi masters forced their party head in Jammu and Kashmir to resign and directed the party to elect a person as its leader who was neither its member nor a member of the legislature. In his government Sheikh Abdulla 'recruited' as ministers men of his own choice who too were neither members of the majority party nor members of the legislature. Such new theories of politics were propounded and acted upon only in this neo-colony where neither democratic principles, nor the dictates of autocracy, nor the decrees of dictators nor the hush of mobocracy is the character of state policies. They are devised to suit one policy of India and that is to continue with the occupation of the territory of Jammu and Kashmir, unmindful of the fact whether people like the policy or dislike it. We will discuss later on the present constitution of the Farooq Cabinet in the same background. This unethical imposition invited reaction and a silent revolt within the state Congress party which had obtained through 'concessional selection' two thirds majority in the legislature.

Notes

1. It was necessary to introduce the readers to the 1971 Parliamentary Elections before we could go into the details of the 1972 Elections but that will make repetition unavoidable because in Part II the subject has been discussed in detail.
2. Syed Mir Qasim in his autobiography edited by Mr. A.R. Kondo has in clear words stated that before these elections he entered into a deal with Qari Saifud Din of Jamati Islam which assertion has not been denied by the latter in his recently published autobiography: 'Mohimati Hayat'. Mr. G.N.Hagro Advocate, a veteran leader of the J&K Jamati Islami, is on record to have persuaded his friend and leader Mr. Qasi to Contradict, but, Contradition has not come. Hence my report carried in "Hazratbal-Central stage of Kashmir Politics" (P.114) gets established that conceeding of 5-Assembly seats in favour of Jamat was yet another facet of fraudulant Elections.

Chapter 12

An Election or Democracy through Intimidation

Veteran freedom fighter, pioneer journalist and great hisorian late Pandit Prem Nath Bazaz qualified the '1977 election' as democracy through intimidation in his book by the same title. Though I am in agreement with the details, factual narration, statistical data provided and placed with the strength of argument, yet, respectfully differ with his ultimate conclusions and qualify the hustings as an 'election', the first and the last in our history.

Even before Sheikh Abdulla could be sworn in as the chief minister, the Indian leadership resiled from the guarantees which its representative Parthasarthy had guaranteed. Though such concessions were totally irrelevant for the people yet, Indira Gandhi again demonstrated the wolf and lamb game. Sheikh Abdulla refused to take oath, but the outgoing Chief Minister Mir Qasim went to Jammu Tourist Centre where Sheikh Abdulla was staying and persuaded him to go to the abattoir where 'the lion within him' was butchered.

Indira Gandhi brought the whole country under 'emergency', but Sheikh Abdulla did not find it necessary to extend emergency to Jammu and Kashmir as this state virtually from 1947 was ruled by emergency laws. He reacted against the terror let loose on Muslims of old Delhi by Indira Gandhi's son Sanjay Gandhi and her sycophant Jagmohan who was the Chief Executive of Delhi Development Authority. These reactions of Sheikh Abdulla annoyed the coterie which had created a nucleus around the Indian Prime Minister. In the meanwhile, the electorate of India punished Indira Gandhi for the crime against freedom and she was ousted. The local sycophants in Srinagar advised by Mufti Mohammad Syed and managed by Ali Mohammad Naik and late Ghulam Mustafa Mir attempted a showdown with Sheikh Abdulla. The newly established rulers of the Janta Party, on the advice of Jai Prakash Narain cashed the cancelled cheque of Indira Gandhi. It is in this background that Sheikh Abdulla lost much of his charisma and the state legislature was dissolved by the state governor - an agent of New Delhi. Fresh elections were ordered. According to the provisions of the Indian Constitution the leader of microscopic minority in the state legislature could not advise for dissolution, the state governor had to ask the leader of the majority party to form the government as it had withdrawn support to Sheikh Abdulla. But, instead, as the new rulers in New Delhi desired Governor L.K. Jha dissolved the house. The Indian leadership at the Center at this time was conscious of the eclipsed stature of the tall political figure of Jammu and Kashmir, but had sufficient understanding that he had enough nuisance value and once he was 'annoyed' he would again be able to fan the flames of anti-Indian feeling. With such clear understanding there were two different and contradictory views dominating the ruling leadership. One view strongly advocated having continuity in the policies in J&K which Jawahar Lal Nehru and his daughter Indira Gandhi had successfully prosecuted in five general elections held from 1950 to 1972. They created their pockets from many contradictory groups and amalgamated them within the fold called J&K state unit of the Janta Party.

This new party was totally devoid of a cadre, had no base among any section of the population, but had a galaxy of big leaders who were soon forgotten by the nation. It also included a group of opportunists and so all these bigwigs were candidates for chief ministership. Sofi Mohi-ud-din had projected Molvi Mohammad Syed as the next leader, advocate Hameed Karra had already started functioning as the agent of the chief minister designate, Khawaja Ghulam Mohi-ud-din Karra, whilst some workers at Kupwara raised slogans:

"*chief minister koun*?" (who is the chief minister)

The reply was, "Mr. Lone, Mr. Lone".

A section of the Shia community had already stitched gowns for the new chief minister Molvi Iftikhar and the brothers-in-law of Shamim Ahmad Shamim had declared Shamim to be the next chief minister. Fans of the Molvi dynasty would not concede the chair to anyone except to Molvi Mohammad Farooq. The integration of these people posed a challenge in 1977 to Sheikh Abdulla under the banner of the Janta Party. This group had propounded a theory that through the known and tested methods of democracy prevalent in Kashmir Sheikh Abdulla could be given a resounding defeat which would have given a blow to his failing health and so have finished the nuisance in Jammu and Kashmir politics.

The other group advocated a wait and watch policy and made the first group put pressure which would compel Sheikh Abdulla to seek mercy. Sheikh Abdulla's family and his life long associate Mirza Afsal Beig advocated surrender of principles upon a guarantee for an election, comparatively free from state interference. Governor L.K. Jha played a vital role.

The Home Minister of India Charan Singh visited Kashmir and openly spoke in restricted gatherings against Sheikh and assured even ordinary workers of the party's state unit that the tradition created and established by the Nehru dynasty was to be carried on with vigour. They even advised the 'old Sheikh' to retire from politics though they were themselves elder to him or equal to him in age.

All these pressures resulted in the collapse of Sheikh Abdulla's health and his fans and followers arranged prayer meetings at Charar-i-Sharief, Hazratbal and Makdoom Sahib's shrines for the early recovery of Sheikh. The largely attended public gatherings had boosted the election prospects of Sheikh's party the All J&K National Conference.

The reader may be bewildered as to how such large processions were organised for Sheikh's recovery when his charisma had gone down. The causes are:

(a) The amalgam of groups brought under the banner of state Janata Party was considered by the people as a deep rooted conspiracy to undo whatever was till then left in the name of 'internal autonomy'.

(b) The people considered the votes against the amalgam

to be a manifestation of a subdued protest against India.

(c) The people dubbed the Janta Party as a device of the All J&K Jansangh and considered the new rulers in Delhi as exponents of expansionist designs.

The National Conference carried propaganda that they would, in case they were voted to power, make efforts to leave open the J.V.C. Road connecting the state with erstwhile trade routes through Pakistan.

The cadres of National Conference, true to its culture, demonstrated muscle power particularly on the day when a caravan of national volunteers under its youth wing visited Pulwama district. They overawed these 'political labourers' who were being engaged in daily wage remuneration by Janata Party leaders.

Sheikh and Beig in spite of their failures and treacheries had contributed greatly in bringing about a political and agrarian revolution. On the other hand, Molvi Syed was dubbed as an 'ambiguous' agent of India, Mohi-ud-din Karra was said to have drained money from Pakistan in his self-interest and A.G. Lone, Shamim and Iftikhar were dubbed as opportunistic sycophants.

The deep rooted 'Sher-Bakre' feud of Srinagar had from 1938 divided the city into two camps. The camp of *sheras* (lions) was led by Abdulla and the camp of bakras (goats) was led by Molvi Farooq. As Molvi associated with Janata Party the traditional sheras though disgruntled, temporarily, as a reaction against bakras threw their weight again on the Sheikh's side.

Lastly, the heart attack of Sheikh, who to his credit had made great sacrifices, created a sort of sympathy wave.

It is against this background that Prime Minister Morarjee Desai visited Srinagar. Though Charan Singh and Jagjivan Ram both had issued directions to rig the elections, but the L.K. Jha administration was reluctant and hence the final word was with the Prime Minister.

Shamim the ruling party candidate from Shopian was more vocal in agitating in favour of rigging. Morarjee Desai was aware of this and as soon as he landed at Shopian, he commented,

"Before my visit the Janata wave has reached J&K."

"No Sir, these people have come to witness an experience of the landing of a helicopter" replied Shamim.

In open public congregation Shamim conveyed the joint demand of the state Janata Party and advocated for the traditional rigging.

In the city the prime minister visited the house of Molvi Farooq where the women of the fans of Molvi dynasty recited a verse in 'wanwon'[1]:

'Sabz Dastars Khuda Chhoi Raazi Pakistanuk Gazi Aaw'

(God bless our green turbaned warrior of Pakistan who has come to our rescue). With this folk verse women commonly welcome the groom when he comes with the 'barat' to the bride's house. It shows a pro-Pakistan tilt in the thinking of the masses.

The women who had assembled at the house of Molvi were not aware of the background of the guest and recited the same verse. Desai on hearing the word 'Pakistan' enquired the meaning of the verse from Molvi Masoodi who conveyed it correctly.

Later Molvi Farooq in a most undiplomatic manner said:

"Here, at this place sir, used to sit Qaid e Azam Mohammad Ali Jinnah"

"Now we are seated here." In these two sentences both made their real feelings transparent. Molvi Farooq exposed himself as a Pakistani, but under a pro-Indian mask to wreak revenge against Sheikh. Desai on the other hand, conveyed that India was deeply entrenched in Jammu and Kashmir and was not in a mood to loosen its grip upon the state.

These unwise comments of both Shamim and Molvi Farooq exposed to Morarjee Desai their weakness and thinking. Molvi Masoodi who headed the J&K Janta Party at that time played a role to make Morarjee Desai understand those contradictory elements who manned his organisation at that time. Intelligent people had sufficient understanding that Molvi Masoodi was completely in favour of 'fair play'. Sheikh was himself conscious that Molvi's presence in the ruling party was bound to weaken anti-democratic tactics of other leaders in that odd combine. This author is witness to the reaction which Sheikh Abdulla expressed when the general secretary of this party Mohi-ud-din Shah and district president Hisamud Din Banday together conveyed their anxiety on the nomination of Molvi Syed Masoodi as the head of the state unit by Nanajee Deshmukh, Secretary All India Janta Party. Sheikh expressed satisfaction and said, "It is well don't worry". Some present there inferred that Masoodi was Sheikh's man in that camp. That was not the position, but Sheikh knew that the Maulana was committed to the principles of fair play.

Maulana too watched the situation and as he found that Sheikh had fallen into an invisible trap and wanted nothing, but merely a fair election, he pleaded with Desai for that concession. He clearly understood that once Sheikh was entrenched in power and kept busy with paraphernalia of the high office; was kept amidst the caravans of pilot cars and jeeps and was engaged day and night in functions and ceremonies, he was bound to forget all commitments made to his people. Hence, to trap him in that invisible net a fair and free election was conceded. In 1972 this concession was limited to a dozen seats out of 75. This time the limit was not confined to any number but to fairness in the hustings - not for the sake of creating a tradition of fairness, but fairness for neo-colonist interests.

P.N. Bazaz was himself a part of that amalgam of contradictions which formed the J&K state unit of the Janata Party. In his book *Democracy by Intimidation* (1978) he has qualified the success of Sheikh's National Conference in 1977 elections as a game of intimidation played by the National Conference. I fear that the assessment is not fair. Bazaz as a defeated candidate was terribly hurt and so cannot be impartial. The intimidation was present on both sides which has become characteristic of elections in the subcontinent. The same was done by the National Conference in several constituencies, but the results which led to the defeat of Janta Party candidates and victory of National Conference candidates were on expected lines though the margin of votes shown in favour of the winning candidates was greatly exaggerated.

The 1977 election was similar to elections being conducted in the subcontinent, but was a device to accord a physical and political funeral to the hero of legends, the Sher-i-Kashmir Sheikh Mohammad Abdulla; a multi-dimensional personality for whom the office of chief minister could only be a feather in his cap. However, he was made to give his head in exchange of the feather.

Notes

1. 'Wanwon': Folk Songs usually sung by women folk during various functions connected with marriage ceremonies.
2. Readers might go through the book of Mr. Bazaz: "Democracy by Intimidation" and assess for themselves the strains upon JK. electorate. Though the late author has been too hurt but the excesses met by opposition candidates convinced the genuine democrats that the N.C. won many seats by their muscle power. However bye and large government machinary did not commit flagrant and naked bunglings but could not remain true to positive nuetrality.

Chapter 13

Communal Verdict

Within three years the All India National Congress of Indira Gandhi staged a comeback to power in Delhi. During this break from power a new brigade of sycophants had emerged who acquired recognition as 'loyalists' and were openly patronised by Sanjay Gandhi—son of Indira Gandhi. In Jammu and Kashmir the state cadre of Congress was confined to a group of concession seekers who had no roots but were always imposed upon the people. They interpreted the excesses of Sanjay as healthy steps towards revolution. They had pinned their hopes on the re-emergence of 1 Asif Ali Road as the centre of power politics. The deliberate failures of the Janta leadership precipitated the recrowning of Indira Gandhi. These concession seekers started playing their game in the corridors of power in Delhi, hence the central Congress leadership under Sanjay Gandhi brought about a temporary lull and so no major confrontation came to the surface. In this war of wits Mufti Bahud Din the acting Chief Justice of J&K High Court was made a scapegoat. In February 1980 when Mian Jalal-ud-din retired the seniormost puisne judge, Farooqi expected confirmation as chief justice, but all the efforts of Sheikh Abdulla failed to get his proposal through. It is about two years after the death of Sheikh that Mufti was confirmed, but was immediately transferred to Sikkim High Court.

This confrontation about the confirmation of the chief justice was meant to convey to Sheikh Abdulla and his organisation the All J&K National Conference that they had to live and die in subjugation and no important post in the state could be filled in on the basis of their choice. They were taught to be docile and tolerate even with the district Superintendent of Police who was the choice of North Block.

The tragic death of Sanjay Gandhi was followed by the

death of Sheikh Abdulla on 8 September 1982. Both these incidents postponed the final showdown between the two families of Jawahar Lal Nehru and Sheikh Abdulla. As is the rule of history Sheikh was yet to shut his eyes that the fight for succcession within the family started with full vigour. Behind the screen Indira Gandhi, managed the crowning of the non-political simpleton Farooq Abdullah, as against G.M. Shah the volatile, ill tempered son-in-law of Sheikh, who nonetheless was skilled in organisational matters. She was certain that Farooq, for the lust of power, non-serious approach to problems and political immaturity could be spoonfed by her and within a very short time, she would get, like Dacca, Kashmir, integrated and that too very smoothly. She was not wrong in her assessment, but acted with too much haste and that too in a slipshod manner. Pressure was so impatiently and forcefully mounted that even a character like Farooq Abdulla had to play a game of hide and seek and so fell into the hands of opposition parties of India. This fraternising by the man installed by her annoyed Indira Gandhi greatly and consequently revenge to dethrone him became inevitable.

Farooq's advisors believed that people might to some extent, take part in elections for the following reasons:

1. Sympathy with the orphan 'simple' son of the man who had spent the major part of his life in jail. Suffering creates sympathy.
2. In the public condolence meeting held in Iqbal Park Srinagar, Farooq openly came out against 'corrupt' colleagues of his father. The outburst had created, in some quarters an impression that he might, to some extent, arrest the wave of corruption which swept public life in J&K after the 1977 elections and under the patronage of Sheikh Abdulla.
3. Kashmiris have developed a sixth sense and can speculate correctly about such developments which might only be in the process and that too secretly. Hence, people felt that Indira Gandhi was inimical to him; so, not out of love for Farooq, but due to the deep hatred for the Nehru family and aversion towards the policies of New Delhi they gave clear indications to help Farooq in this fight.

4. The people made a clear assessment that the state government employees who had been the main agents used against people for rigging the elections, were under the control of Farooq and so their ballot could not be tampered with.

Farooq's advisor's too had information about such an assessment which was being discussed even in barber saloons and during bus journeys.

The cordial relationship revived by the death of Sheikh between Sheikh Abdulla and the Nehru family remained short-lived. The hostility between the J&K National Conference and Indian National Congress was transparent from each statement of the spokesmen of the two parties and through the actions of the cadres of the two organisations. The patronage shown for 'orphaned Farooq' by Indira Gandhi too proved short-lived and true to the National Conference culture Farooq got the most powerful woman of India (whom he had once himself called mother India) humiliated in the historical Iqbal Park (Hazuri Bagh) Srinagar, where she had to deliver an address at an election rally.

She saw herself that all the forces who were against any election under the Indian Election Commission had aligned due to their bias against India, behind Farooq. She always knew that the workers of the state unit of the Congress in Jammu and Kashmir comprised such concession seekers whom she herself had picked up and fed on her largesse, but though limited in number and with no roots among the masses they were her faithful agents. About Jammu she had made a clear assessment that Muslim majority areas would go the same way as the Valley.

In the Hindu majority districts of Kathua, Jammu and half of Udhampur, the Bhartia Janata Party of India had a base and possessed a dedicated cadre. She managed a reaction in these three districts against what her cadre called the Muslimisation of the National Conference. This propaganda caused an erosion in the Bhartia Janata Party base in these two and a half districts and tilted the situation in favour of Indira's Congress. But this double edged sword hurt Indira Gandhi also. In the Muslim majority areas of Jammu division viz. Doda, Poonch, Rajouri district and tehsil of Gool-Gulab Garh in Udhampur district, this communalisation attempted by Indira Gandhi completely eroded even the committed pockets among Gujars (who are Muslims) and among other backward Muslim sections. Hence, these Muslim majority areas of Jammu region, as a reaction, opted for Farooq.

Indira Gandhi took maximum benefit by projecting herself as the savior of Hindu interests in Jammu and Kashmir. She openly argued that it was the ruling party at the Centre and not the Bhartia Janata Party which was able to contain Muslim Kashmir and she alone was able to crush the emerging revival of the J&K Muslim Conference which Farooq's father Sheikh Abdulla had established in 1931. Against this background, ·how the 1983 elections took shape, has been summed up in my earlier book *Hazratbal-Central Stage of Kashmir Politics.* The relevant quote is:

> "Indirajee pressed Farooq to have electoral adjustment with her party and was required to manage safe sailing of her blue-eyed boys in Pradesh Congress Committee, Farooq did not agree. In this clash of personal interests Congress fought elections in Jammu as the sole saviour of Hindu interests and in the Muslims districts of the province Farooq projected his party and himself as the champion of the cause of Muslims. This communal polarisation by two pretenders of secular ideologies reached such a level that only in Baderwah in Doda district of Jammu province the BJP candidate openly propagated for the success of his second rival Congress candidate so that the Hindu vote was not divided. The third candidate representing the mandate of National Conference, himself a Hindu, advised his kith and kin to vote for Congress candidate".

This is how Indira Gandhi and her party forced Muslims to accept, by compulsions of the situation, Farooq as the representative of Muslim interests. Political analysts have attributed the success of Farooq Abdulla in the 1983 elections mainly to two factors. Firstly, it was a sympathy vote as Sheikh Abdulla had died only a few months back and secondly, the communalisation done by Indira Gandhi helped Farooq to win from Muslim districts of Jammu province. He was thus put in a better position in the Valley also.

B.K. Nehru, who occupied the Raj Bhawan during this period has in his autobiography commented upon this election, but has not gone deeper and not shared the experiences he earned during this period of confrontation between New Delhi and Srinagar. He has not given even an indirect hint of communalistion of the situation, but has in a cryptic manner boasted of the advice which he showered on Farooq Abdulla. It cannot be denied that BK Nehru remained faithful to the high position he held and did not dabble in day to day political developments of this state as was the practice of his immediate successor Jagmohan. It is commonly felt that though all the institutions of Indian democracy had caused complete erosion in the values for which they stood, but the sanctity of the gubernatorial post was maintained by the three members of the British Indian Civil Services, Bhagwan Sahay, L.K. Jha and B.K. Nehru.

In Hindu majority districts of Jammu the cadres of Pradesh Congress Committee, Bhartia Janata Party and Hindu officers posted at election duties did not lag behind to butcher the values. It seems that in all circumstances the people of Jammu and Kashmir are destined to experience only fraud and frustration in the name of elections. There have been charges and counter charges in the statements issued during the hustings or after the results, but references to them have been avoided.

In the Valley the National Conference, its allies and local officers posted on election duties carried on with their tradition enthusiastically and thus in both the parts the expression for individual and collective aspirations got suffocated.

After his partial verdict on the confrontation between Indira Gandhi and Farooq Abdulla, Jagmohan has exonerated the former and condemned the latter. He has done so too in the tussle and conflict between central and state agencies. In his book *My Frozen Turbulence in Kashmir* he writes:

> "Some of the returning officers even defied the instructions of the Election Commission of India"

History should not be mutilated in this manner. In the common assessment of the people both state and central governments, both the Indian Prime Minister Indira Gandhi and Chief Minister Farooq Abdulla of J&K, both the presidents of the Indian National Congress and the J&K National Conference were in competition to turn these elections into a mere farce; they communalised the situation and eroded completely the faith in the democratic system.

Jagmohan sums up this fraud, though putting the blame exclusively on Farooq:

> "...there were specific complaints of booth capturing at 18 polling stations spread over the constituencies. At many places a large number of unaccountable ballot papers were found. In Zadibal constituency, for example, the National Conference candidate secured 90% of the votes polled, even during the heydays of Sheikh Abdulla in 1977 the party candidate got 51% votes..."

The learned author comments on the roles played by Farooq Abdulla and Indira Gandhi in the campaign for their parties:

> "Dr. Abdulla himself propagated in the valley, 'This election is a plebiscite to allow the people to say which political party, National Conference or Congress(I), they like.' Mrs. Indira Gandhi and the Congress(I) party, on the other hand, aroused the apprehensions of the Jammuites about Pakistan and the elements in the state who were favourably disposed to it..." ibid.

Jagmohan, as expected, did not state the communalisation of the situation made by the two exponents of secularism. He subtly qualified the regional outbursts of Indira Gandhi as a reaction to the pro-Pak propaganda of Farooq Abdulla. It is a fact that the Kashmiris both in the Valley and hill districts of Jammu have a leaning towards Pakistan and hatred against India. Farooq exploited the sentiment. On the other hand, in the Dogri belt of Jammu, the majority constitutes Hindus who equally, for communal reasons, are committed to Hindu majority India and Indira exploited that sentiment. Thus, the successor of Mahatma Gandhi and son and successor of Sheikh Abdulla practically proved the total relevance of the Two Nation Theory of 'Qaid e Azam' Mohammad Ali Jinnah.

Jagmohan has tried to cover the exposures of the Indian

Election Commission and the organs of Indian democracy, but the reality is patently transparent. The Chief Election Commissioner, the secretaries of the Election Commission, its election observers and the members of the state services borrowed by the commission on election duties from the rank of returning officer up to the rank of counting officers—all collectively and individually from Nirvachan Sadan in New Delhi to the polling officer in Teetwal Kupwara district of Kashmir border area have stripped naked Indian democracy in Kashmir that too under the patronage of the prime minister of India under the auspices of the Indian Election Commission. One inference is logically deduced that the state population stands communally divided and not on regional basis. It appears that the Muslim majority of Jammu and Kashmir has pro-Pakistan leanings and the Hindu minority in the state has pro-India strains. In my view, neither Muslims are pro-Pakistan as appears to Jagmohan nor Hindus are pro-India as some authors contend, but the situation is different. Muslims are anti-India and Hindus are anti-Pakistan and both have genuine reasons for the aversion they respectively feel against the two countries. It is this aversion which the leadership with vested interests has exploited and it is this division against which the people in all the divided regions fight, but the imported interpreters of Kashmiri psyche have distorted the situation and exploited it to promote the interests of their respective clients. With this aim in view Jagmohan projects Farooq Abdulla as a Pakistani agent. Just as Jagmohan compromised with the constitutional office he held, for the benefit of his bosses in New Delhi, similarly Farooq Abdulla exploited the situation for his vested interests. But why should Jagmohan hide the reality that the majority in the state is against India? Had there not been deep-rooted resentment against India how could Farooq Abdulla cash in on this negative cheque?

The leaders of almost all the opposition national parties of India exposed the farce in these elections. The present Prime Minister Mr. Vajpai, his second in Command mr. Advani, late Mr. Sharama vice President of BJP — all condemned these elections as the result of synthesis in central and state frauds. Mr. Khurana, spokesman of the ruling BJPs Parliamentary party gave the statistical data of those frauds in his press conference held in Jammu. Even the great leaders of two Communist Parties Mr. Surjeet and late Mr. Farooqi dubbed these elections as an "unscroplous competition in mal-practices" patronised in Jammu by Mrs. Gandhi and her Govt in New Delhi and in the Valley and mountain belt of jammu by Dr. Farooq and by his state services. It will add to the bulk to reproduce the excerpts herein.

Chapter 14

The Culmination of Fraud

The process to defraud the people of Jammu and Kashmir in the name of elections began in 1950 when they were asked to elect the 75 member house of the Constituent Assembly though its prelude had been written in the limited type of elections during the autocratic rule of the Maharaja. This fraud culminated in the elections of 1987. The first chapter of the fraud was written jointly and consciously by two Prime Ministers—Jawahar Lal Nehru and Sheikh Abdulla. Its concluding verdict was drawn by their respective legal and official successors Rajiv Gandhi grandson of Jawahar Lal Nehru and Farooq Abdulla son of Sheikh Abdulla. Before an assessment is made of these elections it is highly relevant that the situation which formed the background to these elections is summed up.

Firstly, we have seen that whatever happened during and after the 1983 Elections sounded the deathknell of the relationship of the Sheikh dynasty with the Nehru family. Jawahar Lal Nehru had created a plan to dub Sheikh Abdulla as an American agent and a C.I.A. tool and so got him dismissed and arrested. But Farooq Abdulla had not reacted in the manner in which his late father had chosen to react, the young Abdulla sought refuge and asylum with the Indian opposition conclave. In the circumstances, Farooq had thrown himself into the lap of Indianness so Indira Gandhi had to restrain herself. She could not control her anger, but B.K. Nehru the governor did not succumb to pressures to act in a manner which would appear unconstitutional and against the larger interests of the country, so, the search for his successor was the first preoccupation with Indira Gandhi.

To the people of Jammu and Kashmir the 1983 Election was part of the farce, but according to the defined norms and for the sanctity which the affixation of the seal of the Indian Election Commission accorded, it could be deemed nothing but a verdict of the majority—so, a decision of democracy. Farooq had won a two-third majority so he formed the 'democratically elected government' and in his utterances remained committed to the cause of complete annexation of Jammu and Kashmir with India, so, he could not be dismissed or detained as was done with his father. Hence, defections were masterminded under the clear mandate of the Prime Minister of India. Jagmohan masterminded these defections; as a broker he assured the installation of the defector's government. The defectors were led by G.M. Shah. son-in-law of Sheikh Abdulla who had the political clout to succeed the late leader, but was superseded by Farooq the brother of his wife.

Secondly, the dismissal of Farooq Abdulla and installation of the ministry devised out of the fraud of defections created a chain reaction which resulted in a mass upsurge. A situation of people to people contact was a positive contribution of this negative act and for the first time the Indian Opposition unitedly aligned itself with the genuine feelings of the people of Jammu and Kashmir.

The murder of values in Kashmir was followed by the strangulation of the democratic verdict exercised by the people of Andhra Pradesh in favour of the Telegu Desham led by N.T. Rama Rao. People in Jammu and Kashmir found a close similarity in the two actions in the south and north and could empathise. Feelings developed that it was not only in Jammu and Kashmir where aspirations of the people are frustrated, but it was inferred that the Delhi Darbar could not tolerate even any genuine challenge to its authority. But the impression soon vanished as people became disappointed with the ineffective role of the Indian Opposition parties. It is unfortunate that in the political scenario in the subcontinent instead of being led by values the political parties are guided by party prejudices and complexes. The Bhartiya Janata Party for its tacit understanding with Jagmohan, deep-rooted aversion for Farooq Abdulla and anti-Muslim clout did not lend its support to the Indian Opposition for restoration of value-based politics in Kashmir. The failure to force Indira Gandhi to correct her anti-democratic policies in Jammu and Kashmir caused dismay to Farooq Abdulla and the people of Jammu and Kashmir. Farooq Abdulla grasped the point well that the people of Jammu and Kashmir were irrelevant to make him the king, such authority could be derived only from the seat of power in Delhi. He started appeasement of some influential figures connected with the Delhi Darbar, but was not able to win over Indira Gandhi. He could not do so without licking the boots of her blue-eyed boys among whom Mufti Mohammad Syed held a vital position. Particular to the elasticity in his nature, Farooq Abdulla would not hesitate to enter into a deal with Mufti Mohammed Syed, but the latter was arrogantly conscious of his status as a king maker and simultaneously had found that by crowning others as king he could not himself get entrenched in the seat of power. G.M. Shah alias Gul Shah had taught him such a lesson well, so, he could not compromise with Farooq Abdulla short of the surrender of the local leadership in his favour. Against this background, Farooq Abdulla with all the tricks of appeasement was not able to cut any ice in the corridors of power in Delhi.

Thirdly, after the assassination of Indira Gandhi the installation of Rajiv Gandhi as Prime Minister of India made some openings for Farooq Abdulla and in spite of a coterie of vested interests around Rajiv Gandhi, Farooq Abdullah was able to pacify his old friend. Certain equations were built upon—both had childhood associations, pride in their descent, a common history of amity and friendship, a common desire for cementing the Indo-Kashmir relationship and both had the possibility for long rule. Alive to these common interests past, present and future, Rajiv's advisors developed sympathy for the crestfallen Farooq Abdulla. The main reason for such consideration was the assessment that the arrogant man of 1983 was completely tamed and had learnt well the lesson taught by Jagmohan under the tutelage of Indira Gandhi. Farooq gave tacit assurance to everyone that he grasped the point well that the source of power was the goodwill of Rajiv Gandhi and not support of the masses in Jammu and Kashmir. Besides, Mufti Mohammed Syed had for some reasons fallen away from proximity of the Rajiv Gandhi coterie.

Fourthly, the 1983 elections in India conferred unprecedented victory upon Rajiv Gandhi and the capture of a few seats in J&K by the National Conference caused no anxiety to him nor had he cultivated any interest in the defeated candidates of his party in Jammu and Kashmir. More so, he had entered into a tacit understanding with Farooq Abdulla and had received sufficient assurances that all those elected with the pasted label of the J&K National Conference would always remain loyal and faithful to the grand master in New Delhi.

Fifthly, an accord of no consequence, but with a clear understanding to reinstall the dismissed Farooq Abdulla as the chief minister was the end result of a three year old political drama which had, at the start made George Fernandes, Inder Kumar Gujral and a few other opposition leaders in India such as Mirdhula Sarabhai common names in the daily conversation of Kashmiris. They soon understood that Goerge Fernandes and Inder Kumar Gujral could deliver goods to the voters of Andhra Pradesh, but as far as Kashmir was concerned they were either not potent enough to get things corrected or ultimately had no option but to continue with 'their common national interest' a term coined by neo-colonist thinking and expansionist chauvinism.

Sixthly, the same agent Jagmohan who had immorally dismissed Farooq Abdulla was made to crown him which shows that the men who occupy the highest positions in India are devoid of any self-respect and so are unmindful of the dignity of the offices they hold. It exposes the degradation of values of such people who cover their treacheries in eloquence and verbosity. They distort the events of history, exploit the chauvinistic psychologies and create a market for their 'frozen conscience'.

Lastly, in 1986 after two years of his wandering from the opposition conclave to Sonia Gandhi's kitchen garden that Farooq Abdulla as chief minister of Jammu and Kashmir again started fraternising with many forces to muster support for the1987 elections. This swift change in the personality of Farooq Abdulla hung on every neem and chinar tree throughout Jammu and Kashmir portending danger. Warnings were well received and disarrayed groups of the opposition were also forced into a process of alignment.

Before going into detail of the gimmicks played under the umbrella of the 1987 elections, certain ambiguities in the swiftly evolving situation and the personalities involved which followed the 1983 elections must be cleared. The dismissal of Farooq Abdulla in 1984 created a similar reaction which the pages of Kashmir history had recorded in August 1953 at the dismissal and arrest of Sheikh Abdulla. Alistair Lamb opined that this action of Indira Gandhi put the very survival of Article 370 of the Constitution of India in doubt.[1] The uprising in the state was neither in the defence of Article 370 nor in favour of Farooq Abdulla. Before his dismissal, Farooq Abdulla had become not only unpopular but irrelevant for his lack of administrative capacities, political adventurism, selection of an immature and corrupt team, nepotism, favouritism and rampant corruption. He would have fallen under the weight of his own misdeeds and would have been rejected forever had Indira Gandhi 'the only man in India', acted with manly foresight, but she was too strongly led by emotions and to bury the aspirations of democracy she dug a grave in the same Lal Chowk of Srinagar where on July 1, 1950 her father and Sheikh Abdulla had declared their union of 'minds and bodies'.

The logically sound question would arise that in case Farooq Abdulla had become so unpopular why should the people have emotionally offered sacrifices on his dismissal? There is more than one reason.

In 1953 Sheikh Abdulla had lost all his charisma and had himself witnessed the resentment against him and his India from the office of the Principal Government High School Nawakadal (6th Bridge Srinagar) when on 19 June 1953, Kh. Mohi-ud-din Karra addressed the mammoth public gathering in the adjoining locality Sehyaar under the auspices of the Political Conference established by him. As an enthusiastic 19 year old boy, this author was seated in the front row and could experience the madness with emotional outbursts of the masses when Karra asked:

> "utter the suffocated desire, which is touching your lips, don't be terrified of the awe of Indian military or the might of the rulers.' Immediately the lull was shattered by slogans of 'Pakistan Zindabad'—the slogan which was raised in 1947 on the release of Sheikh Abdulla from the Maharaja's Badami Bagh jail. This was witnessed in detail by the lion caged in the chair of prime ministership.

On 9 August and thereafter every street, mohalla and place of worship had become stages to express venom against India and from every such place slogans of 'Sher-i-Kashmir zindabad' and 'Pakistan zindabad' were heard. People were happy to see that the link between India and Kashmir was broken and the man whom they had trusted and loved had returned to lead them against India.

The situation was repeated in 1984. In both the situations it was neither for the father nor for his prodigal son that the nation offered huge sacrifices. Both the situations were created not by the charisma, popularity or affection for Sheikh Abdulla or for his son, but they were treated as symbols to express anger and contempt against the Indian occupation of Kashmir. However, both the situations had some dissimilarities. In 1953, Sheikh Abdulla had revived, to a great extent, his mass base by the postures he adopted and the speeches he delivered immediately after he was forced to sign the Delhi Agreement, but intensified his criticism against India by the start of 1950. In 1984 the son had no equation with his father.

In the1983 elections Farooq Abdulla took advantage of two factors: (a) of communalisation of the situation by Indira Gandhi and (b) these elections took place immediately after the death of Sheikh Abdulla which created some sympathy among the elders and common womenfolk. But the elderly and women both cannot stand up, in any society, to face the revolt of the young. Neverthless, some sections of the electorate were comprised of elders, over-enthusiastic women from down-town or simple village women.

There was a section of voters who had exercised their vote in such localities where the gangster culture of the National Conference in its mad frenzy had posed dangers to their honour and safety.

There was definitely a section which continued to have deep rooted emotional and material attachment with Sheikh Abdulla, his family and the National Conference.

In an electoral constituency having 24,000 voters, the official record in average had shown a figure of approximately 12,000 polled, i.e., 50 per cent. As per our analysis among the 12,000 voters about 4,000 were those who had not even seen the polling booth, were not in the state during elections or had not inspite of pressures, gone to exercise their franchise or were themselves busy with election duty or duty to maintain law and order. Nonetheless, we cannot ignore that among votes polled, 33 per cent, i.e.,17 per cent of total electorate had exercised the right of franchise of their own conviction. They genuinely felt aggrieved and had a reason for agitating.

That section of the population which had always remained critical of Indian policies and avowedly declared lack of confidence in the institutions of India and so had boycotted a struggle through ballot, found a heaven sent opportunity to use the dismissal of Farooq Abdulla as a pretext to revive and revitalise their struggle. Similar to the situation in 1953 people found the occasion suited to express and consolidate an anti-India tirade. This situation equally provided to nationalist and politically conscious leadership in India an occasion to cultivate faith in Indian democracy in Jammu and Kashmir by taking the Indian Opposition parties into confidence and through the good offices of Indian public opinion get Jagmohan sacked, the government of defectors dismissed and the people's verdict as recognised by the Election Commission of India, vindicated. If that was not found to be possible, the same could have been done by allowing the judiciary to interpret the local laws of defection in correct perspective. With such a device the supremacy of judiciary would create an atmosphere of confidence building among Kashmiris. On the other hand, the decision of the state high court on the reference of the speaker of J&K Assembly added one more patent instance of the failure of democratic institutions in Jammu and Kashmir. The impressions so gathered were fortified by the fact that the Hon'ble Judge who delivered that historic judgement was confirmed and continued as Chief Justice of J&K upto the end of 1988 against that very rule of procedure under which Mufti Bhaud din Farooqi was transferred from J&K High Court to preside over the High Court of Sikkim, in the extreme east.[2]

It is our commitment to Indianness which makes us put forth our views as to what would have been in the larger interests of democracy and the Indo-Kashmir relationship, but the totality of events which have, from 1947 till 1997, taken place in Kashmir, shows that either it is the initially conceived and firm decision of India to contain Jammu and Kashmir in any manner they can retain it. Or, otherwise the

Indian leadership had initially taken some wrong steps and multiplied such wrongs and so is now in no position to retreat. Whatever the compulsions, with the decision to appoint Jagmohan as the governor with a clear understanding to create defections and retard the process of self-assimilation of Jammu and Kashmir people with India, the leadership in Delhi committed unpardonable treacheries. There were many chances to retrieve the situation as they did in Andhra Pradesh, but by missing those chances they have compounded their mischief. The happenings of 1984 twisted the circumstances in a manner that G.M. Shah was dubbed as the villain of the drama and was condemned. History probably does not believe in the principles of natural justice and so does not provide opportunities to its moulders of being heard before it could record its verdict. Without having any brief from G.M. Shah the judge within me makes me to explain his position to some extent. Such explanations may not exonerate him from the liability, but we must be fair to our conscience.

G.M. Shah had aspired, as a political sufferer for about 20 years, to get the leadership—at least after Mirza Afzal Beig. Mirza Afsal Beig pre-deceased Sheikh Abdulla that too as an uprooted dry tree. So, after the death of Beig in 1978, G.M. Shah found himself entrenched in the highest hierarchy of the National Conference. Even at this stage Sheikh Abdulla considered his son Farooq Abdulla if not non-political but apolitical and simultaneously was apprehensive about the rash temper of his son-in-law G.M. Shah.

It was believed that but for his ill temper G.M. Shah would have led both the organisation and administration with skill, shrewdness and in a straightforward manner. There were apprehensions too about the commitment, he had for his close relations. The Sheikh couple had a special weakness for their elder daughter Khalida, wife of G.M. Shah. For these reasons the Shah couple felt humiliated and injured by the decision of Sheikh Abdulla to declare Farooq as his heir apparent. By according a warm reception to this decision the cadre gave the decision a common recognition. Though some pockets of the National Conference were in favour of G.M. Shah, but he was unpopular with grass roots workers due to his temper. There was a halo of simplicity, innocence and sincerity created around the person of Farooq Abdulla from Moi Muqqadas agitation days. In building such an image the fans of the Molvi dynasty were equally responsible alongwith the members of the Sheikh dynasty who considered that with G.M. Shah the centre of power would shift to the Buch, Kant and Ashai dynasties to which he belonged by descent and by blood relationship.

Whatever the reasons which made Sheikh Abdulla come out openly in favour of Farooq Abdulla his decision annoyed G.M. Shah. On September 8, 1982, within moments of the death of Sheikh Abdulla, Farooq Abdulla was elected by the manoeuvering of two senior cabinet colleagues of Sheikh Abdulla, viz., D.D. Thakur and G.M. Baderwahi, with the covert support of Indira Gandhi. The two ministers were under the impression that as king makers, they would dictate terms to a 'raw' Farooq, but to their utter surprise, Farooq Abdulla subjected them to public ridicule at the All Parties Condolence Meeting held in Hazuri Bagh Srinagar on the fourth day of Sheikh Abdulla's demise. When Farooq Abdulla made outbursts against the corrupt colleagues of his father, these disgruntled elements joined hands. The duo of D.D. Thakur and G.M. Baderwahi played the role of brokers with Indira Gandhi for the promotion of G.M. Shah, but the latter had more or less assured his mother-in-law (the mother of Farooq Abdulla) that he would be content to play the role of an elder brother. Within a brief period of time he found that not only was his advice treated with contempt, but Farooq Abdulla would deliberately go against such advice. Begum Abdulla too felt aggrieved by this behaviour of her son, yet she sided with him.

To be precise only two instances are quoted. Farooq Abdulla appointed many of his friends to various important posts and for two such appointments G.M. Shah had expressed resentment for valid reasons. Tahir Muztar was dismissed from an organisational assignment by Sheikh Abdulla and Farooq appointed him as his public relations officer. G.M. Shah conveyed through Begum Abdulla that such appointments had left an impression among the cadre and even with ordinary workers that Farooq Abdulla was contemptuously reversing the decisions of his late father.

Similarly, Farooq Nazki a friend of Farooq Abdulla was at that time in the department of Information and Broadcasting

Government of India with the TV Centre Srinagar. His deputation was sought and obtained for the post of Director Visual Publicity Government of J&K. G.M. Shah warned Farooq Abdulla through Begum Abdulla that since Nazki had roots in the Central Government, that his family was known for traditions of opportunitism and for the delicacy in the Centre-State relationship, such an assignment should not have been given to him. Begum Abdulla was in full agreement with G.M. Shah's assessment and conveyed the suggestions to Farooq Abdulla who gave an assurance that he would correct both the decisions, but within a few days he elevated the position of both appointees in stature and status. Tahir Muztar was promoted to the rank of political advisor to the chief minister and Nazki became information advisor. Inflicted with other similar humiliations G.M. Shah played into the hands of Indira Gandhi. Had he kept a political low profile for some time, the post-1989 situation would have, in the process for the search of civil leadership offered a possibility for him to fill in the leadership vacuum.

With this prelude let us revert to our main topic the 1987 elections the culmination of fraud. Alistair Lamb sums up the total impact of these elections:

> The evidence suggests that the 1987 elections were as unfree and unfair as any others held in the history of the State..

Major General (Retd) Afsir Karim with the India Defence Review team writes in *Kashmir*: *The Troubled Borders:*

> People in the valley, however, believed that these elections were largely rigged and this struck a serious blow to the democratic process in J&K.

Dr. Altaf Hussain in his book *The Wounded Paradise*, writes

> ...fresh elections to the legislative assembly occurred in 1987, bringing Farooq Abdulla back to power. This election was a proverbial last straw for the people of the valley. This election was brazenly and massively rigged. The candidates, their election agents and supporters were ruthlessly persecuted. They were jailed and tortured and the die was caste in favour of militancy.

Though the post-election incidents could be discussed

later, it is more pertinent to quote from Dr. Altaf's book again before we go into details:

> In April 1988, a group of young men, harassed and tortured by the establishment during the 1987 elections, crossed the line of control to receive training in the use of arms and explosives.

This post-election persecution and torture will be discussed later on, let us first hear from the horse's mouth—Jagmohan, who at this time was the Governor of the State. Like his predecessors he was not a man to watch from the ivory tower of Raj Bhawan, but was actively involved in bringing about a honeymoon of vested interests of the Indian National Congress and J&K National Conference. He was omnipresent in every department of the state administration and acted through his tested lieutenants Hamidullah Khan IAS and A.M. Watali IPS, neither of whom had undergone any competitive test for entrance into these prestigious services of India, but had acquired sufficient experience to derive maximum benefit from the uncertain political situation which prevailed in Jammu and Kashmir from 1947.

On Jagmohan's initiative Hamidullah was inducted during these elections as Additional Chief Secretary in charge of Law and Order and this posting was made against the guidelines of the Election Commission. Watali was at that time entrenched in the sensitive Kashmir Valley as D.I.G. Police. Hence, Jagmohan had effective say and decisive command to devise the course of the elections. Had he acted as he did in the 1984 Parliamentary Elections, he could have saved the situation to a great extent from slipping away. Muzaffar Shah, son of G.M. Shah was the ruling party candidate in the 1984 Parliamentary Elections from Srinagar. The state government, as was usual in Jammu and Kashmir, planned to manage the defeat of winning candidate A.R. Kabli of the National Conference, but Jagmohan openly and actively intervened. Why? Because at that time secret parleys had started between Rajiv Gandhi and Farooq Abdulla and Jagmohan wanted to humiliate the people of Jammu and Kashmir and force Farooq Abdulla to bow before the king makers in New Delhi. In 1987 Farooq Abdulla enjoyed the patronage of Rajiv Gandhi, and even had a partnership with him so, Jagmohan did not act in the manner in which he had acted during the 1984 Parliamentary

Elections. Instead, he was the third party with Rajiv Gandhi and Farooq Abdulla in perpetuating this fraud. Inspite of his active participation in everything that happened during the 1987 elections Jagmohan shifted the whole blame upon Farooq Abdulla and pleaded an alibi for Rajiv Gandhi and for himself.

These observations from eminent people who based their views on the information received are both relevant and useful. Let me now depose solemnly before the apex court—the court of world public opinion as an eye witness.

At this time the author was secretary J&K Delimitation Commission of which Peri Shastri Chief Election Commissioner of India was ex-officio member. The Chief Election Commisioner was all praise for my work and as Secretary Law and Justice Government of India he had appreciated my views about the *modus operandi* evolved for translation of the Indian Constitution in the Kashmiri language. He was pleased to appoint me as Central Election Observer for three important electoral constituencies in central Kashmir-Budgam, Beerwah, and Khan Sahib in Budgam district, inhabited by politically conscious and aware people. The constituencies of Beerwah and Budgam have both remote rural pockets and urban elite. The posh colonies of Sant Nagar, Bagat Baarzulla, Barzulla, Haider Pora, Peer Bagh form part of Budgam constituency. Similarly, the city has expanded on the Srinagar Gulmarg road beyond Narbal and to Beerwah on the outskirts of Tosh Maidan.

In these two constituencies the National Conference had fielded my erstwhile colleagues in the Praja Socialist party and Plebiscite Front Syed Ahmad Narbali and Syed Gulam Hassan Geelani from Beerwah and Budgam respectively. We had experienced great suffering together and both of them had made great sacrifices. In Khan Sahib constituency, the father of my close friend G.N. Mir, i.e., Mir Lasjan was fielded jointly by the Congress and National Conference. The opposition candidates were more or less novices and not known to me so they were probably apprehensive about my impartiality. But within the first round of the three constituencies, my friends, the candidates of the ruling coalition received sufficient indications that someone himself wronged at the hustings cannot be unfair to the cause and equally the apprehensions of opposition candidates were also dispelled. The electorate too, more so the older generation of the electorate knew me as one who had in the 1962 elections broken the ice in this area by contesting from two constituencies though upto midway. Even after quarter of a century the lyrics composed by the poets of this area to boost my chances of winning were still fresh in the memory of the older men and women. Fairness in the dealings was dictated by my conscience, but to be transparent fairness was a must for the historical commitment I had made to the electorate of this area for clean polls. This commitment felt heavier because I was simultaneously a judge.

But unfortunately, the 'observer' is just an observer—a mute and impotent watcher. After I submitted my report I got a chance to discuss these elections with Peri Shastri at his New Delhi residence and expressed the helplessness of the observer and excessive authority vested in the returning officer. Peri Shastri had, at the dawn of his career taught Mohammadan Law at the university level, so he explained it in that terminology:

> "Muslims believe that two Angels are posted with each man and woman who write the deeds and misdeeds of that individual."
>
> "Yes Sir, that is correct, one is believed to be at my right shoulder and the other at the left", I said.
>
> "The one seated at your right records your good actions and the one seated at your left writes your vices. But can either of them stop you from doing good or bad?"
>
> "No Sir"
>
> "Exact is the position of an observer posted by the Election Commission. He has to observe and record."

I had used the same analogy to educate the people—the electorate, party workers, candidates and their agents about the powers of the observer and assured that I would record even minor incidents, but all my sermons could not kindle even a ray of hope in the fairness of the system. One political worker recited a locally coined Persian proverb:

> "One who goes into a salt mine becomes but salt".
>
> "These elections appear but a street play of a folk theatre."

With all this background—a bit lengthy—let me sum up

what I saw and observed in these three constituencies and the other two of this district, viz., Charar-i-Sharief and Chadoora. Curiously this author was recorded voter in both these constituencies as he owns houses in both these electoral segments. The picture of these five constituencies forms the specimen for the whole of the state.

1. The election was mainly fought between two fronts—the Congress and National Conference ruling combine and the Muslim United Front (MUF). The Bhartia Janata Party had a limited role to play, but was confined to two and half Hindu dominated districts of Jammu. Independents added just cosmetic value to the hustings.
2. The Muslim United Front was an odd combination created on the spur of the moment, its dominant constituent, Jamait-i-Islami had a disciplined and organised cadre, but its pockets of influence are limited in certain areas. The other constituents of the front were only leader based parties or freshly sown plants which had yet to spread roots. This position made the MUF mainly the Jamait dominated combine. The Jamait had the veto power in this combine.
3. Alistair Lamb is correct in his assessment that: "The Awami Action Committee, of course, had never been a conventional political party which contested elections; it was a pressure group.."[3]

   This 'pressure group' which never did try to expand its sphere of influence beyond a few committed localities in downtown Srinagar, this time extended support to Farooq Abdulla. The latter accommodated three nominees of Molvi Farooq as the candidates of the National Conference in these limited pockets of the city. This move was a sort of revival of 1964 tactics when during the Moi Muqqadas agitation the union of two Farooqs was hailed, but this time the traditional bakras (fans of Molvi Farooq) were against this grouping. Thus in the city the MUF had virtually no base because neither Jamait-i-Islami nor any of the constituents of MUF could ever muster support in the city.
4. The city people have in the past to a great extent shown lack of political wisdom by aligning themselves traditionally both on locality basis and for their tradition

of dynasties either to the cult of Mirwaiz or to Sheikh Abdulla. The villager too has not been politically conscious, but for his immediate interest never tied his loyalties to one or the other. Against this background the city people refused to think beyond the shera-bakra (the pro-Abdulla and pro-Mirwaiz factions). There have been small pockets of influence both for communists and the Jamait-i-Islami, but virtually of no consequence. Thus the MUF had no base in the city; in rural areas too the situation, except in some defined localities, was no better.

5. In view of all these circumstances the MUF had to create, recruit, train and introduce both candidates and cadre within a short spell of time. The shortage of men was so acute that the combine did not find candidates for two important constituencies out of five in district Budgam. Although at the eleventh hour it introduced a new person—a junior advocate and an aspirant of Kashmir Administrative Service—Abdul Rashid Hanjoora for Charar-i-Sharief constituency, but the MUF had to own an unknown independent candidate from Khan Sahib.
6. The MUF could not cling only to disgruntled aspirants so the Budgam constituency witnessed a triangular contest and the Shia candidate posed a formidable threat.
7. Inspite of all these weaknesses in the newly established agglomeration of 13 parties called the Muslim United Front (MUF) it posed grave dangers for the strong National Conference-Congress combine with the added might of Molvi Farooq as they had nothing but aversion and contempt for the masses. But it had a few definite advantages. Being in power the traditional spineless corrupt civil servant was a formidable base for this combine. The concession seeker, contractors, licence holders, brokers of ministers and higher civil service—all were readily made available cadre for the ruling combine. Besides, all the three—the National Conference, Congress and Awami Action Committee had a large number of dedicated but rough workers who had all qualities to terrify, brow-beat and harass the people.

But the main advantage for the MUF was that the people were against the Rajiv-Farooq Accord which appeared to them to be a conspiracy to perpetuate the misrule of two dynasties and was commonly considered a clear challenge to the will of the people. The pro-Pak element in the cadre of the Awami Action Committee developed an aversion against Molvi Farooq and his association with this anti-people combine, consequently the MUF which had no positive achievements or qualities received sufficient mass backing. But to derive capital out of this mass anger the MUF required a tactful leadership, disciplined and organised cadre and mature advice. All these three were lacking.

8. As electioneering had never been allowed so neither the people nor the cadres of the opposition, nor even the workers of the ruling party showed the slightest maturity to achieve their respective ends. The so-called public servant had been made to believe that he was not a government servant, but the servant of the ruling party, ruling clique or ruling dynasty. He had experienced that his tricks with the ballot box, ballot paper or ballot table were the only qualifications with which he could rise in rank. His contribution in rigging was the only testimonial which could give him entrance to state administrative, state police and state forest services. The record of bungling was a visa for him to gain entry into similar central services, thereafter remain stationed within the state limits and finally get reemployment after retirement till his death. Hence, he acted shabbily, unintelligently and with immaturity.

9. I could see the immaturity of the people everywhere, but I confine myself to only three polling stations: Soibugh, Nasurullah Pora and Budgam (all the three in Budgam constituency). Soibugh is a big village which gave overwhelming support to the local MUF candidate, a practicing doctor. The village is considered a bastion of Jamait-i-Islami and I found that a large crowd of people did not allow those voters to caste their votes who in their assessment, were not committed in their favour. Similarly, in Nasurullah Pora for the anti-Jamait and anti-Shia phobia the people physically restrained such voters, who in their view would go against the National Conference candidate.

In Budgam, the local Shias did the same for doubtful voters who might vote either for the MUF or for the National Conference candidate.

These incidents will appear familiar to the readers in the subcontinent where it now hangs like a menace, but is surely restricted to sensitive belts whereas in Jammu and Kashmir it is the rule. In the first ever election held for the Constituent Assembly, the expression of dissent was so suppressed that none could dare to file papers. In the election of the first ever Legislative Assembly the ruling party itself opened an intense battle in a constituency. There followed wholesale abductions and rejections in the 1962 and 1967 elections respectively. In all these limited electoral battles the ruling junta created an atmosphere of intimidation and harassment. As a reaction, where the people found rulers strategically weaker they also retaliated similarly, so a culture of fraud and intimidation became a natural consequence. Hence, what happened in 1987 of which three instances have been quoted above can be deemed as the continuation of the process. The word 'rigging' does not convey what happens in Kashmir during elections and leaves an impact upon the people outside this state of the irregularities of which they are aware. In the political lexicon of J&K 'rigging' has different dimensions. It can be defined roughly to a fraud committed by jugglery through which the winning candidate is declared defeated and vice versa or the very process starts with creation of terror, confusion, intimidation and persecutions that even an illiterate person conveys his frustration through an oft-repeated Persian phrase:

"Agar Khawahi Salamat bar Kinars." (If safety is desired be on the shore rather than to go for a swim)

It is what the election authorities did in the constituencies in which this author observed the poll and counting as the Central Observer and was hoodwinked from detecting many things.

In Khan Sahib constituency, for a multi-cornered contest, the fact that the MUF candidate was not known to the electorate and what the engineer son (now recently defected to N.C.) of the ruling candidate did; for these reasons success was presumed to be in favour of the official candidate. But fraud did not abate. The opposition candidates unanimously boycotted the counting. The votes polled in this constituency were counted in the main hall of the District Judge's court at Budgam. Counting agents of opposition candidates did not participate so, the proceedings were all ex-parte and only the ruling party agents were present. The counting officers had to count some 16,000 votes. At mid-day this author paid a round of the hall. Transistor sets were on. In the mid-day news it was declared by Radio Kashmir that Farooq Abdulla had won from Ganderbal Constituency where an equal numbers of votes were counted in the presence and under constant check of the opposition candidate, his lawyers and his counting agents. In this counting hall none was present to object; all the ballot papers, even invalid ones were thrown to the lot of one candidate, nevertheless we had not finished even half of the work. On hearing this news item G.M. Lone, himself a member of the Legislative Council and a leader of the ruling coalition exclaimed: "Oh, how is it possible, here we do the business as if we shuffle the cards to play rummy but are yet in the mid-way. How is it that Ganderbal finished so soon?"

It thus is self-explanatory how even before counting could take off Farooq Abdulla was declared elected. In Budgam, according to the assessment which this author made after he visited each polling station due to vertical division in the opposition vote, the National Conference candidate Geelani a state minister was sure to win. Geelani was perplexed and worried. On his own assessment this author told Geelani that he was winning, but Geelani did not believe it and so was on tenterhooks. Both the candidates against him had better positions; one was from the most respectable family of the religious leaders of the Shia community—Agha Sahib of Budgam; the other was the stalwart of Jamait-i-Islami who had a record of honesty and of public service. But they beat each other badly and in the process the pro-Abdulla vote, fanatic Sunni vote and anti-Jamait vote went to Geelani, but he himself felt that he was sure to lose. The counting was going on in the Town Hall Budgam. This author went to the other counting hall about a kilometre away but soon returned. The returning officer, the DC Budgam and Geelani were locked together in an argument with the chief counting officer—a Kashmiri Pandit.

He was in a furious mood and retaliated:

> "If MUF is anti-national, fundamentalist and communal organisation why should they be allowed to contest. Rajiv and Farooq should have banned them to contest. But I am a trustee..."

On my arrival the trio dispersed and after much probing I learnt that the chief counting officer was approached to do as had been usually done in the past which he resisted. Later it was learnt that he received a phone call from Hamidulla Khan IAS, Additional Chief Secretary for Law and Order and in the meanwhile hoodwinking was done—even though there was no need for it.

A close friend of this author Syed Ahmad Syed Narbali, the National Conference candidate from Beerwah was in trouble. The people had not allowed bogus votes to be polled in a number of polling stations in his constituency, so he had genuine apprehensions. Here also the ghost of Hamidulla Khan played a decisive role and Narbali sailed into the legislature.

In my home constituencies of Charar-i-Sharief and Chadoora the situations were a complete contrast. In Charar-i-Sharief, A Rashid Hanjoora the MUF candidate had many disadvantages. Firstly, he hailed from the same belt from which the National Conference candidate A.R. Rather hailed, so both had common social contacts. Secondly, he was not introduced either as a lawyer or as a political worker in the area, he was lately roped in by the MUF leadership. Thirdly, among the 13 parties which formed the MUF none except the Jamait had any unit in this constituency and Jamait units too were ineffective. All these reasons tilted the scales in favour of the ruling party, but in spite of the culture which the ruling parties had developed—the 'rigging' was rampant here too.

Abdul Samad Mir the National Conference candidate for Chadoora constituency was a perfect gentleman and the embodiment of sacrifice. Inspite of his associations with the National Conference he was unlike the conference members. His counterpart, the independent candidate Gh. Mustafa Mir, who was killed by militants in 1990 had various facets to his personality. He had played an anti-people role in 1953, 1963, 1965, but had served the constituency well in recent times. He had connections both with the Nehru family and friendship with Farooq Abdulla. Mohammad Ismaiel, who was killed by the forces in 1994 was a pious leader of Jamait and as such contested as the MUF candidate. But for reasons which were inherent in the personality of Mustafa Mir, the nobility of Abdul Samad and piety in Mohammad Ismaiel failed to prevail because the voters played a lesser part than rigging played.

In similar manner almost in all the constituencies in Jammu and Kashmir bungling became the rule and seats were deliberately conceded.

It is equally pertinent to make references to a few constituencies where the Election Commission of India exposed this institution. In Wachi constituency of Shopian tehsil (district Pulwama) Dr. Bhalla, Secretary Election Commission supervised the fraud under which the winning MUF candidate was declared defeated by the ruling National Conference candidate. Similar exposure was witnessed by the rural population of Bandipora constituency.

Equally relevant are references of Amira Kadal and Habba Kadal constituencies where ministers from the ruling party Mohi-ud-din Shah and Pairey Lal Handoo contested. In both these constituencies the ministers lost, but not only they were declared elected additionally after the declaration of fraudulent results they got the workers of the MUF tortured in police stations. Strangely the most vocal element of youth had concentrated their activities in these two electoral segments not because the MUF candidates had some halo or importance, but these areas constitute the pulse of the city. Had the Rajiv-Farooq combine allowed fairness especially in these two segments probably the armed movement would have got deferred for some more years. These two ministers otherwise too were a liability for the ruling party rather than an asset. Their defeat would have paved the way for cleansing the administration, but it is not known why Rajiv and Farooq allowed risks for the country to feed the vested interests of two 'national liabilities'. Why the moralist governor Jagmohan failed to act in the same manner he had acted in the 1984 Parliamentary elections during the G.M. Shah Ministry.

It is well established that on the insistence of these ministers, to wreak revenge upon the handful of youth who had exposed them, even after the end of elections, the police summoned Ashfaq Majeed, Hamid Sheikh, Javeed Mir, Yasin Malik and their other young comrades to police stations and tortured them. What could they do? Who could redress their grievances? So they acquired the distinction of becoming the harbingers of armed revolution.

From the very start there was immorality inherent in the political personality of Mohi-ud-din Shah. He got his close relation appointed as his returning officer, who was bound to refuse the assignment due to the close and delicate relationship he had with the main candidate. But, how could one expect morality from the Kashmir civil servants who rose from posts of clerks to super senior scales of IAS, who by mere fraud became successors to famous ICS cadre.

It is from these two constituencies that the militancy was boosted resulting in bloodshed of a lakh of people from all sides. But the magic of Indian democracy is that after such a great setback for these two men, the electorate in J&K changed so fast in its verdict that these two 'popular figures' were elected by the same electorate from the same constituencies in 1996. This is a circumstance sufficient and strong in itself to determine the nature of the 1996 elections which will be discussed later.

Though all the elections and one held so recently are all chapters of the text book of deceit but why have we qualified this one as the culmination of fraud?

It is so because for a decade or so inspite of day to day acts of terror scattered in the vastness of the country and inspite of alignment of the enthusiastic youth against India—the idea of forcing separation through the gun did not recieve popular support. The Alfatah case, the criminal cases against late Mohammad Maqbool Bhat, the hooting of the Indian cricket team and demonstration in favour of West Indies players, the terror let loose in incarceration centres upon Kashmiri youth and many other similar incidents had left the public undecided whether to resort to force or go for democratic methods. They decided on the second alternative—the democratic way to get their grievances redressed. The first grievance of the people was that the promise made to them to decide their future was not fulfilled. Fears that in case a free election was allowed the so elected MUF majority would start a process of constitutional changes, but such apprehensions if expressed at any level were unfounded.

While discussing elections of five electoral constituencies of Budgam district it was perceived that Beerwah constituency was certain to go to the MUF. Due to division in Budgam the National Conference candidate would win on his own. In Khan Sahib and 'Charar-i-Sharief' the MUF would not make headway. After making an assessment of every constituency we have come to the conclusion that instead of 'five' which were conceded the MUF would at best capture 20 to 22 seats. With such a position the MUF would not even be able to get the status of an opposition party. But had the Rajiv-Farooq combine allowed fairness, the people in favour of constitutional struggle would have emerged stronger and the section which argued otherwise, would, for one decade more fall in the background. A pertinent question would arise- does bungling and rigging for 20 to 22 constituencies out of 76 constitute wholesale rigging? It is sufficient to sum up that the whole affair was conducted in such a messy way that in totality it was mired in doubt. Frauds were committed throughout the process—from the preparation of electoral rolls and even during and after counting. As a specimen Jagmohan, quotes only one incident which relates to Zadibal constituency. It is a sort of confession of an accomplice.

> "At many places a large number of unaccountable ballot papers were found. In Zadibal constituency, for example, the National Conference candidate 'secured' 90% of the votes polled. Even in the hey-day of Sheikh Abdulla in 1977 the party candidate got only 51% vote.[4]"

Jagmohan has pleaded an alibi for his involvement in this farce, denied the active patronage of the Election Commission of India and that of the Rajiv Gandhi government. It was a contributory fraud played together by the Rajiv-Farooq combine, the Congress-National Conference alignment, a politically ambitious governor, unscrupulous traditions in Jammu and Kashmir state services, chauvinistic approach of the authorities of the Indian Election Commission and with the active connivance of Molvi Farooq. It is under central patronage that Hamidulla Khan who was in charge of this election nourished political ambitions. He and his counterpart in the J&K Police Service in DIG rank boasted about their role as the king makers. Farooq Abdulla as is usual with politicians, tried to kick the ladder which he had used to climb to the pinnacle of power and as soon as he was sworn in, he humiliated the said D.I.G. and transferred him to Jammu to an insignificant posting. It was his first posting outside the Valley from the rank of sub-inspector police (Government Prosecutor) to the super senior scale IPS, but he too had deep roots in North Block and managed his entry in J&K Public Services Commission through the active support of Buta Singh, the Home Minister of India. Jagmohan protected Hamidullah Khan lest he too be shown the door by Farooq Abdulla. Farooq Abdulla treated such civil servants and even politicians like D.D. Thakur and G.M. Baderwahi with great disdain. Under the strain of a guilty conscience Jagmohan has been too precise in his description about this farce. His narration and analysis has remained engaged in shifting the whole blame upon Farooq Abdulla and state administration and to defend tacitly or expressly the Congress, its government at the Centre and the Election Commission of India. It is needed to sum up the details of his duplicity contained in his book, but that will be going out of the parameterś of our subject. But it is necessary to give a sample of it as a footnote below.[4] In his book *My Frozen Turbulence in Kashmir* this summing up is done:

> "In some constituencies, counting was suspended and the margin of victory for National Conference candidates turned out to be smaller. The margin of victory in Bejbehare was 100, in Wachi 122 and in Shopian 336, while in these constituencies the number of votes declared invalid was 1172, 1703 respectively."

He has dishonestly omitted to mention that in these constituencies these frauds were compounded by the personal supervision and presence of Dr. Bhalla, Secretary Election Commission of India. It is relevant to quote some more lines from the same book:

> "These elections, unfortunately were followed by the arrest of top-ranking leaders of the Muslim United Front (MUF). The unpalatable reality seen emerged on the surface. It found expression in the angry outburst of individuals and leaders".

Here he quoted statements of Kabli, a National Conference member of Parliament and Mustafa an independent MLA. But the latter in my assessment had managed his entry through brow beating and rigging. Mustafa won from Chadoora, but in the same kind of situation.

Later on in connection with the meeting of J&K Delimitation Commission I met Peri Shastri Chief Election Commisioner at his Lodhi Estate official residence and narrated the story of my experiences as an observer, as a voter and sometime back as a candidate. He heard me with rapt attention, but spoke very little and remained non-committal. However, indirectly he expressed his helplessness in the system and agreed that in the 'diseased' set-up in J&K even the officials of the commission catch the disease and contribute to the bungling.[5]

Notes

1. Alistair Lamb, Disputed Legacy.
2. At that relevant time I was posted as Additional District and Sessions Judge Srinagar. On August 24, 1983 (in the morning) an officer of the Indian Intelligence Bureau came to my residence and informed me that the District Judge Syed Sirajud Din was on leave so I had to participate in the oath taking ceremony of the Chief Justice to be held in the Raj Bhawan. "But I have yesterday evening called at the Chambers of Chief Justice and why the oath". It was learnt that the President of India had signed the warrant of appointment of V. Khalid, Judge of Kerala High Court as C.J. of J&K High Court secretly. In a closely guarded secret Khalid was brought to New Delhi where he was briefed by the Supreme Court Judge late Murtaza Fazal Ali (ex. Chief Justice of J&K) and then was brought in a special I.A.F. plane to Srinagar. On 23 August at 4.15 p.m, Chief Justice Farooqi left his chambers where I had met him. He had a function at his house and had invited the Chief Minister and Law Minister to dinner. But they were informed late in the evening from New Delhi of the judicial coup d'etat and so had no face to meet the man who had been sacrificed on the altar of Article 370 of the Indian Constitution and Farooq had shamelessly compromised with the situation. The inability and timidity of Farooq's ministerial team was exposed to us when in the Raj Bhawan Mohi-ud-din Shah (a post graduate in Political Science and a law graduate from Aligarh 1956) senior minister asked his other two colleagues Shafi and A.R. Rather (both law graduates) "Oh, this Handoo (Law Minister) assured us that the Indian Government cannot transfer the chief justice without the consent of the state government. 'How it happened?'" His two colleagues felt equally deceived by Pyarelal Handoo. I could re-collect that an illiterate father of a labourer who received a postcard from his labourer son from Punjab would go to the house of a Pandit and would

hear from him the contents of the letter.In the same manner acted these three law graduate ministers who never care to learn, but only earn through plunder.

3. Alistair Lamb, *A Disputed Legacy,* Oxford Press, p. 329.
4. This author cannot restrain the judge within him so, to appreciate the testimony of Jagmohan we will request the judicial conscience of people to check the veracity on the numerous factual contradictions pointed in his book. I will point out only one. He tried to tarnish the image of the State High Court and its judges by quoting an incident without giving its details. He has criticised the judges who in their administrative capacity had taken stern action against a district judge, but in their judicial capacity stayed the operation of the same order. It is most pertinent to give facts of that case and to assess the 'moralist Jagmohan'. In 1986 G.A. Lone was District & Sessions Judge of Budgam district. It was alleged that without obtaining the requisite sanction from the competent authority he had acquired immovable property in the same district in the name of his wife. The High Court deputed its vigilance commission to enquire, reported that the record about sale deed and other records witnessing the transaction stood destroyed, so the 'High Court' (as the administrative head) decided to refer the case for investigation to the CBI. This order was challenged by G.A. Lone pleading inter alia that neither could any police agency investigate the allegation against a judge nor had the CBI any jurisdiction. The Division Bench of the same High Court found force in the contention and so adjourned its own administrative order. Jagmohan has quoted this case to fortify his argument that the judges shield corrupt people. But the same moralist appoints the same judge of 'doubtful integrity' in 1990 as his Law Secretary. During Governors Rule he enjoyed more powers than the Law Minister; Jagmohan made this entry for him into the ruling syndicate of Kashmir. Exploiting this position and the proximity with the Chief Justice due to blessings of Jagmohan that on 26 March 1991 in judges meeting he got the enquiry against him dropped—without asking him to withdraw his writ petition. Earlier, in the same meeting judges recorded his ACRs for preceeding three years as commendable. Will Jagmohan explain why he had specially chosen the same man whom he had dubbed as' doubtful' for this key post and through whom he sullied the image of the higher judiciary.
5. It will not be too relevant to quote comments of Indian leaders, media men and political analysts in this chapter because all of them, even the patrons of this fraud M/S Jagmohan and late Rajiv Gandhi shamelessly admitted that the gun culture took birth from the womb of elctoral frauds of 1987 elections. Mr. Jagmohan has lacked the courage to make, like a brave man, confession of his culpability. Instead, has tried to shift the blame as if he was a mute spectator. It might be argued on his behalf that being a prisoner of limitations imposed on gubernatorial post he could not intervene. But during 1984 parliamentary elections he actively interfered and frustrated the game of Chief Minister Mr. Ghulam Muhammad Shah and saved mr. Abdul Raheed Kabli of the maneuvered defeat.

Mr. Ghulam Nabi Hagroo was Muslim United Front (MUF) candidate from Pahalgam(Kashmir) segment, he received reliable linformation from Halqa President of Amira Kadal late Mr. Abdul Gani of Solina that his rival Mr. Rafi Mir, National Conference candidate had got a full box of ballots containing "12000" ballots marked in favour of National Conference. He lodged report with DIG Mr. Watali IPS but before the police officer could act, mother-in-law of Mr. Mir exercised influence on Mr. Mohan and connivance of police made that full box of votes to tilt decision in favour of National Conference nominee.

Similarly it was brought to the notice of Governor and Dr. Bhalla, Secretary Election Commission that the counting officer after counting of votes of Amira Kadal and Habba Kadal constituencies were packing those bundles booth-wise in an envelop and seal that. On the so sealed envelops they (the counting officers) would affix signatures and mention the number of votes polled by each candidate. The endorsement was signed by counting agents of candidates also. Latter the same envelop they would contain in another sealed cover on which they would record the highest number of votes polled by National Conference candidate. Neither of the two dignitaries intervened.

Chapter 15

Elections by Corvee (Begaar)

Before describing the 1996 elections, held after eight years a background to this delay is necessary. The intervening period had been so tumultuous with dimensions of a revolution that its narration is thrilling. But, possibly one has to be relevantly selective.

There were various reasons which channelised the trend in the public mind with the freedom movement in India and particularly with Indian nationalism. It should never be imagined that the Kashmiris considered themselves part of the subcontinent, but felt that their independence, prosperity and future was deeply connected with the subcontinent. It should be noted that even during Mughal rule neither the people of Kashmir nor the then Indian rulers considered Kashmir a part of Mughal India as is unambiguously inferred from various writings, proverbs and folk tales. Suffice it to quote from *Hujjati Qasira* of Qalander Beg in which he has versified the history of the Holy Relic at Hazratbal. He attributes it to Aurangzeb that he insisted upon Haji Noorud Din of Ishbera who brought *Mio-Muqaddas* to Kashmir not to take that great treasure out of Mughal India. Though my research has disproved the encounter between the Haji of Ishbera and Emperor Aurangzeb at Lahore at the beginning of AD 1700, but it speaks volumes about such bias in the public mind.[1] Sheikh Noorud Din Wali is popularly known as 'Alamdar-i-Mulki Kashmir'—the standard bearer of the 'country' of Kashmir. The stress on separate independent nature is evident from this epitaph. Kalhana, the eminent historian of the12th Century also mentions Bharat (India) as a country and similarly qualifies Kashmir as a country.[2]

Hence, inspite of this stress on the distinct identity of Kashmir, the Kashmiris considered themselves part of the struggle against the British Raj from which the local Dogra ruler had obtained authority and which was the real sovereign power behind the local rule. The majority in the state was constituted of Muslims and so they identified with the majority in the subcontinent. Consequently, people here aligned themselves with the Indian National Congress, but it was during the beginning of 1947 that Kashmiris felt convinced that what they considered an impossibility was certain to become a reality and Pakistan was in the process of its formation. Rethinking started for various reasons, mainly cultural and geographical. But a section of the leadership remained committed with the Indian National Congress and after August 1947, they declared their priority for accession to the Indian dominion. At this time the literate element, the elite of the society and even a good number of intellectuals from both the communities were openly canvassing for Pakistan with which Jammu and Kashmir was geographically linked and through which the state could get linked with the world. However, the masses were ignorant and so could be led only by the more convincing argument which could be argued only by an acceptable leadership, disciplined movement and cadre based political organisation. At this critical juncture the state was dominated by two political forces, one led by the National Conference and the other by the Muslim Conference. The former had better leadership, disciplined movement and cadre based organisation so was able to percolate deeper in the 'undecided public mind'. This organisation too was divided on this issue from June 1947, but the subsequent developments did undergo a swift and drastic change so those cracks came to the limelight much after. Readers are requested to read *Hazratbal—Central Stage of Kashmir Politics* At this time when public opinion was being churned the tribal raid or the intervention from Pathan sympathisers in the local movement provided a very strong argument for the National Conference against newly born Pakistan and simultaneously provided a fertile soil for it to sow the seeds of suspicion against Pakistan. It was argued that Pakistan was determined to annex Jammu and Kashmir to it by force and to save it from 'such coercive union', India landed its forces in Jammu and Kashmir. Thus, Pakistan at this stage (1947-1948) was made to appear in public assessment as a successor to Pathan tyranny of which a great deal was suffered in the immediate past by the Kashmiris. On the other hand, India was projected as the saviour. The promises, commitments and declarations of Indian rulers and leadership in this behalf made locally or at various places in India including at official fora and in the UNO, convinced the people of Jammu and Kashmir of their bonafide intentions. It was believed that India's only purpose was to save Kashmir from forceful annexation with Pakistan and guaranteed for its people a right of referendum. Such assurances convinced even the pro-Pak elements. But a section which wanted to see Jammu and Kashmir as part of Pakistan, whether people wanted it or not, was not satisfied and remained active against India and against the local administration.

But soon the intentions and intrigues against the interests, freedom and prosperity of the people became transparent. To sum up:

1. The propaganda about the terror and tyranny of raiders let loose in north Kashmir was exposed as soon as the interaction between the north with the city and through it with the south developed. It was learnt with surprise that though these raiders had been brutally cruel they had not caused even a tenth of human loss of life that was caused in Jammu, and exaggerated descriptions propagated by the Indian media about the raiders 'brutalities' exposed to the ignorant and innocent Kashmiris the designs behind it.[3]
2. The most progressive measures taken by the National Conference administration in the manner of Abolition of Big Landed Estates and establishment of Debt Conciliation Boards created strong resentment among the privileged community of Kashmiri Pandits. It formed 5 per cent of population, but owned more than 50 per cent of the agricultural land and was the main money lending community in the state. Their co-religionists in the Indian government and the ruling party in New Delhi reacted sharply against these progressive measures. Even the outstanding progressive leader Jawahar Lal Nehru exerted pressure on Sheikh Abdulla not to be so swift in taking such radical measures. Failing to persuade Sheikh Abdulla he argued for compensation, but Sheikh Abdulla resisted and insisted that such a huge amount was not

within the possibility of the state resources and could be paid only if the Government of India was ready to advance the amount to repay as aid and not as loan. This insistence on both sides created a wedge and it appeared even to the masses that the great secular Jawahar Lal Nehru had a special weakness for Kashmiri Brahmins—the community of his origin.

3. The Quit Kashmir movement was launched by the National Conference under the leadership of Sheikh Abdulla directed against the hundred year rule of the Dogra dynasty. The Indian National Congress actively supported it and its veteran leader Jawahar Lal Nehru got himself arrested in Jammu and Kashmir. Thus the Congress government in Delhi and its sister organisation in Jammu and Kashmir the National Conference—both were committed to guarantee the end of Dogra rule. Besides, the National Conference movement, the ex-soldier insurgency in Poonch and Gilgit Scouts too were fighting to force the Dogra rulers to hand over power to the people of the state. It is under the pressure of this armed revolt supported by tribal Pathans that Maharaja Hari Singh was forced to run away and leave his subjects in chaos in a critical situation. People were made to believe that they had become moulders of their destiny and were free from chains like the people of the subcontinent, but soon it appeared to be merely a mirage. The deceived nation found the minor son of the erstwhile ruler as their king, the difference lay only in the nomenclature. The father ruled the state under the title of Maharaja whereas his son ruled as Yuvraj. Two anecdotes related by none other than the Sheikh himself to his confidants are worth mention. Why has Sheikh not made any mention of these incidents in his autobiography?

Before the Constitution Bill was moved in the J&K Constituent Assembly modalities of its characteristics were discussed by the state leaders with the rulers at Delhi. Salient features of the state constitution were the result of the consultations between Sheikh Abdulla and Jawahar Lal Nehru and it was agreed by them that the state leadership would submit a panel of three men from whom one could be chosen as the official candidate for the post of the head of state (Sadr-e-Riyasat). The panel of three names J.N. Wazir ex-chief justice, G.L. Dogra and Sardar Budh Singh was submitted by G.M. Sadiq on behalf of Sheikh Abdulla directly to Jawahar Lal Nehru. G.L. Dogra for his young age and J.N. Wazir for his closeness with His Highness Maharaja Hari Singh—were not found agreeable to the two sides and hence the choice fell on Sardar Bodh Singh, the veteran freedom fighter of Jammu and Kashmir from Jammu. But, at the time the Assembly had to elect the Sadr-e-Riyasat, Jawahar Lal Nehru backed out from his commitment on the pretext that such a radical step was premature and vulnerable. It left an indelible impact on the mind of Sheikh Abdulla and his associates that the drastic change in Jawahar Lal Nehru was communally motivated. "We, both are committed against Dogra rule and how can I face my people?" asked Sheikh.

"I am under pressure that in case Yuvraj Karan Singh is not elected to the highest post in J&K, the Nawab of Hyderabad cannot be tolerated as Rajpurmukh, so, wait for some time", replied Jawahar Lal Nehru.

"I am, sir, equally committed against every prince, against any autocracy". But inspite of his own inclinations, Sheikh Abdulla had to propose the name of Yuvraj Karan Singh for the high office of Sadr-e-Riyasat.

It proved a setback to the National Conference and a terrible erosion in the credibility and relevance of Sheikh Abdulla. Simultaneously, the very elections for the Constituent Assembly proved the death knell for his charisma and the pro-Pak section convinced people that Sheikh Abdulla had, for his vested interests, deceived the nation, who had given him their sincere love. We have discussed this election under the heading: 'Selection Without Discretion' and so our reader may assess for himself the effect of this fraud played with the people on their credibility.

4. People even living in far flung rural areas could feel that within the first four years of the Indo-Kashmir relationship cordiality had eroded due to the pressures which New Delhi exerted upon Sheikh Abdulla, head of the state administration to surrender each aspect of the

people's suzerainty which vested in them on the abdication of the Maharaja. These pressures were openly demonstrated and Sheikh's absence at Meerajun Nabi function of Hazratbal in 1952 was the subject of discussions everywhere. He returned on the Friday following Meeraj and rushed directly to Hazratbal to be heard by the mammoth public gathering which had assembled there to have a glimpse of the Prophet's Relic. Sheikh Abdulla had lost the admiration of the people and would always snatch opportunities to impose his presence on ready-made public gatherings like the one which he addressed on his return from New Delhi in 1952 after he was made to sign an agreement which became known as the Delhi Agreement. Sheikh Abdulla's assurance to his people that he would not deceive them made people believe in him. The Delhi Agreement is against the mandate of the so-called Instrument of Accession, which provides India with an argument to claim genuineness in its occupation of Jammu and Kashmir.

5. On August 9, 1953 the Indian fraud reached culmination and the same Sheikh Abdulla was dismissed, imprisoned, subjected to the worst type of vilification and character assassination who was till August 8, 1953 represented to the whole world as the symbol of secular traditions of Kashmir and the voice of the people of the state. It was demonstrated to the people of Jammu and Kashmir that like the worst colonial powers of the West, the Indian leadership had developed qualities and expertise to divide them and their leadership to perpetuate its rule in Kashmir. The collective leadership of the National Conference had multifaceted values. The big six of this organisation could collectively pose a forceful challenge to the policies and intrigues against Kashmir, so the six were pushed into three different directions. These Machiavellian manoeuvers were so successfully prosecuted that the same G.M. Bakshi, who in June 1953 had qualified his loyalty to Sheikh Abdulla as the sixth fundamental article of his faith, was made to replace his patron, guide, friend, and leader. G.M. Sadiq felt disgusted with the progressive Jawahar Lal Nehru as he had resisted tooth and nail the suggestion of the

National Conference mooted through him against installation of Yuvraj Karan Singh as the head of state. But he too was alienated from his leader so he did not hesitate to dub Sheikh Abdulla as an imperialist agent. Molvi Mohammad Syed Masoodi was made to wander in the wilderness by the duplicity of Jawahar Lal Nehru. In Delhi he was ostensibly given respect, but in the state he was made to undergo humiliation by the Nehru family agent D.P. Dhar.

It is pertinent to say that some time before this coup d'etat in June 1953 communist leaders Dange and Z.A. Ahmad came to Srinagar to persuade Sheikh Abdulla that the latter should not react against the continued steps of eroding the status of this state. The visiting leaders argued that Jawahar Lal Nehru was surrounded by reactionary forces so was forced to do so, hence the Sheikh should not annoy him. Sheikh Abdulla reacted against the suggestion, such advice tendered was ridiculed by local political lobbies and laughed at by the people.

6. Bakshi who had gone to the extreme indulged in anti-people treachery so he devised unique policies to corrupt the public mind. He too was killed with the same weapon of intrigue with which Sheikh Abdulla was mercilessly butchered. Had Jawahar Lal Nehru been a genuine democrat he could have shown the door to Bakshi through democratic means of the 1962 general elections, but he was sure that such concessions if granted to the people of Jammu and Kashmir were bound to make them conscious of the force in their vote, so, instead finished him through the Kamraj Plan. Later, the same Bakshi was subjected to the worst humiliation, the dead body of whose father was exhumed by the angry people for his pro-Indian and anti-people role. Bakshi died a broken man for his fault of playing the role of an agent for Indian interests in Kashmir. It followed that even traitors of the people and agents of India lost faith in the dealings of Indians in New Delhi matters.
7. The bungling which the Indian government did during the Holy Relic agitation made people believe that it was the Indian leadership which had its hand behind the affair. This author has discussed it in detail in *Hazratbal-*

Central Stage of Kashmir Politics. Pyare Lal Kaul in his book *Kashmir Key Shab-O-Roz* sums up that the "Indian government bungled the matter in a manner as to make people of the state to believe that it was government of India which had hand behind."

8. Bakshi's successor G.M. Sadiq was progressive and a recognised communist so people dubbed him an atheist. He had the reputation of honesty and was considered the symbol of radical ideas and secular ideals. He had a deep understanding with the Nehru dynasty. His credentials as an 'Indian' were beyond doubt, but he was made out to be a communalist by the extra constitutional Pandit lobby of Kashmir which could exercise right of veto against any progressive decision that would disturb their privileges. A few minor incidents kept G.M.Sadiq on tenterhooks and made him react in the same manner against his avowed conscience.

   a. A Kashmiri orphan Pandit girl, who could not find a match in her community for reasons of dowry, developed an affinity with her male colleague in the Co-operative Department where both were employed. Affinity and cooperation matured into love. She converted to Islam, married the same boy G.R. Kanth and was christened as Parveena Akhtar. The documents of her marriage were attested by a Pandit magistrate and identification was made by a Pandit lawyer, but an individual act of love and romance was turned into an agitation. All so called progressive Pandits aligned themselves behind this agitation. The 5 per cent population proved so forceful through the influence it had in New Delhi that Sadiq was forced to appoint a Supreme Court Judge as head of the commission to suggest measures to 'protect the privilege' of this privileged community. The decision made the majority communities assess and feel the power which this microscopic minority enjoyed. The other community especially Muslims, even if killed indiscriminately would not be successful to even get a magisterial enquiry initiated against such brutalities. The same G.M.Sadiq had appointed A.A. Aftab, Sessions Judge as commission of enquiry to enquire about the causes which led to firing in the precincts of Sarai Bala Mosque where dozens of faithful, who were attentively listening to the religious sermon were gunned down in 1964. But what happened to that report is not known till date. These clear measures of discrimination left the impact they logically should have.

b. During the reign of Sadiq a few dozen posts of head masters fell vacant which if filled on seniority basis would go entirely go to Pandits who constituted 5 per cent of the total population, hence the special representations for backward, scheduled caste and other downtrodden pockets of population were devised. Through this at least half of the number of the vacancies could be filled in by two majority communities: Muslims of Kashmir and Dogras of Jammu. The group of Pandit 'masters' moved the Supreme Court of India directly through writ petition known as: Makhan Lal Waza and others v/s State of J&K and others. The Hon'ble Supreme Court set aside the notification for certain defects which were later removed through subsequent amendments by legislature. A new set of writ petitions were the consequence. But Sadiq also adamantly went on correcting the flaws in those notifications which the apex court had in several decisions pointed out. It resulted in a stalemate. In the end, the vacancies were filled in according to the notifications of the state giving representation to various communities, areas and pockets. Contempt proceedings were initiated. On one visit to Srinagar in Cheshma Shahi guest house, the Prime Minister of India Indira Gandhi said to G.M. Sadiq, "The Supreme Court is annoyed with you. We must respect the orders of the apex court".

"Yes Madam, we must respect the institution but the men manning the institution should first respect its dignity", said Sadiq.

"What do you mean?"

"Madam in this matter the Hon'ble Judge had dictated the petition to his steno, the petition was typed in the court, cyclostyled there, the Hon'ble Judge waited till 6 pm in his chamber to pass the interim order because next day the vacation was to start".

Indira Gandhi was stunned to know that G.M. Sadiq knew these details and people were watching all that was happening.

It was a distinct feature with G.M.Sadiq that he would say

the same thing here in Srinagar which he would state or utter in Jammu or in Delhi.

c. In 1967, the All India Integration Conference was held in Srinagar in which all the cabinet ministers including Prime Minister Indira Gandhi and Deputy Prime Minister Morarjee Desai participated. Sometime before this conference a move was initiated to induct a Muslim from the state as pusne judge in J&K High Court for the first time, as the chief justice was an Indian Muslim and two puisne judges were Hindus from two regions of the state. No distinguished Muslim lawyer was acceptable politically so the senior most district and sessions judge Mian Jalal-ud-din was proposed to create this history, but the process got a sudden and immediate setback. It became known that a Kashmiri sitting judge Pandit J.N. Bhat had prevailed at the Centre both against induction of the Kashmiri Muslim judge in the High Court and against the incumbent. Due to the special influence of the community in Delhi the matter of increasing the strength of the High Court went into cold storage.

While receiving the guests in Cheshma Shahi guest house G.M. Sadiq said:

"You have come to teach a lesson on integration to those who have created unique precedents for inter-community and inter-regional integration but you've to prove your credentials because an individual could get the jointly mooted proposal of the state High Court and state government vetoed with you.."

Indira Gandhi gave an assurance to clear the proposal on her return to New Delhi, but suggested deletion of the above remarks of G.M. Sadiq from the minutes.

Only three incidents have been quoted to impress upon the readers of the strains, pressures and pulls which were exerted on the same G.M. Sadiq who left no stone unturned to erode the guarantees contained in Article 370 of the Constitution of India for the internal autonomy of Jammu and Kashmir. People dubbed his actions as treacheries but he was frustrated by the Congress government in New Delhi. The symbol of secular traditions, G.M. Sadiq was dubbed by his co-religionists as an atheist, but before his death he was forced by secular

Indian leaders to think and act like a communalist. It is believed by the people that he was 'killed' in PGI Chandigarh by chemical devices.

9. All endeavours were made by Sheikh Abdulla, his associates Beig and Masoodi and by the leaders of the pro-Pakistan J&K Political Conference 'Karra' to get an assurance for a free and fair election, but were forced to make a formal surrender before they could enter into the electoral arena.
10. With all humility the frustrated and broken 'lion' Sheikh Abdulla surrendered at the feet of Her Majesty, but within days of holding the chief minister's seat he was shown the door. It was just a political miracle which saved him from disgrace. Had not the Congress government at the Centre fallen due to the follies committed during emergency, Sheikh Abdulla would have been politically assassinated—though he had himself committed political suicide.
11. On the economic front Kashmir was turned into a begging bowl subservient for largesse and subsidy. The feudalism which was undone by the progressive measures of Sheikh Abdulla was not allowed to be succeeded by a new economic order nor the crumbled agrarian society allowed to grow into an industrialised economy. Politically, autocracy was not allowed to be substituted by a known and defined political order. In the same manner Kashmir's economic order is but chaos. It lives on imported eggs, milk, rice and all consumer goods.

All these factors political, economic, educational, social, cultural and linguistic together created only one impression on the individual mind and collective thinking that the Indian Government, leaders, intellectuals, Indian media, political parties and the personalities manning the various institutions were not inclined to treat the people of Jammu and Kashmir as part of the Indian nation. It was further learnt by everyone that the agitations, demonstrations, sloganeering and even brickbatting, stone pelting, hurling of fire pots etc. were not sufficient to accord them due recognition and honour for which they had suffered terribly and offered sacrifices. Hence, it is against this background that militancy erupted in 1989 which disproved many old theories about the timidity of Kashmiris and which completely revolutionised the culture of Kashmir.

As described earlier, the main cause which led to the process of alienation was the backing out of the promises which the Indian leadership had made in 1947 to the people of Jammu and Kashmir.

This process could be arrested by building confidence in the institutions of democracy. Ultimately the disillusioned Kashmiri went to the other extreme and the system fell like a house of cards, traces of rule of law too were not visible, the civil administration was buried under the heavy weight of brutal excesses committed on the masses, crackdowns, imposition of curfew, arson, loot, plunder, custodial deaths, random firing, the daily toll of death in cross-firing, molestation and rape of women, sacrilege of sacred places—all these created a gulf which could hardly be bridged. There was no trace of civil administration visible for about a decade.

The Indian position was merely ridiculed throughout the world. It could not explain the breakdown of the system in Jammu and Kashmir, though from 1947 till 1989 it never reflected like an administration established by law.

Section 92 of the J&K Constitution empowers the governor to assume the functions of the government when he is satisfied that a situation has arisen in which the government cannot be carried in accordance with the provisions of the constitution. In January 1990 the situation was really out of control, so the governor was legally justified to act under the said provision of the constitution. Though politically it is debatable because it proved to be against Indian interests which had 76 families aligned to it for their vested interest. However, the governor could not retain the powers of governance with him for a single day beyond six months.

Sub-section (3) Section 92 reads:

> 'Any such proclamation whether varied under sub-sec (2) or not, shall except where it is proclamation revoking a previous proclamation, ceases to operate on the expiration of six months from the date on which it was first issued'.

Hence, by the beginning of July 1990 the governor had to convene the existing assembly which could not be done as he had simultaneously dissolved it with his proclamation so had to seek a fresh mandate from the people. The process for polls had to start simultaneously with the dissolution of the assembly in 1990 which was impossible as the situation had become uncontrollable and the severity was compounded.

The Government of India had since forseen such a situation and had used their docile agent G.M. Sadiq in the 60s who had actually connived to erode all traces of protection of the special status which the Indian Constitution had guaranteed for Jammu and Kashmir. In this connivance he was illogically unaware and unconscious of the conflicts which the constitutional application orders of the Government of India created with the clear provision of the state constitution and simultaneously with the scheme of constitutional relationship of Jammu and Kashmir with India. It is not within the parameters of this book to make a constitutional study, but it is pointed out that Section 92 corresponds to Article 356 of the Indian Constitution.[4] The state constitution maintaining and preserving the scheme of instrument of accession and the guarantees accorded to J&K by the Indian constitution strictly provided the emergency powers to be exercisable only for six months and so does not envisage imposition of presidents rule in Jammu and Kashmir under Article 356. Hence, the governance of J&K beyond 20 July 1990 remained, in nature, illegal occupation. The governments imposed and run from July 20, 1990 could not be at all deemed governments established by law. The state was thus patently being ruled as a colony directly by India without any semblance of even indirect representative character. Though before 1990 there was hardly any representative character to governments installed in Jammu and Kashmir right up from the abdication of Maharaja Hari Singh in October 1947, yet ostensibly they were made to appear so. But after July 1990 that mask too was torn into pieces. There were moves to create an agitation in a legal battle, but no safer pitch was available or can remain available for the wronged people of Jammu and Kashmir who are denied justice in every corner of the world, even by the defender of the cause of Kashmiris, i.e., Pakistan.

It is against this background that the Indian Government had to play some drama of elections, had to install some show boys as the representatives of the people to provide sanction to all illegal and immoral excesses prepetrated on the people of Jammu and Kashmir. Hence, the necessity for holding elections became a compulsion upon the rulers in Delhi.

Pakistan used to exploit this helplessness of India in every international forum in the war of diplomacy—as hinted earlier. Hence, irrespective of consequences after the 'devastation operation' at Charar-i-Sharief the Indian government took a decision to impose an election in Jammu and Kashmir under the circumstances which the situation had imposed upon it. The rehearsal was played in Parliament Elections. The Maharaja had not sought special status that Jammu and Kashmir be ruled as a colony under direct rule of India indefinitely, but special status was sought and guaranteed to enjoy special democratic immunities and positions and hence, Section 92 of the state constitution contained special features distinguishable from Article 356 of the Indian Constitution. The scheme could never be visualised under which the special subjects of J&K state would specially be put to undemocratic burden under the exceptional provisions of both the constitutions. It needs a mention that such constitutional guarantees reflected the spirit of the 'Instrument of Accession' and the assurances which the National Conference received from Congress leaders and the Indian Government. Both these provisions of the two constitutions could, in no case, be burdened upon the people of Jammu and Kashmir. Hence, the special provision contained in Section 92 excluded the application of Article 356 of Indian Constitution which provides the remedial measures, temporary in nature, when constitutional provisions fail in states. This article applies to all the states except Jammu and Kashmir which had a separate constitution of its own and that constitution provides similar remedy for failure of constitutional measures for this state in its Section 92. The comparative study of the two similar provisions will convince even an ordinary student that the very constitutional application order issued in this behalf by President of India even after consultation of the state government has no legal sanctity behind it. It could be done, as rightly pointed out, in his series of articles, by A.G. Noorani (an outstanding jurist and journalist of India) by a Constituent Assembly if at all reconstituted. Without going further in legal discussion these points make it patently clear that the continuation of governor's rule with a changed nomenclature of presidents rule was unconstitutional, illegal and immoral. It has been said that Parliament elections never evinced any public interest and reasons too have been explained; further study on this subject will be made during discussions on Kashmir's representation in the Indian Parliament. The Indian Congress (I) had no base in Jammu and Kashmir. Mr. G.M. Sadiq converted his bandwagon of leftover rejected stuff of the National Conference into Pradesh Congress (I) in 1964, but it was always fed through concession of permits, contracts, agencies and other benefits. Such a cadre of Congress workers had emerged under leadership of Mufti Mohammad Syed. This small cadre too had vertical division immediately before the advent of militancy in Kashmir. A larger group joined with Mufti's-Janta Dal which had formed a ministry in New Delhi under V.P. Singh. The remaining cadre was disarrayed and disgruntled. But, immediately after the people aligned themselves with armed struggle and with increased reign of terror let loose, a complete alienation made this leftover group also align their fate with the collective destiny. But some militant organisations too committed some blunders in this respect and made a section of these old Congress workers feel insecure and they went into security zones. Some of them did so to carry with their vested interest. However, this small leftover group of Congress workers became a dead stock which was consigned to security zones, had become a liability for the government and so remained politically ineffective and impotent. This was the case with Janta Dal and the oldest cadre based political party of the state the J&K National Conference. Hence, the leftover smaller numbers of workers of these pro-Indian political parties had either migrated to Jammu and Delhi or had taken refuge in security zones; they were unable even to meet their kith and kin, so how could they be used for any election activity even minor. In 1991 Parliament Eelections were not fought from the state. For a full term of five years of P.V. Narsimha Rao's rule, Kashmir remained 'unrepresented' in this house where even its insignificant representation has always remained ineffective; yet, absence of six members from Kashmir in a house of more than 500 members was not conspicuous, but to the keen students of history and politics, it held much importance. It was considered a defeat inflicted upon 'sixty crores of people' by sixty lakhs that six seats reserved for Jammu and Kashmir in the Indian House of Representatives remained unoccupied for a full term. Working under this 'defeat psychology' the top brass of the Indian Army imposed its viewpoint upon the divided Election Commission to have an attempt of a rehearsal for imposing an election so as to avoid further humiliation. It would logically be exploited worldwide, against India had Indian Election Commission insisted upon the principle that the situation of law and order in the state was not congenial for an election. In India's history its Election Commission was at this time headed by a strong man who did not bow under government pressure. Though the top brass of the Indian paramilitary forces engaged in Jammu and Kashmir and the Indian Civil Services for their common vested interests were against 'elections' and would not allow any other agency to share their booty in this unfortunate state but a section of the central cabinet had agreed to the suggestion of the army. Such a division in the cabinet was not based on principals, but was due to personal differences. Rajesh Pilot, a junior minister in the Home Ministry was not in favour of immediate elections, but Home Minister S.B. Chavan and his secretary Padhmanabhia both were for imposition of elections. The author's brief meetings with both of them in June 1994 had convinced him that they treated Jammu and Kashmir as a colony and do not care for the people, but the territory. However, their insistence could not stand against the instransigence of the Chief Election Commisioner Seshan, so S.B. Chawan had spare card available in Prof. Bhim Singh, an embodiment of political obscurity. Prof. Bhim Singh could prove helpful to ex-Prime Minister of Azad Kashmir Sardar Quyoom Khan and even to Mehmoodur Rehman, an Indian civil servant. He was made to file a writ petition in the Supreme Court of India which did not care what would be nature of elections in Jammu and Kashmir where every nook and corner was in the assessment of rulers, an arena of proxy war, where the writ of death ran large and where any political activity was an impossibility. The scheme of the Indian Constitution leaves it to the discretion and decision of the Election Commission to examine and decide wether it can hold a 'fair' and 'impartial' election. This is the determination of fact. On the basis of the ground situation the Election Commission had decided that the situation was not one which could be considered congenial for holding elections in a free atmosphere. The Election Commission had to borrow from a class IV official to an election observer from the civil services of the state. The confederation of J&K subordinate civil services had declared complete non-cooperation with elections. In the circumstances prevalent the decision of the Election Commission was sound both on fact and law, but the apex court of India accorded judicial sanction for imposition of elections on the writ petiton of Prof. Bhim Singh briefed, drafted and financed by the Home Minister.

These circumstances disappointed even those few people who considered that there should be some 'effective voice' in the Indian Parliament which could actively present the agony of the people of Jammu and Kashmir. All voters were individually and collectively of the view that no 'free' election could be even dreamed about in the situation. Hence, wholesale indifference leading to a situation of active boycott became the self-imposed decision of the people. On the other hand, after the Supreme Court ruling the forces demonstrated by strong words, threats, and deeds that they had decided to hold elections. As a reaction people decided to resist, thus a situation of 'election' between 'elections' and 'no elections' was initiated rigorously. On the one hand, the voter is utterly indifferent, has no faith in the system, has no interest in the Indian Parliament, has no known party or candidate in the fray (not even the J&K National Conference) had no knowledge whether his name existed on rolls or not; but on the other hand, the army had gathered together from security zones and from among renegade militants a third group, which was paid in cash, provided vehicles and security and managed a show of filing nominations. All the candidates belonged to one party, one platform and one manifesto. The common party which provide them themandate after fixing labels of

Congress (I), Janata Dal, BJP, 'Independent' or Awami Conference or Panthers Party upon their collars was the Indian Army. The common platform was provided by the army and the manifesto was 'to impose an election'. It is relevant here to quote from my book: "Military Operation".

> This author was a guest of our most credible eye-witness on the actual devastation of Charar-i-Sharief about the incident that the commanding officer of Rashtriya Rifles accompanied with his men entered into the lawns and warned our worthy host: "do cast your vote, we will examine your fingers to see indelible ink mark. You will not force us to cut your hands."

Before we could make some comments on this election stage managed and imposed by Indian forces, let us acquaint the readers about the integrity and reputation of the highest officer in the state who administered these elections as incharge of the state administration.

During our discussions on the 1967 elections qualified as 'Election by Rejection' it has been said that the returning officer of Rajpur constituency tampered with the nomination papers of all the opposition candidates and cleared for him the way to reject all those nominations. It is in this most obnoxious way that he declared the speaker of the Legislature (established under the fraud of 'Abductions' in 1962) G.M. Rajpuri elected unopposed from this constituency. The election was challenged through an election petition; in view of a good number of election petitions the government borrowed the services of two retired high court judges, who were appointed ad-hoc judges of the J&K High Court to dispose off these petitions. Late Justice Anant Singh from Patna High Court and Justice A.N. Gurtoo ex-judge of Allahabad High Court filled in these two vacancies for the limited purpose of hearing these election petitions.

G.Q. Mir Muran and M.S. Simnani—two defeated candidates filed two separate petitions against this election of Rajpuri, the petitions were heard and decided by Anant Singh, who quashed the election of Rajpuri, subjected the returning officer Ashok Kumar member of the Indian Civil Services and his assistant Safaya to severe strictures and made strong directions to get both of them prosecuted for criminal actions committed by them as returning and assistant returning officers. Ashok Kumar IAS the returning officer of Rajpura constituency in 1967 indicted by the Indian Judge of High court (who was not able to get those strictures quashed) was in 1996 the sole administrator of J&K as Chief Secretary of the government run from Raj Bhawan by Governor Retd. General Krishna Rao who himself had remained a prisoner of Raj Bhawan and the administration was run by Ashok Kumar. To quote the relevant paragraphs of the judgement of Anant Singh:

"Before parting with the case, I must observe that Kumar and Safaya, have abused their office as responsible public officers. They appear to have entered into a conspiracy to have brought about most wrongly the rejection of the nomination papers of all those three candidates, obviously to facilitate an uncontested return of Mr.Rajpuri, to the assembly. In order to carry out their sinister and evil design they have freely indulged in fabricating and tampering the evidence without any fear of subjecting themselves to the charge of even committing or having forgeries committed.[5] Mr.Kumar has by his own hands, committed forgery by making interpolation, at least in his order, exhibit PW 6/4, apart from fabricating other evidence, to which Safaya also contributed by abetting or even by acting as principal in scoring out the various lines in the endorsements X2, X3a and Xa although he did so under the direction of Mr. Kumar.

A serious view must be taken up of their conduct. A grave suspicion must also be lurking even with regards to Rajpuri, who was once a sitting minister in charge of tourism under whom Safaya was working at Srinagar, that he had influenced these two officers in acting in the manner as they had done, and he could have as well been found guilty of corrupt practices within the meaning of the act. But in fairness to Rajpuri, I may observe that mere suspicion, however, strong cannot take the place of evidence.[6] There is no evidence brought on the record to connect Rajpuri with the misdeeds of these two officers, who could have, after all, acted on their own, only to woo the erstwhile minister in Rajpuri, with a view to earn his grace, little realising that they were not serving the cause of justice, or the cause they wanted to serve. I can understand a public officer, catering to the wishes of his boss, but he should not, in doing so, exceed the legitimate bounds. These two officers have brought ignominy not only to themselves, but they have brought it also to Rajpuri, and to the government they have been serving, it cannot suffer them any more. Kumar had brought ignominy also to the exalted decree of the Indian Administrative Service to which he belongs. I have had by now, since March last decided a number of election petitions, perhaps 18, and have also allowed a few of them, merely on some technical grounds. But I have not come across such Returning and an Assistant Returning Officer, so daring and with no scruples.

Although Kumar is a junior officer and might have been duped by his ARO, who is a much senior and experienced officer, no lenient view should be taken of the conduct of either. I think it will be quite expedient in the interest of purity of administration of justice and with a view to eradicating the evils of perjury and forgery and that committed at the hands of responsible public officers, a separate processing under section 476 of the Criminal Procedure Code should be drawn up against both, calling upon them to show cause within a time to be fixed hereafter in that proceedings why they should not be prosecuted for perjury fabrication of evidence and committing or had forgeries committed in the various nominations papers.

This judgement should also serve as a warning to all the wrongdoers, who may be, that the arms of justice, given due light, or long enough to reach their ears.

In the result, the two elections petitions are allowed with cost and pleader's fee of Rs 5,000 in each payable by respondent no.1 to each of the two petitioners in the two cases.

The election of respondent no. 1 G.M. Rajpuri is declared void and set aside. Let the result be communicated forthwith to be followed by a copy of the judgement to the Election Commission, New Delhi and speaker of the J&K, Legislative Assembly.

By Order,

(sd.) K.S. RAJGOPALAN
SECRETARY TO THE ELECTION
COMMISSION OF INDIA
published for general inforamtion

(sd.) S.A.S. Qadri,
CHIEF ELECTORAL OFFICER,
JAMMU & KASHMIR

Srinagar
28th August, 1968

In the last but three paragraphs the hon'ble judge has in most befitting phraseology expressed his anguish and anxiety about the frauds prevalent in Jammu and Kashmir and warns: "The judgement should also serve as warning to all wrong doers, who may be, that the arms of justice, given due light are long enough to reach their ears."

The phrases 'wrong doers' who may be, exposes the suffocation created in the system of elections during the chief ministership of the so called most progressive democrat G.M. Sadiq. The readers could well imagine the position which might have prevailed during the rule of the dictator and despot Sheikh Abdulla and corrupt and nepotist G.M. Bakshi.

Anant Singh also left as a broken man from this state as the 'arms of justice' even given due light, could not reach to the ears of the concerned. No action was initiated against Ashok Kumar, who reached the highest civil services office of Chief Secretary. Even this judgement was not allowed to be reported though the judge had approved it for reporting. Now it must become clear to our readers that what could be the nature of the elections fought in 1996 for the Indian Parliament and J&K Assembly under the administration run under the guidance and authority of Ashok Kumar whose actions as returning officer were dubbed as evils of 'perjury and forgery by the highest court of Jammu and Kashmir.

It will become too lengthy if we quote the instances booth-wise or even constituency-wise about the force used upon people by the forces of India by dragging them to get their fingers marked with indelible ink marks at the polling booths. To give an instance of what the author witnessed in his locality:

Kralpora is a big village of tehsil Chadoora extending from 8th kilometer to 10th kilometer on Srinagar Charar-i-Sharief road. On the western part of this village is situated the military aerodrome and so the village on that side initially falls within the military zone. On the north, towards Srinagar two camps of Rashtriya Rifles and BSF are situated in Baghi-Mehtab colony. Both camps have a good number of uncontrolled and violent groups of renegade militants who are used as mad dogs to bite everyone. On the southern side, towards Charar-i-Sharief a camp of Rashtriya Rifles is situated at the end of 11th kilometer in the house of late Ghulam Rasool Shah, whose widow and children were forced out and the house was occupied immediately before the elections. It is only on the eastern side that the camps of the forces are at a comparitively farther distance of two kilometers.[7]

Two days before the polling day, groups of Rashtriya Rifles and BSF accompanied by renegade militants paid house to house visits like candidates making a house to house campaign in the democratic world. They did not stress or seek a vote for any particular candidate because all were 'their' created candidates. They did not argue in favour of any manifesto during this campaign nor did they request for taking part in the elections, but warned in their particular way that in case the inhabitants did not participate, their houses would be burnt and they would see their families butchered. A group made its entry into 'Durji Gauhar', the house of this author. A renegade militant informed them that the house belonged to the community of lawyers, nevertheless while leaving, the junior military officer said, "they know the consequences, they will themselves poll their votes". A few locals sought our advice and finally elders met the army in the house of Ghulam Rasool Shah and a truce was arrived at that one member from each family would go and cast the votes of their family members. But we must be fair to the polling staff imported from outside that they did not succumb to allow impersonation and resisted the pressures of the army. In this situation the particular member of a family who was deputed to cast votes for the whole family was able to cast his vote only. The picture of other places was more grim and terrifying. In Soibugh, Budgam tehsil the brother and sisters of the chief of Hizb-ul-Mujahidin Syed Salahu-din were not only forced to cast their votes, but were forced to face the camera. The same force was repeated with the close relations of Dr. G.N. Fai, Chairman American Council for Kashmir. In this farce the electronic media of India was not only a conniving but active partner. Eye witnesses and well informed sources have attributed this media farce to Farooq Nazki, Director

Doordarshan Srinagar and to his news producer Malik Bashir Athar.

The 1996 Parliament Elections was a prelude for imposition of a general election in the state which was conducted in the manner partly explained before and further details will follow. Had Congress (I) won and formed the government, they would have played the same game, but with different actors. The Janata Dal supported by two other Communist parties, on the other hand, roped in Farooq Abdulla in the hustings—an even bigger fraud. Before we discuss the elections of 1996 for the state legislature, we will expose to the public gaze, the vitally important ingredients of the process of an ordinary election.

Delimitation Process

Yuvraj Karan Singh asked the people of Jammu & Kashmir to elect an assembly for drafting the constitution and simultaneously made the orders regarding the delimitation of electoral constituencies for the same house. But, thereafter, The J&K Constitution Act 1956, provided in its sec 47 the strength of the state legislative assembly and fixed the number of elected members of the erstwhile state of Jammu & Kashmir at 100. Under sec 48, twenty five seats were reserved for the people of Pakistan held area of the state. Thus in all 75 members constituted the legislative assembly of Indian administered Jammu & Kashmir. It was later on exceeded by one bringing the number to 76. Elections in 1977 were held for the same number of territorial electoral constituencies and thereafter, in 1982 a Delimitation Commission was constituted under the chairmanship of late J.N. Wazir, ex-Chief Justice of J&K High Court. Other members included retired High Court Chief Justice, Justice Mian Jalal-ud-din and G.M. Mir a retired IAS officer. This commission was appointed in terms of sub sec (2) to sec 47 of constitution read with sec 4 of the State Representation of Peoples Act. Besides, the chairman and so nominated two members, the Representation of Peoples Act provides that the Chief Election Commissioner of India shall be ex-officio member of the Commission and as such, the then Chief Election Commissioner Chaturvedi was its ex-officio member. These were permanent members but legislature had also power to nominate five members. Hence nine members constituted the Commission. According to Representation of Peoples Act the Commission had to divide the state into 76 territorial constituencies in such a manner that the ratio between the population of each constituency 'can practically as possible be same'. The population figures of 1981 census have been relevant for division of constituencies. Though it should not have been the census based population but the number of registered voters. However, while drafting the state act, the legislature had probably copied the Indian Representation of Peoples Act.

In census process the enumerator is bound to reckon every person resident of that particular place where at the time of census such citizen of India is located. The state constitution does not grant right to vote to every citizen of India, but only to the permanent residents of Jammu and Kashmir state. Hence, the words: 'the last preceding census' contained in explanation to sub sec 2 of sec 47 of J&K Constitution are against the spirit of this very constitution. However, it is not very relevant to our discussion. Wazir presided over many meetings and the proceedings under which on the spot representations from the people were heard, but he died before the Commission could finalise its report, so Mian Jalal-ud-din, another retired Chief Justice of State was appointed as chairman and sitting high court judge Justice K.K. Gupta was included as member. The Commission was yet to make its report that two elections in 1983 and 1987 were held on the basis of existing position of the territorial constituencies. It is during the visit of the Commission to Ladhakh and Kargil districts that the modalities of increase in the constituencies were informally discussed at the Dak bungalow Drass-Kargil. This author was at that time the secretary of the Commission. Peri Shastri the Chief Election Commissioner India accompanied the Commission and the MLAs who were members nominated by the assembly including its deputy speaker Ghulam-u-din Malik were also present as co-opted members. The Chairman and Chief Election Commissioner between themselves agreed to add 11 seats. This author could probe into the proposed distribution of the additional 11 seats and felt that it would jeopardise the interests of the Valley and ultimately an attempt to shatter the majority position of the

Valley. Meanwhile, Farooq Abdulla again took over under accord with Rajiv and so the apprehensions were conveyed through Sheikh Nazir Ahmad, the General Secretary of the ruling National Conference. But it soon transpired that Dr. Farooq Abdulla had lost interest in the numerical superiority of the Valley as he had learnt the reality that the source of power was not people, but the pleasures of Delhi. This author canvassed with Syed Ali Shah Geelani, leader of MUF group in the assembly and co-opted member of the Commission and with his counterpart in Jammu Thakur Baldev Singh, leader of the BJP group in the assembly and other co-opted member of the Commission. Geelani assured that he would stall any constitutional amendments adding 11 seats but, for some consideration voted in favour of it. On the other hand, the BJP group voted against the constitutional amendments but for different reasons.

Inspite of all this canvassing, the ill advised and ill intentioned, 'Constitution of J&K (20th Amendment) Act 1988' was passed and became law on 22 February 1988. According to this amendment the words 'one hundred' in sub sec (1) sec 47 of Constitution was substituted by the words: 'One hundred and eleven'. Similarly, thereafter, amendment was made to sec 4 of J&K Representation of Peoples Act and words 'seventy six' were substituted by words 'eighty seven'. Thus, the strength of the J&K Assembly was raised from 76 to 87. The J&K Delimitation Commission created in 1982 was, thus through fresh terms of reference asked to divide Jammu and Kashmir instead of 76 electoral (territorial constituencies) into 87 constituencies. The Commission had yet to take off through its visits in the parts of the state, it had yet to hear people, groups of individuals, political parties and others interested in this behalf; it had yet to make study of adjustments to be proposed, and it had yet to examine the maps and other records that militancy broke out. It made governance an impossibility and more particularly the movement of the Commission too became impossible. To make fair adjustments it was imperative upon it to pay visits and hear the people. In 1990 the assembly was dissolved and so the Commission felt handicapped as its five co-opted members—the integral part of it—the nominees of the assembly from its elected members ceased their membership of the Commission. The governors administration pressurised the chairman Mian Jalal-ud-din to submit a final report distributing 11 additional constituencies in the manner in which Raj Bhawan desired. The illegal and immoral direction wanted him to allot two additional constituencies to Ladhakh region, one each to Gurez and Tangdar, and the remaining seven to Jammu urban areas. It was argued by emissaries of the governor that Ladhakh, Gurez and Tangdar were far flung areas though scarcely populated so deserved an increase. The Chairman in reply argued that on that assumption the additional seats in Jammu province be distributed in far flung areas. It was sometime in 1988, immediately after the constitutional amendments, that the senior Congress-I leader G.N. Azad, the forest minister of Jammu and Kashmir Kitchloo, both from district Doda and this author had together studied the topography of the Doda district, made assessment of the census report of the district and other reports and had prepared a strong case for allotment of one additional electoral segment for district Doda. This case was before the Commission and a convincing one, but the Governor would not concede additional seats for Muslim majority areas. The Commission chairman argued that Ladhakh region Gurez and Tangdar were scarcely populated. Ladhakh had two seats which on population basis was much more than the quota. they deserved according to the ratio of population in these areas, but this was done due to official insistence and the pressure mounted through state Chief Secretary R.K. Takkar, IAS. It needs a mention that Gurez, before 1947 was part of the frontier districts and Tangdar, part of Teetwal tehsil, Wazarati Muzzafarabad now in Azad Kashmir. Uri, Tangdar, Gurez, Leh and Kargil constituencies are almost within the military areas and so it became practically impossible for candidate other than from the ruling party to have any election campaign worth the name in these areas. Even during peace time, Uri, Gurez and Tangdar though presently part of Kashmir division have for the last five decades remained virtually ruled by the military. In the 70s, Dulo a judicial officer posted at Tangdar was detained in an army bunker as he had forgotton his identity card in his office. One can, therefore, understand the psychology of Indian rulers to concede full status of electoral constituencies to Tangdar and Gurez and to Nobra and

Zanskar in Leh and Kargil districts. Finally, the Chief Secretary deputed his Law Secretary, Lone to the residence of Main Jalal-ud-din (ex-Chief Justice J&K High Court), chairman of J&K Delimitation Commission and made him submit his resignation through him. Though the sacked chairman is said to have submitted his resignation for personal reasons, but Lone had claimed that he was 'asked' to do so probably under threat that he too might be roped in under the draconian law of TADA. Anyone could be involved under such a law merely on an unfounded allegation that such person provided a hideout to militants.

After his resignation, Justice K.K. Gupta, a member of that Commission was appointed its chairman without any member/members. Law provided the strength of the Commission to constitute upon the chairman, two members, ex-officio member (CEC) and co-opted five members from legislative assembly. The assembly had been dissolved so there were no coopted members. Justice A.M. Mir, sitting judge of J&K High Court was appointed as the member who never participated and finally resigned without joining the Commission. No Chief Election Commissioner of India after late Peri Shastri ever attended any meeting of the Commission and Seshan on being appointed as the Chief Election Commissioner of India considered it below his protocol to be the member of a Commission which was headed by a High Court Judge. Thus the single member Commission was persuaded and pressurised to allot one seat each to Nobra, Zanskar, Tangdar and Gurez and the remaining additional seats to Jammu urban areas. The dominant interest was to confine Kashmir Valley within 42 and bring the Valley to minority status without making demographic changes. Justice Gupta sought through the good offices of G.R. Kar an audience with the prime minister so it was decided to make the Commission again at least a three member body and to allot additional 11 seats in a manner so as to appear that a large share was taken by Kashmir division, but should appear otherwise. To erode the numerical superiority of the densely populated Muslim dominated Valley. Hence Justice Kuchai on his retirement as puisne judge of Kashmir was immediately appointed a member of the Commission in 1994. Though he had wandered in the corridors of power in Delhi for reemployment, but refused this membership for 'risks and dangers' inherent for his relations who were not privileged to live in security as he himself was. Hence, Bilai Nazki was assured elevation as judge of state High Court with the condition to 'sign' as a member of the Delimitation Commission, the report prepared by Gupta without having made any enquiry or on the spot examination of people and without having toured any of the constituencies. He was offered elevation to the state high court so how could he, therefore, miss the opportunity. To be fair to him as a judge he discharged his duties with competence and dignity, but the manner in which his appointment was made invited debates.

Seshan nominated his secretary as a member of this Commission after he rejected the first report which K.K. Gupta had submitted. It was rejected because it had no legal sanctity. The reconstituted Commission consisting of two judges and a nominee of the Chief Election Commission. suffered all those infirmities which were pointed out by Seshan while rejecting the chairman's earlier report. However, to stitch the jacket to the size of compulsions created, the 'occupying governor's regime' made amendments about induction of five co-opted members from the assembly. Similarly, amendment was made to substitute the nominee of the Chief Election Commisssioner for this post as ex-officio member. It has been discussed in detail that sec 92 of state Constitution envisages Governors rule for six months. There is no provision in the said constitution about imposition of President of India's rule in Jammu and Kashmir and it is also the case that application of Article 356 of Indian Constitution has no legal and constitutional mandate. It can be done only by dissolving the legislative assembly and then to constitute a fresh constituent assembly. Hence, all the amendments made in the laws or the new laws promulgated after July 1990 when Governors rule came to an end are but a nullity. There is, therefore, strong opinion among law knowing people to challenge the 'delimitation' made by such a defective and illegal Commission. But where to agitate? The history of political litigation in Jammu and Kashmir has taught the people to confine these discussions within the precincts of different bar associations only.

In 1996 when the 87 member assembly elections were ordered to be conducted the state had properly defined and delimited 76 electoral constituencies, but the constitution amendment had increased the strength by 11 constituencies so the existing territorial definition of electoral segments had ceased to have any effect. New territorial definitions given were both immoral and illegal, so the elections for the 87 member house is largely a nullity. Any court may not grant such declaration but the court of the people has adjudicated its verdict.

Electoral Rolls

An election is constituted of several stages and the process culminates into the final exercise of the ballot which is called polling. To arrive at that stage the process had to undergo many other stages. The first is the definition of various segments for which the returning officers and the assistant returning officers are to be appointed so that the nominations are invited. At the first the voter must be definite as to what electoral constituency he belongs to, thus the delimitation is *sine qua non.* We have seen that there was no 'legal' delimitation. The other stage must follow or proceed to prepare the voters list as those who, according to the principles and laws can exercise franchise. The election office had got prepared electoral rolls some time immediately before the 1983 elections. Thereafter, in 1984 faith in the system got a fatal knock at the hands of Jagmohan and after the 1985 Rajiv-Farooq accord, the voters had come to the inevitable conclusion that they were merely pawns in the power game and licence quota for power in Jammu and Kashmir could be allotted only by the ruling party at the centre. Hence, though a brief spell of time was announced from media for submission of objections and review petitions for electoral rolls but none availed of the opportunity. That assembly did not live its normal life of six years and within four years the election of 1978 was held on the basis of five year old electoral rolls. During that period thousands had died and lakhs of voters had reached the franchise age, but none was registered as a voter. This assembly 'died' a premature death in January 1990 and preparations for new elections of 1996 were ordered under the suffocating effects of the devastation of Charar-i-Sharief under the force of the Indian Army and under the threats of militants not to participate with any process of the election. Neither had people hope that any election worth the name was possible in the circumstances, nor had they any faith in the system nor could any one dare to make enquiries about electoral rolls, nor did the state machinery cooperate with the preparation or review of rolls; the state electoral officer only copied the electoral rolls prepared 14 years earlier in 1982. The chief electoral officer of J&K Jalil Khan IAS (an Indian Muslim whom people in J&K call a parasite) made an announcement just before 'polling day' that some 24,000 voters had approached for revision or registration. On enquiring it was found that they all related to the refugee camps of Kashmiri Pandits who yet figure in the rolls of their constituencies where these helpless people lived a decade or so before.

In the intervening period more than a lakh of people were martyred, yet they live in the voters list. Similarly, more than two lakh people might have died of natural death, but were voters in the 1996 elections. During these past 18 years more than seven lakh inhabitants reached the age of franchise, but none of them was registered as a voter to cast his vote.

Election Machinery

The state employees had to a large extent remained away from election duties so the officers to conduct the election were imported from outside the state who had no knowledge of places where they were posted, had language difficulties and were not able to understand the situation which they faced. True to their traditions like in the rest of India, they did not initially surrender to the pressures of army jawans posted at every booth ostensibly to maintain law and order though in reality to force the polling, but in the existing situation, they proved ineffective. In such a situation how can we imagine an election of any kind, even one qualified as rigged?

Candidates

In June 1996 the Jammu and Kashmir National

Conference did not participate in parliament elections, rather they had declared a boycott on the grounds that the situation was not conducive and congenial for holding an election in the state. Even Ab Qayoom President J&K Pradesh Janta Dal (ruling Janta at the Centre) had in unequivocal terms convinced Sumantra Bose about the inherent impossibilities to hold any sort of election.

Our readers are now familiar with the Chief Secretary Ashok Kumar who enacted all the major roles of this drama of elections. He called a meeting of officers of the army, paramilitary organisations, state police and top brass of the state administration, mainly constituted of imported officers from India. The meeting was held in Nehru Guest House at Srinagar situated in a sensitive security zone on 9 and 10 April 1996. An extract of minutes contained below will sufficiently reveal that the government installed by India in Jammu and Kashmir was not at all interested in free and fair elections, but in holding the polls in any manner under any circumstances. The extract reads:

> "...It is apprehended that in view of threat from subversive elements to the electoral process, employees of the state government may not actively participate in making all the arrangement for the elections..."

The meetings were being held in Srinagar, but simultaneously the decisions were being taken and implemented from Delhi. On 9 and 10 April in Srinagar the chief secretary informed his officers about the ground situation and said "the state administration had been paralysed by the refusal of its employees to participate in electoral process". However, in Delhi before the conclusion of this meeting on 10 April 1996 the Government of India vide its order No. 13015/31/94-K(DD-1) Vol-1, Dated 10.4.1996, ordered to export from Delhi and other adjoining states to the occupied state, officers and subordinate officials to conduct elections here. Thereafter, Jammu & Kashmir government issued two government orders Nos. GAD (adm) 16/95 Elect.II dated 30.4.96 and 355-GAD (adm) of 1996 of the same date under which such daily wagers were to be ordered to be regularised who would take risk to associate with the conduct of elections. (b) The deputy commissioners (collectors) of districts were authorised to appoint, on contract basis, at least five persons (officials) for each assembly segment on a consolidated pay of Rs 5,000/pm for a period not exceeding 60 days.

In view of the high percentage of educated unemployed in Jammu & Kashmir a large number of 'qualified' poor youth risked their lives and offered their services. Particularly ex-militants got these Contractual appointments. The militants too knew that the majority of them were living below the poverty line so, did not harm them. These newly recruited young people were under order No. 355 GAD of 1996 taken to nearer army camps where they were supposed to receive the training as how to conduct elections. They were given only one lession that they should assist the army and other forces. They were made to believe that they would be given permanent jobs after elections and would be protected from militant attacks only if they were able to show 'participation of voters' whatever the means might be. After elections they have neither been so far regularised nor considered for employment, but left to face the dangers of death. But the militant organisations are aware of the compulsions which made them risk their lives and they have pardoned them probably with a game that this frustrated youth will soon be left with no other alternative, but to take up the gun. But the present Chief Secretary Jatalay is least interested to fulfil the commitment of his predecessors. These people have once again learnt that Indian rulers derive pleasure in defying their promises with Kashmiris, even those which they make to their agents.[8]

The 1987 elections culminated the process of mistrust in the National Conference. The all India parties—Congress (I), Janta Dal, Communist Parties stood since rejected. The agglomeration of leadership which emerged under the banner of the Muslim United Front had disappointed and dismayed the masses for its ineffective role to protect the vote of the people and the policies for its 'elected' group adopted thereafter. Thus, a complete vacuum of leadership had spread gloom. It is against this background that the 'militant' emerged as the saviour and filled in the vacuum. Politicians who took refuge under the umbrella of newly emerged leadership could rehabilitate themselves with the masses, though with a broken image. But the ruling National Conference, its cadres, leadership and workers were subjected to the peoples' wrath for various reasons the main one being their corrupt practices in the immediate past. Similarly, the brunt of condemnation fell on other pro-Indian leaders too. The people's hatred was initially given a vent by the new JKLF leadership against those workers of the National Conference who for reasons that either they were dubbed as 'informers' for government forces or were accused of having engineered persecution of those young enthusiastic people who had taken active part in the 1987 elections. But as soon as Jamait-i-Islami jumped in militancy it also targeted the National Conference cadres for obvious reasons. In this situation either the cadres of the National Conference and other pro-Indian parties had to associate with militancy or had to face death or had to take refuge in security zones.

The heirs of the leaders and workers who were killed either severed all political associations or maintained rapport with the exiled leadership which lived in security either in Srinagar or in Jammu or in New Delhi. Similarly, the National Conference leaders who had to live in security had by compulsion to mortgage themselves to Indian forces and so could not avoid their dictate. Nonetheless as they insisted on going by party discipline, therefore during parliament elections the Indian authorities could not force any National Conference worker from the security zone to contest though some wanted to do so. Shafi Bhat had decided to jump in against the party whip.

The ruling Congress-I had initiated parleys with Dr. Farooq Abdulla, but it was confined to the joint strategy of the two parties which was almost the same argument which Indira Gandhi had stressed in 1983. It pivoted around the theme to concede near about half the seats to Congress-I in the arrangement of electoral alliance. Farooq Abdulla was conscious that within the short period of assuming office he would have to vacate in favour of the Congress-I in the arrangements of electoral alliance. Hence, the parleys failed. The 1996 June elections ultimately brought a minority agglomeration of odd groupings—the United Front to power in Delhi. The Janta Dal, the biggest partner in the ministry had no stake in the J&K National Conference, but Farooq Abdulla to prove an effective Chief Minister, demanded two-third majority and offered to accommodate a few boys of the three major partners of the United Front, i.e., Janta Dal, CPI and CPM in the legislature. At this particular juncture the Janta Dal in Jammu and Kashmir had only three names worth the mention—the two named above in Kashmir viz Mufli Mohd Syed and Abdul Qayoom and Dhan Raj Bhalgotra from Jammu. The Communist Party, Marxist had one prodigal son in M.Y. Tarigami and the Communist Party of India had adopted a volunteer of late Abdul Sattar Ranjeer. The major partner Janta Dal had introduced as their leader Deve Gowda, who had no understanding of national problems and moreso had no information about Kashmir. Hence, the matter was decided with Farooq Abdulla by the CPM leader Harkishen Singh Surjeet who was associated by late Farooqi of CPI. Both these Communist leaders had remained connected with the communist movement in Jammu and Kashmir, but were responsible for weakening in this state.

In 1953 the undivided Communist Party was the only cadre based pro-Indian party in the state. It had made sufficient entries among the working class and trade union movements in Jammu & Kashmir. At this critical juncture Jawahar Lal Nehru pressed that the local communists should merge with the leftover National Conference cadres. The idea was resisted by a sizeable group of communists in the state including N.N. Saraf, M.L. Misri, G.M. Malik, R.P. Saraf and others, but Dange supported Jawahar Lal Nehru's idea. Ajay Gosh opposed Dange's policy. Harkishen Singh Surjeet, as secretary of the Punjab unit aligned with Gosh, but in 1996 Surjeet mustered a forced election so that two unknown workers of the two Communist parties could get rehabilitated.

Harkishen Singh Surjeet thus became the broker in this power game. Mufti felt annoyed, left the Janta Dal in a huff and joined the Congress-I again. The Governor appointed by India then made Farooq Abdulla accommodate some of the favourites of some partners in the ruling front under his umbrella. The party supporting the central government from outside—the Congress-I was also assured accommodation even in the cabinet and that too in an unprecedented manner unknown to democratic polity. In return Farooq Abdulla was assured two-third majority of his own, so he agreed to jump into the hustings; but, a show of elections had to be made.

The Congress (I) workers too were confined to live in security areas. Some civil servants who had risen under the patronage of Congress leaders to the higher cadres and had amassed huge assets and were forced to remain in tight security, were also roped into the hustings. The Janata Dal had neither leadership nor cadre. The state unit chief of the party on the eve of elections was made to join the National Conference under an arrangement worked out by the main broker Harkishen Singh Surjeet, with a clear understanding to give him a ministerial berth without his joining the electoral fray. However, to give a show of its presence, the ruling party in centre had to rope in the rejected members of the Congress (I) or non-political humbugs.

The intelligence agencies of the country and leaders of the armed forces and paramilitary forces dissented with the civil leadership and projected their own candidates from the ranks of renegade militants.

This was an election between various sections of rulers which showed clashes of policies regarding Kashmir. However, all the confronting sections of the rulers had one common aim to impose a rule which would remain subordinate to the forces. The views of ruling politicians prevailed as they argued to make the result of imposed elections, to some extent, a saleable commodity in the world. It was argued that Farooq Abdulla's installation would serve three purposes. Firstly, the National Conference had locally, inspite of all erosions, some scattered cadres. Secondly, in some Western countries Sheikh Abdulla's name could be exploited as both the parties to the Kashmir Dispute—India and Pakistan had projected him on different occasions, with different aims as the credible voice of Kashmir. Thirdly, there was consensus among all the politicians in New Delhi to get the Farooq and Sheikh dynasty completely discredited with the people, so that it was used for some time and then thrown away. Since the installation of the Farooq government, the toll of custodial killings has gone very high; the death toll has reached almost 20 per day on an average; the number of occurrences of arson and devastation of civil property by forces has increased terribly and all these misdeeds of the Indian forces are attributed to Farooq Abdulla's connivance and so add to his alienation even among his left over minor base scattered in the countryside. The role of renegades has also discredited him. Thus, it is intelligible to all that why the Indian leadership granted unprecedented political concessions to Farooq Abdulla and conceded such a large majority in his favour. In the process the nuisance of the Sheikh dynasty in Kashmir politics is to be buried forever.

These three factors carved out a new destiny for Farooq Abdulla and his dead National Conference received an artificial lease of life by the mercy of powers, that too only confined to the civil secretariat.

This time the power was not allowed to be received on a silver platter as Farooq Abdulla's father had received in 1975 in an uncontested game. This time a 'mock fight' was to be played for public consumption. Hence, other reserved divisions of politicians living in security areas were thrown into the electoral battle under the labels of Congress, Janata Dal and BJP. The army particularly the Rashtriya Rifles did not succumb to the heavy weight of political consensus and created their own parties out of renegade militants. There was no rapport between these individual militants who had taken up the gun either to create or to obtain powerful positions or who fell apart from their organisations again due to their own intolerance of discipline or for unnecessary victimisation by the high command of those militant outfits to which they belonged. Hence, the Rashtriya Rifles was not able to create an organisational set-up nor there was any such necessity for them because this concerned military wing had its own organisational strategy. At the time of the parliamentary elections the 'RAW' and 'IB' (main intelligence agencies of India) associated with the Rashtriya Rifles deputed a Kashmiri Pandit migrant connected with these agencies and pasted an organistional label upon a scattered body of these renegades. But the gulf of disagreement among those renegades was so deep that a violent reaction followed and under various organisational labels emerged the growth of those pro-Indian militant outfits officially involved in the process of elections. The leaders and workers of these ostensibly political bodies, but in reality pro-government gunmen constituted amongst themselves the workers and the cadres. All were operating from army camps. The different divisions of these pro-government militants operated as candidates, proposers and propagators from three districts of the Valley. They did not require the polling agents or other allied workers necessary for polling and counting of votes as their interests were safer with their masters in the Rashtriya Rifles, the Border Security Force and other regular army units.

Ultimately the views of 'politicians' prevailed as the other viewpoints were propagated clandestinely. But those other elements did not completely surrender and Farooq Abdulla had to rationalise with the humiliation which his organisation met in Sonawari constituency in district Baramulla of the Valley where Kuka Parray was the candidate of Indian intelligence agencies and of the Rashtriya Rifles the counter militancy wing of the army.

In Kulgam, district Anantnag Farooq Abdulla assured the main broker of power Harkishen Singh Surjeet of CPI(M) to give safe return for the state legislature to the sole communist in Kashmir Yousaf Tarigami—though neither the Communist Partyof India (Marxist) nor Tarigami had even a scattered base in the area and nor could in this stronghold of the Jamait-i-Islami a non-believer be at all considered a candidate worth the name.

In Jammu province Farooq Abdulla had to accommodate the sworn enemy of his father Dr. Karan Singh and his son. Though in politics neither friendship nor animosty has any permanency, but the void between the two families was so deep that only various phases and prolonged process of reconciliation could bridge the gulf. Power brokers in New Delhi had made Farooq Abdulla yield even against the wishes of his mother, the patron of the National Conference and against the humble persuation of Sheikh Nazir, general secretary of the National Conference.

Thus all the rejected elements disarrayed as they were, had, perforce, to surrender to their common patrons in New Delhi. All these elements held allegiance to varied agencies and parties. They had deep rooted differences and clashes of interest, but had to yield to play in the drama of 'elections' as tutored knowing full well the part which was to be played by each character and being consciously aware that the role of 'hero' was allotted to their common enemy, Farooq Abdulla. None could resile because the remuneration they had been receiving in the form of doles from the Government of India in the security zones where they lodge, the necessities, comforts and luxuries as well as security of life were all met by their Delhi masters. Let us now discuss the election imposed in Charar-i-Sharief constituency as a sample.

Charar-i-Sharief Constituency in 1996

Abdul Qayoom of Charar-i-Sharief is now a familiar character to our readers. It has been said that inspite of his non-political inclinations Bakshi Ghulam Mohammad, for his own interests, imposed upon Qayoom the role of a political worker. Belonging to a petty burgeoise mentality and feudal background he too succumbed. In the bye-elections of 1957 he was imposed as representative of Charar-i-Sharief Assembly segment. The game was repeated in subsequent elections till 1977. Thus Abdul Quyoom had assumed the role of hereditary ruler of this area but he was dethroned in 1977 when the kingdom was allotted to a political novice Abdul Rahim Rather of an adjoining village Badipora. This author too played a role in baptising a non-political ex-school teacher and budding pleader Abdul Rahim Rather into a local leader when in the 1972 elections this author and Abdul Gani Mir a dynamic teacher made him pose a threat to Abdul Quyoom. Abdul Rahim Rather frustrated with the bungling done by the returning officer and concerned superintendent of police under the dictates of A.G. Lone, then a minister in the state cabinet made endeauvours to join 'the national industry in Kashmir' that is the government service as D.P. Dhar described it. In September 1975 he submitted an application with this author (still preserved in my records) to be absorbed as translator in Kashmiri law translation cell which was under contemplation of the state government then for which this author was appointed by the new chief minister Sheikh Abdulla to head a committee to suggest measures, but the recommendations did not materialise. This author pulled him out from frustration and made him wait in the corridors of Mujahid Manzil. Within two years he entered the legislature with the miraculous mandate from Sheikh Abdulla; he did not look back and soon found himself in the high command of their party. In the1987 elections though he had all chances of success, but his success too remained a part of the culmination of fraud played in the name of elections.

Inspite of the fact that both Abdul Quyoom and Abdul Rahim Rather created a rapport with the local Jamait-i-Islami and its militant wing the Hizb-ul-Mujahidin, both had to seek asylum in protected security zones. Abdul Quyoom as the head of the state unit of the ruling Janata Dal had either to vacate the office and declare his retirement from politics or had to live in security. Later it transpired that he expected a formidable threat to his life not immediately from the Mujahideen, but from his colleague and patron the union Home Minister Mufti Mohammad Syed. Abdul Rahim Rather had deep interest in the careers of his children who were busy in studies and had to enter professional institutions. He preferred to build their career so remained in Jammu. Abdul Quyoom had in the hey days of his power crossed that stage, so both severed their links with the constituency, but Abdul Quyoom's availability in the city did try and test his relevance to power politics by 'lodging' written recommendations in favour of victims of official terror. These 'letters' usually were thrown by BSF officers, army officers, CRPF cmmandants or by the officers managing JIC's (Joint Interrogation Centres) in waste paper baskets. Rather pleaded guilty by his escapism. These two ineffective rulers of this constituency possess certain common qualifications - both are gentlemen with no political base, both like creepers stand erect with borrowed support, both have created some pockets of concession seekers and both are self-centred and have no politics beyond their own children. However, Abdul Quyoom has theoretically some political notions and even is honest in his assessment about the failures of Indian politics, but within his limited circle. Due to such an assessment that some time before the siege of Charar-i-Sharief in a restricted social get-together he has admitted that India has occupied Kashmir in the manner in which colonial powers do. He was then in agreement with this author that the erosion of the organs of Indian democracy in Jammu and Kashmir were responsible for the alienation of the people of the state. In this context it is pertinent to quote in original his conversation with Sumantra Bose the author of *The Challenge In Kashmir* (New Delhi: Saga Publications).

"...holding (assembly) elections will be totally counter productive and have disastrous consequences."

He had unanimity of thought with Farooq Abdulla who held the same view. He had fallen apart with his mentor Mufti Syed and through the good offices of the Governor General Krishna Rao; he walked too close to Farooq Abdulla.

A mention is relevant here that the Surjeet-Farooq accord consisted of only two unwritten clauses, viz., to share the power in Jammu and Kashmir and to install Krishna Rao as governor as his first term was cut short on the eve of the outbreak of militancy. Farooq Abdulla had made a point to get him back again to this paradise and the obliged Krishna Rao cultivated all avenues to reinduct Farooq Abdulla. In this game for their common vested interests General Krishna Rao was successful to create a wedge between Mufti Syed and Abdul Quyoom. He provided new support to the latter as he cannot stand in the political arena on his own.

In the summer of 1996 Farooq Abdulla took the decision to array the scattered left over cadre of his party the J&K National Conference and jumped in the fray. Abdul Quyoom exploited the situation and without moving to New Delhi the centre of power he was assured by General Krishna Rao of his political rehabilitation. The Janata Dal government in New Delhi had no stakes in any specific person or group of persons in Jammu and Kashmir, but had interests only in Mufti Syed and Abdul Quyoom. Mufti Syed reacted against the United Front deal with Farooq Abdulla, left it and re-joined his parent organisation the Congress (I). Thus, there were only two persons to be rehabilitated Abdul Quyoom in the Valley and Dhanraj Balgotra in Jammu. So a deal was entered under which the two stalwarts of the Janta Dal would be given positions in power, but both through nominations and without being troubled to wander in the muddy field of elections. Abdul Quyoom was all set to the join state cabinet in the Education Ministry, the department he had supervised as state minister upto February 1975, nevertheless he was convinced that this game would, instead of narrowing the gulf between the people of Jammu and Kashmir and India, widen it. These were the remarks which he would make with his friends on the eve of declaration of party mandates announced by various self-styled parties from security zones.

On the other hand, Abdul Rahim Rather assured of success showed his keen interest to retain his domain. To be fair to Abdul Rahim Rather he has catered for the needs of his village, relatives and of the limited number of his workers.

Immediately after joining the Congress Party, Mufti Syed on the eve of elections arrayed all those elements who had acquired status and remuneration due to their pro-Indian clout. These elements in district Budgam are connected to each other through common vested interests and they strengthened political connections by creating marital relationships with various families. It is out of this dual relationship that engineer Ghulam Nabi Mir Lasjan was thrown in the fray by policy makers of India under the Congress label from Chadoora constituency and he recommended services from the 'Lone' family from village Hanjoora with whom he was interrelated. So, advocate Ghulam Nabi Lone was made to file nominations from Charar-i-Sharief constituency on a Congress (I) ticket.

Ghulam Hassan Muqiem had been propped up by Chauduary the BSF commandant as a 'viable' candidate from this constituency.

On the eve of these elections, the town of Charar-i-Sharief was facing the agonies of the first anniversary of its destruction and so the anger and hatred mounted against all the contributory characters, individuals, groups or countries who had contributed to this tragedy. Destiny dragged the APHC leadership to the spot where hatred had started erupting and so they burnt their fingers. Ghulam Hassan Muqiem led this violent demonstration and was even beaten up. Such courage increased his purchase value with military forces and so he got encouragement. People unmindful that he too was a 'purchased' man liked his courage as they too had resentment and so planned to humiliate the duo of Rather and Quyoom. The town people decided that if they could not resist the pressure of the milliary and were made to line up in fron of polling station and affix their seal on ballot paper they would affix the seal of approval only upon the symbol of Ghulam Hasaan irrespective of his party affiliations.

During the proceeding few days they were brought to bunkers and threatened with consequences if they did not go to the booths. The majority of local population lived in refugee camps but the sub-localities of Zinpanchaal, Gundi Shams, Hapat Naar, Arzan Garza, Satellite Town, Gulshandabad, etc., were even then under a siege like situation. From the high peaks around—all occupied by the army, even the movements within the houses were visible to the armed forces. The situation of the people particularly in this constituency generally resembled a vast war prison where the authorities were determined to impose a situation upon the prisoners to express their choice to get the warden of the jail 'elected.' However, the voters here and equally in other constituencies in the Valley did not yield to threat to take all members of their families to booths. So, a day before polling a gentleman's agreement evolved between the frightened heads of the families and the forces that at least one member from every family, whether registered as a voter or not would have to get his finger dyed with indelible ink mark at the booth. This agreement was even evolved in the locality where the author lives, viz., Kralpora in Chadoora constituency.

It should not be construed that no one was in favour of elections, but in our assessment, no one liked the manner in which this farce was being imposed as a begaar (corve) upon the people.

Certainly a section of people was in favour of elections for more than one reason. Firstly, the struggling Kashmiri disgusted with the peaceful struggle from 1947 to achieve the promised self respect restored, ultimately preferred the use of force against the 'policy of per force occupation'.

They had clear assessment that as the situation goes out of control for India, Pakistan will intervene in the same manner in which India intervened in erstwhile East Pakistan. During 1990-93 the total involvement of the people with the armed struggle against India created apprehensions in the minds of both the policy makers in New Delhi and among their military forces, but Pakistan did not avail of the opportunity. In the assessment of the people, it was Pakistan's weakness or it was made to miss the situation or it feared a defeat. Hence, a section of people desired to experience both the forms, have armed as well as constitutional struggles simultaneously.

Secondly, the 'foreign governor' advised by imported advisors and assisted by forces of occupation and the prejudiced civil service had pushed the victimised Kashmiri to the wall. Hence, this victim of the situation wanted some local pockets of authority who could, at the least hear his grievance even if could not redress it. The majority of the people had no faith on any individual or group of individuals or on any political party that could have courage in the circumstances, to give him a patient hearing. In discourses discussing permutations and combinations the people would dismiss even the Hurriyat leadership if it was elected to power to assuage their pain. They had sufficient understanding that in this vast Joint Interrogation Centre of Army, BSF, and CRPF no civil administration could prove effective. Inspite of this clear understanding a small section wished to experiment with a civil administration, no matter how ineffective.

Thirdly, thanks to Bakshi Ghulam Mohammad the pockets of concession seekers are omnipresent at every set up and at every place. Though many of them had substituted their devices and had joined with militants directly or indirectly and had made their fortune, but their exposure had made them to hunt out new sources for their appetite. Many of them wished to play as proposers or election agents so as to receive the booty.

Fourthly, the renegade or 'sarkari' militant or the armed

informer of the forces had created terror (though in a small degree in the constituency of Charar-i-Sharief) for the people. Under their threat of assault, humiliation and challenges, the voter felt that he might be dragged to booths. The rural population scattered in small villages preferred, on the other hand, a negotiated settlement with the forces to depute one male member from every family to cast the vote of the whole family and so save them from persecution at the hands of the state terrorist. The forces too were satisfied so as to provide material to the video cameras of the agencies from India and other countries.

Some readers may dub us with the stigma of partiality if we fail to admit that there exist some pro-democracy elements too, though small in number, who stand convinced in the viability of the democratic process even in the suffocating situation of Kashmir. A study revealed that such a group too was not at all inclined to take part in such elections which, in their view, were bound to prove fatal for the very faith in the system and organs of democracy. They believed that such imposed elections would establish that gun culture was the only viable solution in the situation in Jammu and Kashmir. Hence, such genuine democrats resisted the pressures of the army and prefered to dye their fingers in their own blood rather with the indelible ink-mark.

This author provides a living example. A retired judge, an advocate of repute, a writer of all India recognition was threatened by a major of Rashtriya Rifles :

"Oh judge Agar Tum Vote Daalney Naa Gaye Too Hum Tumar Ungli Kaat Dengey".

(Oh Judge, if you do not go to cast the vote, we will cut your fingers).

But neither did we go to cast the votes nor did anybody did cut our fingers. The game was not in the translation of threat into action, but to derive dividends from it by way of establishment of fear psychosis.

This conscious pro-democracy element actively and consciously boycotted these elections not in response to the call of the APHC or gunmen, but to the call of his conscience. Having reasons to believe that these imposed elections would drive the final nail in the coffin of democratic aspirations as he had to exercise his right of choice only between rejected and anti-democracy corrupt parties and persons.

Fifthly, the misguided, mismanaged and ill timed campaign of the All Party Hurriyat Conference against elections insulted the self-respect of the electorate. They were against hustings out of their own conscious commitment and so inferred from the so 'launched campaign' that the leadership, with all the conscious sacrifices of the people, considered them dumb driven cattle. Few citizens at Gaw Kadal after being approached and advised not to take part in hustings remarked:

> "They would have taken part as candidates themselves, but for the fear of popular awakeness."

This campaign also caused a reaction. Had there been a genuine approach New Delhi could cultivate a bona fide interest in elections and could create a formidable pocket committed to the process of democratisation of this society. But right from Jawahar Lal Nehru down to I.K. Gujral—all leaders in New Delhi have been interested only in imposing puppets. In the early 50s Jawahar Lal Nehru had gameplan in the imposition of Sheikh Abdulla and Harkishen Singh Surjeet, the brain behind the Deve Gowda Ministry (Deve Gowda was himself ignorant of Kashmir and its politics) had a gameplan in the imposition of Sheikh's son—Farooq Abdulla.

These five reasons had made a pocket of 10 to 15 per cent electorate convinced to try the exercise of the vote. Had the Election Commission of India guided itself by the assessment of its head Seshan and imposed strict vigil that the turnout remained completely and constructively voluntary, such cautious and genuine effort would have created a basis for pro-democracy and given a pro-Indian twist to the churning of events in the political process. His two colleagues however, Dr. Gill and Krishnamurthy were, patently against their conscience, led by the charisma in the myth of 'national interest' created by the debased values of the occupants of South Block from 1950 till date. Their guilty conscience was quite transparent from their cryptic remark:

"No one had come forward to allege and establish rigging in elections."

Both these members were sufficiently conscious that it was the voter in general who was defrauded by all the contesting candidates who were thrown in the fray by the single proposer, master and mandate holder i.e.the Government of India.

Had the two communist leaders Harkishen Singh Surjeet and Inderjeet Gupta taken lessons constructively from their own memories and experiences about Kashmir politics they would have preferred the genuine play and ignored the percentage in the turnout of voters. There is no provision in J&K Representation of Peoples Act fixing any specific percentage for valid election; even if only 5 per cent cast their vote that would not invalidate the elections, but would cultivate faith in the institutions and organs of the system. Thereby Kashmiri voters would feel that the authorities in New Delhi had taken proper lessons from the seven year history of destruction and disaster which was a natural consequence of their undemocratic policies. Such feelings would reciprocate a feeling of confidence and would have paved the way for a constructive pro-democracy shift.

However, the policy should have remained under the umbrella of protection to the voter from the threat which would deter him to go to the booth. Instead, to protect his frightened desire he was dragged under a sword hanging upon his head and 'choice' was forced upon him. The gun which had come to protect him was used to impose upon him the rulers of the common choice of the Surjeet, Inderjeet and Kesri clique.

The small limited section which felt viability in democratic struggle were convinced that New Delhi would never, under any rule, allow even a minor voluntary assimilation of the democratic urge of Kashmiris with that of the people of the rest of India. This is the policy initiated and consolidated by Jawahar Lal Nehru in 1950-51 which was carried forward by his successors and Deve Gowda treaded the beaten tract.

Investigations made by the author in selected pockets of the state make him claim with certainty that even if any individual looked enthusiastic at the polling booth, that meant to demonstrate the indelible ink-mark on his finger was to enjoy a little peace—from the terror which he apprehended from the military bunker nearest to his home. Such satisfaction might have been detected by the Door Darshan Indian TV video camera from the hypocritical smile dancing on the squeezed lips of Gulam Qadir at the polling booth of Doda in Jammu. It was all done to save his skin. We do not dismiss his claim that he had come to the booth due to his hatred for strife and threat. No human being more so a peace loving Kashmiri would have ever approved and encouraged destruction to his life and property. Gulam Qadir looked jubilant, but for his assured safety from official terror.

It will make this part too lengthy if we contain herein the details of constituency-wise sample survey made in this respect but, we confine details to the devasted town of Charar-i-Sharief. Out of the total number of voters here more than 60 per cent were living in refugee camps scattered in suburbs and the newly constructed incomplete houses in Alamdar colony. Only young energetic members of families supervised the construction work whereas their families continued to live in refugee camps. On the polling day which came after 400 days of this destruction, all the hill-tops and elevated places were fitted with binoculars and even the entrance or exit of a pilgrim was visible to all the three inspection bunkers of the army. The movement of soldiers in the heart of the town and its extended localities was so frequent that any visitor or pilgrim would get frightened. Every local man was looked upon with suspicion, anger and contempt for the hospitality he had showered on Mast Gul and every woman, whatever her age, was treated with disrespect for her fault that she too might have cooked food for the militant. It is in this psychological fear that the army jawans and officers in batches would enter into every semi-gutted dwelling place or in an incomplete new construction or in the tent or shed where the uprooted 'voter' of the town lived and he would be made to realise that Mast Gul wished to frustrate elections from this town but "we turned it into ashes and we believe that you are wise to understand". Similar threats were conveyed daily from the date when the four candidates were made by their master, the Government of India, through its various agencies, to file nomination papers. Hence, the brains of the town collaborated on their action plan. They conveyed with confidence that they would not be allowing women to vote nor would cast votes for absent voters living in refugee camps. The forces had full assessment of the determination of Charar-i-Sharief residents and assured that they would themselves cast votes for absent voters, but would like a show of voters near all booths and so the truce was arrived at.

The second phase for collective decision was to express the choice of compulsion. Lone of the Congress (I) had hijacked the party mandate so was not considered for the favour of the 'forced choice.'Abdul Rashid Rather the National Conference candidate and his old foe and new friend Abdul Quyoom were both targets of general contempt and hatred not only for their political affiliations but for their 'roles' during the Charar-i-Sharief siege and after its devastation. It was commonly known that Gulam Hassan had remained for two decades a political worker committed to the Congress party. People of the town decided that from each house a male member would get his finger dyed with colour at the polling booth and they also decided to affix the seal on the election symbol of Gulam Hassan for the following reasons a)hatred for Congress and National Conference candidates and b)to further appease the tyrannical BSF commandant as he alongwith his juniors and seniors openly propagated for Gulam Hassan, who had arranged (after Hassan was treacherously ignored by Congress-I) for him to contest from Janta Dal.

As the polling concluded each person who was made to dye his finger with an ink-mark on his own ballot paper or on the paper of a dead, migrated person or jailed voter, declared that Gulam Hassan was winning hands down. Choudhary of BSF and Panday of Rashtriya Rifles and their subordinates did not feel shy to say that they had marked bundles of votes in favour of Gulam Hassan and had dropped those in the box successfully without any objections being raised. This time even close relations of Abdul Quyoom and A.R. Rather had contemptuously rejected both of them and marked Hassan's symbol. The closely committed puppets of both these rivals were annoyed with them not for their anti-people activities, not for their active and passive connivance to get this sacred town gutted and not for their discourtesy that after this destruction they failed even to render mere lip service to the wronged inhabitants but for different reasons. Abdul Quyoom's sympathisers were annoyed with him as to why had he joined the National Conference which he had condemned for his whole political life. Rather's confidents were displeased with him as to why had he allowed 'entry' to a sworn enemy of Sheikh Abdulla in the family organisation of Sheikh, i.e., the National Conference. Hence, Rather's score was very poor and Lone, the Congress candidate was not able to open one for him. So, out of 27 per cent votes polled by all means—by the intimidated voter, by frightened impersonator, by the agencies of forces or by polling staff themselves—all these players who had played the game claimed that Gulam Hassan would win and the security deposits of the National Conference and Congress candidates would be confiscated. But the results were greatly against these expectation of locals and in favour of Abdul Rahim Rather who had declared in his native village during the election campaign "votes or no votes we have arrangement with Deve Gowda and I am a cabinet minister". So the result declared stunned the wings of the forces and paramilitary forces too. An officer of the BSF A.S. Singh said:

> "Wah kya haath ki safai hai"
> "*This haath ki safai* (jugglery tricks) made us to take arms", said a young man, Mushtaq Ahmad.
>
> "Similar jugglery tricks imposed Beant Singh upon the Punjab" whispered A.S. Singh in reply so that his senior Hindu colleagues could not hear him.

The moral of this story is precisely that the results were declared as were worked out at the time of parleys between Farooq Abdulla and Harkishen Singh Surjeet. The ruling Janata Dal at the time of initiation of parleys had no idea that they could be able to sacrifice their own winning candidate in the fray (in the Valley) at the alter of fraud.

The trend was similar in every constituency and each one had its own peculiarities. For example in Kupwara electoral segment the National Conference candidate was a novice who had failed to make his entry felt in the local district Bar and had after the outbreak of militancy migrated to the city. On the other hand, Choudhary Jalal-ud-din, a leading renegade militant and a stooge of the army had the support of the all defected militants, the military, BSF and local administration. It is alleged that in the early 90s the Hizb-ul-Mujahidin chief had issued a death warrant against this man who was even then known as an infiltrated malignancy within the bossom of militants. The warrant was entrusted to a 'constable turned Mujahid' Gulam Mohammad Hajam who was arrested by the army at Drugmulla military headquarters near Kupwara and was detained in Police Station Kupwara. According to allegations contained in FIR No: 59 of 1993 Mohammed Hajam escaped from custody and head constable Mohammad Mukhtar and a few other constables of police station Kupwara were booked for offences punishable u/secs 224/225 RPC and 3/4 TADA and also were detained under Public Security Act. Readers can well grasp the importance of Choudhary Jalal-ud-din for army and intelligence agencies. It is widely known that Kupwara is the border town where from 1947 several divisions of the regular army and equal number of paramilitary forces are stationed. Almost every village has some 'defence' installations with full protection of armed guards. Political activity in the district had come to a halt in 1989 and all the known workers of the National Conference and Congress were either eliminated or had migrated or had themselves joined arms revolt. So, no political party had any base; on the other hand, Choudhary Jalal-ud-din had a base in army and para-military forces. He had a group of disciplined workers among his defected gunmen and had a 'social base' in his Gujar community. Many Gujars considered it a haeaven sent opportunity to see an MLA from this 'neglected' and 'oppressed' community. This constituency is divided into four areas each having clash of interests. Both Saifud Din, the National Conference candidate and Jalaud Din hailed from the same area Trehgam. The third candidate migrant Gujar heavyweight Din Mohammad Cheta also hailed from the same area. The other three areas Hai Hama, Kupwara township and Drugmulla belt opted for boycott. During counting of votes Choudhary Jalal-ud-din was winning but the National Conference candidate was declared elected. Some junior army officers (committed to Choudhary) from Trahgam Brigade protested, but were pacified by their higher authorities that things had to go according to the political truce entered into with Farooq Abdulla.

In Sonawari constituency a similar tussle ensued between folk singer turned militant, turned politician Kuka Parray and Mohammad Akbar Vakil of Nayid Khai. Here the National Conference had to eat humble pie at the eleventh hour, the earlier truce superseded the later arrangement. The candidate of the forces Kuka Parray was declared elected and became the sole visible spokesman for the extra-constitutional rulers in the assembly.

Before we conclude, it is pertinent to quote from some Indian authors on these elections:

Major General Arjun Ray in his book *Kashmir Diary* (New Delhi: Manas Publications, 1997) has side-tracked this most vital information somewhere through indirect references. The index of this book indicates that the topic of the elections has been treated at page 147 of the book, but this page does not even contain the word 'election.' It shows that Indian authors either mischievously suppress facts or publishers censor details.

To quote from Sumantra Bose *The Challenge in Kashmir.* This author has moved around the region extensively, has interviewed cross-sections of the public and has gone into the genesis of the hustings held in Jammu and Kashmir for six seats of the Indian parliament and for 87 constituencies of the State Legislature. On page 139-40 the learned author comments on the basis of his on the spot enquiries:

> "A coercive and fraudulent exercise cannot, in any event, be dignified as a reintroduction of democratic process. As one Kashmiri told me: 'the root cause of all problems here has been the government of centre (New Delhi) by the centre for the centre.' But even though they are exhausted by incessant violence and repression most Kashmiris are today no longer willing to passively tolerate the imposition from Delhi of an unrepresentative, unaccountable and corrupt puppet clique. Even the small pro-India segment of opinion in the Valley is unequivocal on this score: the mere imposition of essentially discredited politicians like Farooq Abdulla or Congress leader Gulam Rasool Kar."

The coercive fraud ultimately imposed Gulam Rasool Kar as 'Kashmir voice' in the Indian legislature and Farooq Abdulla's elevation alienated even the handful of pro-Indian segments though very small but genuine and sincere. About the massive threat made transparent from the huge number of forces he commented the "valley was saturated with armed men and that one soldier was present for every three or four voters..." Had this huge number of soldiers with strict army discipline protected voters from threat to deter them to cast their vote such constructive discipline would not only create faith in the Indian democracy, but would make a situation emerge which would clearly convince the people of Jammu & Kashmir that whatever the excesses committed by the forces during the last few years they essentially had come to protect their ego and self respect rather than to occupy the land.

This book (referred Supra) exposes the mandate given to the discredited National Conference in 1996. It is compared to the mandate which this party, with all its power, hooliganism 'charisma' of Sheikh Abdulla and sympathy wave created after his death got respectively in the 1977 and 1983 elections: "Prior to the elections, the National Conference had been widely expected to emerge as largest single party in the new legislature at the very least, and probably as the winner of a narrow majority of that 87 seats (46 in the valley, 37 in Jammu and 4 in Ladakh) at stake. But the scale of the National Conference's victory turned out to be simply overwhelming.. In an ironic, indeed bizarre twist of fate and circumstances the party that had completely discredited itself with its mass base did better in the elections in 1996 than it had ever done."

The term 'ever done' includes the hey days of the charismatic leadership of late Sheikh Abdulla, the elections of 1983 when communalisation of the situation, the sympathy wave and the position of the National Conference then ruling the state benefited the party with traditional official misuse and when the successors of Sheikh Abdulla were united. On the other hand, the position of 1996 was quite a contrast even by the assessment of Indian rulers in the following ways:

1. There was a proxy war being fought in every nook and

corner, so the safety of the individual was in immediate danger or at the least apprehended threat.

2. The imposition of boycott call added to the immediate threat to life of a voter and there was no immediate gain for him or long term definite gain for which he would sacrifice his life.
3. There was no sign of building faith in the system and it was the erosion of faith which culminated in 1987 and so gun culture started in 1989.
4. During the intervening period of a decade every village had added to its locale a cemetery of martyrs conspicuous with the plaques on their graves. Such graveyards are in close vicinity to mosques where villagers go for prayers five times a day. Thus, parents and kith and kin of every slain youth would five times a day, get his memory refreshed and hatred would get compounded.
5. For all this destruction the nation had without any reservation, dubbed the Sheikh dynasty guilty of this widespread massacre. Even pro-Indian pockets, Kashmiri Pandits, Jammu Dogras all had declared Farooq and his bandwagon responsible for the destruction.
6. This can be deemed only the effect of mesmerism in Indian polity that the victims of the full decade of devastation forget, within a night, the role played by the two stalwarts in the 1987 Elections, Mohi-ud-din Shah and Piare Lal Handoo. As ministers of the National Conference Government they forced by continued persecution after their 'real defeat' and 'imposed success' at the hustings, the "wronged" candidates, their election agents and supporters to take up the gun and the result is evident. People held them squarely responsible for militancy. But the same victims in the same constituencies and the same migrants from these two constituencies, after about a decade, returned the same condemned persons elected from the same constituencies which had rejected them in 1987. This can happen only under Indian occupation. Deve Gowda, Inder Kumar Gujral, H.K.Surjeet, Inderjeet Gupta, Sitaram Kesri and other players of Indian politics had no sense of discretion that they would have asked

Farooq Abdulla to change the constituencies of these two living symbols of mass destruction. Mohi-ud-din Shah and Piare Lal Handoo should have received honour from Pakistan for they did what even General Zia-ul-Haq or Zulfiqar Bhutto could not do.

Had the political pandits in New Delhi ever cared for the inferences which reason and logic deduced from their actions they would have conceded only bare majority to Farooq Abdulla, that would, at lease blunt the argument which reasonable intellectuals like Sumantra Bose have so logically deduced. The feeling exists that the Indian administration is so transparent in its misdeeds that it does not care for any cover.

We have argued that an election is constituted of various stages of process and does not mean the mere exercise of affixing the seal upon the symbol of the candidate of choice and throw the so sealed sheet of paper in the ballot box. We have put before the court of the people the actions of the Indian Government, the Elections Commission, the army, the paramilitary forces, the renegade militants, the Mujahideen, the Hurriyat Conference, the polling staff, the common voter and the manner in which various political segments, which had deep rooted enmity with each other, were brought to the arena to fight a tug of war with borrowed chivalry and vigour from the Indian government for the pleasure of the rulers in Delhi who have always hoodwinked and deceived their own people. We have depicted the 'occurrence' of historical fraud with full details.There are certain consequences besides forming the government which are the logical outcome of every election fought on party or individual basis, but such incidents or consequences are quite absent from this mock drama.[9]

I have in this chapter made study of sec. 92 of JK Constitution and the Corresponding Provision in Indian Constitution Article 356. In those discussions reference to the book of Dr. A.S. Anand has been frequently made. This eminent Judge and author has been conscious of the fact that both the provisions of both these constitutions providing one and the same remedy cannot be made applicable to J&K. Therefore in his book" "The Constitution of J&K. Its Developments and Comments" (3rd Edition page 313) against his own evolved modus operandi, the learned author avoids to discuss Art 356 of Indian Constitution. On page 311 Sec 91 is discussed in the light of Article 213 and under Sec. 93 (P:314) he quotes Articles 214 to 216 of Indian Constitution. The same has been manner of his discussion about almost every clause of JK Constitution Sec. 92 had a similar provision in Indian Constitution in Article 356 but the EX-CJ censors comparative study particularly here. Why? Because had he done so he would have to express himself that the constitution (application to J&K Amendment) Order 1964 was in conflict with J&K Constitution and inspite of "Concurrence" it could not be enforced. To avoid embarrassment to his 'career' he censored the comment. Pertinent is to state that Delhi Agreement of 1952 expressly stipulated that though Article 352 will have limited application to J&K but Articles 356 and 360 will have no application.[10]

Notes

1. Read G.N. Gauhar, 'Hazratbal Central Stage of Kashmir Politics' (New Delhi: Virgo Publications)
2. Pandit Kalhana, Rajtrangin.
3. Alaister Lamb is his book: 'Disputed Legacy' adds note 26 to chapter VII describing atrocities of these battalions, their impact on command and the exageration made by the India media and leaders.
4. Detailed discussions on the Constitutional ambiguities and contradictions will get treatment, in the introduction to Parliament Election in J&K,1967-99 (part II)
5: Free indulgence in 'fabricating and tampering of evidence' has been rule with returning officers in J&K. However, in this specific case the opposition candidate Muran was a very strong and courageous fighter of causes and dedicated to human dignity and civil society, so, he was able to carry the fight to the end. He gave exposure to these inherent qualities rampant in the largest democracy in the world. It is the fearlessness of Muran which achieved martyrdom for him. He was killed by militants for his commitment to fair play. In the white paper on the 1996 Elections APHC mistakenly calls Muran a National Conference candidate. He was an independent and Sumnani was the National Conference candidate.
6. It is practically impossible to prove by any sort of evidence, involvement of the benefited candidate in such situations. Though logic can adjudicate the active involvement of the beneficiary, but the law requires proof.
7. G.N. Gauhar, 'Military Operation in Kashmir' see map showing military

and paramilitary bunkers on the 30 km. Srinagar—Charar-i-Sharief Road, pp. 139 and 169.

8. A group of such scared cheated jawans of Kupwara district preferred a writ of mandamus Mushtaq Ahmad versus State and Others. SWP No. 120 of 1998 and sought a direction against the state government to fulfil its promise as these youths had no alternative to death at the hands of militants except to take up the gun and join militancy. This author argued vehemently that such promises which were never fulfilled, created alienation. The writ was not admitted and my argument was qualified as a political rather a legal one.

9. In its white paper the APHC referred to this author in this respect and made mention of his book 'Bless N Blaze' which was latter published under another name, viz., 'Military Operation in Kashmir'.

10. The discussions made on Sec. 92 and article 356 respectively of the two constitutions and mention of Delhi Agreement might create suspicious in the minds of our readers about our honesty as it is hardly believable that Government of India can act so mischievously and an author of the stature of reitred Chief Justice of India (CJI) can deliberately suppress fair comments. Hence, contain herein the provisions of both the constitutions and excerpts from Delhi Agreement 1952 (copied from Hon'ble Dr. A.S. Anand's book 3rd Edition page 123).

The following is the extract from the Delhi Agreement.

"(viii) Government of India insisted on the application of Article 352,. . . . But the state delegation was however, averse to the President" exercising the power to proclaim a general emergency on account of internal disturbance.

In order to meet the view point of the state's delegation, the Government of India agreed to the modification of Article 352 in its application to Kashmir by the addition of the following words:. . . .

Both the parties agreed that the application of Article 356, dealing with the suspension of the State Constitution and Article 360. . . was not necessary".

Thus this agreement excludes J&K from the ambit of Articles 356 and 360 so the state consembly was left to have its own provision in this behalf which it devised in Sec. 92 of its Constitution Act 1956. It is unfortunate that Indian Government in 1964 acted against Delhi Agreement and Ghulam Muhammad Sadiq who was on J&K delegation involved with Delhi Agreement should, as head of the state government concur with this fraud. The act and concurrence both are but illegalities and against clear constitutional scheme and agreed treaties.

However the texts of Article 356 and Sec. 92 are annexed as appendices.

By the comparison of these two provisions from two constitutions added with the particular study of Delhi Agreement 1952 para (viii) even a layman, not conversant with legal and constitutional intricacies will, without hesitation, hold that the two parties to the Delhi Agreement 1952 have with full understanding and after study of all pros and cons excluded the application of Articles 356 and 360 to J&K and have left it to the JK constitutent Assembly who was then in seizen of the matter, to legislate a distinct provision to meet the emergencies within its own ambit in similar manner in which the senior consembly had provisions contained in Articles 356 and 360. In the light of this discussion, the 2nd Amendment Order of 1964 extending President of India's powers under Article 356 to J&K, is illegal. The concurrence accorded by the gobvernment imposed by an assembly which was created by wholesale abductions cannot validate it. Therefore the rule of President from July 1990 upto October 1996 was but ultra virus of constitution. Even if the matter is agitated before any court in India, the chauvinistic interpretation of the term: "National Interest" will validate it in the same manner in which Pakistan Suypreme Court has created a history of frauds with its nation under the misuse of the Doctrine of Necessity.

Chapter 16

Elections Petitions (Disputed Elections)

Section 87 of J&K Representation of People Act provides that anyone aggrieved with results of any election may file a petition in the state High Court challenging such an election. We have discussed that elections were never fought in the manner in which they are conducted in the rest of India so the people had generally no enthusiasm for delayed court cases relating to elections. No one in Jammu and Kashmir dared to invite the wrath of Sheikh Abdulla by challenging any of the uncontested results nor was there procedure then to file a petition in the High Court; it had to be filed before the J&K State Election Commission. No such petition was even preferred against the selection of 1957, but after the 'Selection by Abduction' (i.e., 1962 Election) some petitions were preferred and the elected ruling MLA from Basoli (Jammu) was unseated. There was no tradition even among pro-Indian politicians to challenge the fraud of such elections. This author experienced both 'rejection' and 'abduction' during the 1962 elections alongwith communist leaders G.M. Malik, R.P. Saraf and P.S.P. leaders like O.P. Saraf and P.L. Koul, but none of us chose to prefer an election petition.

The 1967 Elections have been qualified as 'Selection by Rejection'. This election was fought between the two sides of the same coin, the National Conference of Bakshi Gulam Mohammad and the ruling Congress of G.M. Sadiq. Both received support from the All India National Congress, New Delhi. G.M. Sadiq had the support of the Congress whereas his rival received undeclared encouragement from what was then called the Congress Syndicate. It consisted of Morarji Desai, Jagjeevan Ram, S.K. Patil, Nijlingappa and Neelam Sanjeeva Reddy. Indira Gandhi on the other hand, had given a green signal to G.M. Sadiq for any and every fraud and hence all his candidates were returned. To keep up the morale of Bakshi's cadre the Congress Syndicate advised him to challenge all the elections and so, to cope with the rush of election petitions the High Court of J&K sought and obtained the services of two ad-hoc judges, Justice Anant Singh and Justice Gurto retired judges of Patna and Allahabad High Courts respectively. Some returns were so fraudulent that the so elected MLAs were unseated. One such case discussed earlier was the one wherein the returning officer of Rajpura constituency in Pulwama district Ashok Kumar IAS, was subjected to severe strictures. However, the majority of petitions involved in such allegations were totally factual in nature. It is an admitted rule of evidence that a civil servant is presumed to have acted honestly and fairly, while discharging his duty, though in J&K the presumption should be otherwise. The party alleging fraud has to prove it and give convincing evidence, thus an issue involving the fact of bogus votes requires examination of hundreds of voters. Besides, in the society created by colonial agents even strong witnesses are tempered with minor concessions or by forceful intimidation. Filing of election petitions did not invite hope for fairness, but the device was considered as an alternative to political activity, hence Bakshi financed his cadre to remain engaged in the legal battles to keep the ruling party on tenterhooks. The supporters of Bakshi (Congress Syndicate) had generated the hope among Bakshi and his 'defeated' cadre that the sooner they weakened Indira's grip at the Center they would influence the decision of petitions in a manner that fresh elections became inevitable.

Ultimately the Congress Syndicate was liquidated by Indira Gandhi and so the Bakshi cadre gave up any hope to get power not through vote. The same device which he had invented was used against him.

After the 1972, 1977 and 1983 general elections some results were challenged through the medium of election petitions with the dominant interest of creating uncertainty about the ruling party MLAs. But after the 1987 elections even for that limited purpose no election was challenged. The petition was to be filed within 40 days and for that entire period the 'defrauded' candidates of the MUF and their polling agents, election agents, counting agents etc. were either continuously persecuted in police stations or were detained in jails. Hence, no returned candidate had to experience any uncertainty and all elected rulers enjoyed undisturbed power for two years till the gun made them run away and live in the wilderness. Within those 30 months they depleted the central funds of aid and subsidy, looted the state resources and created huge assets through each and every corrupt practice. In 1996 the communist theoreticians of CPI and CPM imposed the same gang of dacoits as rulers so as to close all avenues of future understanding between the people of Jammu & Kashmir and the people of India. Inspite of this wholesale 'rigging' which was not visible to the two Election Commissioners Dr. Gill and Krishnamurthy. Not a single election out of six to Parliament and 87 to the J&K Assembly was challenged in the High Court which proves that the two Election Commissioners were not blind to the situation. Let us make our reader ponder upon why even the Janata Dal candidate, who had initially won from Charar-i-Sharief did not challenge his defeat, why Choudhary Jalal-ud-din of Kupware who yet believes himself the elected MLA did not move the court against the imposed National Conference MLA and why M. Akbar Vakil of Sonawari, a blue eyed boy of the National Conference was warned not to challenge the election of Kuka Parray a candidate propped up by RAW. It is because the 1996 elections were fought between the agents of the same master. Though in 1967 rival parties of both Sadiq and Bakshi had the same source of inspiration, but the two situations were in complete contrast. That contest reflected the sharp division in All India Congress(I), but in 1996 all political parties which are ideologically poles apart had a common objective to impose an election upon J&K against the wishes of the local voter. Neither Kashmiri Muslim concession seekers nor unpaid Kashmiri Pandit agents of India nor committed Dogras nor pro-Beant Singh Sikhs wanted elections. Hence, neither Gulam Hassan, nor Jalal-ud-din, nor Akbar Vakil nor any other 'defeated' agent was allowed by their masters to challenge sham verdicts.

The 'Consembly' was constituted in such mystifying circumstances that it became known to people after its first session was convened and the names of the Constitution givers became known to the elite after their names and photographs were mentioned and printed in the Urdu daily

Khidmat the official organ of the ruling National Conference.

In 1957 people totally indifferent to elections had boycotted them. The Jammu (Dogri-Punjabi belt) based Praja Parishad was forced to declare this electioneering as a Nazi type Fascist system. Their leaders and cadres had received a thrashing. Goondas were taken even from Srinagar to beat and terrorise cadres of the Parishad. Besides, there was no confidence in the State Election Commission to which the election petitions were to be presented. It was a unique procedure that the Election Commission the very institution accused of bungling had power to constitute a Tribunal to hear such petitions. The Election Commissioner too was an officer of the state of the rank of a collector/secretary to the government whose promotion, transfer, posting, re-employment after retirement and all avenues of career were dependent upon the ruler Bakshi Ghulam Mohammad who had become so arrogant as to treat the heads of departments, secretaries to government and even High Court judges as subservient to his mercy. He would treat His Lordship Wazir Janki Nath, Chief Justice with respect, but would call him by the locally abreviated form of his name, viz., 'Jane Wazeer'. It can be imagined, how a subordinate judicial officer in such circumstances, could act to undo a legislator created by the same Bakshi. The judiciary was browbeaten from the very start of rule in 1949 when Masood Hussain J. was forced to leave this state in utter frustration. In 1962, (the selections by abductions) the petitioner had to establish by cogent evidence within an election petition facts of his abduction. Who could come to the witness box to state that G.N. Gauhar's agents were abducted in the open market of Budgam by the local police? Such a witness might suffer his daughter, wife or mother to be abducted and assaulted. In 1967 'Selection by Rejections' who could prove that the candidate had sworn the oath form, but it was stolen by none other than the custodian of records, the very honourable judge—the returning officer. Here the system of Anglo-Indian Law comes to the help of the returning officer, his official behaviour is protected as his act is presumed to have been done and performed with honesty. This principle is repeatedly enunciated in scores of decisions of various High Courts of India and the apex court of the country. Our readers may only study AIR 1974 Supreme Court P.405, AIR SC 242; AIR 197 SC. 24 and AIR 1967 A.P. 155.

The 1972 elections have been qualified as 'Selection by Concessions' as in two divisions Jammu and the Valley the Jan Sangh and Jamait-i-Islami were both given as concession five seats each. The two parties had been compensated and in those circumstances they felt content with their 'significant entries' into the legislature and so had no reason to agitate through election petitions. The independents who were subjected to humiliation had neither resources nor courage to go for this remedy.

The 1977 elections entitled 'An Election' had strains of intimidation and, therefore, P.N. Bazaz discussed these elections in a book *Democracy by Intimidation.* The party which intimidated voters during hustings when it was out of power and even terrorised supporters of the Janata Party which could have terrorised and victimised any voter who would have opted for legal action against election results or if he was scared himself his witnesses would never dare to depose the facts before such a forum. The parties behind the action were the Janata Party and Congress; Janata under Morarjee Desai after 1977 elections was for an 'elected' National Conference government as through the electoral process the party blunted the power of Sheikh Abdulla (which Jawahar Lal Nehru and his daughter were not able to do) and obliged him to be the most faithful co-traveller with them. So the central leadership did not approve the Pradesh unit challenging any of the results even if sufficient reasons were at hand.

The second party which was humbled by the National Conference was the Congress. Though its local unit was keen to challenge results especially in the Gojri-Kashmiri belt of Jammu division, but Indira Gandhi vetoed this suggestion because the Sheikh had openly spoken against the victimisation of Indira Gandhi by the Janata Party. Sheikh Abdulla had strongly expressed even against subjecting Indira Gandhi to a commission of enquiry so no petition was moved. The 1983 verdict which we have discussed was undone by Jagmohan so the defeated Congress(I) candidates were assured to wait and watch.

The 'Culmination of Fraud'—1987 election was conducted, as explained, in such a manner that the 'defeated candidates' who were declared elected had developed so deep a desire for vengeance that they victimised the opponents and their sympathisers to such an extent that instead of going to seek justice from courts they were forced to seek justice through the gun.

The Parliament was not represented upto 1967 directly and after 1967 these elections invited neither confidence nor enthusiasm nor any interest.

The post-insurgency elections for three parliaments and the current legislatures have been elections between the forces imposing boycott and the forces imposing a sham in the name of hustings so none was aggrieved and none, therefore, had to seek any remedy.

Who is blind...voter or...

It was the 1987 election which made the people on the whole 'agree' that only the gun provides the solution. Though from 1947 unabated 'armed' struggle against Indian occupation has remained, but it never achieved popular support upto 1987. It is thus the treachery of the Rajiv-Farooq accord which widened the gulf between Kashmiris and Indians. It was the result of these treacheries that 50,000 to 60,000 Kashmiris died, lakhs were victimised, the whole community of Kashmiri Pandits is continuously facing pangs of separation from their home. It is an adultede fact that army and para - military forces to have under gone so many coasulties during this proxy was that such number exceeds to total casualities — suffered by India during three regular wars. Mr Advani has recently accepted so. Even Indian analysts agree that the militancy took birth from two constituencies of Srinagar city Amira Kadal and Habba Kadal. Here the two ministerial colleagues of Farooq Abdulla, viz.; Mohi-ud-din Shah and P.L. Handoo not only got themselves declared elected, but the wining opposition candidates and their sympathisers were put to all types of persecution; and a reign of terror was let loose. It is either due to the faults in the memory of the people or the Indian rulers devised their policies vis-a-vis Kashmir in frustration that these two who caused deterioration in India-Kashmir relationship have been returned from these very two segments. Would the electorate of Amira Kadal and Habba

Kadal, after the full decade of devastation which turned heaven into hell, elect them to ministerial berths from those very two constituencies? Will the communist thinkers Surjeet and Inderjeet think about it? Will the intellectual ex-PM Mr. Gujral ponder upon it.

Farooq Abdulla has invited danger by borrowing two-third majority from sources where he had to share his political base with his worst adversaries. His post-election follies are unpardonable in the view of his own party cadre. In the election for J&K upper house he accommodated all disgruntled elements including one from the Hindu communal party the BJP. He had no voice in the Indian Lok Sabha (Lower House of Parliament) so required formidable voice in that House and it was occasion for him to take all the four seats of Rajya Sabha which were to be filled by members of the J&K Assembly. But the arrangement which granted him power made him helpless and out of that helplessness and not for his spirit of accommodation, he surrendered two of these four seats to his political enemies Dr. Karan Singh and Gulam Nabi Azad, both indirectly or directly tied with the fate of the Congress (I).

Coalition, Diarchy or Anarchy

Molvi Iftikhar Ansari was elected from Patan constituency in Baramulla district on a Congress(I) ticket though with National Conference support. In the distribution of power in Jammu and Kashmir the lion's share was allotted to Farooq Abdulla, but other elements were accommodated. The Congress(I) too was given a few seats including one from Patan in this arrangement, but opted for the role of opposition and neither entered into a coalition with Farooq nor opted to support the government from outside. When Congress was the opposition party in the legislature one of its members Molvi Iftikhar joined the Farooq Abdulla government as a minister. This was declared by the group leader of the Congress(I) as 'defection,' but why was the anti-defection law not invoked? Why did the Congress high command under Sitaram Kesri not object to the behaviour of their member who till date continues to be simultaneously member of cabinet and member of opposition group in the legislature. Such political behaviour is licensed by the protagonists of Indian democracy and can be allowed only in case of satellite territories and subjugated colonies. By the end of the millennium Farooq Abdulla has dropped Molvi Iftikhar from the cabinet, he had to consult none in this behalf, his party high command is his family. Molvi Iftikhar and Abdul Qayoom both were always considered enemies of the dynasty and the National Conference. The former dared to fight elections against 'Madari Meharban' Begum Abdulla and the latter had dared to get her molested in 1971 by getting her shawl snatched, so, their inclusion in the state cabinet and admission in the National Conference had caused annoyance among the family and family loyalists. Farooq Abdulla had unfettered power to drop any minister and more so these infiltrated elements, but Farooq Abdulla did not dare to drop him. Farooq Abdulla requested this minister to resign which he declined, so on 10 December 1999 he had to rush to New Delhi to consult 'many' elements to get a signal to drop this minister who was a defector of Congress-I, was not a member of the Bhartiya Janata Party or of any party in coalition at the Centre. Then from whom Farooq Abdulla sought permission to drop him is pertinent.

These post-election measures constitute a policy of imposition of rulers through the fraud of ballot.

Imposed Elections Consequence of Imposed Situation

After June 1990, when the six month term of Governors Rule imposed by Jagmohan u/s 192 of J&K Constitution expired, the rule extended under Article 356, Constitution of India upto October 1996 was illegal and unconstitutional. This illegality was covered under the mask of Presidential Application orders. We need not discuss again vires of such orders, but suffice it to say that Indian rulers were now under constitutional, legal and moral pressures to install some government which could be labelled as a 'representative' one. In the situation which continues till date it was impossible for India to hold any elections; notwithstanding the exported and local threats the main impediments to hold an election were: the complete erosion of faith in Indian democracy and its institutions and in the viability of elections to put an end to the Kashmir imbroglio. No right thinking government could under such compulsions devise measures to build faith, thus the remedy was left in 'destruction' so as to construct the edifice of faith. There was no alternative left for India, but to impose an election not with the aim to give power to a particular family or group of families, but to open avenues for future voluntary participation in the democratic process out of the present imposed situation.

The post-election happenings show that the rulers in New Delhi, whoever they may be, have no intentions to cultivate faith in democracy in J&K.

The question arises as to why the Indian rulers wanted to impose an election upon the people of Jammu and Kashmir who were neither ready to face one, nor had any choice available, nor had a congenial atmosphere to think about the exercise of a choice nor had faith in the system which had to elicit their choice? We have seen that militancy and involvement of people with it had resulted in the breakdown of governance in Jammu and Kashmir, the stalemate continued for six years. Under section 92 of the state constitution this constitutional breakdown is tenable only for six months. It has been said that beyond July 1, 1990 the continuation of direct rule by New Delhi was though covered under the mask of Presidents Rule, constitutionally unwarranted and immoral. The position was being exploited by the adversary ie Pakistan. In these circumstances India had no option, but to manage an election to blunt the Pakistani argument in world fora. Pakistan and some movements in Jammu and Kashmir both were conscious of this helplessness imposed on India and they tried vigourously so that the Indian position continue in a stalemate (which to a great extent was its own creation). Hence, India was pushed against a wall and had to play a drama of elections. However, out of this drama they could cultivate confidence had Indian leaders intentions beyond occupying this state as a ruled territory. They could have created a sense of voluntary assimilation had they conducted these imposed elections with possible caution.

Had the rulers strictly allowed only voluntary participation in the hustings and confined law and order agencies to protect such voters who voluntarily participated, various groups would have emerged, from the hustings so a coalition would have been the logical consequence. It would inevitably go in favour of democratisation as it would fail and early dissolution of the hung house would have resulted in increase in the number of voluntary voters for the second election.

It can be argued that frequent elections involve huge expenses, but could even three elections within a normal term (which is six years for J&K Assembly as compared to five year term for Lok Sabha and the other state assemblies) be deemed wasteful in comparison to the huge expenses spent to contain Kashmir by force?

But the manner in which the forces and paratroopers behaved during both parliament elections of May 1996 and later in assembly elections convinced even the microscopic section of people which had undergone the process of rethinking about participating in 'democratisation' that the leadership in Delhi both in power or out of power was concerned only about installing a coterie under the label of representative government. Had the forces and agencies for maintenance of law and order strictly confined their activity to the extent of providing protection to the interested voter who was being threatened and had they not acted in a manner as to force the populace to make a show of participation; a silent process of confidence building would have, in probability, been the result.

The soldiers of these 'forces' have from their childhood aptly heard the story of how coming out of the invisible line of demarcation drawn by Laxman in the forest of Dandakvana resulted in ultimate devastation. Had they drawn a lesson from that store of wisdom they would not have ignored their conscience. But what could they do? The broker of power at the Raj Bhawan was committed to repay with compound interest to Farooq Abdulla, who had given him a second entry to the Valley. Similarly, the leadership in Delhi, ignorant of the Kashmir psyche were equally committed. These commitments created one more obstacle in the Indo-Kashmir relationship.

Post-election day to day happenings compounded the view of the people that the 'illegitimate' representation has become the hard reality of the destiny of Jammu and Kashmir. Does it, therefore, once again prove the relevance of terrorism?

Chapter 17

Azad Kashmir Elections

The author has no direct information about the situation in which the people of the unfortunate Jammu and Kashmir divided by the tragedies of expansionist chauvinism of their own brethren, live and die across the Line of Actual Control (LAC). No opportunity could be so far availed by us to elicit correct information directly from that part of Jammu and Kashmir lying across the LAC. Hence, we cannot discuss it with the same certainty with which we have narrated the events in Jammu &Kashmir which we ourselves have experienced. We depend on secondary sources which include:

1. The details provided about the various facts of governance in that part of the state in various books, journals and reports written either by Indian authors and reporters or by Western intellectuals.
2. The details which we have been able to elicit from various friends, acquaintances, kith and kin who either from that part, at various times, visited this part of the state or who from this part of Jammu and Kashmir have sometime got an opportunity to visit that part. It must be borne in mind that the two parts of the same state are divided with such cruelty that they are hardly able to interact; even the divided families, might be of real brothers. Neither Indians nor Pakistanis face such restrictions to visit either country as Kashmiris face. The conditions have become more severe since 1990. Hence, the second source is very weak.

3. What we, here in Srinagar can guess from the Indian media, Pakistan TV or Radio, BBC news service and from other world media about the happenings on political scene in Muzaffarabad (capital of Azad Kashmir).

As regards the first source we have to make a cautious and careful sifting of the material because writers are of many hues. The lobbies working for the countries have engaged intellectual manpower with conflicting beliefs and so literature on 'Kashmiriology' based on confusion and conflict has piled up. Careerist writers with political ambition and material interests, have in both countries of the subcontinent tampered with historical truth. It is therefore, that we have to carefully study this contemporary record. We have no document, book or report available from Pakistan about the elections in Azad Kashmir. Thus, we will mainly refer to Alaister Lamb's *Kashmir—A Disputed Legacy*, Sumantra Bose's *The Challenge in Kashmir* and Maj. Gen. Afsir Karim of Indian Defence Review Team *Kashmir-The Troubled Frontiers* .

In the estimation of the common Indian Alaister Lamb's book has a tilt towards Pakistani policy on Kashmir. We, will therefore, quote from him selectively where the tilt appears closer to Indian perceptions or where to impartial assessment his views appear critical of Azad Kashmir governance. Sumantra Bose is an Indian intellectual and so his assessment cannot be dubbed as pro-Pak, nor is it so. To be fair, we as eye-witnesses have found his testimony correct by and large though as a true nationalist he is conscious of lapses in Indian policy on Kashmir and views that such lapses are but causing damage to the Indian case. The third book referred to above has such strains which a semi-official document must possess, but deals honestly with certain references. Alaister Lamb sums up the characteristics of political culture which emerged initially in Azad Kashmir as:

- First: in its actual political structure it demonstrated great instability. Presidents came and went with extraordinary rapidity, particularly in its early years, for reasons which were not always apparent to the outside world.
- Second: its formal constitution tended to reflect whatever regime was in force in Pakistan.

(Kashmir—A Disputed Legacy, p. 188)

The 'extraordinary rapidity' with which presidents in Azad Kashmir were changed carried impressions among the fans of 'free Kashmir' everywhere that these changes were imported from Karachi to suit the whims of Pakistani rulers. Logically it was inferred that unfortunate Kashmiris in both the countries were being given the same treatment and both the parts were being subjected to unrepresentative rule. Such impressions were fortified by the fact that rulers in Muzaffarabad reflected the colour of the ruling party in Pakistan. It is an exception that Nawaz Sharief the Muslim League ruler of Pakistan is yet (these lines were written in September 1998 and Sharief took over office in February 1997) to change the rulers in Muzaffarabad to reflect the colour of his party flag.

It is not totally attributable to manoeuvered elections, but many attribute it to genuine public opinion. In this part of Kashmir, the people generally tend to favour whichever government comes in Pakistan, with the hope that the same leader might come up to his expectations and might get the Kashmir tangle solved.

A probe of the voter community of Azad Kashmir reveals the element of fairness in the elections held there. Immediately after the 1977 elections in Jammu and Kashmir a few citizens of that part of Kashmir visited their kith and kin in Srinagar. They were faithfully committed to Pakistan politics, but during discussions a remark, pregnant with an element of deprivation slipped from them:

- "We, in Pakistan were overwhelmed that you have here in Srinagar been able to trounce the ruling party at centre in hustings...."

Alas this impression created by Morarji Desai and L.K. Jha was not allowed by Indira Gandhi to churn the public opinion in both the parts of Kashmir. The Sheikh dynasty made efforts to dispel that impression which Morarji Desai and L.K. Jha had created in 1977. Indira Gandhi got that completely eroded through Jagmohan.

This remark conveyed that in Pakistan held Kashmir people have vote to empower the ruling party in Islamabad or Islamabad manages itself to do that or the public opinion in Muzaffarabad is so built that the 'voter' has no alternative, but to vote for favourites of Pakistani rulers. Or it is that the public opinion itself, with the change in Pakistan politics yearns for an immediate change in Muzaffarabad politics to reflect the colour of Pakistan ruling politics. Such opinion is created by the unending desire to achieve completion of the cause of Azad Kashmir, whatever the cause might be. The moral of the story is that unfortunate Kashmiris have yet, even after five decades of the freedom of the subcontinent, to exercise their right of franchise in a free atmosphere.

Sumantra Bose has made constructive study of the most recent happenings in the two parts of Kashmir and reports about elections held in Azad Kashmir in June 1996:

- "Meanwhile elections in Azad Kashmir continue to be a manipulated farce. In the most recent ones, held in June 1996, pro-Independence political parties were again barred from participating because their candidates refused to compromise their principles by signing affidavits certifying their allegiance to Pakistan....Even the partial contest that did take place, limited to an assessment of Pakistani parties and pro-Pakistani groups were severely haunted by rampant irregularities and fraud."

Challenge in Kashmir p: 177

The author has, therefore, done extensive study to develop the theme that pro-Independence politics is dominant among Kashmiris in both parts thus binding down the voter to subscribe on oath allegiance to either country amounts to denial of vote to the majority of Kashmiris. Some pro-Pak elements argue that as the law of the land envisaged citizens to subscribe to an oath of allegiance, so rejection of papers for non- fulfilment of such formality cannot be deemed a denial of right of franchise. They argue that in this part of Jammu and Kashmir even pro-Pak Jamait-i-Islami candidates have sworn affidavits of allegiance to India and why the same 'tactics' were not adopted by pro-Independence politicians in Azad Kashmir and thereby sneak an opportunity to get elected. They, therefore, make us infer that the pro-Azadi element in Azad Kashmir had in order to run away from elections, adopted a face saving device. This argument compels us to examine the laws on the subject with particular stress on Azad Kashmir. Article 257 of the Constitution of Pakistan states:

- 'when the people of the state of Jammu and Kashmir decide

to accede to Pakistan, the relationship between Pakistan and that state shall be in accordance with wishes of the people of the state'.

This constitutional clause guarantees:

1. The destiny moulders of Jammu and Kashmir are its people and it is only their choice which can make them a part (integral or with some option) of Pakistan. Thus, the political view that this state (J&K) had ipso facto according to the scheme, under which sub-continent was partitioned, automatically become a part of Pakistan is nullified by the constitution of Pakistan itself;
2. All other matters geographical, cultural, religious etc. are relevant only to formulate choice for the subjects of Jammu and Kashmir and are not in themselves a consideration to compel the state to accede with any country;
3. That even after such accession based on free and impartial plebiscite the state of Jammu and Kashmir will not merge into Pakistan. The Punjab, Baluchistan and other provinces of that country form amongst themselves the Islamic Republic of Pakistan. On the other hand, the people of Jammu and Kashmir and Pakistan government will, therefore, decide the course of future relationship between the two characters.

Let us quote from the famous judgement of the apex court of Azad Kashmir para 78 (Azad Kashmir Government v/s Pakistan on the jurisdiction of northern areas). It explains in the light of Article 257 of Pakistan Constitution

- '...it is clearly postulated that the state of Jammu and Kashmir, as such is single entity, its future is yet to be determined in the light of the terms and conditions of accession; have deliberately been preserved by the framers of the constitution....'

We have quoted above an excerpt from Sumantra Bose which describes that in June 1996 elections of Azad Kashmir Assembly the nomination papers were rejected on the ground that candidates from a particular political view did not file affidavits swearing allegiance to Pakistan. It is not only Sumantra Bose who makes mention of it, but we in this part of Jammu and Kashmir listened to Azad Kashmir Radio,

Pakistan electronic media and world news services and daily during that period, learnt the names and party affiliations of the candidates who were barred entry into the electoral fray on the grounds mentioned above. The news items would state that it was prescribed under the law governing People's Representation in that part of J&K such a provision is clearly in contravention to the spirit of Article 257 of Pakistan Constitution and against the Azad Kashmir Supreme Court judgement. It is against the principles of Islam too and unbecoming for the Islamic Republic of Pakistan to allow such hypocritical policies. There cannot possibly be direct Hadis (verbal or direct action of the Prophet peace be upon Him) about these political gimmicks, but ample guidance is indirectly provided in His wise and eternal sayings. Sahih Bukhari quotes a Hadis reported by his companion Anas which postulates immorality in such transactions which are akin to speculation. "A fruit of an orchard while just one of the bud".... Pakistan on the one hand strives for plebiscite in Jammu and Kashmir and on the other has 'speculated' the result of such plebiscite (yet an impossibility) in its favour. It is, in our view not in consonance with straightforward policies of Islam, but more or less resembles the practices of hypocrites (Munafiqueen). Pakistan might defend itself as does India that it does not interfere with the legislation in Azad Kashmir, but such claims are only pretensions and hypocritical. In both the parts under both the countries even day to day amendments in laws and even drafts for notifications are imposed upon Muzaffarabad by Islamabad and upon Srinagar / Jammu by New Delhi. Here a precise digression may not be out of place.

In this part of Kashmir we have found that Pakistan unintellegently copies or reacts to Indian actions and policies. To bar the anti India majority to enter into the electoral arena India made a provision in J&K Representation of People Act that every candidate who contests elections must take an oath of allegiance to India. For this reason hundreds of the nomination forms in the 1967 elections were rejected and hence, that election was dubbed: 'A Selection by Rejection'. Pakistan immediately got its puppets in Azad Kashmir to copy the law and it was made incumbent to swear allegiance to Pakistan. In Indian Kashmir much before the 1967 Elections the majority had developed an aversion against Indian policies and were anti-India. Pakistan for hypothetical reasons or very feeble causes created a situation which developed a formidable public opinion in Azad Kashmir for Independent Kashmir and so was anti-Pakistan. It is again the policy of imitation or reaction by which Pakistan encouraged dissension and division in the freedom struggle of Jammu and Kashmir. India had a policy to divide so as to perpetuate its rule, but Pakistan is 'dividing' Kashmiris to facilitate Indian domination.

The above quoted Azad Kashmir Supreme Court Judgement in para 204 issues the following directions as:

"I (a) the Azad Government to immediately assume the administrative control of the northern areas and to annex it with the administration of Azad Jammu and Cashmere.

(b) The Government of Pakistan to provide an adequate assistance and facility to the Azad Government in attainment of the said objective.

II. The residents (state subjects) of the Northern areas shall enjoy the benefit of fundamental rights conferred by the Act of 1974. They shall be provided representation in:

The Government:
The Assembly:
The Council:
The Civil Service and
Other national institutions, in due course of law."

It is a clear judicial admission that these unfortunate people of northern Jammu and Kashmir have been deprived of self-governance, representation in elected bodies and the civil service. In this part of Jammu and Kashmir deceptive laws are in the statute book which make this unfortunate land appear part of the democratic world, but Pakistan, inspite of its high claims and inspite of the directions of the highest court of Azad Kashmir refuses to grant those Kashmiris basic human rights who have created history as the first Kashmiris to hoist the Pakistani flag upon their land. Is not it shameful to agitate plebiscite at world fora for with such a unreasonable and valueless record. Pretensions and contradictions in practices bring the greatest code of human values—Islam under criticism.

We are thankful to the *Indian Defence Review* team which had contained major portions of Azad Kashmir Supreme Court judgement (supra) in *Kashmir—The Troubled Frontiers* with acclaim. It has proved beyond doubt that the standard of judicial functioning in that part of Jammu and Kashmir comes to the expectations of civilised people, but how the system has been systematically eroded in this part of Kashmir after the abdication of His Highness Maharaja Hari Singh is discussed in the: *J&K Militancy Evil or Necessary Evil?'* chapter entitled: 'Judicial Erosion'. It has been hinted in *Hazratbal—Central Stage of Kashmir Politics* too. Many references are contained in this book also.

At the stage of final reading of the computerised manuscript the results of the Elections in Pak occupied J&K for the Legislative Assembly of Azad J&K held on July 5, 2001 were declared. I am not concered as who won or lost, but am concerned with the manner in which it was held. We have earlier shared the view that according to Section 257 of Pakistan Constituion and as per the spirit of the Azad Kashmir Supreme Court Judgment (Supra) the clause added to Azad Kashmir Peoples Representation law binding any candidate to solemnly declare himself as a 'Pakistani' is immoral, hypocritical and against the spirit of the establishment of Azad Jammu and Kashmir government established on October 24, 1947. The declaration made on this day has been reproduced by their Lordships of Azad Kashmir. Supreme Court in their judgment on Writ Petition filed by the Azad Kashmir Government against Pakistan Government Para 94. It opens:

> "The provisional Azad Govt, which the people of Jammu and Kashmir have set up a few weeks ago with the object of ending untolerable Dogra tyrannies and for securing to the state, including Muslims, Hindus and Sikhs. The right of free self government...."

Has the Azad Kashmir government achieved the goal assigned to it on October 24, 1947? Had it reached the destination pin pointed in this declaration? No. It is yet in the midst of struggle. It has not attained for Muslims, Hindus and Sikh subjects of erstwhile Jammu and Kashmir free self governance so, its decision to impose an embargo upon the right of vote amounts to the denial of that right.

In an article recently published and reproduced by a Srinagar daily *Kashmir Monitor* July 10, 2001 Gulzar under the heading 'A Peep into PAK Elections' has hailed the matured democratic tradition of the people of Azad Kashmir and pays complimentary tributes to Azad Kashmir Election Commission and Pakistan Government for holding these elections with utmost care, honesty and freedom. The wisdom of the electorate that they have rejected religious parties, proves their political emancipation and shows that they have fared well in the discharge of their duties as voters. However, this contributor has not made even any indirect reference anywhere of the rejection of scores of papers of those candidates who had not sworn their allegiance to Pakistan. This contributor could have justified those rejections or might have felt that the rejected candidates would not, in his view, cut any ice in the hustings. But, he had to discuss this important aspect with due reference to the relevance, morality and legality attached to such provision of Election Laws of Azad Kashmir which binds a candidate to 'swear in the name of Pakistan'. Gulzar had to be fair whether in view of the unfinished task of establishment of provisional government in Azad Kashmir and in view of the fact that the aim of establishment of the said government is yet to be achieved. The values and vires should have been discussed with such a rider. The mysterious silence on this vital issue makes one infer that Gulzar has not rendered justice to the topic and projects a tainted view. One can draw only one conclusion that residents of Azad Kashmir like the 'state subjects' of erstwhile Dogra Mahraja living in Indian occupied Kashmir have been by and large denied the right to vote. They are in a situation where Pakistani stooges are imposed upon them and in this part of Jammu and Kashmir the people are put under similar imposed governance which easily surrenders the national ego before ordinary civil servants, police officers and army commanders imported into Jammu and Kashmir from India. This is the exact position in Muzzafarabad.

Chapter 18

The Boycott Policy

Under the subtitle 'Selection without Discretion' it has been discussed that the two great leaders Jawahar Lal Nehru and Sheikh Abdulla frustrated all democratic aspirations of the people of Jammu and Kashmir in 1950. Had Kashmiris been allowed to participate in the Election of the Constituent Assembly the disarrayed and frightened opposition would hardly have taken one third of the seats and those too would have fallen within the lot of the parties with contradictory political attitudes. But, we cannot ignore, nor can the rulers dismiss the fact that these two veteran leaders too had made an assessment of the situation. They had sufficient information through their informers, ground level cadres and the state agencies that the hatred against the Indo-Kashmir relationship was about to explode, hence, they tried to prevent this. They must have grasped that the masses would register their verdict which would defeat their joint exercise to impose a constitution through which they planned to confuse the people; as is evident from the remark made by Jawahar Lal Nehru: 'the luxury of democracy cannot be conceded for J&K.' Thus came the imposition of a constitution against the wishes of the people without allowing them to participate in the process in any manner and the people but developed an aversion. This document which otherwise should have been an article of faith for the people caused doubt about the whole political process which was nourished with the blood of our martyrs. Its immediate consequence was that the masses suspected very political thought and attributed malafides to the very system. This is why that immediate reaction was not visible on the surface.

Immediately thereafter, the very active partner of this joint fraud Sheikh Abdulla demonstrated his reaction and the conflict of his mind became transparent from the contradictions in his speeches and from the choice of words he used in his public utterances at different places. Break of relations between Sheikh Abdulla and Jawahar Lal Nehru became the theme of common gossip during the exercise of pressure on Sheikh Abdulla to enter into an accord with India and his subtle expressions against the very Delhi Agreement which he was made to sign with New Delhi in 1952. The shift in the situation diverted public opinion and it ultimately rejected this election and the assembly formed under the same leadership. Hence, the dismissal, arrest and detention of those stalwarts who had imposed this assembly followed. Its very creation was illegitimate as was admitted by Sheikh Abdulla who had conceived and delivered this assembly. He, alongwith his close associates who had imposed this assembly and through it themselves as representatives of the people, were kept in illegal detention. Thus, in a camera session a group of defectors Bakshi and Sadiq got a document passed which qualified as the constitution of Jammu and Kashmir. It has niether legal sanction nor moral values as its basis nor is it a product of genuine political process. It is summed up:

1. All the 75 members from Indian occupied Kashmir were imposed without any duly prepared, circulated, revised and reviewed electoral rolls, without providing opportunity to the people to create a situation for emergence of even feeble opposition arrayed in a party or disarrayed in groups. The delimitation of electoral segments was made so secretly that it is after declaration of imposed members that the masses could locate their respective electoral constituencies.
2. ...less than half of Jammu and Kashmir under Pakistan occupation was (as India had earlier declared) not liberated to join in the election process.
3. ...That soveregnity is not divisible. It had at the end of British Raj or abdication of the ruler of the state passed to his subjects divided by the artificial cease-fire line and so unless the two parts were joined together none could bind the other by a proxy decision.
4. ...Even if New Delhi had to impose a system of governance it would not cause so much public resentment, as was caused to validate the fraudulent relationship of Kashmir with India. Peoples were able to

understand that India had only imperialistic and neo-colonistic designs to prosecute through this imposed constitution.

5. ...That the 'installed head' Yuvraj Karan Singh son of the abdicated ruler had declared constitution of a 100 member House for the state. Twenty five seats were reserved for Pak-occupied part of the 'domain'. About the same number of members were (including the creator of this Assembly Sheikh Abdulla) behind bars. A few of them under the leadership of Mirza Beig were brought from jails in 1956 to address the house. In their speeches they exposed the fraud which was conceived in New Delhi, but was being enacted in the Amargarh Palace (Assembly Hall) Srinagar. The Bakshi regime hired 'goondas' and policemen in civil clothes who made murderous attacks on Mirza Beig and other detained members of the assembly and under that state threatened to eliminate them physically whence they were again boarded in police vehicles and were thrown in prison cells in Srinagar, Kud, Jammu etc.

6 ...Other twenty one members involved in the voting session of that house, were under threat that they would be involved in criminal cases and after mock trial would be convicted and punished. It is thus that out of the house of 100 members only 50 were actually involved in constitution making and 21 of them were involved through force and persecution. Only 29 of the 100 members voted of their own free will for the constitution.[1]

7. ...That 9 to 10 members, of the Constituent Assembly, were part of the Indian game in Kashmir either by their conviction or due to the directions which they used to receive from Moscow as sympathisers of the world communist movement. Others were purchased agents. In 1964 India itself exposed agents like G.M. Bakshi for amassing huge assets. They were allowed to create assets in lieu of their conscience and once their conscience pricked them and their treachery became transparent they were eliminated through Enquiry Commissions. The Ayanger Commission was the last reward Bakshi got for his treachery to impose a constitution upon the people

suited to the expansionist and neo-colonist designs of New Delhi.

8. ...The main game in the imposition of this document was to widen the ambit of the imposed Instrument of Accession purported to have been executed by the Maharaja of Kashmir. The Indian government and leaders of its freedom movement had, on all occasions, declared that it was the people of a princely state who had option to accede with one or the other dominion of the subcontinent. Against this avowed, declared and publicised stand Indian rulers had made the 'bastard' (Maharaja of Kashmir as qualified by Menon in his book *Integration of States)* to sign the document of Accession. Government of India required to accord some sanctity and that too through imposed fraud to the act of the'bastard'.
9. ...The second party to the dispute which rarely grasped this game as a matter of routine and so a protest was lodged by its foreign minister Sir Mohammad Zafarulla at the U.N. Security Council. In reply the Indian permanent representative in U.N. Sir B.N. Rao declared the provision of 'accession' contained in the draft constitution as a 'one-way traffic' and not acceptable to India.
10. ...That it was the elected group of Jammu and Kashmir Praja Sabha (Assembly) elected in December 1946, which had amongst themselves to elect four members to the Indian Constituent Assembly. On the other hand, the Indian Government managed the nomination of those four persons as members of Indian Constituent Assembly who had not taken part in Praja Sabha elections. So Jammu and Kashmir had no representation in the Indian Consembly. It will be discussed in Part II.

All these facts created a stir in the public mind against the constitution and governance under that constitution. Participation with it through elections was considered a game of fraud for the sake of fraud with their own collective interests.

Hence, the first election held to the first Legislative Assembly was consciously boycotted by the electorate in Jammu and Kashmir and we have under the subheadings:

'Selection with Discretion' discussed its manner and impact.

Before the 1962 Elections (which has been qualified as 'Selection by Abductions') Maulana Masoodi in his house at Ganderbal started a whisper campaign that for immediate and day to day economic and political difficulties we must create some opening in the legislature to give vent to the pressing public demands. Hence, this author too was swayed by the idea and joined with other pro-Indian elements in the Democratic National Conference and Praja Socialist Party and with other like-minded independent candidates and took part in elections. r. We were all taught a lesson. We all found wisdom in the alternative of positive boycott so this author, Malik Gulam Mohammad, late Abdul Satar Ranjoor, G.M. Lone, Bahaudin Zahid, K.D. Sethi, and R.P. Saraf (all communists and avowed pro-Indians) O.P. Saraf, P.L. Koul, Kh. Umar Bhat and others (all socialists linked with Delhi) signed a document under which we affirmed faith only in non-participation in elections and committed that democratic participation for Kashmiris was a prohibited pleasure.

Wisdom in this discussion was further fortified by the drama of 'Rejections' played in 1967 and the farce of concessions granted in 1972. Finally, the 1977 elections which invited public participation later on proved that it was also a 'device' to frustrate the aspirations of the masses. This election proved to be a sugar coated poisonous drug which finally killed the leadership created during the sacrifices of four decades. Finally, the Jagmohan formula of 'Defections' administered in 1984 proved that any 'democratic' verdict of the people of Jammu and Kashmir for assimilation with India was not acceptable to New Delhi which has provided only one alternative to the people of Jammu and Kashmir and that is a complete surrender of their regional identity and national ego.

Jagmohan made the people of Jammu and Kashmir revert back to the policy of non-participation and taught them that even within the ambit of 'imposed constitutions' Kashmiris cannot go contrary to the unwritten directions of Delhi Darbar.

1987 proved to be the culmination of this continued fraud and vindicated the decision taken by the people and imposed upon the leadership in the mid 50s for complete non-participation in this game in the name of elections.

This summary (above) teaches us a few lessons so vigorously taught by the process of history. They are:

1. ...It is the constitution of a particular political society which defines the powers, limitations and the working of the governance of that society. Within the ambit of so defined situation do work the executive, legislature, judiciary and other organs of governance. Thus, the constitution is the fountain source of authority for the people of that particular society. Likewise the constitution of Jammu&Kahmir provides two directly elected and indirectly chosen houses of legislature. The house of representatives is the electoral college for the upper house. Immediately after the selection of the house people found that pressures were being exercised to surrender authority to New Delhi. They apprehended that a 'system' which works, conveniently, as a stooge,* was to be imposed upon them. The signing of the Delhi Agreement made the apprehensions a reality, the coup d'etat of August 1953 consolidated that reality and the manner in which this constitution was imposed in a melodrama played in Amargarh Palace at Srinagar made people reject it as their collective code of conduct;
2. The manner in which elections, thereafter, were turned into a mockery did fortify completely the collective decision of the people that such hustings are only played to ridicule their national ego. Ranjoor a communist assassinated by militants for his avowed pro-Indian political leanings described in a speech in March 1962 at Keegam, Shopian, these elections through the medium of the metaphor used by the great Urdu poet of the subcontinent, Faiz:

   "Haan Joo Jafa Bhi Aap Ney Kee Qaayidee Sey Kee"

   (Yes my beloved! Thou hast committed all treacheries but under a regulated code);
3. Contemporary history has shown that the rulers even if chosen by the people have been caught between the imported head of the state for J&K (governor appointed by Central Government) and the imported and imposed

bureaucracy; the towering personality Sheikh Mohammad Abdulla, even after 'winning' a massive mandate from the people was not able to select officers of his choice. We will have to acquaint our readers with the causes of such compulsions and may provide some relevant information.[2]

4. It has also been proved as a hard reality that even if the people offer heavy sacrifices, force the authorities to provide them a comparatively fair election and after they choose their representatives the verdict of the people can within no time be frustrated, through corruption or intimidation defections are manipulated and thereby the very concept of representation is eroded. In the process the leadership stood rejected by those very people who created them. To quote the instance of Sheikh Abdulla and his dynasty. The leader of the Valley with mass charisma lateSheikh Abdulla is now condemned as a villain and spy by history. His son-in-law G.M. Shah is also discredited. Sheikh Abdullah's son Farooq Abdulla, Mustafa Kamal, Tariq Abdulla all stand rejected; their present is uncertain and their future is tied to the mercy which they are accorded by New Delhi. Irony lies in the fact that the woman, neverred as loving mother by three generations, was, laid to rest by the side of her husband Shiekh Abdulla not under sermons and recitation of holy verses but under the strict guard of the gun weielding army.

5. The 'Begaar Election' (of 1996) has given two third majority to present rulers, but who rules the state of Jammu and Kashmir? Farooq Abdulla and his cabinet, or the Chief Secretary Ashok Jetley and B.R. Singh Principal Secretary to Chief Minister? In reality the rulers are the members of joint command which consist of personnel from military and paramilitary forces and token presence of the civil head of administration, i.e., the chief minister of the state. The decisions formulated there are carried out by the Jammu and Kashmir Police again headed by imported police officers- the Director General Police and assisted by the I.G.Ps all imported from India. Even district level rulers are mainly Indians. The moot point to be conveyed is that the people cautiously preserve and maintain the ego of their right to elect and so are not

interested to elect such rulers who rule for and on behalf of others and are but show pieces. We will elucidate the argument with details later on, but a recent incident of April 24, 2001 is mentioned below as a footnote.[3] The incident of May 9, 2001 which took place at Magam in Central Kashmir further vindicates our argument.[4]

6. We need not go into details of the proceedings of various assemblies which have from 1956 till date claimed representative character, but let us confine ourselves to the proceedings of the present assembly creation of the 1996 election. The print media reports daily about dozens of killings which even include custodial killings. Such victims hail from the one or the other assembly segment and the house possesses 'so-called' representatives from those constituencies. Have such representatives even made a mention of such extra judicial killings on the floor of the House and asked the treasury benches to explain the killings or at least to counter the press reports? Readers may peruse the proceedings of J&K Assembly of the session just held in August 1998 and check for themselves, why the so-called representatives of the people lack such courage. The reply is inferred from the fact that their 'creator' is the killer and so how can they annoy them. Can any self-respecting people waste their vote to elect such a body? It is pertinent here to refer to the statement of the State Minister for Home, J&K who on May 3, 2001 said at Kupawara:

   > "I fear with what face I will account for these misdeeds before Almighty on the day of resurrection because I proved myself and my officers incapable to protect from physical elimination a young boy from Ladakh who had come to me and other officers to know the whereabouts of his advocate brother who was earlier lifted by paramilitary forces but never released nor his dead body given. But the younger brother too probably lost his life to locate the predecessor disappeared brother...."

7. Jammu and Kashmir is a colony in all respects. Its fiscal policies are imposed from Delhi. It has a virtually dependent economy and financial pressures make local leadership remain with a begging bowl in their hands. In 1997-98 the state government headed by Farooq

Abdulla was bankrupt to such an extent that its employees could not be paid as the Sadder treasuries at Jammu and Srinagar and district treasuries were penniless. This author had contributed from his monthly salary towards his provident fund No. 989/Jus. After five years, the 'Chief Accountants Officer' sanctioned payment vide order No: 662/Ac, but due to bankruptcy of the state the payment could not be made for a few months. In such financial subjugation people may elect a government and can such a government move unless it is cordial with the center? Cordiality with reference to Jammu and Kashmir means to remain dependent, obedient and without self-respect and to keep the seal and signature for concurrence of a Central law readily available with New Delhi. Can people offer sacrifices for protection of their precious vote to elect a government which has to remain in a state of impotency due to such impositions?

8. In June 2000 this so-called elected assembly was exposed so badly that had its leader or its members any values they would have either resigned or tried to vindicate the honour of this 'representative' body of the people. An almost unanimous resolution for restoration of the state autonomy, eroded from 1952 was passed by it. Though it had vide u/s 147 of J&K Constitution sufficient powers to restore much of the eroded powers, but probably to seek permission from New Delhi the Farooq Abdulla government tabled the resolution in the State Assembly and got it passed. But this resolution was dismissed in a huff by the Central Government without reference to the Indian Parliament. Two central ministers including the Law and Justice Minister, in an interview to a private T.V. Channel said that Farooq Abdulla and his house has been elected by military and paramilitary forces and so what credibility did the resolution possess? Immediately on the rejection of this 'autonomy resolution' by the central government, a militant leader Abdul Majeed Dar from some unknown hideout declared a unilateral cease-fire. All important central ministers including Hon'ble Prime Minister, without wasting a single minute, expressed jubilation and deputed important secretaries to the government to

enter into parleys with masked militants. The assembly was not accorded reasons for dismissal of its resolution. It shows that the central leaders have openly dubbed the J&K Assembly which had passed the resolution as their own creation and masked militants being a creation of historical process, so, represented aspirations of the people.

It is in the light of these hard facts that the critics of Farooq Abdulla who accuse him of political opportunitism have to take mercy upon him. It is usually said that he changes loyalties as soon the 'power centre' changes in Delhi. He was installed by the Janata Dal rulers with the good offices of communist leaders to counter the criticism that J&K is ruled as a direct colony of New Delhi. So, he has to win any body who occupies the office of Prime Minister. Till the fall of Deve Gowda he was always appeasing him as being a great leader of India and within moments changed loyalties and became close to I.K.Gujral. This was an ordinary shift, but by aligning with the BJP he exposed himself to common ridicule. But the circumstances which created him he had to change as directed by his behind-the-screen makers, i.e., the Indian Intelligence Bureau and the Research and Analysis Wing (RAW). He was taught this lesson by Sheikh Abdulla in 1977 which that leader learnt on the eve of installation of the Janata Party Government under Moraiji Desai in New Delhi. On 28 February 1958 three lakh people roared with laughter as Sheikh Abdulla dubbed the then Prime Minister of Kashmir as 'Karam Din'—a pet monkey who danced to the tune of his master juggler. But the irony of history has made his own son to act as Karam Din. After discussions on the 1999 Parliamentary elections, the boycott policy will get further mention. It should not be construed that Kashmiris now have no aspiration to exercise the right of franchise. Kashmiris have nourished that aspiration for the last one century and made heavy sacrifices to evolve a national code of conduct which can provide them provisions to elect representatives and accountable governing authorities. But he has neither faith nor the will to participate in an exercise in futility even to elect from strong leadership which can by different tactics be cowed down by New Delhi and if such elected leadership resists it can be divided, ruled through the tested methods of 'corrupt and purchase policy'. If any leader resists he will have to face incarceration as a detenu in different jails without trial on mere accusation of seccession which Indian rulers successfully foisted upon one of the tallest personalities Sheikh Abdulla - the Lion of Kashmir.

However, people in Jammu and Kashmir are ready to participate in an interim election till the final verdict from them is sought about their future. They are ready to undergo this limited exercise only to elect their representatives who can project the collective views of the people of Jammu and Kashmir in tripartite deliberations between the representatives of India, Pakistan and Kashmiri people to evolve a solution for the imbroglio which now poses an imminent threat to the existence and prosperity of the subcontinent and to world peace.

People have the will and courage to defend the sanctity of their vote if and when they are referred the matter of choosing their representatives for such deliberations. They opine that such an exercise should be made in both parts as also in those northern areas of erstwhile Jammu and Kashmir which are under direct Pakistani occupation. However, they would like UN supervision for such an exercise, but in case due to the over-sensitivity of India such supervision is not acceptable, then observation by democrats, human rights activists, renowned authors and journalists from the subcontinent, from SAARC and NAM countries should be acceptable. Even sovereign countries have made in their elections transparent through such observations.

Such observation needs to cover the following stages in the process of hustings:

- Delimitation proceedings for defining the electoral segments in both the parts of the state on universally recognised principles of proportionate representation to all regions within this state.
- Preparation, declaration, review, revision and final approval of electoral rolls.
- Filing of nomination, withdrawal, scrutiny of papers and final stage of approving the lists of candidates for each constituency.
- During the interim period of canvassing.

However, these four stages require limited observation

whereas the actual polling, counting of votes and final declaration of results requires to be carefully observed.

In the epilogue the practicability, reason and logic behind these suggestions will be discussed. If treated with sincerity by all the concerned parties, there is no difficulty to find out an efficacious solution to this age-old problem.

Notes

1. About half a dozen among the authors of 1956 Constitution Act are living Mr. G.N.Wani Budgami was at the time of passing of this Act behind bars, Peerzada Crhulam Jeelani of Pampore has no qualms to admit the over-aiding force paspetuated upon him, Abdul Gani Goni was just at the spur of moment purchased from a room of Kashmir Guest House Lal Chowk (A Private Hotel), an affair which he will not deny at his old age. M/s RP Saraf and K.D. Sethi as Communists were actively and enthusiastically involved with Constitution making but, admit the frauds which were played.
2. Shiekh Abdulla during Baig–Parthasarthy talks in 1974 casually sought some suggestions from this humble author. I suggested that before he takes power he should get the integration of Civil Services disintegrated as was before 1957. He agreed. Mr. Banerjee the Chief Secretary of Mir Qasim Govt and Mirza Afzal Baig his own deputy assured him that he can post any officer without such restrictions conveniently for any office. On taking power in Feb 1975 he immediately appointed his scribe, the Secretary of JK Academy of Art, Culture of Languages, Mr. M.Y. Taing as Director Information. But as the rules imposed by center dettered the lion of Kashmir to induct Taing in Indian Administrative Service the latter sought his reversion.
3. The instances if quoted will pile up into a big volume of a book about the helplessness demonstrated by actions, deeds, policies, practices, statements and outbursts of the present government imposed under the 'Selection by Corvee' in 1996. The summary dismissal of Autonomy Resolution of June 2000 by the Central Government will be given precise but separate treatment. Herein, I quote that on April 24, 2001 the'Unified Command', as per Government press note reviewed law and order situation in the state; ' who reviewed the situation'? The names and offices of the reviewers were made public by all newspapers and the state owned electronic media on April 25, 2001. They all are Indian officers—colonial rulers of this colony and all are Indian Hindus. They are:

   Ashok Jaitley (Chief Secretary), Gurpeet Singh Chief of Staff Northern Command, Ashok Suri Director General Police, Lt. Gen. J.R. Mukherjee, Asok Bhan Inspector General of Police, B.S. Chaturvedi Inspector General of BSF, officers of Indian Tibetan Border Police and officers of RAW and I.B. (all non-Kashmiri Hindus). A recently inducted ordinary Muffasil lawyer into the cabinet as junior most minister added ridicule to it as an insignificent costume of no consequence.

4. On May 9, 2001 indiscriminate firing by the BSF at Magam Central Kashmir killed a dozen passengers in a civil bus travelling to reach their homes in villages around Magam. Next day a team of more than three dozen of members of the fourth estate (media) went to cover this berserk action. They were fatally beaten under the directions of Mullick the D.I.G. B.S.F, their cameras worth a crore of rupees were snatched from them and broken into pieces or thrown in the nearby river. On this murderous attack on the vital organ of Indian democracy how did the imposed chief minister react?. It speaks volumes about his helplessness under the system devised by neo-colonist tactics. Dr. Farooq Abdulla said: "I am leaving forDelhi to acquaint the Indian Home Minister of this incident." Can the advocates who preach to us to participate in elections explain why a Kashmiri should undergo trauma of vicissitudes to protect his vote? Is he to offer sacrifices to elect emasculated rulers who have no power to punish a semi-mad Deputy Inspector General of Border Security Force; who, by his actions does not only commit crimes cognizable by our law, but puts to disgrace in the world the largest democracy of the world.

NOTES

Part II

Elections to Six Parliamentary Seats from J&K 1967-1999)
and
Indo-Kashmir Constitutional Relationship

Chapter 19

Representation from J&K in India Constituent Assembly

The development and decline of the British Raj in India, the growth of the Freedom Movement and the causes of partition of India are now oft repeated facts of history and references are not necessary to our study. However, it needs to be stressed that Kashmir had a distinct history as a viable link between the states of the subcontinent and countries of Central Asia. Jammu Province of the present Jammu and Kashmir state forms a constellation of tiny independent principalities. All these smaller states and Jammu state had a deep political, cultural, geographical and religious affinity with the Valley. Though at different times any one of these states was part of Kashmir country or even sometimes the Valley was temporarily subdued either by Jammu Rajas or by the estate holders of Rajouri-Poonch, but they never formed a single political entity till AD 1846. Since then they have become dependent units of one another inspite of continued intrigues against its existence. Its relationship gets more cemented. The Jammu and Kashmir freedom movement had its own strategy and independent characteristics than those of the Indian freedom struggle. But Indian political parties meddled in these troubled waters with ulterior designs and complicated its destiny. On the independence of India the destiny of this state was in an ambiguous and confused situation grouped mischievously, with Indian princely states.

Kashmir and its present associated principalities being surrounded by the grandeur of the Himalayas by and large retained their independent character always. However, the Mongols had for last millennium harboured greed for the riches of Kashmir. It was in prosecution of that lust for plunder and loot that Tier, a Mongola invader attacked and devastated this country. In 1320-21, Zulcho, another Mongol aggressor reduced this country into shambles, killed considerable portion of its population and took thousands of youth from both the sexes as hostages. In consequence to this deep mental shock the faith in the spiritual and political leadership of Brahmin was eroded, search for a more practicable and viable system became common urge. Islam, which had already penetrated in social life, filled this void. Sultanate was established and again to prosecute those defeated Mongol designs in sixteenth century, their Muslim successor Mirza Haider Douglat exploited the sectarian dissensions and tried to lay the foundation of the Mughal empire through Kashmir, but his aspirations were frustrated. His cousin Babur established the foothold of Mughal rule and his grandson Akbar fulfilled the shattered dreams of Mirza by annexing Kashmir with Indian imperialism under a calculated fraud in AD 1556. Inspite of becoming part of the subcontinent as a colony of the Mughal empire Kashmir retained its distinct identity and cherished the deep rooted urge of independence. This is manifest from a Persian poem composed by Mirza Qalandar Baig (though himself a foreigner) in June 1700 narrating the history of the arrival of the Holy Relic (Moi Muqqadas) in Kashmir in April AD 1700. He attributes that Aurengzeb Alamgir resented the taking of the Holy Relic to Srinager as he considered Kashmir not to be a part of India. Even if the reliability of the poem is doubted, but it speaks of Kashmiri national psyche about their subdued reaction against Mughal rule and about the traits of the Mughal Kashmir policy.

The Mughals showed keen interest in certain scenic spots of Kashmir, but their governors, land owners, civil servants and power brokers all exploited the masses as colonial rulers do in colonies. The successors of the Mughal regime the Pathans subjected Kashmiris to untold miseries. The tyrannies culminated during the most cruel rule of Sikhs. Human dignity was subjected to an unparalleled disgrace in 1846 when this paradise on earth with its innocent, beautiful, simple and decent people was sold to Gulab Singh an ordinary soldier. For about a century he and his successors humiliated this nation to the extent that the only alternatives were either to commit collective suicide or to go for revolt. The latter alternative erupted like a volcano as a natural reaction. The pretext was provided by the unwise decision of authorities to close down, in 1921, the only industry viz the state silk factory situated in Solina Srinagar. It took a decade to channelise this reaction into a disciplined, organised and popular upsurge. In 1931 this channelisation earmarked the restoration of national dignity as its collective destination. To achieve this goal the viable and effective source lay in the struggle for pro-people and accountable governance. A common phrase was evolved as a popular slogan for *zimadar nizami hakoomat* (a government answerable for its actions before the people). In other words, the aspirations for democracy were nourished and developed.

During Pathan rule both the communities were equally subjected to inhuman treatment though a small section of the privileged in both the communities exploited the situation by sheer sycophancy. A group of political elite grew among the Pandit community which mastered the Persian language and even masterminded Pathan policies of tyranny. One such opportunist, Pandit Bawani Dass Kachro, lived in Kabul in luxury to advise the Pathans how to rule in Kashmir with an iron hand. During Sikh rule this privileged Pandit lobby became powerful to the extent that it was a Pandit Wazir who warned the Sikh ruler against his designs of blasting the centre of Muslim religious activity in down town Srinagar viz. Khanqahi Moula. Another Muslim centre of worship Shahi Mosque in the heart of the city was turned into a godown. Thus the majority community Muslims of Kashmir were subjected to untold miseries and inhuman discrimination. The Dogra rule continued with the same policies of oppression and discrimination which can be well grasped by quoting a single specimen illustrating discrimination before law. In case of the guilt of murder against any accused in which the victim was non Muslim the punishment was not life imprisonment, but the death penalty and in case the murdered victim was a Muslim and the murderer a non-Muslim the guilty was, on the proof of guilt, to pay twenty eight rupees as a fine. In such a background revolution was a dire necessity, particularly for the majority community—Muslims. Hence, the struggle for accountable governance was initiated, organised, run and fed with the blood of Muslims and so its united nature appeared, inspite of its progressive and democratic objectives, a sort of religious agitation. Hence, the organisation which guided this revolution was also run under the banner which made it appear a single community concern. It was named the All J&K Muslim Conference. It was soon realised that though the elite from minority communities lived on privilege as agents of exploitation, but by and large commoners were not in any better position than the Muslims. Low caste Hindus were subjected to the same treatment which these castes faced in the subcontinent. The Kashmir Valley had virtually no low caste pockets of the Hindu community. The Brahmin even as a petty government employee, or petty land owner or as apetty money lender considered himself to be a 'maharaja' within his limited situation wherein he lived on exploitation and extortion. The smaller community of Rajputs settled in certain parts of the Valley boasted of their kinship with the ruler and were not less than rulers. The Khatri controlled the export and import of the state so had sufficient reasons to foresee a threat in case the masses were allowed to feel conscious of their might and right. In Jammu except the low caste untouchables, Gadies, Jewars, etc. other caste Hindus, inspite of their poverty and utter helplessness considered themselves committed to the Hindu monarchy rather than to the revolution oriented by the majority designs. So, inspite of change of the nomenclature of the people's organisation from the All J&K Muslim Conference to All J&K National Conference the movement remained under communal strains. However, the intra-conflict of Muslim leadership under the two banners of the Muslim Conference and National Conference diverted the mass mind from the main struggle against monarchy to a cult building race with the thought as to which cult should substitute the divine position of the king. On the one hand, there remained aggressive postures of the National Conference to impose the charismatic Sheikh Abdulla, the leader of the party, but on the other hand, the Mirwaiz dynasty exploited the Muslim Conference to preserve its traditional hold on the Muslim sentiment. This clash was exploited by the main two political organisations of the subcontinent - the All India National Congress and All India Muslim League. Britishers also medlled in troubled waters, but surreptitiously with intrigue. The ruler of the state Maharaja Hari Singh found safety of his interest in these contradictions. During the mid

40s, as the independence of the subcontinent and its partition started to appear a reality which was to happen at any moment, the rigour in the intrigues within the political circles of Jammu and Kashmir also evolved mysterious dimensions. The intentions, designs and motives started to evolve certain definite shapes. In this political scenario Maharaja Hari Singh, alive to the changes worldwide found safety for his interests and for the interests of his progeny in an independent status for Jammu and Kashmir. Though as an autocrat he might not initially concede to surrender sovereignty to the people, but the dynamism inherent as a quality of his lifestyle would have adjusted his egoistic patriotism to the status of constitutional monarchy. Such a situation would even consolidate the relationship between Jammuites and Kashmiris. Sheikh Abdulla who with his dynamism and diligence, had emerged as one of the few great public leaders with a definite edge was also, in his heart of hearts, nourishing ideas for a democratic, secular independent country of Jammu and Kashmir, but later events created a chain of circumstantial evidence which provide a strong hypothesis that he was swayed by his dynastic interests. In clear words it appears that he too was for independent Kashmir, but would not like His Highness even as titular head of the state but had definite aspirations to replace dynasty rule by dynasty charisma. Equally the strong Jammu lobby of the All J&K Muslim Conference led by Choudhry Hamidullah Khan openly came out for independent Kashmir. Both the powerful parties of the subcontinent the Congress and the Muslim League, though theoretically avoided practical involvement in the state politics, but the Congress with its offensive designs of greater India would not allow this strategically vital state to remain out of its grip and the Muslim League with fallacious presumption considered Jammu and Kashmir as its conquered territory - a blank cheque to be cashed anytime. Hence, both were busy in hatching conspiracies in Jammu and Kashmir and turned this soil into hot bed of intrigue.Both required services of agencies, hired such services and continue till date with hired crutches in this beautiful Valley; both had an eye upon this land and had no respect for the people. However, despite these malafide intentions, the Congress acted with maturity in its deceit and the Muslim League acted too bluntly thereby proving its immaturity.

It is pertinent here to study the important characters of the political drama in Kashmir through their actions. None could deny that had not the Mirwaiz dynasty played the role of harbingers of educational revolution in the state probably even Sheikh Abdulla's family would not have been able to get that orphan boy of the family educated. Later, had not Mirwaiz Yousuf Shah patronised Sheikh Abdulla from the pulpit of Jamia Masjid he would not have made any headway in politics. But in the mid 40s Mirwaiz was too engrossed in the struggle for survival and to preserve the hegemony of his dynasty. The traditional fans misled him to confine his policies in a negative direction.

Sheikh Abdulla with all attractions in his programme, oratory and personal charisma had by 1946-47 established an image of being a despot, dictatorial in his functions, contradictory in his policies and actions and a patron of corrupt elements. Even his close comrades were fed up with his intolerance, capricious disposal of vital matters; he was deaf to advice and suggestions and was aggressively committed to his own shortcomings.

Hari Singh was regarded as a villain by the masses both in Jammu and the Valley though the privileged Kashmir Pandit, Jammu Rajput, land owners and Zaildars considered him the shadow of the Almighty. But, inspite of his autocratic character, egoistic might and authoritarian functioning, there were progressive characteristics evident in his policies.

Neither Sheikh Abdulla, nor Mirwaiz nor Abbas nor Choudhry Hamid had universal acceptability in the three diverse regions of the state., viz., provinces of Kashmir and Jammu and the districts of Frontier. Jammu province and Frontier areas too had very grave diversities in which no single leader even from those regions could muster wholesale support. In this situation had not Hari Singh inherited ill-will and had he evolved a compromising attitude with the genuine demands of his subjects his acceptability in the situation would not have eroded. From the provisions of Constitution Act of 1939, from other pieces of legislation and from his appropriate judgement of the selection of men to implement his policies it was sufficiently evident that he had progressive ideals as a ruler. Beyond that, expectations could not be nourished from and connected with the autocracy. In this mixed situation his dream of independent Kashmir could not receive even limited sanctions from his subjects, except from a lobby of the Muslim minority in Jammu and Hindu minority in Kashmir. The latter's view was represented by the actions and policies of R.C. Kak, Prime Minister of the Maharaja. He had community interests in ndependent status of Jammu and Kashmir. He was conscious that for survival of a nation with independent identity human resources are an essential prerequisite to explore other sources. He knew that it was his community, though a microscopic minority which could gain from the then prevalent situation, fill in the void as other majority communities- Muslim in the Valley and Jammu Hindus lagged behind in the field of education.

On the eve of Indian independence Sheikh Abdulla and his colleagues in the National Conference were in prison. The Maharaja decided to hold elections to Praja Sabha and convened the newly elected Assembly in January 1947. Sheikh's party the National Conference had boycotted the elections. Though the Muslim Conference had also joined the Quit Kashmir movement, but it decided to participate in the elections held under J&K Constitution of 1939. However, in midstream the fraction of the Muslim Conference led by Mirwaiz boycotted. Both parties did not opt for boycott for positive reasons, but pretexts were so shallow that their non-participation did not effect the participation of the registered electorate.

In this background Sheikh Abdulla's term of punishment awarded for commission of sedition was reduced under a covert intervention of the Congress, the *persona non grata* for the Indian National Congress R.C. Kak was sacked to crown their installed agent, Meharchand Mahajan, who created the opportunities to mould the destiny of Jammu and Kashmir. The obliged Sheikh, on his release, demonstrated confusing stands which confused the people about his real stand and his superior muscle power imposed this confusion which was confounded with the tactical blunders of Pakistan to instigate and abet the Pathan armed intervention which provided India a pretext to rope in the ruler of Jammu and Kashmir and it intervened to occupy the state. The envitable happened.

This state turned into a battle field; unethical, unreasonable and illogical division of the state was imposed in a manner which dissected the very heart of Kashmiris. The absurd line drawn by an unreasonable blind referee from far away U.N. Head Quarters hung a sharp edged sword upon the heads of every state subject. In this swiftly evolving and confusing situation the Indian Constituent Assembly was formed and later the same Assembly framed the Constitution for the Indian dominion—'Bharat'. Presently we will discuss this formation; the *modus operandi* evolved for its formation, representation of the people of erstwhile British subjects who became citizens of a free Indian dominion, the representation of erstwhile princely states which acceded with Indian dominion, the nature of representation from the state of Jammu and Kashmir direct or indirect in the formation of the Indian Constitution.

Before us the constitutional 'pandits', jurists and eminent authors like Serivai, D.D. Basu and Dr. Anand have discussed the aspects of constitutional relationship between Jammu and Kashmir and India, but none of these stalwarts have dealt with the delicate matter of the representation of the people of Jammu and Kashmir in the Indian Constituent Assembly. I am an ordinary student of political history so am of the opinion that without going into the history of involvement of the people of Jammu and Kashmir with the decisions of the people of India many serious inferences are deducable which need to be discussed without any reservations. These discussions might make us comment upon the intellectual integrity of those constitutional 'pandits' at appropriate places. The cabinet mission outlined in its statement of 16 May 1946 the scheme of setting up of the constituent assembly. It needs a mention that the cabinet mission did not approve the method of election by adult franchise, "which is the most satisfactory basis for the constitution of an assembly. It would result in wholly unacceptable delay in the formation of the new constitution". Therefore, it was resolved that the only practicable course was to turn the "recently elected provincial legislative assemblies into the electoral college." The Cabinet Mission outlined the "fearest" and the most practical plan as:

1. To allot to each province a total number of seats proportional to its population roughly in the ratio of one

to a million, as the nearest substitute for the representation by adult sufferrage.

2. To divide this provisional allocation of seats between the main communities in each province proportionate to their population.
3. To provide that the representatives allotted to each community in a province would be elected by the members of that community in its legislative assembly.

The Cabinet Mission added:

> "We think that for these purposes it is sufficient to recognise only three main communities in India; General, Muslim and Sikh. The 'General' community including all persons, who are not Muslims or Sikhs....."
>
> *Select Documents 1,48(1) p.214.*

It is under this scheme that an assembly of 235 members was constituted for the Indian Dominion. The table by Subha Rao contained in *Framing of Indian Constitution* giving province wise details and communal distribution is reproduced below:

Province	**General**	**Sikh**	**Muslim**	**Total**
Madras	45		4	49
Bombay	19		2	21
West Bengal	16		5	21
United Provinces	47		8	55
East Punjab	8	4	4	16
Bihar	31		5	36
C.P of Berar	16		1	17
Assam	6		2	8
Orissa	9			9
	197	**4**	**31**	**232**
Delhi				1
Ajmer-Merwara				1
Coorg				1
				235

The scheme of allotment of one member to a population of one million entitled the princely state of Jammu and Kashmir to elect four members for the Indian Constituent

Assembly in the manner in which British Provinces or other princely states did. Under this scheme on the basis of the proposals of the Cabinet Mission elections were held in July and August 1946 to the 292 seats allotted to the British Provinces. The already elected Provincial Legislative Assemblies formed the electoral college for this number of Constitution givers from erstwhile British India.

With regard to 93 seats allotted to the princely states under Cabinet Mission plan, paragraph 19 (ii) of Mission's statement of May 17, 1946 the method of selection of these 93 members was also devised. The method was determined by the consultation between the princely states and British Indian Section of the Constituent Assembly of 292 members entered into negotiations with a 'Negotiating Committee of the Chamber of Princes.' For some time the two negotiating committees remained busy in deliberations. The British Indian Constituent Assembly was represented in these negotiations by Sir N. Gopalaswamy Ayyangar and Dr. P. Patabhai Ramaya whereas the Chamber of Princely States was represented by Sir Sultan Ahmad and Sir V.T. Krishnamachary. Besides, Sir B.N. Rao participated as Constitutional Advisor of the Constituent Assembly of British India. H.V.R. Iyengar Secretary Constituent Assembly of India and Maqbool Ahmad, Secretary, States Negotiating Committee were also involved in the deliberations. After prolonged, detailed and exhaustive discussions and deliberations it was evolved:

1. That there were 20 single states with a total population of 61.86 million.
2. That the total number of seats were allotted with the following break-up:

Hyderabad	16
Mysore	7
Travancore	6
J&K	4
Gwalior	4
Baroda	3
Jaipur	3
Udaipur, Jodhpur, Reva & Patiala	8 (2 each)
Cochin, Bikanar, Alwar, Kotah, Indore, Bhopal, Kolahpur, Bahalpur and Mayurbhanj	9 (1 each)
Total	**60**

Four seats were allotted to the Frontier group principalities with an aggregate population of 3.32 million. Twenty nine seats were given to states classified as interior groups with a total population of 27.82 million. This total number of members of the Constituent Assembly of undivided India (including) princely states was as under:

Provinces of British India	296
Single-State	60
Frontier Group States	4
Interior Group States	29
Total	**389**

The two Committees—one appointed by British Indian Constituent Assembly and the other appointed by Chamber of Princess evolved the following agreed principals:

> *"50% of the total representatives of the States should* (stress added) *be elected members* of the legislatures of the states concerned or where such legislatures did not exist by other electoral colleges. The states ...would endeavour to increase the quota of elected representatives much above 50%..."

The state of Jammu and Kashmir had elected a Praja Sabha (State Legislative Assembly) by the end of 1946 which was convened by January 1947. One of the tasks for this Elected House (elected under J&K Constitution Act of 1939) was to elect from 'its elected members' four persons at the most and two at the least to Indian Constituent Assembly. However, even if it could elect only two or three of its elected members of the Constituent Assembly, the remaining one or two were also to be elected by the house, but could not necessarily be from its elected group of members. They could be from the nominated group of the J&K Legislature, but in both the cases the electoral college was the J&K Legislative Assembly. In Part 1 the 1946-47 State Assembly has been discussed. Though it was a lopsided representation, but it was the only body which under this scheme had right to elect four members to Indian Constituent Assembly; at least two from its elected group of members. Almost similarly situated systems had evolved legislatures in the majority of princely states which 'houses' did elect their alloted quota to the Constituent Assembly of India.

It is pertinent here to quote Subha Rao *Framing of Indian Constitution,* first edition, chapter 2, under the heading 'Membership of the Constituent Assembly' p. 98:

> "With regard to 93 seats allotted to the Indian states under the Cabinet Missions Plan, paragraph 19 (ii) of the Missions statement of16 May 1946 had stated that the method of the selection of these representatives have to be determined by consultations between the states and the British Indian Section of the Constituent Assembly. Mainly for this a Negotiating Committee was set up by the Chamber of Princess and a Corresponding States' Committee was appointed by the Constituent Assembly."
>
> This book is a quasi state publication of the Indian government with the foreward by the first premier Jawahar Lal Nehru and publication authority from the first speaker Mavlankar.

It is by the mutual consultation and thereby arrived at decision of the Committee set up by the Chamber of Princes and the corresponding states committee of the Constituent Assembly that the formula quoted Supra was evolved and it was decided that the legislatures of the princely states as electoral colleges would elect the allotted quota of its representatives for Constituent Assembly of India and at least 50% of such elected representatives would be from its own elected quota or group. J&K Praja Sabha (Legislature) had to elect four representatives - two at least from amongst its elected members—to the Indian Constituent Assembly.

It is a known fact that from January 1947 when the J&K Legislature was convened till October 1947, no such initiative of election of these four representatives took place. In October 1947 the ruler of the state under the weight of Quit Kashmir Movement, Poonch Insurgency, Gilgit Mutiny and Tribal Armed Intervention left the state in anger, but neither did he dissolve the recently elected legislature nor did it cease to enjoy its character in any manner. Every subsequent act, thereafter taken in the name of the so abdicated ruler or by his regent Yuvraj Karan Singh was taken only under the J&K Constitution Act of 1939, under which the said assembly was elected for three years. Under section 15 of the said Constitution Act the said Assembly had life upto January 1950. Under the proviso to the same section the ruler could dissolve it before expiry of its term or could extend its life beyond three years. But it neither stood dissolved nor its life was extended. So during the deliberations of the Indian Constituent Assembly from 15 August 1947 upto 26 November 1949 there existed an Elected Legislature for J&K which according to the decision taken by the Committee set up by the Chamber of Princess and Corresponding State's Committee of Constituent Assembly of India (in accordance with the Cabinet Mission Plan) had declared the same state legislature as electoral college for election of four members from J&K to the Constituent Assembly with a clear rider that at least two of such four members should have been from its elected group of members. Now let us examine wether this J&K Praja Sabha (Legislature) did elect four members (two from its own elected members) to the Indian Constituent Assembly. If so, inspite of being an insignificant (a microscopic) minority, their involvement with the adoption of the Indian Constitution would bind the people of Jammu and Kashmir in the same manner in which the involvement of so elected three members from Baroda or Jaipur do bind the people of those two erstwhile princely states with this national code of conduct. If in such process either no one is involved from Jammu and Kashmir or if anyone is involved, but he/she has no representative character as agreed by the two committees then such fake involvement cannot contain the people of Jammu and Kashmir within the phrase 'we the people of India' used in the preamble ofthe Indian constitution or any provision (maybe even Article 370). It amounts to imposing of a code of conduct upon the people of Jammu and Kashmir in the same manner in which Government of India Act 1935 was (or any other imperialistic law) imposed by Britishers upon India.

Post-October 1947 events were made to take such turns which were both mysterious and confusing. The mystifying situations, intriguing circumstances and confusing matters were facets of deliberate manoeuvering. In this mystery, confusion and ambiguity the realities were shrouded and not only were people of the world confused, but even the minds of the people of Jammu and Kashmir were bewildered. It is essential to acquaint the readers with the Constitution of J&K Assembly as it stood on 27 October 1947 - the date when the Instrument of Accession was formally executed though the Indian army had since landed in Jammu and Kashmir. The elected members of this house were:

(1) Col. Sansar Singh, (2) Rao Bahadur Thakur Kartar Singh, (3) Capt. Fazal Rehman Khan, (4) Pandit Bala Kak Dhar, (5) Choudhri Birbal, (6) Pandit Dina Nath Kilam, (7) Th. Haqiqat Singh Jamwal, (8) Choudhary Hamidulla Khan, (9) Choudhary Ghulam Mustafa Tur, (10) Malik Ghulam Mohammad, (11) Mirza Mohd. Hussain, (12) Choudhary Shihab-ud-Din, (13) Choudhary Khurshid Ahmad, (14) Sardar Yaar Mohd. Khan, (15) Sardar Mohd. Ibrahim Khan, (16) Ghulam Ahmad, (17) Hakim Mohd. Sadiq. (18) Ghulam Nabi Gilkar, (19) Abdul Gani, (20) Ghulam Mohammad, (21) Malik Gh-Mustafa, (22) Molvi Mohammad Abdulla Shah, (23) M. Habibulla, (24) Safdar Ali, (25) Anayatullah Kakro, (26) Mian Ahmad Yaar, (27)Pandit Prem Nath Dogra, (28) Lala Gopal Dutt Mengi, (29)Capt. Gandharab Singh, (30) Choudhry Mohd. Yousuf, (31) Munshi Ali Mohd. Vakil, (32) Th. Dhantar Singh, (33) Wazir Ganga Ram, (34) Ch. Ram Lal, (35) Pandit Amar Nath, (36) Pandit Shiv Narain Fotedar, (37) Pandit Janki Nath Bhat, (38) Lala Thakur Das Malhotra, (39) Sardar Kulbir Singh, (40) Sardar Baldev Singh.

Among these 40 elected members none was from the weaker sex and only 22 were Muslims representing about 80 per cent of the population whereas 18 were non-Muslims (only 20per cent of total population). Nevertheless, it was an elected house under the constitution which was then in vogue.

None of these 40 members was elected, nominated or selected to the Indian Constituent Assembly nor the four members sent to that Constituent Assembly in June 1949 (when the Constituent Assembly of India had almost completed all the readings of the Constitution) were elected or selected or even nominated—even by fake exercise - by this State Assembly. History does not record that after January 1947 this Assembly was ever allowed to have a Session—even a brief one.

The Maharaja was persuaded to sign the notification of such nomination drafted in South Block, but he declined on the basis of the argument that it was the elected group of the Praja Sabha which could, under agreed formula, elect four members, at least two amongst themselves, to the consembly of India. The hard and 'arrogant' Maharaja prefered to live as a refugee rather than be dictated to by the Private Secretary of Jawahar Lal Nehru. So in June 1949 he signed the proclamation appointing Yuvraj Karan Singh as his Regent. However the notification does not bear any date or number.[1]

But it transpires that much earlier Karan Singh has been made by the masters in South Block New Delhi to act as Regent when according to their claim Hari Singh was well in control of his rule upon Jammu and Kashmir. This conflict is evident in their 'bluffing lies.'

According to Press Communiqué number 36 of 5 March 1948, the Maharaja 'held a Darbar' in Jammu. Conspicuously this Darbar is held three months earlier, i.e., on 11 January 1948 and this royal act bears extraordinary mention of a witness to make it 'believable'. The contents thereof show that the Maharaja of Jaipur was seated on the right side of Hari Singh. (Please refer *Gazette Extra Ordinary J&K Govt. of 5-3-1948* and also *Constitutional History and Documents* by Dr. Teng, Kaul, Bhat Kaul. Further read the book with similar title of Justice. Raja Jaswant Singh retired Judge Supreme Court of India, pp. 190-92). Certain logical questions which throw this proclamation in the mist of doubt will be given precise treatment later on. However, according to it upto 5 March 1948 he was allegedly in authority of his ruled country Jammu and Kashmir. According to Teng, Bhat, Kaul Koul (four Kashmiri Pandit contemporary writers on Kashmiriology) in their book *Supra* quote that the Notification appointing Karan Singh as Regent was published in the *Government Gazette Extra Ordinary* dated 7 Asuj 2006 corresponding to 9 June 1949 ref. p. 547 *Supra*) but the quoted gazetted notification does not give any date of the issuance of this proclamation. Justice Jaswant Singh in his book *Supra,* p. 201 also contains this proclamation under the signatures of Karan Singh, but it too does not bear any date nor mentions in its contents the dates from which the ruler intended to cease to function and from which date the Regent on his behalf would function. Even let us take that Karan Singh was appointed Regent on the same day i.e. 7 Asuj 2006 (9 June 1949) but a proclamation issued in his name as Regent of J&K, contained on p.301 of White Paper Government. of India (ref. Justice Jaswant Singh's book *Supra*) shows that Karan Singh had acted as Ruler of J&K

seven months earlier, i.e., even on 25 November 1948 when he proclaimed:

> "...The Constitutional relationship established between this state and Dominion of India should be continued and Constitution of India as drafted by Constituent Assembly of India, which includes duly 'appointed' representatives of this State....
>
> Now, I hereby declare and direct that the Constitution of India shortly to be adopted by the Constituent Assembly of India in so far, as it is applicable to the state of J&K shall govern the Constitutional relationship...."

This proclamation shows that on 25 November 1948 the four persons from Jammu and Kashmir had already occupied their seats as members of the Indian Constituent Assembly. It further shows they were neither elected by State Legislature nor were selected by the ruling clique nor were nominated by His Highness the Maharaja, but were 'appointees' as civil servants of any class are being appointed to the cadre of that service. While drafting this proclamation in South Block New Delhi in the name of the 18 year old boy ruler installed by political bluffs, the craftsmanship of bluff expertise lost sight of the prevalent position - it neither consulted the secretariat of the Indian Constituent Assembly nor in haste consulted their agents in Srinagar/Jammu. So this factual blunder crept in. It stands exposed by the document issued by the Ministry of Information and Broadcasting Jammu & Kashmir as an introduction to the Instrument of Accession and to the statement of Sheikh Abdulla made on 11 August 1952 explaining the 'Delhi Agreement' before the J&K Constituent Assembly. This pamphlet of 24 pages has suffered deliberate and willful destruction, but one copy has missed this wave, which is preserved under ACC No: 545/G/ACC re-registered on 1 November 1996 and stored with Reference Collections of J&K Archives Srinagar.

Paragraph 4 contained on p 3 of this brochure of J&K Government is a very important source of evidence pointing towards the undercurrent pressures made from the first day of Independence and partition with the designs to merge with manoeuvering, tricks and intrigue all the princely states against the express guarantees enshrined in Cabinet Mission

Plan of 12 May 1946. However, I will confine myself to the theme as when four members of Jammu and Kashmir were enrolled as constitution givers of India and what was the manner of their 'appointment', 'nomination', 'selection' or 'election'. In this context lines 21 to 28 have been quoted:

> "A large number of Indian States were represented in the Constituent Assembly right from the beginning and took full share in the framing of Constitution of India. While the Indian Constituent Assembly was passing through its final stages, four representatives from Jammu & Kashmir were *nominated* to it in June 1949..."

From the first day of Indian occupation of Jammu and Kashmir, i.e., October 26, 1947, the Maharaja was even 'coerced' to nominate four persons (names dictated by South Block) to the Constituent Assembly of India, but he flatly refused and argued to adhere to the Cabinet Mission Plan of 12 May 1946. Sheikh Abdulla tried to persecute and persuade a large number of Praja Sabha members, but neither men from Jammu nor from the Valley obliged him. Finally a fake proclamation of 7 Asuj 2006 (9 June 1949) was forced into being and immediately thereafter on 24 June 1949 a list was issued in which Karan Singh made mention of appointing four persons to the Indian Constituent Assembly and under that authority four 'imposed persons' viz. Sheikh Mohammad Abdulla, his Revenue Minister Afzal Beg, his General Secretary Molvi Masoodi and an office bearer of the ruling clique of the National Conference Moti Ram Baigra took seats in that house with the fathers of Indian Constitution without any locus standi or without opening their lips on its merits and demerits, but to be filmed as signatories of the document so that the viewers are bluffed by occasional display of that film.[2]

This notification does not state these four names, but the annexed list attached in the name of a junior state officer of the rank of under secretary Sardar Teja Singh mentions these four names. The contents of the notification do nowhere mention that a list was annexed to that notification. Inspite of this intriguing circumstance we will not dispute that it was issued by the regent Karan Singh, but why this discrimination? Why was the State Assembly not asked to elect four members? It was because none of these nominated four was an elected member of J&K Assembly, nor would the elected members of Jammu and Kashmir oblige the Indian Prime Minister to elect his four blue-eyed boys Sheikh Abdulla and his lieutenants Beig, Masoodi and Baigra. Thus the State of Jammu and Kashmir was in no manner even indirectly or remotely represented and involved in the framing of Indian Constitution in the manner in which other princely states which acceded to either the dominion of India or Pakistan were involved. It is most unfortunate for the people of this state that they are sandwiched in a mess of Constitutions - Indian Constitution, J&K Constitution, Azad Kashmir Constitution and even Pakistan Constitution, but in the adoption of none of these four constitutions have the people of Jammu and Kashmir or any section been involved in a manner which could be called a democratic manner. Thus for more than five decades the people of Jammu and Kashmir have been subjected to imposed disciplines.

By the so-called consultations with the imposed governments of Jammu and Kashmir various provisions of the Indian Constitution were extended upon Jammu and Kashmir under the orders of the President of India. It takes us to other relevant topics covering the involvement of the Jammu &Kashmir people with presidential elections.

Notes

1. See original notification contained in Note 6 Chapter 6 Part I.
2. Suppression of even a minor fact amounts to a treachary with history and when such suppression of a fact relates a person— (a character connected with moulding of history) amounts, positively to Character assassination. Deeply rooted with such values it is my duty to mention that Shiekh Abdulla refused to associate personally or with his group of the other three with Indian Constituent Assembly unless assured that their participation will be only under Article 7 of Instrument of Accession (Ref. "Kashmir The Troubled Fronters"— India Defence Review Team headed by Maj. Gen Afsir Karim Page 316)

   Article 7 (Accession Deed) reads.

   "Nothing in this Instrument shall be deemed to Commit me in any way to acceptance of any future Constitution of India or to detter my discretion to enter into arrangements with the G.O.I. under any such future Constitution."

   Shiekh's dismissal and detention was due to the Confrontation on this Article and interpretation of the words "me" and "my" used in this article. Shiekh Abdulla insisted the 'me' meant people of J&K and 'my discretion' meant discretion of, his people. But, India had a plan to devise a scheme for creation of such "puppets" who would exercise the peoples, discretion through fradulent proxy. Hence the fraud in the name of elctions has become our destiny.

Chapter 20

Elections of the Presidents of India and J&K Representation

Article 54 of the Indian Constitution provides the procedure and method to elect the President of India. It reads: "Art 54: The President of India shall be elected by the members of the electoral college which consists of:

a) Elected members of both the houses of Parliament.

b) Elected members of the Legislative Assemblies of the states.

According to the explanation the Union Territories of Delhi and Pondicherry also fall within the purview of the definition of the state as far as this article is concerned.

At the time of the elections of the first, second, third and fourth presidents, Jammu&Kashmir had no elected representation in either of the houses of parliament, so, according to the mandate contained in Article 54, the nominated members from this state both to the Lok Sabha and Rajya Sabha could not be included nor were actually included in the electoral college which elected these first four Presidents of India. Readers will share our view about these nominations in the discussions that will follow and will agree that this nomination was completely devoid of any element of representative character. It is during this period that the President of India issued important constitutional application orders extending provisions of Indian Constitution upon Jammu and Kashmir. As far as the second group of the members of the electoral college is concerned, viz., the elected members of J&K Assemblies (Constituent and Legislative) our readers have appreciated that they were not elected. Members of the Constituent Assembly were imposed under a selection without discretion, members of the first Legislative Assembly were imposed under a selection with discretion, members of the second Legislative

Assembly were imposed under a selection made by way of abductions, and the third legislature was the creation of an electoral fraud by way of mass rejections. In these circumstances the inclusion of such members in the electoral college envisaged by Article 54 amounts to political immorality and legally it has similar character for Jammu and Kashmir which the British Crown possessed vis-à-vis British India before 15 August 1947. In the light of this submission made before the court of public opinion we desire to convey that the character of the crop of Presidential Application of Constitutional Orders upon Jammu and Kashmir are similar to the ordinances the British Crown imposed upon its subjects, the citizens of India.

In his address to the J&K Consembly on 11 August 1952 only 362 days before his dismissal, arrest and detention, Sheikh Abdulla declared:

> "Article 324 of Indian Constitution already applies to the state in so far as it relates to elections to parliament and to the offices of President and Vice-President of India". But in reality this article had no application upon J&K upto 1967.

Chapter 21

Popular Leadership

The documentation about the facts and events that took place with the execution of the 'Instrument of Accession' relate to a very vital matter that the offer of accession was accepted with a precondition to install popular leadership of Jammu and Kashmir as rulers of the state so as to facilitate the Indian Government to intervene in these troubled waters.

Meharchand Mahajan the Prime Minister of Maharaja of Kashmir at the relevant time who had, according to his description gone with the letter from the Maharaja to the rulers in New Delhi to seek their intervention writes about this part of the episode in his autobiography: *Looking Back*, (Bombay: Asia Publishing House, 1963):

> "Give us the military force we need. Take the accession, give whatever power you desire to the 'popular party'."

Now who was this popular party? The reply is contained in an excerpt from the same book:

> "It appeared that Sheikh Abdulla had been listening to all this talk while in one of the bedrooms adjoining the drawing room where we were."

We defer the discussion on the veracity of this statement, but presently confine it to discussion on the 'popular party' whom Jawahar Lal Nehru wanted to make the successor to the Maharaja of Kashmir who was waiting in the Corridors. It was Sheikh Mohammad Abdulla whom later on India projected locally, internally and on international level as the only popular leader of the people of Jammu and Kashmir, rather the symbol of their aspirations. Though in 1953 the same Indian leadership projected him as 'an imperialist agent, a communialist and as the traitor of his people.' This stance taken by the Indian leadership from 26 October 1947 to 8 August 1953 that the Sheikh represented the sentiment of the people requires logical analysis.

There are only democratic methods on which popularity or otherwise of a person more so of a leader claiming representative character is to be ascertained. If we determine the popularity of a person on the basis of listeners he attracts as a speaker then the street juggler can claim more popularity than any thinker or an ideologue. It cannot be denied that Sheikh Abdulla would attract thousands as an orator and as he launched the Quit Kashmir movement in June 1946, he received mass support and shook the entire state. Simultaneously, the Poonch Insurgency had caused more threat to the autocracy than Quit Kashmir and Gilgit Scouts shook it completely. The response that these movements received was not for the charisma of one or the other party. On June 19, 1946 the Working Committee of All J&K National Conference rejected unanimously the idea to launch the Quit Kashmir Movement, but next day not only the same leadership of the party supported the move as they found people ready to undo monarchy, but even the Mirwaiz faction of the All J&K Muslim Conference supported the movement. Why? It was charisma in the slogan, the thrill in the adventure, the lava of hatred against the monarch that burst with this slogan and it was a century old reaction against that shameful sale-deed under which a nation along with succeeding generations was sold.

But no sooner as it appeared that Britishers had decided to quit from India, the people understood that this 'hangama' was unnecessary, within one year the tempo in the movement waned so drastically that when Sheikh Abdulla and his colleagues were convicted and punished for sedition no revolution took place not for the reason that the people were overawed by the autocracy, but for the reason that passing of Independence Act by British Parliament had diverted the attention of the people of Jammu and Kashmir towards their immediate future. Initially this movement received good support from the Valley, but it had no support from Jammu. Even the Jammu based Muslim Conference leadership did not support it. It is on the basis of the reaction of Jammu people that Alaister Lamb in his book *Disputed Legacy* writes in particular about the Muslim Conference:

> "It adopted a policy of non-involvement in what is perceived to be a political ploy on the part of Sheikh Abdulla's faction in alliance with Indian National Congress..."

Jammu Hindus were for other reasons, averse to the Quit Kashmir Movement. They considered it broadly a 'Dogra Rule' though common Dogra (Jammu Hindu) did not have a better lot than a Kashmiri common Muslim. On the other hand, districts closely situated to 'would be' Pakistan viz Poonch and Mirpur, had lost any interest in the present or future of autocracy. In their perception the autocracy would immediately cease as the state became part of Pakistan and so took to armed insurgency to force the ruler to adopt a realistic policy. To be precise, at the relevant time when partition and independence of India both had become imminent realities the people had lost interest in Quit Kashmir, they had understood that both, the All India National Congress and All India Muslim League had opened their respective agencies for roping in Jammu and Kashmir in either of the would be dominions. People had understood that Sheikh Abdulla too had compromised with the ego, identity and self respect of the people of Jammu and Kashmir and it is in this background that in the autumn of 1946 only nine or ten months before Indian Independence Sheikh Abdulla's National Conference had adopted a cunning device to run away from the people and boycotted the 1946 elections to the J&K Legislative Assembly called Praja Sabha. It had sufficiently grasped and understood that it would, in the circumstances which were prevalent then, hardly bag any seat from Jammu Province and from the districts of Frontier. In Kashmir Province, i.e., Wazarati Muzzafarabad it would not take a single seat and it would from two wazarats of the Valley, viz., Baramulla and Anantnag, in all bag four to ten seats. Thus, among elected members of 40 legislators it would, at the minimum bag four seats and maximum ten seats. That result would have proved the All J&K National Conference a political group confined only to two wazarats of the Valley. Now what yardstick was adopted by the great democrat of the East, Jawahar Lal Nehru on which he declared and projected Sheikh Mohammad Abdulla as the popular leader of Jammu and Kashmir and on what basis his party National Conference was made to appear as popular party of the state, is easily intelligible. It was just to confuse the democratic forces of India and the world so as to build a fake mandate to the decision of a virtually abdicated monarch, Hari Singh.

We have by the references to 1946 Elections provided valuable clues and inferences to our readers which are reasonable and logical and more so aptly relevant as they relate to happenings which have taken place just immediately before the installation of the so-called popular leader as the ruler of Jammu and Kashmir. Now let us examine the inferences from what happened immediately after this installation.

Firstly, a popular leader and party when comes to power either under the mandate of the people or under the weight of circumstances naturally meets the aspirations of the people to a great extent and to establish the popular rule such a leader or party immediately abrogates the measures of repression let loose by the predecessor rulers against whom this popular leadership had fought and made sacrifices. It is meant to convey that on coming to power Sheikh Abdulla and his party should have undone the harsh laws under which the 'unpopular' autocrat had suppressed the aspirations of his subjects. Instead they introduced new draconian laws like Enemy Agents Ordinance under which scores of people were persecuted and prosecuted. Ban on expression of views and holding of assemblies was so vigorously imposed that the tyrannies of early Dogra rule were put in the background. A British missionary had visited Jammu and Kashmir in 1867 and issued a statement in London. In that statement he had summed up the psyche of the Kashmiris in the following excerpt:

> "The poor Kashmiri is like a mouse trying to drink milk with an army of cats in the same room with him. Spies, reporters, bribery, treachery are all among and around them. They sometimes are afraid to speak much to each other and afraid to talk... to each other, everyone is suspicious of his neighbour."

Under Sheikh Abdulla's so called 'popular rule' the situation in 1948-53 had surpassed the agonies which our forefathers were subjected to and were hinted about in *Supra*. To quote a few stanzas from an Urdu poem, 'Taqdeer-i-Kashmir' (Destiny of Kashmir) by a lesser known poet of Kashmir G.A. Zehri, (composed in 1948-49). It has been composed on the style and diction of the poem 'Tasweer-i-Kashmir' (Picture of Kashmir) by the great Urdu poet of the subcontinent Hafeez Jalandhri. The stanza is:

"Aaj Kashmir kee woh Dilfareebi Hai Kahan,
Dast-i-Qudrat Ney Banaya Thaa Jisey Janat Nishaan.
Baagh Murjhayaa giyaa hai ujdaa Howa Hai Aashiyaan
Ghath main sayaad hain mamnoon hai aaho fugaan
Bulbulon main Howslaa baaqi nahey Taamer kaa
Ek Aanso yeh bee hai kashmir key taqdeer kaa"

(Why have vanished today all those charming attractions of my Kashmir. That Kashmir to which natural craftsmanship had carved into a paradise. Alas! The garden is now a devastated desert, the nests of birds shattered in storms. The hunter (to catch and kill the perching birds) keenly waits behind the bush, Prohibitions are imposed upon the sighs and moaning of so caged and semi-butchered perching birds. The nightingales have been cowed down upon to rebuild (their shattered nests in this wide desert). These expressions only unfold the miseries of its bloody tears.)

'Shiddati Aflaas say har ek sina chaak hai
Aysey wairaaney mein jeney kaa mazaa kiya khak hai
Jow kooyee shahbaaz bhee hai bastayey fitrak hai,
Hai kahan bhonchaal ab tak aah key tabkheer kaa
ek aanso yeh bhi hai kashmir key taqdeer kaa'

Each bosom stands dissected with the acute pangs of poverty, It is to lay on the bed of thorns to live in this desert. In these ruins which convey echoes of cries of agony and frustration the hawks and phoenix have been semi butchered and bundled in bags. To be carried to the rich kitchen of the hunter.

Alas! it is all against the natural process,

That the sighs and lamentation of the victims had not created a stir. Yet no earthquake has shattered the edifice of terror.

Depicting the position of the imposed 'popular' rule in Jammu and Kashmir the poet says:

"Is now aabadi riyasat main hai dilee kaa Nizam
Jis kow bhi chaha Banaaya apney matlab kaa gulaam
Markazi haathon main hai kaarey hakoomat kaa qiyam
Bandayee bay dam hain majboor kashmiri awam
Hai Tasalut har taraf is desh main andheyr kaa
Ek aanso yeh bhi hai kashxmir key taqdeer kaa"

> The writ of Delhi runs in this occupied colony of India.
> It is they who impose rulers upon us only to obey and implement their dictates
> The whole system of governance here is run (on remote control) by the central government in Delhi
> This country (of Kashmir) is on all sides wrapped under blanket of terror.

This stanza provides historical proof that the very installation of Sheikh Abdulla in 1948 generally appeared to the common perception as a neo-colonist imposition because the hawkish eye of the young poet has detected the undercurrent colonist strains on the work culture of the rulers of Jammu and Kashmir. Though till then neither the consembly was by farce imposed nor the agents were changed as we witnessed thereafter. But the strain of terror which remained dominantly transparent on the functioning of Sheikh Abdulla, first as Emergency Administrator and then as Prime Minister (the head of the so-called popular government) provided speaking evidence of the facts that (a)Jammu and Kashmir was ruled as colony; (b)Not only through proxy, but by direct rule from Delhi; (c)This rule had known strains of purchasing the conscience and throwing away such purchased personages with utter contempt; (d)the people of Kashmir were trapped but in an 'invisible' trap, and; (e)the reign of terror was rampant on all sides.

Other stanzas unravel a situation in which the Nazi camps opened particularly in Kothi Bagh (Srinagar) Police Station called Special Staff, other police stations in the state and generally in all the offices of the ruling National Conference on Halqa, village and Mohalla levels. All those were turned into the worst interrogation and persecution centres where people were terribly tortured. All the newspapers which were in circulation during the autocracy were forced to cease publication except the official organ of the ruling party the Urdu daily *Khidmat.* People were forced to subscribe to this newspaper only to feed themselves and their youngsters with false propaganda for and against India and Pakistan respectively. The same impact sums up the situation in this stanza:

> "Bravo, thy journalistic values of the daily paper: "Khidmat", its subscription is obligatory for every person. Thereby

immunity for one year is guaranteed for the subscriber from the unreasonable victimisation. It conveys the news of leaders to the led. Besides that it amounts to the filth and spits of a piles patient."

School children and college students were subjected to forced sodomy by special staff under the overwhelming terror of Ghulam Qadir Ganderbale in charge of this special cell of torture. The respectable members of the gentry were put to public disgrace. With hot irons their bodies were given electric shocks; the women of respectable families like the Khan dynasties of Zachaldara in present Handaware Tehsil of Kupawara district and of village Zogo Kharian in Budgam district were molested; the same tyrant was accorded as a police officer, a Presidential award which he received from the first President Dr. Rajendra Prasad. This recognition to a tyranny eroded the image of the office of the President in the eyes of the Kashmiris.

During this very period the Sheikh government introduced drastic, radical and popular agrarian reforms in the form of Big Landed Estates Abolition Laws, Debt Conciliation Boards established and similar progressive measures were taken. But as human dignity, the self-respect of the people and their political aspirations were subjected to the worst contempt these progressive measures (which are yet to be introduced in the subcontinent), could not pacify the injured sentiments of the people. How could these measures dispel those deep-rooted impressions that were left by this unabated and unparalleled repression? The same leadership which was nourished with love and sacrifices by the people had deceived them mercilessly and compounded the deception and fraud by worst measures of torture. The same leadership which had created awareness in the ranks of the masses about their individual and collective honour perpetuated contempt upon them. This fraud and terror culminated in the shape of imposition of an unopposed 'Selected Constituent Assembly'. Had there been even an iota of truth attached to the claim of the popularity of Sheikh Abdulla neither that tall politician nor his 'democrat' mentor Jawahar Lal Nehru would allow a situation under which such fraud could become a necessity for them. Both would not keep a permanent disability with the J&K Constituent Assembly which had to play a great historic role of far reaching consequences. But as Sheikh Abdulla and Jawahar Lal Nehru were conscious that in spite of the fact that they had wiped out the chances of the growth of any opposition party, they could not win elections, if at all allowed; so the imposition of the 'without discretion selection' of the 75 member assembly became inevitable for both of them.

We have seen that immediately before installation of this, so called popular rule, those new rulers had boycotted elections as per their analysis and assessment that they could not win more than ten seats from elected 40 seats of Praja Sabha (State Legislature). We have seen that immediately after the installation of this so-called 'popular rule' within two years it had no face to face with the electorate of the state, so, the imposition. We have seen that during this intervening period the so-called popular rule had to survive with the measures of terror which in the words of the great Hindu leader from Jammu Shri Prem Nath Dogra, "Nazis too would fear to describe." This discussion exposes the myth that Sheikh Abdulla and his party was at all commanding any popularity with the people of Jammu and Kashmir when under that label of popularity this rule was imposed in October 1947. Maharaja Hari Singh and his Prime Minister both were also conscious of the deception in the phrase 'popular rule' so Meharchand also quotes it in his autobiography within the commas of sarcasm.

Jawahar Lal Nehru had consciously wished the imposition of unpopular leadership under the deceptive label of popularity so as to hoodwink the democratic opinion of the world and accord 'popular' colour to a forced unpopular act of the virtually abdicated ruler. In this purpose he was greatly successful, the other party to the dispute too was not able to expose this fraud. This deception was exercised so tactfully that even English authors like Campbell-Johnson were also hoodwinked. They have observed that in exercise of his sovereign powers Hari Singh acceded to India. It takes us to another sub topic 'The Paramountcy.'

Chapter 22

Myth of Paramountcy and Fiction of Accession

Almost all the analysts in India, even in Jammu and Kashmir and many foreign authors who hold the view that like other princely states of undivided India the ruler of Jammu and Kashmir had also surrendered paramountcy to the British Crown and from August 15, 1947 to October 26, 1947 the Maharaja enjoyed, as an independent ruler, unfettered sovereignty. Sheikh Abdulla, in his August 11, 1952 speech in the J&K Assembly says:

"On 26th October 1947, when the state had become an Independent Sovereign State..."

Let us now examine this position. It is an independent topic which requires separate treatment, but brief hints are necessary here to convey our views on the Indo-Kashmir relationship. Let us quote from the Memorandum of Cabinet Mission dated 12 May 1946 regarding 'states treaties and paramountcy' issued on 25 May 1946:

"...This means that the rights of states which flow from their relationship to the crown will no longer exist and that all the rights surrendered.

They were under British paramountcy which after 14 and 15 August 1947 ceased to vest in it and transferred to the people of those provinces which constituted two independent sovereign countries India and Pakistan. Similarly, the people of Jammu and Kashmir acquired sovereign power upon their state, as it ceased to vest in the British Crown.[1] It is this very strain which dominates Sheikh Abdulla's speech of August 11, 1952 before consembly and his insistence on this position resulted in his dismissal, arrest and detention in 1953. Later, for more than two decades he had the same views.

Here a pertinent question arises. The Maharaja ruled the

state for two months and ten days so it could be construed that he did so as the sovereign power i.e. successor of the British Crown. It requires us to describe the position of this brief spell of his rule from 15 August 1947 to 26 October 1947. The points in brief are:

1. We have known details of the Quit Kashmir Movement which had politically, legally and morally shaken the administration and had exposed the rule of the Maharaja beyond 1946 as one of usurpation.
2. It has also been described that the armed revolt of Poonch had completely eroded the ruling authority of the Maharaja. Alaister Lamb in *Kashmir A Disputed Legacy* writes:

   > "On 23rd October 1947 Ponch rebels formally declared their independence from Maharaja as the state of Azad Cashmere."

3. Gilgit Scouts had ceded the northern districts of the state immediately after the Britishers left India.
4. Finally, the intervenors from the North West Frontier Province mounted such pressure upon the Maharaja that he was forced to quit in a huff and left his state to be ruled by chaos.
5. That formally the Instrument of Accession is reported to have been executed on October 26, 1947, but much earlier than that date Indian forces were detected by locals active in fighting positions around Srinagar city and particularly around the only aerodrome situated on Damodhar Karewa. The small section of conscious group of people which could make out this distinction in time factor were immediately terrorised, thrown across the cease-fire line or were contained through soft measures. In this confusing situation villagers around the aerodrome had to migrate to safer places. G.A. Zehri, an outstanding Persian, Urdu and Kashmiri poet also migrated from Ichigam to Charar-i-Sharief (the home town of this author) and deposed about the presence of the Indian Army in his area much before 26 October 1947.
6. The fleeing caravan of the Maharaja demonstrated frustration in such a manner which consolidated the

communal anger of the Jammu RSS cadre. This consolidation found the scattered Muslim population unprepared, undefended and confused and targeted them under royal instigation. This massacre was unprecedented in the history of Jammu and Kashmir. Sheikh Abdulla, in his autobiography *Atish Chinar* gives a lucid description as to how in the caravan of the Maharaja, his wife Maharani Tara Devi, stood like a symbol of divine wrath on the platform of the vehicle. She had unravelled her tresses like a stone image of angry Mahakali and made the communal sentiments to rise in anger against her own subjects which could be done only by such a ruler who out of revenge, leaves his domain to destruction.

7. The record vill show that after mid October 1947 till his death the Maharaja never paid even a brief visit to Srinagar, his summer capital.
8. The record seems to have been fabricated and distorted in a manner which provides the presumptive inferences that the ruler had been abdicated in real sense of the term, but his ghost in the shape of his minor son was imposed by the cunning manoeuvering of the Prime Minister of India Jawahar Lal Nehru in which the Prime Minister of Jammu and Kashmir Sheikh Abdullah was outwitted. These circumstances prove that Sheikh Abdulla too was imposed under intriguing developments of the situation. Here we will make reference to a royal proclamation about holding of the Darbar on January 11, 1948 and its publication in *Government of J&K Gazette (Extra Ordinary)* on Friday 5 March 1948. This proclamation is contained herein:

> "In accordance with the tradition of my dynasty I have from time to time, provided for increasing association of my people with the administration of the state with the object of realising the goal of full responsible government as early as possible and in pursuance of that object have, by the J&K Constitution Act 1939 established a constitutional government with a council of ministers, a legislature with a majority of elected members. I have already appointed the *popular leader of my-people* Sheikh Mohammad Abdulla (stress added) as the Head of

Emergency Administration. It is now my desire to replace the emergency administration *by a popular* (stress added) interim government with powers...."

This proclamation has two exceptional characteristics which no royal proclamations before ever had. Firstly, it specifies the time of holding of the Durbar on 11 January 1948. Secondly, it specifically mentions that the Maharaja of Jaipur was seated on the right side of Hari Singh. Now let us put the following questions for the consideration of our conscious readers:

a. Why was this peculiar deviation made in this proclamation to specify time and mention the name of a 'witness' to the otherwise royal act which attaches presumption of truth to it? Does it mean that there was some guilty conscience which made the authors of the contents of this proclamation deviate from usual tradition? It is more so because the deviation in both the cases was irrelevant or at least unnecessary.
b. What necessitated the authors of this proclamation to make it believable subject to the testimony of a royal quest? Before this proclamation a number of Durbars have been held by His Highness the Maharaja under the benign presence of his close friend the Maharaja of Patiala, but no proclamation issued after such sessions of the royal court made direct or indirect mention of the presence of that royal guest. Does it therefore mean that this Royal Court was held under such suspicious circumstances which required testimony of a witness?
c. This proclamation makes a clear admission that the 1939 Constitution Act was in vogue even on 11 January 1948, it had not been abrogated.
d. That there existed a government established under the said Act of 1939 with a council of ministers with a mandate from elected members of the state assembly. It is a clear admission in the deed.
e. That the ruler had appointed the popular leader of people viz. Sheikh Mohammad Abdulla as head of the Emergency Administration.
f. In presence of a popular government consisting of the council of ministers with a mandate from elected members of legislature how was the Emergency Administration

established? Does this mention in the proclamation connote that the popular government was dismissed and in its place the Emergency Administration was established, or does it mean that the very popular government was converted into Emergency Administration. This assertion is against facts. After the election of 1946 the ruler did not appoint any popular government with a direct or indirect mandate from the elected members of the Praja Sabha. Instead he dismissed his Prime Minister Ram Chand Kak, a person not acceptable to the newly established Indian Government and appointed Meharchand Mahajan, the choice of the Indian Home Minister Sardar Vallabh Bhai Patel in his place. Thereafter, in the last week of October he appointed Sheikh Abdulla as Head of Emergency Administration who according to democratic norms had no popular support as he and his party had not faced the electorate. We have earlier discussed in detail that at the time of taking over as Emergency Administrator Shiekh Abdulla had neither popular mandate nor did he dare to face the electorate immediately after his appointment as Prime Minister under the proclamation supra, but he imposed a selected assembly in 1950.

Thus it is stressed that the claim made in this proclamation about the so-called popularity of Sheikh Abdulla was nothing but fiction. After January 1947 the State Legislature never met and neither Meharchand government nor Abdulla Government were established under the 1939 Constitution.

g. The Maharaja had sufficient understanding of the mass support which Sheikh Abdulla enjoyed. He had assessed that inspite of the fact that Sheikh Abdulla attracted huge congregations he had no solid mass support in all the regions of the state. So the Maharaja had never accepted Sheikh Abdulla as a popular leader. It, therefore, becomes manifestly clear to the students of contemporary Kashmir history that there had been some extraneous force which imposed these phrases and words in the proclamation. Such inferences make this proclamation a doubtful document with many discrepancies and contradictions.

h. Under the J&K Constitution Act of 1939 an elected legislature existed even during January-March 1948 with majority of the elected members whose names have been given before. Sheikh Abdulla who was appointed Prime Minister under this proclamation (Supra) was not a member of that assembly nor had his deputy Bakshi Ghulam Mohammad contested elections for the assembly nor had any of his cabinet colleagues G.M. Sadiq, Mirza Afzal Beig, G.L. Dogra, Col. P.M. Khan and S.L.Saraf contested elections for this assembly. How can the government consisting of such people who had not faced the electorate be qualified as a popular government? For more than three months after holding of this durbar why was this proclamation not published? All these circumstances are intriguing and greatly erode credibility of this proclamation. Hence, this proclamation with eroded credibility becomes an important ground to doubt the presence of the Maharaja in Jammu and Kashmir and these eight points lead to the conclusion that the Maharaja of Kashmir did not command sovereignty on Jammu and Kashmir which on 15 August 1947 lapsed in the British Crown.

9. According to records on November 7, (2006), i.e., June 9, 1949, Hari Singh appointed a Regent, but the Regent acted as the Ruler even on 25 November 1948 when he bound this state to the would be Constitution of India and appointed four representatives (unnamed) to the Indian Constituent Assembly. It fortifies the propaganda of the National Conference cadre, its leadership and the public speeches of Sheikh Abdulla as Emergency Administrator that he had 'overthrown' the Dogra dynasty and made the royal family petty refugees of Bombay. Most pertinent here is the speech which he delivered while 'mutating' the landed estate of late Maharaj Kishen Dhar and his first cousin Maya Devi at Gopalpura Chadoora(a kilometer from my residence of Durj-i-Gauhar) among their tenants. The speech is covered in the Urdu daily *Khidmat*, Srinagar.

After Hari Singh abdicated he settled in Bombay, as Indian city, where he was an ordinary citizen, subject to Indian laws and governed by the municipal laws of that city. From Bombay the Indian Government made him appoint his minor son Karan Singh as his regent. The abdicated king assumed to himself sovereignty and India which had militarily occupied Jammu and Kashmir in the name of the same 'disqualified' power, facilitated this appointment. By this Bombay-based proclamation the so appointed regent Karan Singh acquired the power which vested under the provisions of J&K Constitution Act 1939 in the Maharaja. After imposing an assembly to draft the constitution for the state and before the constitution could be passed the so appointed regent surrendered his regency and opted for the elected post of the Sadr-i-Riyasat (Head of State). Hence, whatever paramountcy or absolute power vested in the dynasty till this regency automatically ceased and it now vested in the people.[1] Consequently, the sovereignty in unambigious terms vested in the subjects of the erstwhile ruler ie the people of divided Jammu & Kashmir. In the Constitution Act 1939 no necessary amendments, defining the powers of so elected Head of State, (Sadr-i-Riyasat) were made. Those powers were defined in the Constitution Bill which had yet to become a law, so there was no document or code of conduct which would have provided powers, duties and prerogatives of this new office of Sadr-i-Riyasat. Those provisions had to become law which in the Constitution Bill provided the specific course in that direction. But the law in vogue (1939 Constitution) did not even make a mention of the office of the Sadr-i-Riyasat.

This assessment will get fortified if we quote the existing provision and its amended nature. Section 5 of 1939 Constitution Act reads:

> "Notwithstanding anything contained in this or in any Act, all powers legislative, judicial and executive in relation to the state and its government are hereby declared to be and have been always inherent in and possessed and retained by His Highness."

It is pertinent to contain herein the amended provision in section 7 of this Constitution Act. It reads:

> "The Council shall consist of the Prime Minister appointed by His Highness. Prime Minister and other ministers shall be collectively responsible to the Legislative Assembly...." (Act No. XVIII of 2008 (1950 A.D.)"

The Amendment Act of 2008 (Bik) read with the 20 June 1949 Notification almost deleted such power in His

Highness and its effect as summed up by Dr. Adarsh Sen Anand (Chief Justice of India). The excerpt is quoted below:

> "So there was no longer any inherent power of legislation vested in Yuvraja Karan Singh."

On the basis of this amendment supra and comments (within lines) of Chief Justice Dr. Anand bring us to square one that after accepting the elected post of Sadr-i-Riyasat for temporary period the 'powers' contained in the almost ineffective document of 1939 Constitution Act were also erased like those of misspelt words. A repetition is needed to show how the Constitution Act of 1939 was ineffective. We know that by the end of 1946 the state elected a legislature under the said Constitution Act. The said legislature was convened in January 1947. It transacted business by electing its President and by having some discussions about the nature of the relationship of the state which it should prefer to adopt with India and Pakistan as Independence and Partition had become a reality then. Views were expressed both by elected and nominated members. Either opinions for accession with Pakistan were expressed or a strong case for independent Jammu & Kashmir country was made out. But no proposal was adopted. The Royal Proclamation supposed to have been issued on January 11, 1948 and issued in *Government Gazette Extra Ordinary,* March 5, 1948 made a farce with this Constitution. It makes mention of a constitutional government with a council of ministers established in the state. Without abrogation or amendment of the 1939 Constitution Act which would suit the installation of Sheikh Abdulla he was imposed under the label of 'popular' leadership. This installation had neither a popular mandate nor was made voluntarily by the ruler. It was rejected by the subjects and fraudulently done by the rulers of India where he lived as a refugee.

All these events which took place from August 1947 upto 1950 (till passing of the Act No. XIII of 2008 bill) created such a confusing situation that the sovereignty claimed for the Maharaja of Kashmir appears only a myth. It is a rather puzzling riddle which can hardly be solved by any direct evidence. The situation which emerges from these circumstances is to be given the pro-people, pro-democracy and pro-freedom interpretation. It cannot be interpreted in favour of autocracy or in favour of a despot nor in favour of the consequential relief derived from a sale of land. The origin of occupation of Jammu and Kashmir sought to be accepted is the sale-deed of Amritsar in 1846 under which English usurpers had transferred their rights to Gulab Singh, the predecessor of Hari Singh. The core point and the result of these discussions, therefore, is that the people of Jammu and Kashmir had challenged this usurpation and its authority was by stages overthrown. The abdicated ruler was used to create a fiction of accession by the new occupant of Jammu and Kashmir, i.e., the Indian government.

Paramountcy stood transferred to the people of J&K by the circumstances indirectly and by direct surrender of it by Yuvraja Karan Singh in 1950 hence, some pertinent questions arise for consideration of students of jurisprudence, international law and constitutional law. These questions are formulated as:

- Is the sovereignty divisible? If so has it partly vested in the erstwhile subjects of the ruler living on this side of the LAC and partly in the people living in PoK?
- Have the divided people ever collectively or through 'untainted' representation exercised their sovereign will in any manner to constitute their code for national life?
- If people on any side have done so can their decision bind the other side?

In the first part we have seen that the Constituent Assembly of 75 members was purely an immoral imposition and soon became discredited it was against those very norms and cannons for which this imposed body had been established. It has also been seen that passing of the 1974 Constitution for Azad Kashmir was a similar fraud. Both these 'exercises' have been the result of neo-colonist imposition on the occupied people of Jammu and Kashmir.

The above discussion is relevant to assess the legal, political and moral grounds of the Instrument of Accession executed by the ruler logically, abdicated much earlier than 26 October 1947 which date this deed bears as the date on which it was executed.

Azad Kashmir was declared independent four days before execution of the claimed instrument of accession.

The common assertion of the people supported by the statements issued by Sheikh Abdulla and the National Conference was that on August 15, 1947 the sovereignty had passed to the people of Jammu and Kashmir. Does it, therefore, mean that, that part has inherited sovereignty on behalf of all the erstwhile subjects of the Maharaja. Is Azad Kashmir the real successor to paramountcy vested upto August 15, 1947 in the Maharaja or does the 'action' of eroded monarchy imposing authority upon this part of Kashmir attribute genuine sovereignty with such imposed schemes?

Confusion has been created by the connivance or suppression of facts by eminent commentators of the Indian Constitution like Chittaley, Serivai, M. Hidayatullah, D.D. Basu and even by other eminent scholars of Kashmiriology like Crambell-Johnson, Alaister Lamb (who is charged with a pro-Pak tilt) and many others. They have not cared to discuss the involvement or otherwise of the people of Jammu and Kashmir in framing of the Indian Constitution nor have they dived deeper into the intricacies of the subject of sovereignty. They have all presumed that like other princes, the Jammu and Kashmir ruler had surrendered paramountcy which reverted to him on August 15, 1947 and then from 26 October he exercised unfettered sovereign powers. They did not consider the impact the Quit Kashmir Movement left upon the claim of sovereignty nor did they consider the effect of the Gilgit Revolution, the consequences of tribal intervention nor did they consider the nature of the rule of the Maharaja's dynasty.

These authors have, besides arrived at some conclusions without a rational study that Sheikh Abdulla was a popular leader of Jammu and Kashmir in 1947 who 'avoided' to take part in the 1946-47 elections and who for apprehensions about an unfavourable mass verdict imposed an unelected Constituent Assembly in 1950.

Such conclusions at which they arrived without study could be accepted as genuine had these authors made a rational and unbiased analysis, with constructive approach, of all these matters. But the manner in which they based their conclusions, without a probe, fortifies the local contention that either they were swayed by the halo around leaders of independent India who then projected the values in the aspirations of struggling colonial people or were won over by the 'big' Asian democracy.

Characteristics of the only commentary on the J&K Constitution by Dr.A.S. Anand: *Constitution of J&K—Its Development And Comments* shows how facts have been suppressed. Dr. Anand has acted under known pressure as is evident from the manner of his discussions about the relationship of Sheikh Abdulla with India or when he comments upon Sheikh's dealings with Pakistan. In the former case when Sheikh Abdulla is cordial with India the learned author appreciates him, but when his relationship with India is under strain the author's assessment tilts in favour of India. Similarly, the author usually lauds Sheikh Abdulla for his role when it is tough against Pakistan. Dr. Anand occupying a great position in the Indian judiciary, has not cared even to consult the book by Subha Rao *Framing of Indian Constitution* as to the constitutional relationship of Jammu and Kashmir and India. He has been remote successor of M.C. Mahajan who for the script of drama of accession reached this highest pinnacle of the judicial heirarchy.

These discussions are meant to convey that facts have purposely been suppressed. The great Urdu poet Mirza Ghalib inferred unpleasant realities lie behind suppression *"Kuch Too Hai Jiski Parda Daari Hai"* (There is something for which veils and masks are worn).

The second point which invites discussion is the scrutiny of evidence which has so far come forth on the documentation of the Jammu and Kashmir 'accession' with India. This 'occurrence' as emerges from such depositions took place at York Road (Moti Lal Marg) the official residence of the Indian Prime Minister Jawahar Lal Nehru. It was witnessed by Jawahar Lal Nehru, Meharchand Mahajan, Vallabh Bhai Patel and Sheikh Abdulla. The fifth man K.P.S. Menon was not present on the spot. Meharchand Mahajan tried to persuade Jawahar Lal Nehru, the latter rebuffed him, Patel pacified Mahajan and stopped him from proceeding to Lahore. Meanwhile, the presence of the fourth character emerges. Sheikh Abdulla prevailed upon Nehru and Mahajan finally presented the letter of accession and requested Nehru to 'give power' to the leader, who, in his estimation, had popular support in Jammu and Kashmir.

Thus this narrative makes four characters conversant with the actual happening of the accord called accession. These four persons are: Jawahar Lal Nehru, Sardar Vallabh Bhai Patel, Lala Meharchand Mahajan and Sheikh Mohammad Abdulla. The first two have not left any written memoirs of this incident whereas, the latter two had occasion to contain these details exhaustively in their autobiographies. It is on the basis of details provided in the autobiography of Meharchand Mahajan *Looking Back* (New Delhi/Bombay: Asia Publishing House,1963) that Lt. Gen. (retd.) M.L. Chhibber in his book *Pakistan's Criminal Folly in Kashmir* puts discussions on Accession of J&K with India under a very appropriate heading viz.: 'The Drama of Accession of J&K to India.' The qualification of this act as a 'drama' is but a natural conclusion after reading these details provided in Mahajan's book. To be precise we have this evidence from the main character, rather the broker of the deal. Maharaja Hari Singh lived many years after this drama, but never broke his silence nor kept any record about it.

Another important witness who 'deposed' the facts about this drama is Sheikh Abdulla who has given detailed treatment to the drama in his autobiography *Atish Chinar* (Srinagar: Ali Mohammad Sons) In this he has quoted extensively from *Looking Back*. Thus, while writing these details he had constantly followed the earlier deposition of Mahajan. In spite of this there are certain deviations which cannot be considered ordinary omissions or natural variances which in narration of an event logically creep into the testimony of two witnesses. But, on the other hand, in the circumstances, such deviations amount to deliberate suppression of details and further amount to contradictions in the testimony of the two statements. Such contradictions between the depositions of the two main witnesses of the 'occurrence' provide very serious implications and even erode the veracity of both. To appreciate this contention let the readers of this book get access to both the relevant portions of these depositions.

The following excerpt from Mahajan's book is most relevant:

> "...I requested immediate military aid on any terms. I said somewhat empathically that the town of Srinagar must be saved at any cost from loot and destruction. During the talk the

Prime Minister said even if the town was taken by the tribesmen, India was strong enough to retake it. Its recapture, however, could not have undone the damage that would have resulted. I therefore formally but respectfully insisted for the acceptance of my request for immediate military aid. The Prime Minister observed that it was not easy at the spur of moment to send troops as such an operation required considerable preparation and arrangement, and troops could not be moved without due deliberation merely on my demand. I was however adamant in my submission; the Prime Minister also was sticking to his own view. As a last resort, I said, "give us the military force we need. Take the accession and give whatever power you desire to the popular party. The army must fly to save Srinagar this evening or else I will go to Lahore and negotiate terms with Jinnah." When I told the Prime Minister of India that I had orders to go to Pakistan in case immediate military aid was not given, he naturally became upset and in an angry tone said; 'Mahajan go away'. I got up and was about to leave the room when Sarder Patel detained me by saying in my ear, 'of course, Mahajan, you are not going to Pakistan'. Just then a piece of paper was passed over to the prime Minister. He read it and in a loud voice said 'Sheikh Sahib also says the same thing'. It appeared that Sheikh Abdulla had been listening to all this talk while sitting in one of the bedrooms adjoining the drawing room where we were. He now strengthened my hands by telling the Prime Minister that the military help must be sent immediately. This came as a timely help for the success of my mission to New Delhi. The Prime Minister's attitude changed on reading this slip..."

This episode had taken place in the official residence of the Prime Minister of India at York Road now Moti Lal Nehru Marg New Delhi on 26 October 1947 when V.P. Menon and M.C. Mahajan flew to Delhi from Jammu. They drove straight to the Prime Minister's house, but V.P. Menon was not with them in that room. There were only three persons Nehru, Patel and Mahajan. Sheikh Abdulla did not enter this room, but sent a slip from the adjoining bedroom where he was listening to the conversation. The slip of paper mentioned 'military help must be sent immediately.' This slip came as a timely help to the broker of the deal.

Now before we examine the statement of Mahajan, let us quote relevant excerpts from *Atish Chinar* the autobiography of Sheikh Abdulla. It has mainly quoted Meharchand Mahajan. His account corroborates the details of discussion amongst the trio, but gives a different version about his intervention. After quoting Mahajan's remarks to Jawahar Lal Nehru 'either to send the military or he would go to Pakistan,' Sheikh Abdulla describes Jawahar Lal Nehru's anger and his intervention. He says:

> "How could Jawahar Lal tolerate such warnings, he lost his temper and when he used to lose his temper, the situation could take any untoward turn. He in angry mood warned Mahajan that if he was eager he might go to Pakistan and warned him to vacate forthwith from his place. Panditjee was incoherently uttering some words that like a burning flame he came out of the room (where?) I saw him in that infuriated angry mood and enquired cause from him. Then I with love pacified and impressed upon him that situation did not demand to lose temper and in case appropriate decision at the nick of time is not taken the situation would slip away from our grip, the snake will run away and we will remain beating behind the bush...." (translated from Urdu)

He writes that after he got Nehru pacified the document of accession was signed.[2]

I am conscious that I am not as a presiding officer of some civil court sifting the evidence recorded about the execution of an agreement deed involving a promise about creation or extinguishment of some right upon a petty immovable property. I am consciously aware that I discuss the nature of an international treaty. It is admitted by the parties to the treaty that they both had sovereign powers and were executing the treaty in that character. But it is to be borne in mind that this deed affects my honour, my safety, my present, my future and even the fate of my progeny.... So I have every right to sift it on the touchstone of reason and logic. The matter, I am sure, is not subjudice before any court of law, but really is under trial before the world public opinion, before the genuine democrats of India who are above chauvinism. I believe in their inherent values of Indianness and believe that they are above intrigue and do adhere to fairness. Hence, the sifting of these two statements—the only evidence available about the drama of accession—is exclusively made for such sections who love and cherish to remain informed, who resist to feed their sentiment with misinformation or disinformation. The discussion in brief is contained within a few points.

Mahajan had stated that Sheikh Abdulla was in the adjoining bedroom of the Prime Minister's residence at York Road New Delhi where Mahajan alongwith Jawahar Lal Nehru and Patel all were busy in discussions. Sheikh Abdulla on the other hand, contradicts Mahajan about the location and says, "That angry Nehru came out from the drawing room probably strolling towards the lawn in an angry mood" when Sheikh Abdulla met him. Thus, firstly Sheikh Abdulla contradicts the assertion of Mahajan that the former was at the relevant time in the adjoining bedroom. Secondly, Sheikh Abdulla contradicts the assertion of Mahajan to the extent that former overheard what transpired between the two prime ministers. On the other hand, Sheikh Abdulla enquires the cause of anger from Nehru who conveys to him what had transpired between him and Mahajan. Thirdly, Sheikh Abdulla falsifies the statement of Mahajan that he had sent a written slip to Jawahar Lal Nehru which he read and remarked that, "Sheikh too had approved the request of Mahajan." It could be argued that these contradictions were natural as the two could not have remembered the details of the incident, but we have seen that while making this historical deposition Sheikh Abdulla had refreshed his memory by regular study of Mahajan's biography. Sheikh Abdulla in these descriptions quotes extensively from Mahajan's book *Looking Back* had refreshed every detail of the occurrence for Sheikh Abdulla and he had known from reading that book where Mahajan had located him. Instead he provides different location of his placement and different mode of his reaction. This is not merely an ordinary omission, but a material contradiction. Here certain questions do logically arise: Why Sheikh Abdulla 'intentionally' is at variance with the statement of Mahajan when Mahajan's testimony was constantly under his study?. The variance is about the location where from Sheikh Abdulla intervened in the discussions. According to Mahajan Sheikh Abdulla was in the adjoining bedroom and overhearing the conversation sent in a slip. Sheikh Abdulla either deliberately hides his location of the bedroom and so denies flatly that he overheard the conversation or Mahajan intentionally drags Sheikh Abdulla to that location or both deliberately hoodwink their contemporaries and successors. Lt.Gen, (retd.) Chhibber rightly infers from this dramatised situation that 'accession' claimed was a drama.

Sheikh Abdulla compiled his autobiography after his reconciliation with India in 1975 so corroborated Mahajan's testimony. Had he written it when he was interned as a prisoner it would have been quite different. Had he written it during his period of penance from 1970 to February 1975 when he was totally engrossed in the reconstruction of Hazratbal Shrine; he would have been truthful to history. It needs to be mentioned that as soon as Mahajan's book came in the market, late Kh. Mubarik Shah of Baramulla provided one copy to Sheikh Abdulla, but the latter qualified it as a 'bundle of lies.' But while giving his own account, he made the same 'bundle of lies' as his source. The question arises as to why he should particularly create contradictions about his location. The reply is inherent in the psychology of his people of which both Sheikh Abdulla and Mahajan were conscious. The introduction of 'bedroom' was either intentional mischief committed by Mahajan aware of probable inferences which the sensitive Kashmiris would draw about the character of Sheikh Abdulla or Sheikh was sufficiently conscious of those inferences which the sensitive masses would deduce and deliberately ran out from the 'bedroom'.

The episode as put by both these characters of the drama: Mahajan and Sheikh has all the characteristic of Indian 'filmi' (Bollywood) fiction. It has similar development, characterisation, suspense, etc., as Indian movies have. By introducing the location of bedroom Meherchand makes it not a political or legal fiction, but a romantic fiction. The 'bedroom hero' the so-called popular mass leader of Jammu and Kashmir is conscious of this mischief so contradicts, without formal denial, his presence at that specified location and invites formidable cracks in the veracity of the statements of both.

It has become a material variation between the only two available depositions. Mahajan makes Sheikh Abdulla a witness who without any intervention fully heard the conversation between the two prime ministers - the small prime minister who had come to assimilate his being with the bigger prime minister and the bigger who was reluctant to allow assimilation. But Sheikh Abdulla on his part denies overhearing what had transpired between the two and states that he gathered information of details from a party to the conversation.

The impact which the comparative study of these two books leaves upon the mind of the common reader is only one and that is that both versions are concocted fiction.

It also remains unexplained as to what happened to that letter which Mahajan had with him for Jinnah? It is also not explained whether both the letters of accession had signatures of the ruler because Mahajan had started from Nehru's house for the journey to Lahore with the Maharaja's letter when he was stopped by Patel. 'It shows that he was equipped with two documents from the same executant'. Does it mean that without canceling the other (in favour of Pakistan) that became automatically ineffective as only one letter of accession was acted upon. Conscious of these infirmities in this confused affair of accession, Jawahar Lal Nehru himself offered to the people of Jammu and Kashmir, to Pakistan and to the world at large the exercise of right of self determination to be exercised by the real sovereign authority—the people of Jammu and Kashmir.

It is unfortunate that the Pakistan Government was at the relevant time though manned by the best talent available, but was devoid of maturity or had no credibility in the world to expose the Indian policy of transparent bluffs. They could neither expose the myth in assumed sovereignty,[3] nor could erode the basis of the claim of popular leadership in Jammu and Kashmir nor were able to understand and highlight the fiction of accession scripted by Jawahar Lal Nehru and woven around the fictional personalities as its characters. In my earlier book *Hazratbal—Central Stage of Kashmir Politics* I have stated that Pakistani rulers and leadership of the All India Muslim League was ignorant of the geography of Jammu and Kashmir; reference is made to the following extract:

> "Probably both the Muslim League leadership...were not fully aware of the topography of the state of J&K or they committed strategic blunders by leaving that entry unsealed which the Redcliff commission had mischievously opened for India at Pathankot...."

My contention stands fortified and statement corroborated by the admission of Shaukat Hayat Khan's admission. I am thankful to Molvi Wahi-ud-Din Khan who has quoted the excerpt relevant to my study in his monthly *Al-Risala*. With gratitude to both the Khans I quote from the Urdu translation of Shaukat's book, *The Nation that Lost its Soul* (as contained in *Al Risala* June 2001-No 295):

> "I met Liaquat Ali Khan Prime Minister as the minister connected with Kashmir affairs and told him that we must accept the offer from Sardar Patel Home Minister of India and disengage ourselves from meddling in Hyderabad state so that reciprocally India keeps its hands off from Jammu and Kashmir, but Liaquat Ali said that he was not ready to undergo this bargain under which he is asked to surrender Hyderabad, a bigger region than the Punjab, for the hills and mountains of Kashmir. It showed his ignorance of geography..."

To conclude it is summed up that on 15th August 1947 on the lapse of sovereignty in the crown it was transferred to the people of J&K. The Maharaja continued as ruler under the authority of Amritsar Treaty from 15th August to 23rd October or at the transferring sovereignty in favour of J&K Maharaja Pro-autocracy inferences cannot be drawn. But it is to be presumed that he either unsurped the authority after the expiry of the "Amritsar Lease" or exercised such authority on behalf of his people. Because, in the situation which took place after March 1946 and particularly after the British did quit India, the ruler whose basis to rule and authority to rule, both had eroded, could not claim sovereignty. The topic will get seperate treatment in my next book.

Notes

1. Under Treaty of Amritsar executed in 1846 the British has retained sovereignty of of this state with it and did not transfer to Gulab Singh, hence the question of reversion of sovereignty to State Maharaja under Independence of India Act does not arise. It was before the execution of Amritsar Treaty with British Crown, continued with British Crown under Clause X and so was transferred to the people of Jammu and Kashmir in the similar manner in which the British sovereignty upon provinces of British India was transferred to the people of those provinces. Pertinent is to quote the relevant excerpt from the Treaty of Amritsar:-

   "(X)Maharaja Gulab Singh acknowledges that the supremacy upon the state shall remain with British government. He will in token of such supremacy present annually to British government one horse, twelve perfect goats of approved breed. . . ."

2. The selection and choice of words reveal that tilt in the sentiments of a narrator. Here Meharchand Mahajan justifies the reaction of Jawahar Lal Nehru ". . . .he naturally became upset. . . ." Use of the qualifying word "naturally" justifies the reaction of Nehru to the requests of the narrator. It reveals that the narrator (Mahajan) had identity in sentiments with the listener (Nehru). It thus lends support to the view of Ram Chand Kak that Mahajan was installed by the Indian Government as Prime Minister of Jammu and Kashmir at this critical juncture and later he was paid for his role of confusing the 'word' by his elevation as judge and then as Chief Justice of India.
3. The "Instrument of Accession" on which India based its superior claim on J&K reserves for the ruler the acts in exercise of sovereign rights, though it had since transferred to his subjects. It is in the circumstances untenable and unintelligible as under which authority the Delegation of J&K Government imposed by New Delhi under a bluff of popularity participated in the deliberations with Government of India delegation in 1952 and agreed the erosion of the conditions laid down and accepted in the Instrument of Accession. Para (7) of this document binds that 'nothing shall be deemed to commit me in any way to acceptance of any future Constitution of India to fetter my discretion. . . ." In this behalf the Government of India White Paper (page 371) discloses that the Regent Karan Singh had on 25, November 1948 committed his government to future Constitution of India which was then in making but two points need to appreciate.

   (a) Regent was appointed on June 9, 1949.

   (b) Four "nominees" were appointed to India (See Note 6 Chapter 6 ante) Constituent Assembly much after, though the Notification issued in the name of Regent (office never existed then) on 25, November 1948 falsely claims that four members had been earlier appointed to dominion Consembly. A mere bluff.

Chapter 23

The First Three Indian Parliaments: J&K Representation

The first Indian Parliament was constituted after passing of the Indian Constitution. It is explained and elucidated in the first chapter of this part that Jammu and Kashmir had no representation in that dominion consembly. Such was the case with the first three parliaments elected by the people of India (except the people of Jammu and Kashmir) in 1952, 1957 and 1962. In such a situation the provisions contained in the constitution of India regarding Jammu and Kashmir including Article: 370 were all a one way traffic and such provisions amounted to the assurances and commitments of the people of India and do, in no case, bind the people of Jammu and Kashmir. However, such assurances and commitments bind all successive Indian people which the forefathers of the Indian Constitution made or granted as commitments to the people of Jammu and Kashmir. Similarly, the 'erosions' made by these three parliaments or by the apex authorities elected by such parliaments in those very assurances and commitments which Indian Constitution had made with the people do also amount to one way traffic. Such decisions, provisions of legislation or presidential orders of the applications of the provisions of Indian Constitution are also a unilateral exercise which does not bind the people of Jammu and Kashmir. It is in this background that the people of Jammu and Kashmir dismissed these constitutional intrusions as acts of consolidating the occupation rather to involve the people of Jammu and Kashmir to assimilate their political and economic aspirations with the similar aspirations of the people of India. Each act of intrusion added causes to the process of alienation.

It is pertinent to explain in categorical terms the nature of representation to the Indian Parliaments from Jammu and Kashmir.

The First Parliament

Six seats were allotted from Jammu and Kashmir to the Indian Parliament. Neither the electoral segments for these six constituencies were delimited nor defined nor any specific *modus operandi* was evolved for distribution of those seats. It has been succintly explained in this chapter that the J&K National Conference government under Sheikh Abdulla was imposed in 1948 under an attractive, but mischievous use of the phrase 'popular government'. We have exposed the mischief and explained the selection without discretion under which Sheikh Abdulla put the seal of elections upon the selection which was in reality an imposition. We have stated the manner in which he managed '75' members of his party to become unopposed representatives of the people. It was to hide his unrepresentative and unpopular character. Hence, in the situation just before and after the convening of the first Indian Parliament there was no representative government in Jammu and Kashmir. It was a government imposed by occupying forces of India upon the people of Jammu and Kashmir. The same imposed government was asked to nominate six representatives to the Indian parliament and Sheikh Abdulla in a similar manner of selection without discretion picked up six persons and despatched them to New Delhi to 'represent' people of Jammu and Kashmir (including those in Azad Kashmir) in Indian Parliament.

The Second Parliament

In 1953 Sheikh Abdulla, described as a 'popular leader' of Kashmir in the formal drama of 'accession' was informally degraded from 'popularity' and dubbed an unpopular traitor, an American agent and a conspirator and so was dismissed and arrested. We have discussed that a fraud too has certain norms and in dislodging the imposed fraud no norms were adopted. He was dismissed from the leadership of the same House which he, himself, had created by his 'without discretion' selection. He was not afforded any chance to face his own created parliamentary party for any no-confidence move nor was there any move even in whispers among the jackals created by the lion. Even Bakshi the new agent in the process of installation, just 39 days before his crowning as the next king spoke publicly that "all the Muslims have to adhere only to five fundamentals, I have to follow the sixth foundation of my faith and that is loyalty to my leader Sheikh Abdulla." It is thus that Sheikh Abdulla rightly claimed in his statement u/s 342 Cr. Pc. before special magistrate Nila Kanth Hak that the Government created and established with his dismissal was 'one not established under law but by illegalities.' The same illegal government imposed an assembly in 1957. Its nature has been discussed in the first part under the heading 'Selection by Discretion.' We have quoted therein the statement of Praja Parishad leader P.N. Dogra which he made as sole opposition member on the floor of that very house in which he had qualified as one established by 'illegalities.' It is this government, which on the ground realities, on the basis of political morality and democratic cannons was declared by two big personalities of the two regions viz. Sheikh Abdulla and Prem Nath Dogra as a government not established by law. The same government nominated six persons (including the brother of the then Prime Minister) to Indian Parliament as representatives of the people of Jammu and Kashmir. We need not, therefore, make further discussions on the representative character of this parliament viza-viz this state. Hence, its decisions, pieces of legislation and the actions of authorities elected by it involving Jammu and Kashmir have no binding effect upon the people of this state who were not represented there even through proxy, but through fraud. Such decisions by the authorities elected by it were similar in character to those laws and decisions the British Parliament passed for imposition upon its colonies before 1947.

The Third Parliament

It has been discussed under the heading: 'Selection by Abduction' that the Legislative Assembly of 1962 was imposed by Bakshi Ghulam Mohammad by abduction of opposition candidates, by kidnapping their proposers by detaining their close kith and kin and by creating a reign of terror. The same house elected Bakshi Ghulam Mohammad again as Prime Minister who constituted a Cabinet from amongst the members of the same house and these very members of legislature constituted an electoral college which elected unopposed the son of the abdicated ruler as the 'elected (popular)' head of state. The same government recommended names of six persons to the Indian Parliament and on the same recommendation the Sadr i-Riyasat made the nomination and these six nominated persons represented 50 lakh people of Jammu and Kashmir.

It was the miracle of special status granted to the people of Jammu and Kashmir under Article 370 of the Indian Constitution that for three Parliaments the people of Jammu and Kashmir were represented by a Himalayan fraud. May we, therefore, leave it to the conscience of democrats worldwide and particularly from India to assess the value of the following Presidential Orders of the application of Constitutional Provisions (of India) upon Jammu and Kashmir. Some are as under:

> The Constitution (Application to J&K) Order 1954, The Constitution (Application to J&K) Amendment Order 1958, the Second Amendment Order of 1958, the Constitution Amendment Orders—first and second of 1959, the Amendment Acts of Constitutional Applications enforced in 1960, Amendment Order of 1961, order of 1963, Amendment Orders (first, second and third) of 1964, the first and second amendment orders of 1965, the Amendment Order of 1966 and the two Amendment Orders of 1967."
>
> The people here in Jammu and Kashmir consider all of them devoid of any legal, moral or democratic sanctions.

In 1967 a similar defective order was passed which accorded a concession to the people of Jammu and Kashmir that they would also hold elections for six representatives from Jammu and Kashmir. Before we discuss the manner of elections conducted for these six parliamentary constituencies it is most pertinent that we introduce the so defined six segments and the manner in which the delimitation committee delimited areas which fell under each segment. It is also relevant to state once again that for Parliament elections every adult ordinary resident who at relevant time of elections was stationed within this state has a right to vote from Jammu and Kashmir irrespective of the fact whether such resident is or is not a permanent resident of this state. On the other hand, under Jammu and Kashmir Constitution it is only Permanent Resident of this state who is entitled to exercise right of vote to elect representatives to

J&K Legislative Assembly. This political hypocricy has caused confusion even to the state legislature which provides the delimitation of J&K Assembly segment to be made on the figures of current census report. However, according to the Indian Representation of the People Act the six segments in the state are to be defined on population basis. Hence, it was the 1961 census which had relevance for delimitation of these six segments.

Chapter 24

Delimitation of Parliamentary Constituencies

J&K consisted of three units: the provinces of Jammu and Kashmir and united districts of the Frontier. From ancient times the Valley of Kashmir consisted, administratively two divisions Maraz and Kamraz which were divided into 36 parganas. Maraz is the south valley situated from Srinagar up to the Banihal, i.e., villages situated on both sides of Pir Panchal range of hills. Kamraz is situated on the north of Srinagar. It also include some parts of central Kashmir, i.e., from present Tehsil Budgam. Sir Walter Lawrence who is the father of prevalent land settlement of Kashmir and who reconstructed the land record, recommended in 1892 the creation of two *wazarats* out of these two divisions. The scheme was evolved and each wazarat was put under administrative control of an officer called wazir-i-wazarat. Under Criminal Procedure Code of the State he enjoyed powers of an S.D.M. and was subordinate to the Governor. Each province was administered by a Governor who was empowered for the whole province as District Magistrate under the Code of Criminal Procedure. Under J&K Land Revenue Act the Governor of the province was designated as Commissioner and wazir-i- wazarat was also collector of the wazarat. Province of Kashmir consisted of three wazarats: two were the two divisions of the Valley and the third was 'Wazarat-i-Muzzaffarabad'. After 1947 whole of the Valley viz Maraz and Kamraz divisions fell within the Indian side of Kashmir whereas the whole of Muzzafarabad wazarat except a part of Uri pargana and near about half of Tehsil Teetwal fell within the Indian side. The rest of the wazarat forms part of the Pakistani side of Jammu and Kashmir. The province of Jammu and districts of the Frontier were vertically divided by the imposed Line of Actual Control, which is the consequence of the illogical ceasefire. The ceasefire was to end hostilities and to reunite the state so as to finally decide the fate of this disputed state.

But the usurpation has been subjected to a process of rationalisation. Immediately after the acceptance of the ceasefire resolution of UNO, both the occupying countries made such administrative changes which suited their neo-colonist designs and disturbed the rationale of the decision, which Sir Lawrence had on geographical, topographical, cultural, linguistic and economic considerations rightly devised. The inclusion of the parts of Uri sub area and Teetwal Tehsil viz present Tangdar area with Kashmir division had some rational basis; though both these small pockets got so merged in their minority character devoid of the distinction which they enjoyed on linguistic and cultural basis. They became satellites of majority interests. On the other hand, inclusion of Gurez with Kashmir had no reasonable basis except that it had a narrow hill terrain connecting it with Bandipora Tehsil in Baramulla district. Before 1947 it was part of 'Frontier' which included besides present Gurez the present districts of Kargil and Leh and northern districts directly ruled as a 'colony' by Pakistan now. These regions are Askardo, Gilgit, Honza, Chitral, Nagar, Yasin, Punial, Koh Khizer and Ashkomand. Hence, Gurez due to its history, geography, ethnic considerations, economic parity - rather for several reasons forms a part of the erstwhile frontier. It should have been amalgamated with Parliamentary constituency of Ladakh which was formed on only the present two districts of Leh and Kargil which were at the time of delimitation in 1966-67 a single district known as Ladakh district. Though it can be argued that it had no closer communication link with those districts, but that was the position even before 1947. None of these 'frontier areas' had formidable plain links with one another. The communication lines were and are through hill passes and similar hills separated Gurez from Bandipora at that time and it is after decades that India built a road for its military purposes. Where there is a will there is a way. Had Indian occupying interests given any weightage to the rational consideration an easier and similar link being available from Drass to Gurez could have been developed. Why this gerrymandering? It will be addressed later.

As 'frontier' districts of this country and Wazarat of Muzzafarabad were unevenly cut by the cease-fire resolution so was the fate of Jammu province where even families were divided and problem of displacement of state subjects severed their roots with the soil of origin where they had taken birth, lived and had woven dreams of life. Wazarati Mirpur and a major part of the tiny principality Poonch became Azad Kashmir on October 23, 1947 which is now 'Azad' by name, but in reality an occupied part of Pakistan. Thus the present Jammu culturally, linguistically and on the basis of economic considerations can be divided for giving proper and effective representation to all inhabitants into two areas: 'Kashmiri Gojri' speaking belt and 'Dogri Punjabi' speaking area. The former consists of hill tracts, is economically backward and has internal links of communication. It consists of present districts of Doda, Poonch, Rajauri and sub district of Reasi in Udhampur district. The latter belt is situated in the plains, is industrially and economically developed and has with each other easier communication links. It should not be considered that their common aspirations in these two segments can be divided and prevalent administrative set up requires any change, but these considerations had to effect the delimitation of parliamentary and assembly segments. So are the directives and guidelines succinctly contained in the relevant provision of Representation of People Act of J&K and India. But what has been done needs to be explained in the light of this background.

With a rational approach Kashmir Valley has been divided in three parliamentary segments. It has largely been done on the basis of the evolved administrative pattern and could in no case be disturbed. Though central Kashmir in the good old days had no separate identity—but this delimitation recognised its larger size. Hence, Srinagar district (after 1979 districts of Srinagar and Budgam) constitute the central parliamentary constituency. Kamraz (present Baramulla and Kupawara districts) is the northern constituency and Maraz (present Anantnag and Pulwana districts) form the southern constituency.

Ladakh constituency, as far as area is concerned is the largest belt of all the six constituencies. On population basis it is the smallest, rather as small as an assembly segment is, in both Srinagar and Jammu. But on topographical, cultural, ethnic, economic and even on other grounds the committee could have not deleted any area from the Valley from the southern side of Zojila pass so as to include that with Ladakh. But as far as detachment of Gurez from Ladakh (Frontier) constituency and coupling that with Baramulla constituency in the Valley is an erroneous decision fraught with consequences fatal to the interest of those few thousands of voters who live there. Such detachment and inclusion greatly amounts to denial of representation to those ill-fated Dardas who have, since the formation of Jammu and Kashmir state, remained part of Frontier sub-division. This tehsil has culturally, geographically, economically and on the basis of language been closer to the Shina speaking population of Drass and Kargil and so formed part of that area. They are bottle-necked and have to cover difficult terrains to enter into the Valley. They could face similar difficulties to reach Drass and Kargil, but just as a temporary fair weather communication link was improved between Gurez and Bandipora the same could have been done to connect this area with their original administration units. More so, it was not the Dard of Gurez who had to wander after representatives, but the representatives had to go to Gurez to beg votes as he presently goes from Kargil to Chishole, a remote area bordering Tibet. In the circumstances in which susceptibilities of this erstwhile 'frontier' division of Jammu and Kashmir have been fed both by India and Pakistan it is reasonably felt that Gurez has been detached from Ladakh constituency merely on communal basis. In spite of the propaganda that Ladakh was a completely Buddhist populated area it is proved that the said constituency is populated in equal proportions by Buddhists and Muslims. Even the population balance tilts, if census is correctly conducted, in favour of Muslims. But upto even 1981, the Kargilites were mostly uneducated; women confined to purda and men also were uninterested to reveal correct figures to census enumerators for many reasons, resulting in this incorrect census record of 1961 that was made the basis for delimitation in 1967. In the estimation of communally fed views of the members of the delimitation committee if Gurez was tied with Ladakh constituency that would make this constituency a Muslim majority segment. Hence, Gurez was dropped and it was merged into the ocean of Baramulla. These 16,000 'frontier' voters were forced to lose their cultural and geographical identity in the ocean of more than six lakh voters of pure Kashmiris. Hence, they have always remained indifferent to parliament elections and as a military zone, their votes are always bundled with the votes of government candidates.

In Jammu province too with similar mala fides gerrymandering of the two constituencies is patent. We have seen that geographically, culturally, linguistically and on the basis of economic backwardness the Kashmiri-Gojri population living in the hill tracts of Jammu would form a compact 'hill constituency' comprising Poonch, Rajouri, Doda districts and Reasi sub-district of Udhampur. On the other hand, the 'plains Constituency' comprising Dogri-Punjabi speaking areas in the plains, economically forward, educationally emancipated and inter-linked by several road and rail connections would form a separate constituency consisting of Udhampur, Ram Nagar, Chenani assembly segments and districts of Jammu and Katua. But on the other hand, gerrymandering has patently been made on communal malafides. The most backward Gojars, Kashmiri Muslims and Khatris living in Poonch or Doda districts, the Bakerwal nomads, Punjabi (Rajput) Muslims—all have been so divided that in this division they have not only lost their respective identities, but have to merge their subdued aspirations with sweepingly powerful aspirations of the urban elite, monopolists in trade, hoarders of essential commodities and an emerging class of industrialists.

However, in devising constituencies as shown above would give more populated areas to the plains constituency and the hill constituency would get comparatively lower number of voters. That would not make any discrimination as according to the 1987 voter list Ladakh Parliamentary Constituency had only 1,64,363 voters whereas Baramulla Constituency had 655,738 voters; that means Baramulla Constituency is bigger in population than five constituencies like that of Ladakh. Similarly, if the urban areas of Jammu-Kathua and Udhampur plains exceed in some thousands to rural (hill) constituency of 'Poonch—Rajouri, Doda and Reasi,', it would hardly matter. That belt too could not hit the local population because Udhampur and Jammu has lakhs of army jawans enumerated as residents of those areas. It is similar as is the case in Srinagar Assembly segments of

Zainakadal (down town) and Sonawar. The former is densely populated, but records lesser voters as compared to Sonawar which as part of Badami Bagh cantonment area been occupied by about one lakh Indian army jawans, registered as ordinary residents there and so are voters for Parliamentary elections.

It becomes pertinent to digress and give a reference to the on-going census operation in Jammu and Kashmir. As soon as the process started ex-central minister from Jammu and Kashmir S.D. Soz, without coming up with concrete proposals, issued a statement of penance to wash off his earlier sins. In the statement he accused the government of India of creating a distorted record of demographic changes by recording six lakh men of the Indian army and paramilitary forces as residents of Jammu and Kashmir. The exercise in this direction is really fraught with dangers. But neither Soz came up with concrete positive suggestions which could keep the record on the right tract nor was there positive reaction anywhere. The Government of India dismissed the idea as 'mischievous'. Its local civil servant superintendent Jammu and Kashmir census operation issued a press statement in which he tried to plug the flow of misinformation and disinformation that might ensue from such lopsided census exercises. Militant organisations issued a threat to the civil employees to boycott the census duty and similarly a directive to the people not to associate with the process. It ensued that like other jobs paramilitary forces were deputed on this duty too. Such practice bears support from tradition created in Pakistan where the 1991 census was conducted mainly under army supervision. In the process the paramilitary forces that cannot invite death to move from house to house did so from their bunkers and consequently a record prepared against Kashmiri interests. Immediately after S.D. Soz's statement this author wrote a detailed article which was published in *Kashmir Monitor* (Srinagar). In this article a case was built in support of involving locals with the census process, but made a small suggestion to the Government of India. It was confined to the basic form of record of the inhabitants domiciled in Jammu and Kashmir at the time of census. It was suggested that as it is only Jammu and Kashmir which has a special status, has a separate constitution, the Indian Constitution also protects the interests of permanent residents of Jammu and Kashmir and a distinction between 'Indian Citizen' and the 'Permanent Resident of J&K' is maintained and respected, so, to protect that distinction from dilution the 'forms' provided to enumerators in Jammu&Kasmir should bear an additional column specially mentioning whether the man/woman/child/girl recorded as resident of a place in Jammu and Kashmir is its permanent resident or not. The heading of the column was suggested as 'Permanent Residents or'. The reply would be yes or no. It would facilitate the work of the delimitation committee appointed by India for delimiting Parliament Constituencies and for the work of J&K Delimitation Commission to delimit Assembly Segments. Besides, such census report would become the basis for framing, revising and review of electoral rolls. But, as the suggestion goes against nefarious interests so it did not invite any official comment, even hostile. On the other hand, officers in the State Census office have, with appreciation sent these recommendations to the Central government but with no directions therefrom. Unfortunately, the so-called representative agglomeration of leaders of the A.P.H.C. has pegged all these problems to the single hanger on which Kashmir imbroglio has hinged since 1947. They are least conscious of the situation that the irregularities piled up during this half century will consume another half a century after the solution of Kashmir to resolve these ambiguities. The Hurriyat agglomeration is indifferent to this taxing situation. They are not conscious that the time spent to undo these irregularities could involve the Kashmiris in a confusing situation and they could be used by agencies with undercurrents of intrigue. Jammu and Kashmir could became a victim of such politics or would become a second Afghanistan.

As far as the rulers are concerned, they are only aware of self-interest that lies for them in the status quo. The suggestion made by the author in the *Kashmir Monitor* amounts to a safeguard to Farooq's propaganda stunt for the myth of autonomy. Farooq Abdulla and his government should have at least tried to activate the matter with N.D.A. Central government of which National Conference is also a part.

In the light of the discussions made above among six

parliamentary constituencies only three in the Valley were devised correctly. They could not indulge in gerrymandering in the Valley for the reason that the Valley is well knit compact unit and communally unipolar. It has no district, tehsil or segment which has predominance of any community other than Muslims and that too Sunni Muslims. In 1962 when this author filed nominations from Budgam constituency (Budgam is the seat of leading Aghas of Shias) and was under the impression that it must have been a predominantly Shia majority constituency, but the perusal of electoral roll of the constituency belied our estimates. It too is a predominantly Sunni constituency. Similarly, Kashmiri Pandit concentration has been in Haba Kadal assembly segment and Sikhs are domiciled in Baramulla and Tral Constituencies, but all these constituencies bear a tilt in favour of the Muslim population. Hence, the delimitation committee headed by Hon'ble Justice Kapur could not get any material to indulge in gerrymandering in the Valley which would suit interests of occupation. On the other hand, communal decision was imposed in Jammu and Ladakh. In Jammu it was done by deliberate fragmentation of Muslim pockets and in Ladakh the communal flames were fanned by allowing a very narrow difference between the two communities living in that frontier region. We will now see how under the patronage of Jawahar Lal Nehru the communal void in Ladakh was turned into a gulf of hatred which was widened by his great daughter and by the Congress—a secular party. To be fair the least contribution has come from the RSS and Jansangh for widening the gulf between the communities.

It is pertinent to mention that Ladakh and not the Valley was the real laboratory of secular traditions. As Chief Judicial Magistrate of Ladakh, I have witnessed, appreciated and eulogised the communal fraternity which existed upto the mid 70s though under the ongoing intrigue of division. A close confidant of Indira Gandhi's home minister Mehmood-ur-Rehman who was the 'favourite' deputy commissioner posted there had fed waves of anger against Kashmiri Muslims and this venom was in due course directed against local Muslims also. It will be treated as an injustice with that outstanding secular family if I do not substantiate my argument. These circumstances if connected together build a convincing case that the Nehru dynasty imported communalism from New Delhi within the rank and file of Ladakhis who were tied with each family by inter-marriages. At the outset I will quote only one example. In 1977 I was invited to a dinner party by one Yaqub Ladhakhi who retired recently as Assistant Commissioner of Nobra division. I was received at the gate of his house by Ghulam Qadir and Sonam Gelson and was told that both were brothers of our host Yaqub Ladhaki. After the death of her Buddhist husband the mother of Sonam Gelson had married a Muslim. Sonam was a baby when he was orphaned and was brought up as a devoted Buddhist by his Muslim stepfather and on his death Sonam brought up Yaqub like his son, but as a sincere Muslim. It was not an isolated instance, but a rule in Ladakh. During my tenure of office a lady named Dolma was married to Asad Zargar. It was the first inter community marriage which invited some reaction. In the same Ladakh where many Muslims and Buddhists were uterine brothers, but imported hatred made them bloodthirsty for each other. One of the causes which led to this confrontation was the very formation of Ladakh Parliamentary Constituency, the other cause was to project Ladakh in India and elsewhere as an only Buddhist region, Ladakhi culture was mischievously depicted as Buddhist culture. This depiction caused a chain reaction.

I was elected as executive member of the Sahitya Akademy New Delhi. I was posted then as CJM Leh and proceeded from there to attend its first meeting. Eminent writers of India who were on the Executive Board of this National Academy of Letters disputed my contention that Ladakh had a composite society and insisted that it was solely a Buddhist region. They all dubbed me as a communal Muslim and I was silenced. But the oldest Telegu member Dr. B. Gopala Reddy, ex-Central Minister of Information and Broadcasting and ex-Governor of U.P. bailed me out. He disclosed that as Finance Minister of Madras state he had visited Ladakh to keep up the morale of Madrasi jawans who were deputed there on duty. But, surprisingly this testimony too was disputed. The impact of the propaganda created was that even the great scholars of India refused to be corrected.

Let my readers share the secrets as to when this tirade started.

Late Mirza Afzal Beg, a close confidant of Sheikh Abdulla, had proved by cogent facts that the letter which Chiwang Regzin[1] had addressed to Prime Minister Nehru in 1948 was drafted and even typed in South Block. Earlier, his letter addressed by the same Lama to the Maharaja was also drafted by the same agency. Both the letters contained tutored material and complained that Kashmiri Muslim civil servants had exploited the Ladakh region. In 1948 the representation of Kashmiri Muslims was so poor that three lakh Muslims in present district Budgam had two graduates, one trained teaching graduate, 16 Patwaris, 21 school teachers and no gazetted officer. The most advanced elite among Muslims too had no spare staff of petty government officials who could be posted in adjoining areas of Budgam which then formed part of the extended city. Who then were the Kashmiri Muslims who had exploited the resources of Ladakh in 1948-49? A researcher can even today consult records from state archives and will be satisfied that it was neither Kashmiri Muslims, nor Jammu Dogras and nor even Ladakhis who ruled Ladakh those days. It was Kashmiri Pandit who ruled all the three regions. It is after 1948 that all these secular traditions were subjected to strains and finally it was the old ally of the All India National Congress & All J&K National Conference which after February 1975 exploited the sentiments of disgruntlement among Ladakhi Muslims and encouraged communal confrontation. The National Conference could have if it had belief in secularism enunciated policies to expose the Congress game of creating a communal void in Ladakh, but for petty political reasons it added fuel to the already burning issue of 'the amity' which had been laid by the outstanding secular family of Allahabad Pandits with Kashmiri descent. Sheikh Abdulla also with same origin from a Brahmin Prohit of a Badipora (Budgam) Shavistic Mandir organised and channelised Muslim reaction.

During the discussions on delimitation of six parliamentary constituencies we have made some relevant digressions and stated that the severance of Gurez segment from the Frontier Constituency reflected strains of the communalisation in politics. Had Justice Kapoor remained true to the administrative history and political geography of Jammu and Kashmir he would have devised 'Frontier'

Constituency instead of Ladakh Constituency—as the area was known during the Maharaja's rule as United Districts of Frontier.

Notes

1. In this letter Rigzin further demanded that either Buddhist Ladakh should be allowed to merge with its cultural mainstream Tibet or along with Hindu majority areas of Jammu it be annexed together to be made administratively part of Hindu Punjab. In the use of the term 'Ladakh' he did not separate or gift away Muslim Kargil. The tutors behind, the great secular democrats of Congress high command, were more than conscious that the demand for annexation with Tibet was just a camouflage devised to convey the real strain which is presently projected through the slogan of tripartisation of the state. It furthur shows that the Indian leadership who had tutored those simple Lamas of Ladakh had made an assessment that ultimately they would have to bow before the will of the people and so initiated an alternative of communal division at the earliest. It will be a treachery both on the part of our leadership in all the three units and for Pakistan leadership to succumb to such demands. 'Hell or heaven we go together'— is the slogan of commoners.

Chapter 25

The First Parliamentary Elections from J&K

It is pertinent to quote from the brochure issued by the Chief Electoral officer J&K[1] about the date of Parliamentary Elections held in this state during 1971 General Elections through the booklet which deals mainly with 1971 Elections, however, as introduction it provides some information about 1967 Elections held for six Parliamentary seats from J&K. The relevant extract is quoted:

"Before 1967 nominated members were sent to the Lok Sabha from J&K. During 1966 Delimitation Committee was constituted under the Chairmanship of Justice J.L. Kapur....[2] the said Committee set up territorial Constituencies into which the whole state was divided."

Then the schedule annexed sets out these six constituencies with their names and the extent of area each such devised constituency contained in it.

The report then goes on:

"It was for the first time in the history of J&K that in the year 1967 that the direct elections were held to the Lok Sabha from the above (quoted in schedule) Parliamentary six constituencies simultaneously with the Legislative Assembly of J&K."

The report further shows:

"From Anantnag and Ladhakh Constituencies two candidates of the ruling party in the centre and state, viz., Mohammad Shafi Quraishi and Kaushik Bakula were elected un-opposed." Thus, in other words nomination as has been our destiny remained undisturbed inspite of the 1966 Constitutional Application Ordinance which changed the system of nomination into election. At this time neither in Jammu nor in the Valley was there any formidable pro-Indian opposition party. Even the ruling Congress was hoisted and imposed as discussed earlier. However, the Valley and district Doda of Jammu province were completely under the influence of All the J&K Plebiscite Front. Besides, the other dominant political forces the J&K Political Conference and J&K Awami Action Committee were also strictly committed to boycott. In some obscure lanes and merely in name existed offices of the Indian Communist Party headed by A.S. Ranjoor and of Socialist Party. They had neither cadres nor public support. The communist cadre had rejoined the ruling clique from 1960 and were mere volunteers of G.M. Sadiq, the C.M. and had deeply involved themselves with state largesse. Much earlier the socialist workers had merged their identity with the Plebiscite Front. Similarly, in Jammu (Dogri-Punjabi belt in Jammu, Kathua and sub district of Udhampur) Jana Sangh had some cadres confined within some Thakurs and Mahajans. But to be fair, the Jammu Hindus (high caste) had in the process of elimination aligned themselves with the political party in power at the Centre. They considered such political moves as providing guarantees and sureties for further merger of Jammu and Kashmir with India. It has been discussed in the first part that the ruling Congress party at the Centre was on the verge of a split. Indira Gandhi, Prime Minister and party high command nicknamed as 'Congress Syndicate' were in open confrontation in which clash Bakshi was aligned with the Syndicate. From its creation in the 30s the All J&K National Conference was under this deceptive label state unit of All India National Congress, but in 1964 in his over enthusiasm G.M. Sadiq was made to take very drastic steps to erode Jammu and Kashmir special status and in this tirade he had buried this organisational identity in the graveyard of the Congress Party. But Bakshi on his defection from the State Congress unit used this rejected label to organise his loyalists who mainly consisted of concession seekers and the power hungry. Hope was nourished among them that the Syndicate had assured guaranteed fairness at the hustings, at least for Bakhshi's party. Hence, the main contest was between the Sadiq group patronised by the Congress Prime Minister and the Bakhshi group backed by the Congress leadership.

Thus the 1967 Election particularly for six parliamentary constituencies was a fight of strength between the two agencies of the waring groups of the ruling party in New Delhi viz. Congress Party. Bakshi represented the Org-anisation and Sadiq had agency from the ministerial group. To sum it up, the former had a mandate from 24 Akbar Road, New Delhi (head office of the Indian National Congress) and the latter had open support from 1, Asif Ali Road (official residence of Indian Prime Minister). Before taking over as the chief minister Sadiq had a reputation of being an idealist democrat, clean politician and a fellow traveller of the Indian Communist movement.

Bakshi was considered a Great Mughal or Budshah Saani (the Second Sultan Zainabidin ruler of Kashmir from 1420 to 1470) who by distribution of largesse and for his philanthropic nature had influenced different pockets of sycophancy. But after 1964, when Sadiq became the chief minister he eroded all myths about his image. He emerged as a despot who could not tolerate even a dummy like the unknown Kashmiri Pandit Matoo to file nomination papers against him though Matoo could hardly gather the support of 2 per cent of the electorate. Sadiq was so scared of the might of the mass resentment that he arranged for abduction of the opposition Jan Sangh candidate and managed his own uncontested return. While he was an administrator, inspite of his personal cleanliness had established a kitchen cabinet of three women Mehmoda, Zainab and Sajida who paved the way for emergence of a civil servants syndicate consisting of J.L. Kaul, Ghulam Shah, Peer Ghulam Hassan Shah, and Sheikh Ghulam Rasool. They showered two cousins of Sadiq viz. Rashid Kara and Rehman Kara with concessions. Thus Sadiq emerged as a petty 'traitor' who to suit his vested interests, treacherously eroded the distinctive character of the J&K Constitution which as a member of the drafting committee from 1951 he had, by his own personal commitment devised and which as President of Constituent Assembly he had imposed to keep Jammu and Kashmir a distinct but distinguishable part of India. Those distinct and distinguishable traits he got eroded with such swiftness and in such a slip-shod manner that it appears to serious students of history that the Holy Relic was displaced from Hazratbal to create a wave of hatred against the Bakshi dynasty and under that wave to impose this 'agent' with a clear understanding as to what he had to do. He did so. However, he could not get the aggressive lust for turning Jammu and Kashmir into a colony for vested interests of a privileged community reduced. That will be discussed at the proper time.

His rival G.M. Bakshi had earned the reputation of a traitor of his leader, an enemy of the mass interests, corrupt ruler who created a political culture based on concessions. He was a symbol of gangsterism, persecution and devised original methods to involve his political opponents in false cases. He had looted the exchequer and amassed money through embezzlement. In spite of all these ills he had appeased all odds and contradictions by free distribution of largesse. He had developed personal rapport with priests of all communities which included peer families, Imams and Mujawirs of Muslims, of Hindu Mandirs and Ashrams, Aghas of Shia community, Buddhist Lamas and Christian priests. He would, with devotion call, at the cottages of soothsayers and interact even with petty musicians. In spite of mass boycott he had a definite edge upon Sadiq. Boycott would facilitate the success of Bakshi's candidates as he had definite committed pockets of sycophants who benefited from his philanthrophy. On the other hand, Sadiq had no following even smaller or more insignificant. The smaller fraction of intellectuals who had pinned hopes in the idealistic democrat Sadiq had developed aversion against him after seeing his actions as the chief minister.

As stated earlier Ladakh was treated as a private family asset of Indira Gandhi-Nehru Dynasty so to keep the great Buddhist Lama Kushak Bakula obliged, the papers of his rivals were got rejected and he was returned unopposed.

Sadiq had assessed that M.S. Qureshi who from one pro-Pak extreme had jumped to pro-Indian political extreme had through Dinesh Singh cultivated deeper contacts with Indira Gandhi so directed the 'Rejection Master' Deputy Commissioner Anantnag (Returning Officer Anantnag Parliamentary Constituency) to manage unopposed the return of Qureshi to the Indian Parliament. Dinesh Singh was then Union Minister for Commerce and was considered very close to the Prime Minister and Qureshi was his deputy. Qureshi was an infiltrator from Srinagar into South Kashmir Constituency. Neither his party had any base in this bastion of pro-plebiscite politics nor Shafi Qureshi had any personal contacts in any of the assembly segments nor had he any social contacts in that area. So, he was scared of the threat from an insignificant and unknown independent rival who could, in spite of strict boycott policy, manage to persuade his kith and kin and personal friends to participate. On the other hand, even local ruling Congress cadres were annoyed with this infiltration so, even the minimum participation of voters would get Shafi consigned to the shameful disgrace of a defeat. The services of 'Rejection Master' were hired and he was returned 'unopposed'. Again South Kashmir saw the same previous nomination, but *'fazool hangama'* of useless paper filling.

Ali Mohammad Tariq was the first political Pichlaka[3] whom the center desired to impose rudely. That imposition was resented even by Sadiq, Qasim, D.P. Dhar and their cabinet colleagues in the state ministry. It is relevant to sum up herein his political geography. He was as a young man devotedly involved with the National Conference, but the party had nourished expectations beyond his stature so took to political hermitage. In the 60s he used to go during winters as a hawker of Kashmir handicrafts to Bombay. There in the electoral historical fight of the two giants; J.B. Kriplani and Krishna Menon from north Bombay he worked as an ordinary volunteer of Menon and so later on came closer to him who took him to Jawahar Lal Nehru. There he was encouraged to form another pull upon Srinagar leadership. This game was immaturely played by him and even by Krishna Menon as a result of which he created, a good number of enemies, more so, in the state unit of the ruling Congress.

Indira Gandhi had a game plan to get Bakshi humiliated from Srinagar Constituency from where he had filed nomination papers as the candidate of his family party the National Conference. Indira Gandhi had a personal grudge against Bakhshi and anecdotes about this are part of political folklore. Sadiq and his cousin the pro-Pak leader Mohi-ud-din Karra and even the Plebiscite Front leadership had a common cause to get Bakshi consigned to political humiliation, but the candidate imposed by Indira Gandhi from the ruling party A.M. Tariq was not acceptable to any of these adversaries who held a common grudge against Bakshi. Beig as an expert of Land Laws knew that Pichlakas usually destroys out of vengeance clans of their origin and under acquired big brother chavinism exploit the families where they are brought up but denied recognition. Karra and Sadiq too understood this, so preferred the discredited Bakshi to the budding agent Ali Tariq. Beig and Karra got the call of boycott strictly imposed which facilitated Bakshi's fans to participate. D.P. Dhar a close confidant of Indira Gandhi convinced that grand lady that the naked bungling was bound toprovide an argument for the syndicate. Bungling was restricted to allow fairness hence this sole seat went to a National Conference candidate who was the agent of the organisational syndicate of the ruling Congress. Total percentage of votes polled was shown as 55.16 per cent, but as per our study and in the assessment of the local media the participation did not go beyond 30 percent which included 12 per cent non-Muslim voters of the constituency. This time Kashmir Pandit worked (for the first time) against the Nehru dynasty mandate and due to their developing aversion against Sadiq (who before 1964 was considered by them to be an athiest, but was now being projected as a communal Muslim by that community) voted for Bakshi. Sikhs had a preference for Bakshi and Muslim priests, Mujawirs and soothsayers played a positive role for him; Gojars and backward kandi inhabitants had sympathy for Bakshi, who, in their belief, was a devotee of shrines and was sacrificed for the interests of an atheist.

The ruling party had no candidate to field from North Kashmir (Baramulla constituency) whereas the old National Conference stalwarts from the area like late Sufi Mohammad Akbar, late Khwaja Mubarak Shah, late Hakeem Habibulla, late Peer Yalgam, and young activists like A.A. Vakil, Sheikh Mohammad Maqboul, Ghulam Din Shah, Malik Ghulam Rasool and others had all joined the Plebiscite Front. The left over cadre Kabir Khan (Jail Baba) Malik Abdul Gani, G.Q. Masala, G.N. Sogami and few others all had aligned themselves with Bakshi.

The left over cadre with the National Conference (NC) after the 1953 camp had always felt it a punishment to be nominated to the Indian Parliament. The same dearth was faced by this party while making nominations to the second Parliament and so a search started from the civil service. Agha Syed Ahmad retired from civil service and was inducted in J&K Public Service Commission. On completing six and a half decades of his life he was nominated to the second parliament. The old retired civil servant turned young under the magic treatment of Indira Gandhi and became an activist as a 'Young Turk' with Chander Shekhar, Mohan Dharia and others. Thus, he was adopted as a political pichlaka by the Congress. Under the dictates of Indira Gandhi this infiltrator in politics, infiltrator from elderly age group to the youth, an elitist from a posh city colony to the backward rural areas of northern Kashmir was imposed as the Congress candidate for Baramulla Parliamentary Constituency. Bakshi fielded Malik Abdul Gani from the most influential apple town Sopore. Malik was a freedom fighter who had deeper political personal and social links in all the areas of the constituency. Though the main towns like Patan, Sopore, Baramulla, Hundaware, Kupawara and Bandipora gave positive response to the boycott call of the Plebiscite Front, but in remote villages and particularly in the assembly segments close to the LAC friends and 'contacts' of Malik Gani defied the boycott and voted for Bakshi's close confidant; yet he lost by 20,515 votes. In the towns which showed total boycott the civil servants of the democrat Chief Minister Sadiq filled in ballot boxes with bundles of votes marked in favour of Agha Syed Ahmad. In this constituency hardly 22 per cent voters actually participated, whereas records showed that half of the total number of voters in the constituency exercised their right of franchise. Only 28 per cent counted ballot papers were fake.

During our discussions on delimitation of Parliamentary Constituencies, it has been stated that the two Parliamentary segments in Jammu division were devised in an intended and designed manner. Backward Gojars and downtrodden Kashmiri speaking belts in the undeveloped hill tracks were thrown into disintegration in such a manner that they had to subordinate their political aspirations to the aggressive interests of economically stronger people living in three important and developed towns - Jammu, Kathua and Udhampur. The Gojars, Kashmiris and converted Rajput Muslim families living in the districts of Rajouri and Poonch are so closely situated to the LAC that this artificial dividing line has divided their heart and minds. At certain places this division is unrealistic. A single village or a belt of villages have been divided in such awkward manner that if the pasture ground of the village area fell across the line, the drinking water facility tied with a spring or stream fell on the other side. Consequently, these divided families cannot avoid crossing over from one side to the other. I have as Additional District Magistrate of Poonch 1970-71 myself examined this on the ground situation. Hence, these victimised divided families have usually been subjected to cases under Ingress and Egress Act, Enemy Agents Ordinance and other penal offences. The majority of such cases are a fabrication to force them to work as spies and runners for the army and in this competition of using the citizens living near the LAC for nefarious activities the forces of Pakistan also persecute them only to use them as their agents. In this competition families are divided. If the father works for the Indian army the son is on the pay scale of the other country. In this situation these people live with a complete fear psychosis which has caused a suffocating situation throughout. In such a situation these backward Gujars, Kashmiri speaking people and Punjabi Muslims living in these two districts can hardly afford to align themselves with the Valley or with the Doda voters in favour of boycott.

In view of the Hindu communal threat from Praja Parishad these minority communities have to align themselves usually with the ruling party. Thereby, they can in a situation full of risks, save themselves and their kith and kin from further persecution.

Doda district is a Muslim majority area consisting of old tiny semi-independent estates or principalities which were brought under Dogra rule during the 19 Century and formed a hill district in between the plains of Jammu and the Valley. The district is predominantly a Muslim district. The gap between the two communities is not as big as in the Valley. The ratio of Muslim and non-Muslim population is 60:40 respectively. During the 1967 Elections the Hindu vote included the Sikhs as well; the Sikh community has a good chunk of population in an area of this district. After 1984 Sikhs stand alienated from Hindus, but that was not position in 1967.

Hence, on the known lines the result of both these constituencies came in favour of Sadiq's ruling party. Brigadier Gansara Singh and Inderjeet Malhotra won respectively from Udhampur and Jammu defeating Sheikh

Abdulla Rehman and Thakur Baldev Singh respectively.

The result is evident that the shift from nomination to election was one more deception act which disappointed even those sections of the Indian population which considered that extension of the jurisdiction of the Indian Election Commission would initiate the process of revival of faith in the Indian democracy. But the 1967 Elections, both for State and Central legislatures, eroded the faith in the institutions of Indian democracy completely. The negative politics of boycott was vindicated as a positive reaction to neo-colonist designs.

Notes

1. Any state officer of the rank of a collector or a secretary to the government is given charge of the office of Chief Election Officer in addition to his own job. Such an officer has service career, promotion avenues, facilities of favourable/lucrative postings and after retirement hopes of re-employment all connected with the party in power.
2. Younger brother of Justice Kapur was a forest lessee in District Doda of J&K, and so had deeper connections with the then Home Minister and Forest Minister D.P. Dhar and Trilochan Dut. In a criminal case (private complaint) this author as Judicial Magistrate Doda issued several warrants for his arrest, but none were executed. Then I got him arrested once through my prosecution officer from the official residence of S.P. Mr. Duchan.
3. "*Pichlaka*" is a status recognised by the customs prevalent among Kashmiri rural (Muslim) agriculturists. On the death of a young married agriculturist who predeceases his father his children under the principle of representation recognised by Mohammadan Law of Inheritance, do not inherit the peoperty of their grandfather. A widow on remarriage within another agricultural family takes with her the suckling son by her deceased husband. The son is brought up in the stepfather's family as '*Pichlaka*', but finally neither inherits the stepfather's identity, nor retains his original identity. Later on many persons obtained this clout of political pichlakas who presently include M.L. Fotedar, G.N. Azad and many others.

Chapter 26

Prelude to Concessions

The Lok Sabha constituted in 1967 was dissolved by the President on December 27, 1970, though normally it had to live upto 1972. Hence, there arose the necessity of a mid term poll. We need not go into the detailed background of this dissolution, but even during the 1967 general elections, political analysts felt that the conflict which was transparent during the 1967 elections between the two dominant groups of the ruling Congress party would inevitably result in a division and the inevitable happened. The inner party rift in Delhi had clear implications on the political developments of Jammu and Kashmir. For two years Bakshi sustained his cadre with the hope that the Congress leadership was destined to overpower the antiparty and pro-dynasty strains of Indira Gandhi, but it worked otherwise and hence, in utter frustration Bakshi's cadre disintegrated.

On the eve of this mid term poll a process of rationalisation with occupation and imposed division of the state was going on. There were few reasons responsible for this situation. It should not be construed that forces to undo the occupation had disintegrated, but their sacrifices too were not creating any impact in Srinagar. Under the chapter 'Selection by Concession' we have provided sufficient hints that the leadership was disillusioned. The pressure from his family to compromise had mounted excessively upon Sheikh Abdulla. In 1959-60 an eminent freedom fighter and outstanding world peace activist remained in Srinagar in the ancestral house of Khwaja Ghulam Mohammad Shah son-in-law of Sheikh Mohammad Abdulla. Saifud Din Kitchloo as the special emissary of late Jawahar Lal Nehru had come with special proposals. G.M. Shah was also released from preventive detention. Kitchloo had a clear plan for Jammu and Kashmir. It should have Sikkim, Bhutan like status and the author was authorised to communicate the message to Sheikh Abdulla in the special jail in Jammu where he faced trial as an accused in the Kashmir conspiracy case. As a 23 year old boy this author trembled to convey the message to the Sher-i-Kashmir. He roared like a real lion and retorted:

> "You might have been briefed by Shah about this cryptic message of that old communist leader. Tell Shah that if the status of being my son-in-law does come in his way to compromise with status quo, let him divorce my daughter."

To be fair I was not briefed by G.M. Shah.

The same determined Sheikh Abdulla had within a few years become, at least, tolerant to the persuasive arguments of his grown up children, but was as yet undecided about any shift in his policies. However, a sort of disappointment swept over the common cadres of pro-plebiscite political parties. In 1965 the internal political rivalries and rifts in Pakistan pushed suicide squads into this part of Kashmir from Pakistan occupied J&K. These trained cadres were dubbed by India as infiltrators and by Pakistani media they were qualified as Mujahideen. Though this time they were warmly and enthusiastically received by the Kashmiri masses, but there was no earlier groundwork done which could have created awareness among the masses as to how to assist, lead and derive capital from them. They had no supply line provided by their senders, but were purposely thrown into death traps. However, the anti-occupation hatred made common Kashmiris feel penitent for follies committed in 1947 when they deceived and misled the tribals and created overwhelming fear about them as they were painted as being horrible people in the local folk anecdotes. It was the determination of common Kashmiris that these Mujahideen/infiltrators could safely come out of the death traps. The commoners had helped them with an aspiration that they were an advanced party of a permanent infiltrating force which would, in their estimation, at least loosen the Indian grip on them. But it fizzled out soon and the indecisive 1965 war disheartened the Kashmiris. They came to the logical conclusion that an unarmed population of few lakhs with an army of spies, runners, traitors, purchased agents and corrupt leadership they were not able to liberate themselves. The 1965 abortive attempt of armed infiltration and then the 1965 war, which yielded ambiguous results made Kashmiris believe that even active Pakistani involvement would not help them to come out of the trap in which they had fallen in 1947. Against this background, a feeling swept over the people to take concessions, improve individual economy, exploit the political situation for careerist interests and so a sort of compromise with the situation became an undeclared policy of both the leaders and the led. This shift in thinking could have been exploited positively by both the interested parties to suit their respective interests had they sincerity, determination and a correct assessment. They lacked all these three qualities. Pakistan could channelise such disillusionment towards armed revolution by providing training, weapons and support as they later decided to do in 1989, but instead its negative policies consolidated frustration.

India, on the other hand, could have sown confidence among the people. It could have encouraged the institutions of democracy to grow on solid and genuine basis in Jammu and Kashmir. Thereby the people of Jammu and Kashmir, who had nourished aspirations for democratisation, would have felt, and genuinely so, that they were better placed than the unlucky Pakistan for whom rule by the people for the people had been frustrated by contradictory political experiments.

Unfortunately for Jammu and Kashmir and even for the whole subcontinent neither was Pakistan able to create a post-1989 situation out of the post-1965 stalemate, nor could India come out of its neo-colonist designs. Neither was Pakistan able to keep India and the occupying forces of India on tenterhooks and nor did any Indian leader avail of this opportunity to assimilate the democratic aspirations of the people of Jammu and Kashmir with similar aspirations of the Indian masses. The result was that both fed the masses on their largesse, and made their national ego a purchasable commodity.

It should not be construed that this phase had either universality or had swept all sections of the people. On the other hand, during this period frustration was leading towards the idea of armed revolution. The pioneers of this revolution—young boys, enthusiastic young men and even grey haired old people were persecuted by a local group of police officers who for entry to the lucrative Indian Police Service had become equally enthusiastic to involve even the masses in false cases. A Nazi type of interrogation centre was opened in Baagi Mehtab at the 7th kilometre on the Srinagar—Charar-i-Sharief Road where now a developed colony under Srinagar Development Authority stands. A good number of the people including innocents were lodged there who were involved in a case partly based on real facts and partly concocted called the Al-Fateh case. It was really after 1556 A.D. when Akbar the Great both with force and corruption unarmed the Kashmiris that Kashmiris had again started to pick up lethal arms. However, from October 1947 there had been stray incidents of resorting to armed actions against the Indian occupation, but such attempts had fizzled out. At times even huge quantities of arms were thrown in lakes at Sudrabal near Hazratbal, Srinagar, but this Al-Fateh group of militancy could not gain peoples' sanction as a process of rationalisation with concessions was more strong a wave than to undo ties with India. But, unfortunately for the general cause of democracy, the leadership in Delhi did not rise above its neo-colonist and expansionist designs; instead of the expansion of the ambit of institutions of Indian democracy, Indira Gandhi and her blue-eyed boys both in Srinagar and New Delhi were interested in further integration and erosion of 'special status'.

It has been discussed in the first part that the tallest leader of Kashmir Sheikh Abdulla had imposed upon himself a sort of political hermitage. He had channelised all sorts of his activities for rebuilding the historic mosque at Hazratbal, housing in its chamber, the Holy Relic of Prophet Mohammed (S.A.W). The pro-Pak political Conference Leader G.M. Karra cousin and brother-in-law of the chief minister G.M. Sadiq had goal through his cousin whereby his Karra dynasty had snatched the rule from the Bakshi dynasty who had snatched it from the 'Sheikh' dynasty. Hence, Kara had lost interest in pro-Pak politics, but did not formally close his political shop. The successor of the All J&K Muslim Conference leader Maulana Molvi Yousuf Shah, viz Maulana Molvi Farooq with the committed fans of his traditional waaz (religious sermon) was also devising a permutation and combination for selection of an appropriate field where he could reap political dividends. He had not severed his traditional links with Pakistan as he owed his political career to the manoeuvering of Pakistan, but disappointment over the situation made him conscious of tapping other sources. The All J&K Plebiscite Front had become a liability for bankrupt families of its leaders and cadres. Intellectuals mainly constituted of civil servants, teachers of government educational institutions, technocrats (all state employees), lawyers, judges, creative artists including poets, story writers, painters, sculptors and all others connected with creativity, one and all, had fallen prey to greed. Even preachers, clerks, priests and religious leaders did not lag behind in this race. Immediately after the 1953 coup G.M. Bakshi had cultivated the mentality as a distributor of largesse than as an accountable pro-people ruler and made the malaise of corruption second nature among the people of Jammu and Kashmir. Hence, as the patron of this 'lust' for wealth he had deep-rooted connections in all the corrupt streams of public life. Therefore, Mohi-ud-din Karra, Molvi Mohammad Syed Masoodi, Mirza Afzal Beg and the Sheikh family considered even the emasculated Bakshi a potent threat who might outwit them in this competition for opportunities. To be precise Bakshi with his whole cadre had become inconsequential which required either support of khamba (wooden pillar) or a khamba was required to demolish that dilapidated political ruin. Hence, all the five leaders of the United National Conference, vis., Sadiq, his first cousin the pro-Pak leader Mohi-ud-din Karra, the unintelligible political ambiguity Masoodi, the so-called wisest of political fools M.A. Beig and the members of Lions' Den (the Sheikh family) with common criminal intent formed an unlawful association to commit the political murder of the half dead Bakshi.

Though in 1967 Sadiq had created history of ' Selection by Rejection', but the Sadiq government was particular this time to afford chances for electoral fight from Srinagar Parliamentary Constituency. To be more transparent in this display of fairness a close relative of Bakshi, viz., Agha Iftikhar Ahmad I.A.S. (nominated)Deputy Commissioner (Collector) Srinagar was appointed Returning Officer of this Constituency.

It is also highly relevant as to why at this critical juncture the Kashmiri Pandit community had made a drastic shift in their policy. From 1947 to 8 August 1953 the community revered, even virtually worshipped Sheikh Abdulla, in spite of the fact that they did not hide their reaction against his radical policies which were pro-downtrodden. It was Muslims who had for about two centuries been exploited and the Pandits had enjoyed privileges. Even as a petty village chowkidar of a remote and backward village like Kanikot near Yusmarg, in district Budgam a Kashmiri Pandit represented himself by his actions as an agent of autocracy and so was a member of the privileged community. Nevertheless, Kashmiri Pandits politically supported the same radical Sheikh Abdulla who to them was the 'only link' between Kashmir and India. On 9 August 1953 the same Pandits accused the Sheikh of treachery and shifted their loyalty to Bakshi because, in their estimation, he had saved Kashmir from the secessionist policies of Abdulla. Similarly, they reserved their unqualified support for Sadiq after 1963, but later a shift was not only visible but dominant.

Though this shift was in no case one which could cause some irritants in the Indian policy of occupation of J&K, but to the assessment of Kashmiri Pandits Bakshi and Sadiq, as agents of this policy had different altitudes. They had assessed that though the latter had gone too swiftly in the moves of integration, but by keeping such a pace he had not cared to protect their privileges. Their reaction expressed through the influential Pandit lobby in New Delhi had fallen on deaf ears for the reason that Sadiq had the reputation even within the household of Indira Gandhi of a staunch leftist, being an unparalled secularist rather than an athiest. Hence, Kashmiri Pandits this time did not toe the Nehru-Gandhi family policy. They chose Bakshi who in their estimationn played the role of a better agent and had protected the interests of this privileged community to a great extent.

Two important developments took place during the Sadiq regime which alienated the Pandit community from the progressive Sadiq and got them aligned with Bakshi. The voluntary conversion of a 'major' (overdue for marriage) Pandit girl to Islam and her love marriage with a Muslim youth provided Pandits a pretext to air their grievances of erosion in their privileges. Sadiq withstood this agitation of 5 per cent population, but it exercised an extra-constitutional force upon New Delhi. Simultaneously, Sadiq had to fill in some vacancies in gazetted ranks of school education which if filled on the seniority basis would give 85 per cent jobs to Pandits, then only numbering 5 per cent of the population. So, Sadiq devised a policy which made it possible for him to promote some Muslims, Dogras, Sikhs and Buddhists also. About 50 per cent vacancies were to be filled in by Kashmiri Pandits when their share according to their population could be only 5 to 6 per cent. Sadiq could not force the major girl to undo her decision and could not ignore the claim of majority communities for headmasters' posts, so, this influential Pandit community started working against him in New Delhi. Their unabated tirade against Sadiq was, to the assessment of Molvi Syed Masodi, going to help Bakshi in the current situation. Hence, the Molvi joined hands with two cousins Sadiq Karra and Mohi-ud-din Karra to dislodge Bakshi even as M.P. But all the three had no image in public. So, Molvi and Karra persuaded Beig and through him won over Sheikh Mohammad Abdulla. The point was successfully conveyed that unless Bakshi was completely uprooted in New Delhi no accord with the rulers there was possible. Now the question arose as to how to finish him politically. The weapons of the Plebiscite Front and J&K Political Conference had gathered rust in the neglected armoury of boycott policy and without lifting of the 'boycott' neither of the parties could jump in the fray. They could not choose only one constituency if they fought at the party level. They would have to fight from all the six constituencies. But that required a guarantee of fairness in the elections which Sadiq, would neither allow to be granted nor would New Delhi grant it without complete surrender of Sheikh Abdulla, without winding up of the Plebiscite Front and until the tall leader merged with Sadiq's state unit of Congress. Sheikh Abdulla was not ready for that. Hence, consensus was reached to remove the main hurdle of future alignment or accord so a formula was evolved to uproot Bakshi. "But whom to use as a weapon against Bakshi" enquired Sheikh Abdulla? "A khamba (a non-constant wooden pole)" replied Maulana Masoodi. The search for a wooden pole started.

Shamim Ahmad Shamim, a firebrand journalist, fearless literary critic, an impressive orator was considered to be 'politically unreliable' and an 'opportunist'. He had already looked into the pros and cons of the situation, had found fertile soil to sow the seeds for his political career and had declared his candidature from Srinagar Constituency. Though as an MLA he had dominated the assembly proceedings with his wit, eloquence in literary rhetoric, but had exposed that his oratory was devoid of due awareness of the rules and procedures of the House and his discussions hardly reflected his commitment to his electorate. He had represented Shopian Constituency, an important electoral segment in district Anantnag. The citizens of Shopian town commenting on Shamim's deliverance for his constituency, convinced other important segments in this district that their representative had turned the assembly like his weekly *Aina* (an Urdu weekly which people called the 'Shamim Gazette') into a theater to impose his verbosity rather than to project the situation of his people. Hence, Shamim decided not to contest from his home constituency. Secondly, Sadiq had revealed his mind that his government was not ready to do things in 'proper form' which might endanger the safe return of Qureshi, a junior minister in the Indira Cabinet. Shamim on the other hand, was conscious of the contradictions in the ruling party and had received direct encouragement from G.M. Sadiq. Firstly, he knew that city people have looked down upon the rural intellectuals and would prefer a candidate from Srinager city rather than a villager. Though a limited section of literate people liked Shamim's forceful writings, but common people had no such conception. Secondly, he was aware that following the reputation of his grandfather Molvi Abdulla he was dubbed as a Mirzai or even Bahayee. Thirdly, he knew that the swift changes from being a close ally of Bakshi's son-in-law Mir Nasurullah to alignment with his enemy Sadiq he was considered an opportunist. Fourthly, he had a clear assessment that the city was divided between two loyalties—loyalty for Sheikh Abdulla and commitment to the Mirwaiz dynasty. He figured nowhere in the two.

Despite these odds against him he decided to jump into the fray just to gain from the contradictions which were inherent in the situation then.

Sheikh Abdulla initially refused the suggestion of a khamba because he was beaten the most by such khambas (wooden posts). The collective canvassing of the trio: Molvi Masoodi, Beig and Karra and ultimate approval by Begum

Abdulla made the tall leader lend his support. It was decided that neither Sheikh Abdulla nor the president of the Plebiscite Front, Mirza Beig would directly involve themselves in the campaign, but the question was how to project among the masses that Shamim was the blue eyed boy of Sheikh Abdulla. Though he was not accorded political patronage by Sheikh Abdulla he was accorded political support by Begum Abdulla. In the campaign run together by Begum Abdulla and Molvi Masoodi the two were beaten by the 'goondas' of Charar-i-Sharief MLA Abdul Qayoom who snatched the blanket of Molvi Masoodi and the shawl of the Begum. As Charar-i-Sharief has been the citadel of Bakshi's influence so the incident went deeply against him throughout the constituency. To be fair to Bakshi, in spite of his devotional attachment with Noor Ud Din Wali (R.A.) and with Charar-i-Sharief he had never exploited this politically as Sheikh Abdulla his family are doing with Hazratbal and the Mirwaiz family is doing with Jamia Masjid. But he had committed a grave folly by giving undue patronage to the Mujawirs there and had by sheer nepotism created a class of hypocrites who were willing to appease new masters saddled in the power, but had mere sympathy for Bakhshi. In discharging their debt of gratitude to Bakhshi, they did this mischief which caused a deep resentment against him.

Thus, many factors along with the support of government machinery of Sadiq, political symbolism of Maulana Masoodi, closed door pornographic jokes of Mirza Afzal Beg, legendary underground work (for which he had earned fame during the Quit Kashmir Movement) of G.M. Karra and use of Sheikh Abdulla's name by his wife—all factors put together made a wooden khamba—an independent candidate, Shamim Ahmad Shamim trounce the late G.M.Bakhshi.

This concession was granted not in the interests of nourishing democratic institutions in Jammu and Kashmir, but it removed a person who by his rehabilitation, could in the process prove beneficial to lay the foundation of a democratic opposition party with a pro-Indian programme. But Indian rulers never intended the emergence of a democratic opposition in Jammu and Kashmir as they never wanted democratic institutions to grow. They have always encouraged paid agencies. Besides, according to current political 'folk tales' a personal grudge also worked; Indiraji was revengeful and under this strain a viable link was broken by the defeat of Bakhshi. Beyond this concession all the other five constituencies saw the usual and traditional manner of elections as has been destiny of the people of Jammu and Kashmir. It is not ordinarily possible for an independent to fight and win elections unless there is a party or parties backing him. In Jammu and Kashmir no individual, during the lifetime of stalwarts like Sheikh Abdulla, Mirza Afzal Beig, Molvi Mohd. Syed Masoodi, Kh. Mohi-ud-din Karra, Bakshi Ghulam Mohammad, Gh. Mohd. Sadiq and the scion of Mirwaiz dynasty Molvi Mohammad Farooq could cut any ice. It was by the collective support of these five stalwarts that the khamba selected by Molvi Syed uprooted Bakshi. In view of this collective support Bakshi would have been sidelined, but the committed fans of the Mirwaiz dynasty came to his rescue and saved his deposits. Overall this was ostensibly a fair deal, but in reality this was tantamount to stabbing in the back the party candidate, and also politically an immoral act—a deathblow to the emergence of rule of law in Jammu& Kashmir. But it was not the case with other independents from three other constituencies Anantnag, Baramulla and Ladhakh.

In the 1967 elections, neither M.S. Qureshi nor Agha Syed Ahmad had any personal base in both these constituencies nor did the Indian National Congress have any footing there in both these segments. During their three year tenure (1967-70) they were completely unmindful of the problems of their respective electoral segments and had dismissed their voters with utter contempt and unmistakenly conveyed to their respective electorates that they would be imposed again. Without any ground work, hard labour, a contest worth the name or campaigning, but by arranging picnics in Dak bungalows, guest houses and tourist huts and enjoying the hospitality of district and tehsil level government officers, these two official candidates M.S.Qureshi and Agha defeated the two independent candidates Peer Ghulam Nabi (alias Hakim Ghulam Nabi) and Syed Ali Geelani respectively. Who were they? It is pertinent to introduce them to our readers.

Both Peer Ghulam Nabi and Syed Ali Geelani were learned religious preachers and orators who could hold their audience spellbound for hours while delivering sermons on any topic on Islamiyat (Muslim theology). Both belonged to J&K Jamait-i-Islami which from 1945 attempted to create raw material for Islamic revolution which could replace man's sovereignty upon earth by the absolute sovereignty of the Almighty. They propagated that man has defined duties of being His viceroy to implement only His dictates in letter and spirit. With its unabated spread of Muslim literature, mainly the writings of late Maulana Abdul Ala Maudodi the Jamait had successfully arrested the trend of atheism which the success of Soviet revolution had infiltrated into the student community during the 50s and early 60s. This literature, sermons, the eloquence in their oratory, metaphors and anecdotes had introduced the Jamait within the literate Muslim group which upto 1970-71 constituted hardly 12 per cent of the population. Almost all of them were either government servants or connected with the state establishment. Thus, the raw material which they created, would after joining services or other fields of life fall prey to the same practices of earning by 'all' means as is prevalent in the other ranks. In this process of elimination hardly 2 per cent to 3 per cent group was committed to Jamait ideology in 1971. Outside the active members even their fellow travellers were not so committed that they would sacrifice their jobs. To be precise, the Jamait had penetrated its influence to the level of schoolteachers or had a localised support among college teachers and had virtually no representation in legal, medical and engineering professions. As far as the civil service was concerned many of them would enjoy the gripping diction of Maulana Maudodi's literature, but beyond that were worshippers of the rising sun. Jamait had no base among women, had not percolated in the city working class or rural agriculturists. But none can deny that the Jamait schools, libraries and study circles were busy in laying foundation for a revolution which would take at least one generation to achieve some result that might provide them enough vitality to nourish political ambitions. With these inherent shortcomings the Jamait had some odds against it. Briefly, they are as follows:

1. They were dubbed as *kotas*—the non-believers of the shrines. The majority of Kashmiri Muslims constitute the t*sekas* (such Muslims who are committed to the pilgrimage of shrines)

2. The traditional *kotas* (Wahabees or Ahli Nadis) also had deep rooted theological differences with the Jamait.
3. Even the limited pro-Jamait section considered politics a game devoid of ethical values and so considered these religious leaders ineffective. In their view politics being a game of falsehood so it required similar tactics to defeat the adversary. This group believed that Jamait leadership was incapable of doing so.
4. The pro-Pakistan majority in Kashmir had developed a bias against the Jamait for the reason that Pakistani people had rejected the Pakistan Jamait-i-Islami in the elections so considered the local Jamait incapable of delivering results.
5. A major section of the cadre of the Jamait was not in favour of election politics and so this inner contradiction too was a weakness for its candidates.

Conscious of these circumstances and aware of the results, it took a calculated step to fight the parliamentary elections in these two districts with the view to assess the situation whether to jump in the fray in the coming general elections for the state legislature. The Jamait was further handicapped as it had no trained cadre of workers who could counter the malpractices of the ruling party and could protect the sanctity of the vote. They had expectation of the participation of the electorate. In view of the active support of P.F. and P.C. in favour of independent candidates in Srinagar the boycott call of these organisations had no effect at all in these two constituencies and in Jammu province. In spite of the prejudices against the Jamait and that its candidates had no modern political training, even then voters were adamant about rejecting the official candidates at the hustings. Therefore, the ruling party took all steps to turn these two elections into a farce. The official machinery involved itself on behalf of ruling party candidates and indulged in bungling, such as loot and plunder of ballot papers and ballot boxes.[1]

These elections once again exposed that the democratic and progressive claims of Sadiq were a big fraud and his pretensions of honesty were exposed. In this context the Srinagar elections provided a lesson for the people of Jammu and Kashmir that honesty and dishonesty are tools which neo-colonist India uses to facilitate its game of occupation of Jammu and Kashmir.

With dishonesty and undemocratic means they created Bakshi's political persona and with immoral fairness they killed his political existence. Hence, the election result at Srinagar did not contribute any positive element in restoration of confidence in democratic institutions, but provided vicarious pleasure to Kashmiris that India had itself demolished one more link, one feeble but dependable bridge.

In Ladakh the inaction of Kushak Bakula for two terms as M.P. had convinced the voters that he may be a great religious leader, but had not evolved himself into a dynamic political personage. Hence, they were for Sonam Wangual who had worked as an activist at the lower ranks. Besides, the contradictions among various Lamas of important gumpas had also eroded the base of Kushak Bakula. The Zananskar Buddhists had felt completely alienated from the leadership at Leh and so were averse to Bakula. The Kargil area (which is now a separate district) had developed a strong reaction against the impressions deliberately created in India and elsewhere that Ladakh region was only a Buddhist district. The census figures had shown the ratio of population as being 50 percent for each. Hence, to dispel this impression Kargil Muslims devised a tactic to shatter Leh hegemony by dislodging Kushak Bakula. Therefore, all these disgruntled elements constituting more than two-third of the electorate joined together to reject the Congress candidate and elect the independent political worker. But, the government machinery from deputy commissioner down to village patwari all committed irregularities which are very easy in this region as the population is sparse and smaller villages are divided by great distances. Therefore, in carrying the election material, mischief is usually committed. It is practically impossible for an independent candidate to recruit a huge number of agents who can detect such bungling. This time the election held for Ladakh seat added one more fraud to the history of the elections. Finally, it provided will and courage for comparatively backward people of Kargil to assert themselves politically.

The results in two parliamentary segments in Jammu region was on expected lines, but achieved through undemocratic means. Had the government acted morally and had the Election Commission impressed upon the government to adhere to the norms and rules the result would have been the same even by strict honesty. However, these expected victories too were dubbed by the people as illegitimate for the transparent acts of fraud played by government agencies.

We have earlier discussed that the devising of these two electoral segments in Jammu province by the Delimitation Commission had led to gerrymandering, for many reasons including communal. In both these constituencies the Muslim vote had to go to the Congress candidates because they had a challenge only from the Hindu communal party the Jan Sangh. Besides, the large number of candidates in these two constituencies from Hindu community divided the Hindu vote; low caste Hindus are also against Jan Sangh and lastly, the Congress had a base among secular Hindus. All these circumstances put together provided a guarantee for the two Congress candidates Inder Malhotra and Gansara Singh to win these elections. But the manner in which the Sadiq administration behaved too, left an indelible impact that democratic norms shall always be ignored in Jammu and Kashmir and Kashmiris will in no circumstances witness fairness in value based polity. The subsequent exercises in this field did not dispel the impression but established truth in this assessment with increased vigour.

During these elections I was posted as Additional District Magistrate Poonch and so had opportunity in my dual capacity as a judge and as an important organ of the law and order machinery to witness, analyse and study the strains on every political party, on the minds of the voters and on the work culture of government servants who were deputed in bulk for the elections. It is relevant to mention that in 1968 Judicial Separation on magisterial level was introduced and implemented in the entire state of Jammu and Kashmir except in districts of troubled border Poonch and Rajouri. It can be well grasped that where the government did not dare to extend separation of judicial functions what can be the situation regarding freedom of expression in such areas. The immoral Line of Actual Control or ceasefire line, as it was then called, has so badly divided this area that even a village is unevenly divided. I have witnessed many such villages part of which with drinking water facilities fall under Indian occupation and the other part consisting of agricultural land and pasture ground has fallen under Pakistani occupation. In such imposed topography, forces and paramilitary forces impose restrictions and censor the speeches of candidates lest the opposition to the policies of government, its weaknesses and shortcomings do not provide material for propaganda to the listeners so closely situated on the other side. Can an election campaign bear any impact if the opposition is not allowed to highlight the failures of previously 'elected' members and the government? On my return to Srinagar immediately after these elections I did collect material about all the constituencies in Kashmir division and maintained relevant excerpts in my diary.

However, I found the leadership and cadres of Jamait-i-Islami enthusiastically inclined to participate in electoral politics. But a section, even closer to Amir Jamait Peer Saad-ud-Din was reluctant and apprehensive of the consequences. But after the death of Sadiq, the new chief minister Syed Mir Qasim wooed[1] the inclined section to participate mainly to convey to protagonists of boycott that if they failed to review their stand they might have to vacate from public life to make place for others. Both the inclined group of Jamait and rulers had felt the common strain of mass thinking which was unmistakably one of revision in the policy.

Notes :

1. Only twelve hours before polling a religious clerck of Bijbara mosque declared that Jamati Islami Chief Election Organisor Mr. G.M. Bhat (The Presant Amir of Jamat) had declared boycott. But in spite the electorate exercised their votes in Anantnag Constituency for which this partial boycott was declared. Ninety per cent of the polled votes went to Jamat Candidate Hakim Ghulam Nabi Shah as now admits the returning officer of that Segment Mr. M.A. Khan (retired I.A.S.). It was openly steted (next day) in Anantnag Bar Association by Mr. Narain Bakshi Advocate, Chief Election agent of Mr. Qureshi, Congress-I Candidate. Mr. Khan admits that had Jamat participated even at latter stage in the counting it would become impossible for him to declare results in favour of Mr. Qureshi as he latter did. The electorate and analysts hold that this sacrifice was offered by Jamat as a corrupt deal to get 'Concessions' in the forthcoming 1972 electionś of J&K Assembly.

Chapter 27

Betrothal for Divorce

After the 1971 elections great events created three distinct phases in our history. The end of 1971 gave birth to an independent country out of the subcontinent, the emergence of Bangladesh in December 1971. It left a mixed impact of hope and despair. It spread despair in the minds of leaders and ranks of political parties in Jammu and Kashmir which had pinned hopes in the political and military strength of Pakistan. To them Pakistan lay shattered and could hardly consolidate again, at least in their generation. So, they became apprehensive for two different reasons. One set was apprehensive about its very existence and other was apprehensive that a victorious Indian government might, in all probability, to suit its convenience, alter the demography of the state. The Indian government had much earlier initiated canvassing to make drastic changes in their policies and the Bakshi dynasty was the only hurdle in their way and so they liquidated it. By the start of 1972 the efforts were initiated to persuade the tall leader for a complete change. The other factor which also contributed to accelerate the process of change was the death of chief minister G.M. Sadiq who had eroded the special status of Jammu and Kashmiras no other political agent for India could have done. But ultimately the strong Kashmir Pandit lobby—the extra-constitutional force in the corridors of power in Delhi turned the dedicated outstanding secular comrade into a different Sadiq. This difference is evident from an incident which took place only a few months before his death. During the 1971 war as the fall of Dacca was felt certain Sadiq was in Delhi for treatment. A cabinet colleague, a Kashmiri Muslim rushed to his room and enthusiastically discussed the inevitable which was to happen. The annoyed Sadiq rebuked the minister and told him, "Oh! you fool, don't you understand that your safety and Indian integrity lie in strong and united Pakistan, disintegrated Pakistan is a threat to the safety of Kashmir, Muslims of India and it shall ultimately disintegrate India."

But, due to this victory on the Dacca front, there was widespread jubilation in India which created widespread frustration among pro-Pakistan and pro-plebiscite leadership in Jammu and Kashmir. A strong section led by Sofi Mohammad Akbar, Haji Mohammad Ishaque, advocate Mohammad Yasin Siddiqui and many others, on the other hand, argued with Sheikh Abdulla that breaking up of Pakistan had paved the way for the balkanisation of the subcontinent which ultimately would facilitate independent status for Jammu and Kashmir. Common people also contributed to this theory. Hence, there was no disappointment among the masses though they believed that a long drawn battle was necessary. Sofi bluntly told Abdulla, "it cannot be during our lifetime but history has to dictate a lesson to India".

A section of intellectuals who provided theoretical and moral support to the movement for plebiscite felt more apprehensive that India under the frenzy of its victory in war might erode, whatever was left in the name of special status and might even get the law about 'Permanent Residence' of original Kashmiris abrogated under which non-state subjects acquire immovable property in this state. They felt that by abrogation of such laws rich Hindus from various states of India might acquire property in the state and process of demographic changes might be set in motion. It is under these circumstances that a great pro-Pakistan intellectual Prof. Mohi-ud-din Hajni who was known for his views against Indian occupation of Kashmir conveyed to Sheikh Abdulla through late Khwaja Mubarak Shah in my presence that Sheikh Abdulla must take measures to protect, at least, the permanent residence status. The conversation took place in a hut within the sacred environs of Baba Payamud Din Rashi's shrine near Tangmarg when Khwaja Mubarak Shah sought the advice of late Hajni whether the former should join Syed Mir Qasim's ministry as an emissary of Sheikh Abdulla or not. This inclusion of Sheikh's trusted comrade and leader of the Plebiscite Front Khwaja Mubarak Shah in Mir Qasim's Cabinet as a powerful minister with maximum portfolios was a form of probation to test as to how the future relationship between India and Sheikh

Abdulla should evolve and to gauge the reaction which ensued from the people.

Here history repeated itself. In October 1947 the Indian Prime Minister Jawahar Lal Nehru to accord democratic character to the autocratic action of the Maharaja created a myth of mass popularity for Sheikh Abdulla and under that propaganda covered the so-called accession of the abdicated Maharaja. In the post-1971 scenario Indira Gandhi the daughter of Jawahar Lal Nehru, had similar designs.

In 1947 Sheikh's popularity was related to the Quit Kashmir Movement which had proved a flop and hence in the changed situation in the subcontinent his personal charisma had dwindled. In 1972 Sheikh Abdulla had merely a nuisance value and to deprive him of that value too Beig-Parthasarthy talks were initated. M.A. Beig President J&K Plebiscite Front represented Sheikh Abdulla and Parthasarthy represented Indira Gandhi. Sheikh Abdulla had no popular mandate as he had boycotted all elections and nor was the electoral process free in Jammu and Kashmir. However, through the defeat of Bakshi at the hands of the 'political pygmy' Sheikh Abdulla had conveyed his nuisance value and his intentions to undo the policy of abstention; the drastic action of Jamait-i-Islami to involve itself with active politics and in the electoral fight had provided a pretext to the pro-election cadres in the Plebiscite Front even to Sheikh Abdulla's family that the people were desirous to take part in elections. It was argued that in case Sheikh Abdulla confined his activities to negative policies the inevitable result would be to get the political vacuum filled in by others. The Mirwaiz party was also eagerly in search of an occasion, but for decades the old confrontation with the Sheikh dynasty and its political party the National Conference the leader of Awami Action Committee, Molvi Farooq and his associates were eagerly watching as who would bell the cat as he himself had no 'courage' to do so.

Immediately after the 1971 Parliamentary elections the establishment of Bangladesh frustrated even those limited sections which formed a persuasive force behind Sheikh Abdulla to leave the matter to history rather than hasten his own political downfall. Here let me make a reference to a historic speech of late Sufi Mohammad Akbar, the veteran leader of the Plebiscite Front who till the last moment of his life maintained that in any manner, whether by concessions or accords, India would never grant democratic privileges to Jammu and Kashmir. Therefore, he worked against any kind of accord with India and after the 'Indira-Sheikh Accord' he remained against this 'marriage of inconvenience'—as he called it. In December 1974 fell the 10th Muharram, the day of martyrdom of Imam Hussain grandson of Prophet Mohammad (SAW). In this connection a leading member of the Shia community, a superintendent in J&K police Syed Wali Shah made a request to me, as President Kashmir Cultural Organisation to convene a 'mushaira' (poetic symposium) in honour of Imam Hussain. The Kashmir elite, from all parts of the state, assembled in the house of Syed Wali Shah at Munawarabad, Srinagar. Syed Wali Shah requested me to invite Sheikh Abdulla to preside over the mushaira. Instead Sheikh Abdulla persuaded me to offer Sofi Mohd. Akbar to have that honour. Sofi Mohd. Akbar in his presidential address said:

> "Hussain had lived from his childhood under the shadow of swords in the lap of great military strategist Prophet Mohammad. He was brought up by the greatest warrior, his father Ali. So he was not unaware of the consequences he would face in the adventure he was undergoing. He had only two alternatives—either to offer his head or he had to compromise with vice, with falsehood and with degradation of human values. Similarly, are we situated presently. Either we have to offer our heads for sacrifice or have to make compromises. Compromise will kill us as a nation and determination with our mission is bound to grind us in the mill of vicissitudes, but ultimately history will not condemn us as traitors."

Sheikh Abdulla either had no belief in the contention that history shall come to the rescue of its victims or had no hope beyond himself and so believed that only he would be able to save Kashmir from a demographic invasion; or he had lust for power which made him compromise with his historical stature; or he was under heavy pressure from his wife, three sons, two daughters, two sons-in-law and their families. Whatever the reasons the ultimate happened. In February 1975 terms agreed and executed between two individuals without any representative character became a pretext for Sheikh Abdulla to enter the cage of power with two others, from the herd of Indira Gandhi. Sheikh Abdulla had no representative character at this time too. He entered into the Accord as an individual. He was not even elected president or office bearer of the J&K Plebiscite Front or J&K Political Conference. He had never participated in any election. Indira Gandhi too did not enter this accord as Prime Minister of India. At best it was an accord between the self-imposed president of J&K National Conference from which Sheikh Abdulla was dismissed in 1953 and which in 1963 was converted by G.M. Sadiq into the state unit of All India National Congress. Sometime later, probably on the eve of the 1967 elections Bakshi did again revive this organisation which was literally usurped by the Sheikh Mohammad Abdulla company in 1975. Had Sheikh, Beig or his other colleagues been its members they could have divided it in any manner and even as a minority group Sheikh Abdulla could have usurped the good offices of the political organisation. On the other hand, they claimed that 22 year earlier in 1953 they were illegally dismissed from the party, ran for more than two decades to different organisations, but ultimately under patronage, abetment and advice from New Delhi removed the existing members of this organisation and became its masters. In 1975 Sheikh Abdulla with his close confidant headed the state cabinet as the leader of the National Conference which did not have a single member in the J&K Legislature. This party was not on the rolls of the J&K Assembly, but strangely enough Sheikh Abdulla as the usurped leader of Bakshi's organisation, the National Conference was elected leader of the All India Congress Parliamentary Party in place of Syed Mir Qasim. Such neo-political theories can only be propounded and implemented in Jammu and Kashmir alone; everything is democratic which suits the colonial interests of the biggest democracy of the world. The cabinet initially constituted four golden sparrows (*chaar sowni ki chadiyan*). Sheikh and Beig were from pro-plebiscite politics, late Sonam Narbu was a retired engineer from Ladakh and ex-Ambassador of India, so was a trusted man of the Nehru-Gandhi family. The golden sparrow D.D. Thakur from Jammu requires some introduction as he was a novice in the contemporary political history of the state.

D.D. Thakur hailed from a Thakur family of a backward area in Pogul, a hill tract in district Doda, but contiguous to the south Valley. Hence, he inherited composite culture and language. He was the son of an ordinary agriculturist, but successfully competed as a lawyer in Muffasil Bar of Musaff's court of Ramban. Without moving to district court at Baderwah he directly shifted to Jammu where with the blessings and patronage of the Chief Justice Wazir Janki Nath, his ingenuity, practical wisdom and successful lobbying made him develop contacts first with the leadership of the state unit of Praja Socialist Party, then received patronage directly from Bakshi Ghulam Mohammad and finally, came in contact with Indira Gandhi. Simultaneously he received appreciation from Justice Murtaza Ali the then Chief Justice of J&K. These influences caused his elevation as an additional judge of the State High Court. But, his handling of a receivership matter of a Jammu based cinema shook Chief Justice Ali, who, refused to recommend him for confirmation and was even reluctant to recommend further extension in his favour as additional judge. Thus, by 1975, after he completed two years as additional judge he had to return to the bar again which caused him much stress. In this situation he developed close intimacy with Mirza Afzal Beig who with his engagement in the Beig-Parthasarthy talks would also conduct some important lucrative cases before courts of law including the Hon'ble High Court. As the dates for the honeymoon between Sheikh Abdulla and Indira Gandhi were fixed by Beig and Parthasarthy the question arose as to who would represent Jammu in a new compact cabinet of four experts. Sheikh Abdulla was himself strongly committed to install either O.P. Saraf or Balraj Puri or even Roshan Lal from Jammu who had supported him for 22 long years while Sheikh Abdulla and his family were undergoing suffering. Beig vehemently argued in favour of D.D. Thakur whom Shiekh Abdulla did not know. Beig praised Thakur's capacities as a judge and lawyer.

"We will elevate him as the Chief Justice, but he has no political contribution."

"No, Sir, he represents Jammu aspirations."

"No, No. He does not. Jammu people never accept migrants from hills as their representatives. As people of Srinagar cannot, in spite of your great sacrifices, own you as the representative of their aspirations so the Thakur will require two generations to cultivate acceptability in Jammu.' We must choose either of the three who have stood with us. Even I would prefer Sant Singh Teg upon D.D. Thakur."

Sheikh Abdulla's assessment was correct but Beig acted on the advice of some extraneous source or lacked wisdom to understand human nature. Indira Gandhi had a clear perception about O.P. Saraf and Balraj Puri. In her estimation they could not work as agents and therefore, she too exercised pull for D.D. Thakur. It is an irony of fate that in late 1977 or early 1978 due to some ailment D.D. Thakur was not able to attend the secretariat when Sheikh Abdulla convened a cabinet meeting at his Karan Nagar residence. Beig uttered in his despair:

"The man does not call on my residence to see his old ailing friend but has convened cabinet meeting at DD's residence for the known weaknesses of old leader."

"*Ien Hum Awardai Trust*" (it also is your creation) retorted I through a Persian medium. In this brief meeting with Beig I could infer that out of total frustration he was talking loosely with each word being carried across by his sycophants to the adjoining house of Sheikh Abdulla at Jammu. Two of those tale-cariers have their names in the literary history of the state.

With this anecdote I would like to convey that among the four 'golden sparrows' Narbu and Thakur were indirectly infiltrated in the cabinet of four persons by Indira Gandhi.

Immediately after this accord based on suspicion, Indira Gandhi proclaimed Emergency in India. What happened in the country is widely known and it is not relevant to quote its details or even its consequences in these discussions. However, it caused no material effect in Jammu and Kashmirfor two reasons. Firstly, the emergency caused consternation in the situation in India which had developed emotional commitment with freedom of thought, freedom of expression, freedom of association and with other types of freedom relevant to democratic governance. On the other hand, from 27 October 1947 Jammu and Kashmirhas passed through terror, which even India had not passed as a British Colony. So, this development in India neither bothered us nor did it affect us. Instead Kashmiris derived vicarious pleasure out of it. Secondly, Sheikh Abdulla had not approved of the terror let loose by Sanjay Gandhi and Jagmohan in old Delhi so Muslims in general in Jammu and Kashmirhad appreciated the opposition of Sheikh Abdulla against such atrocities. Thirdly, the change in Sheikh's ideology and his accord was initially considered by the people of Jammu and Kashmir as a change in the tactics of his struggle and not purely a power game. Hence, he had no formidable opposition which he needed to curb as was the case with him in 1947-48.

The youth, educated, conscious sections were averse to 'unprincipled' shifts in Sheikh Abdulla's policies, but were unaware how to express their aversion. Fourthly, all the anti-Indian opposition parties completely lacked direction after the fall of Dacca, so, they could not evolve any plan whether to oppose Sheikh Abdulla and if so in what manner and with what programme? The Mirwaiz dynasty had also found its fans in the race for opportunities and so Molvi Farooq too was watching for a clear opportunity to devise his political future. Jamait-i-Islami had initiated pro-Indian politics with anti-Indian slogans so these contradictions posed no challenge for Sheikh Abdulla, instead this duplicity was useful to further his political opportunities.

In this background came the 1977 Parliamentary elections when Sheikh had exercised power for two years walking on the crutches provided to him by the Indian National Congress.

Sheikh Abdulla's party men persuaded the party leadership to try their luck at five out of six places conceding only one segment for its senior ally the Indian Congress, but the deal finally settled at half each. The cadres wanted an organisational division of the state with a plan to leave three parliamentary segments for National Conference candidates and the other three, one in Ladakh and two in Jammu region to the Congress party, but the Prime Minister herself was keenly interested in her ministerial colleagues Dr. Karan Singh and Mohd. Shafi Qureshi. So, the National Conference had to accommodate both these candidates from the two constituencies where they (in their assessment) had an edge on their ally the Congress. The Natinal Conference was annoyed with Shafi Qureshi whom they regarded as a political novice, though he was not so. Besides, they considered everyone who had crossed from pro-Pak or pro-plebiscite to pro-India as a traitor. Qureshi too had crossed from one extreme to the other extreme so, in their perception he had become an Indian agent. Similarly, Sheikh Abdulla had both political and personal grudges against Dr. Karan Singh who was the son of his life-long enemy Maharaja Hari Singh with whom he had fought a long drawn battle from 1931. As ruler of the state Hari Singh had imprisoned him several times, dubbed him as a rootless 'goonda' and made all efforts to liquidate him.

Sheikh Abdulla had a genuine grudge against Dr. Karan Singh. In his assessment Karan Singh was a symbol of autocratic terror and a legacy of the treacheries of history which had resulted into sale of this land with its people and their progeny. He had the conception and a legally sound one that Dr. Karan Singh had neither the mandate nor power to dismiss him as Prime Minister in 1953.

We have discussed under the heading: 'Myth of Paramountcy and Fiction of Accession' that in 1953 the state administration was run under J&K Constitution Act of 1939. Dr. Karan Singh was elevated to the Regency under Notification of 20 June 1949. Sections (5) and (7) of 1939 Act provided, defined and contained powers which His Highness Maharaja Bahadur of J&K could exercise vis a vis the Praja Sabha (Legislature) and his government. After 20 June 1949 Notification, these two sections were not amended nor the said notification made any reference either to these two sections or to the relevant provisions of 1939 Act. However, for arguments sake it could be said that 20 June 1949 Notification by inference conferred those powers which the Maharaja possessed under Sections 5 and 7 of J&K Constitution Act of 1939 upon Karan Singh. The Regent, while exercising legislative powers invested in the Maharaja made drastic amendments to both these sections, viz., Sec 5 and 7 of 1939 Act vide J&K Constitution Amendment Act of 2008 Bik (1950). According to this amendment neither the Maharaja nor his Regent could dismiss the council of ministers. So, Sheikh Abdulla had a genuine grudge that Karan Singh had acted as an agent illegally and was conscious that his continuation as central minister was the reward for enacting treachery with the J&K Constitution. These were pretended arguments of grudge otherwise he was conscious that he was the creation of a fraud.

The post of Sadr-i-Riyasat which Karan Singh held on 8 August 1953 was a creation of the J&K Constitution and no presidential notification would vest such power in the Sadr-i-Riyasat to dismiss a Prime Minister who was 'elected' leader of the house, though imposed by a 'Selection without Discretion'. Before establishment of this Constituent Assembly Yuvraj Karan Singh—the Regent of the 'deposed' ruler made the first amendment to the Constitution Act of 1939 in exercise of Sec. 5 of the said Constitution Act. The relevant section is quoted here:

> "Notwithstanding anything contained in this or any other Act, all powers, legislative, executive and judicial in to the state and its government are hereby declared to be and to have been always inherent in and possessed and retained by His Highness."

The power vested in His Highness was exercised by his Regent appointed under proclamation of Hari Singh dated 20 June 1949. So under this power the Regent Karan Singh issued a proclamation to elect a Constituent Assembly for J&K.

In 1950 another Amendment Act (J&K Constitution Amendment Act 2008) was passed under Sec. 5 of 1939 Act read with the Notification of 20 June 1949 by the Regent Yuvraj Karan Singh which caused amendments to its Secs. 5 and 7. Sec. 5 quoted Supra was amended omitting inherent powers of His Highness.

Dr. Adresh Sen Anand, the learned author of *Constitution of Jammu and Kashmir—Its Development and Comments* commenting upon this amendment observes:

> "...So there were no longer any inherent powers of legislation vested in Yuvraj Karan Singh who was acting as the ruler of the state in the absence of his father Maharaja Hari Singh."

This author, an outstanding judge of India has with the dominant focus in his mind to cover all the illegalities in the

Indian case deliberately avoided pinpointing other consequences of this amending order issued by Karan Singh in 1950. My views about the powers which left after this amendment of 2008 are conveyed in the chapter 'Myth and Fiction'. However, some brief points are repeated here:

1. In my views (which I have hinted earlier and will discuss in a separate book: *Myth of Paramountcy and the Fiction of Accession* sovereignty upon J&K had passed to its people in August 1947 yet, if anything in the name of sovereignty vested in the deposed ruler that sovereignty in semblance was also surrendered by his Regent Karan Singh vide amended Sec. 5 of the J&K Constitution Act of 1939 and by his acceptance of the office of Sadr-i-Riyasat an elected office.
2. The substitution of a new section instead of Sec. 7 of the said Act divested the Regent or his source of power the Maharaja of any sovereign power or of any exercise of sovereign authority which after this amendment stood vested in the people. Sec. 7 amended reads:

   "The Council shall consist of the Prime Minister appointed by His Highness and such other ministers of the state as his Highness may appoint on the advice of the Prime Minister. The Prime Minister and other Ministers shall be collectively responsible to the Legislative Assembly of the State...." [Act XVIII of 2008 (AD1950) Sec. 5].

Thus when in August Sheikh Abdulla dismissed S.L. Saraf, his minister, the dismissed minister had ceased to be the member of the council of ministers. Sadr-i-Riyasat was bound to accept the recommendation to drop him from the council earlier. He (the minister) was 'legally' bound to submit and the head of the state was, upon the advice of the Prime Minister, bound to accept or reject the same. Even if the head of state (Sadr-i-Riyasat) was approached that the leader of the house had lost the confidence, he had only one alternative to ask the Parliamentary party of the ruling Junta to act in accordance with its constitution or remove the leader and elect a new leader in his place. Alternately, he could convene a session of the Assembly and to decide the fate of the existing leader and in case he was removed it could be asked to elect a new leader whom the head of state would invite to form a new government. On the other hand, the head of state did an illegal act by dismissing the elected leader of the 'elected legislature'. Dr. Anand, inspite of the fact that he owes the emergence[1] of his career to Sheikh Abdulla is not fair to history and reason. It is against this background that Sheikh Abdulla developed a grudge, rather sworn enmity with Karan Singh. But as he stood on the support from the Congress so had to obey without any commitment to his conscience to the dictates of the Congress high command. Unique contradictions existed in the personality of Sheikh Abdulla; obstinacy and intransigence subjected him to widespread enmity and even to victimisation. The latter added charisma to his personality. But simultaneously, he would not on occasions, feel any shame to surrender his conscience to such ridicule the result of which always was obnoxious. The same hero who received a historic funeral—the second in Kashmiri history—now lies in a grave squeezed into a small military protected area lest the public anger might sacrilegiously exhume his mortal remains. It is all due to contradictions in his personality.

It is in this background that Sheikh Abdulla accepted the nomination of Dr. Karan Singh as a candidate supported by him from Udhampur Constituency where his committed vote bank and the cadre had an aversion to Karan Singh. The Hindu vote was divided; the Hindus 'emotionally' attached to Maharaja Hari Singh considered Karan Singh a disobedient and undeserving heir to the Maharaja; the downtrodden Hindus particularly low castes dubbed him as the symbol of age-old exploitation. Similarly, Sheikh Abdulla had to accommodate M.S. Qureshi from Anantnag where Qureshi was condemned as a 'political infiltrator' and Sheikh Abdulla's party had a herd of candidates with a base. In Ladakh, Indira Gandhi had an interest in a woman named Parvati Devi who had no political base either in Leh or among Zanskar Buddhists or Kargil Shias or in Drass Sunnis. But Sheikh Abdulla too was interested in promoting women so supported her candidature. It is for the failures of Congress itself that it had no formidable candidate in Jammu who could pose a real threat to the respected Praja Parishad leader Thakur Baldev Singh and besides Indira Gandhi found in Balraj Puri—the candidate proposed by Sheikh Abdulla's National Conference to be a genuine democrat committed to socialism and secularism and with known inclinations for 'regional' equalities. In the other two seats Baramulla and Srinagar in the Valley the contest was confined between the National Conference and semi political Jamait-i-Islami. In Srinagar the 'blue eyed boys' of Indira Gandhi in Congress, opportunist political upstarts and disgruntled secular elements jointly but surreptitiously backed an independent candidate Molvi Iftikhar Hussain Ansari who had changed political affiliations too swiftly and so was dubbed by the masses, beyond his Mureeds—a small group of vociferous Qadeemi Shias—as an opportunist. Jamat had a formidable candidate in Syed Ali Shah Gulani in Baramulla alone though there too their influence was confined to the intelligentia only. To get their presence felt, the Jamat nominated a sitting member of the State Assembly late Abdur Razaq Mir who had limited influence in Kulgam Assembly segment only as their candidate from Anantnag. Even that insignificant non-political entity could defeat the Congress candidate had there been fairness in the election.

Only one constituency in the Valley witnessed straight contest in Baramulla where the National Conference leader (present speaker Assembly) Abdul Ahad Vakil faced straight contest with Geelani present head of the 17 party agglomeration called APHC. Akbar Jehan Begum wife of Sheikh Abdulla faced four candidates from Srinagar, but only Ansari was formidable enough to challenge Indira Gandhi's blue-eyed boys in Pradesh Congress Committee who had interest in blocking the Indira-Sheikh Accord. It is with this dominant objective that from my home town which has no Shia influences Abdul Qayoom (presently Farooq's minister) and his kith and kin (the same element which in 1971 in the electoral fight between Bakshi Ghulam Mohammad and Shamim Ahmad Shamim had snatched the woolen shawl of Begum Abdulla) worked openly for Ansari. Qayoom was an office bearer of the Pradesh Congress at this time and bound by the accord of his leader.

In Anantnag besides A.R. Mir of Jamat, four other candidates also were in the fray. For the first time during contemporary history Ladakh constituency witnessed communal polarisation—an imported infection in its body politic. Had only Congress nominated a Muslim candidate from this region a couple of times in five parliament elections having almost equally divided population, the local Muslim community would not have felt it necessary to demonstrate their existence by consolidation of its divided ranks. At this time a resourceless independent candidate Ali Kargili gave tough fight to Parvati Devi who had collective support from Indira Gandhi and her Congress party and Sheikh Abdulla and his National Conference. Though she won with a narrow margin of 2,877 votes, yet, it provided an opportunity for Sheikh Abdulla and his Conference to cultivate ground for grazing of its fat cow. The symbol of Indian secular politics the Nehru dynasty moulded Ladakh politics on communal lines and the symbol of Kashmir's secular preachings—the Sheikh dynasty-completed the so created communal void into a permanent gulf of communal hatred. The truth in Jinnah's theory became a universally acclaimed reality and practical proof was provided by the Nehru and Sheikh dynasties.

In Baramulla, inspite of grave odds against the Jamat, it gave tough fight to the 'vakil' of Sheikh Abdulla. Even the lesser known politician Ab. Razaq Mir who had neither talent in modern oratory nor traditional art of sermon deliverance forced M.S. Qureshi to adopt the same means to get elected which Bakshi had adopted to get him trounced by Pandit J.N. Bhat in the 1963 bye-election from Amirakadal Assembly segment. Shafi had support of powerful Sheikh Abdulla and the whole government machinery was behind him. Even then he would not survive the tough battle given to him by late Mir of Buchro.

It is most pertinent to examine some shortcomings which the Jamat and other opposition candidates had:

1. It stood nowhere among women folk, the labour class and agriculturists forming 80 per cent of the electorate. On the other hand, Sheikh Abdulla was a legend and to common people he was the harbinger of revolution.
2. It had no political cadre trained in bungling of votes which could withstand such bungling. On the other hand, both the Congress and the National Conference had the ability to indulge in this.
3. It had no muscle power, on the other hand, the National Conference and Congress both had only politics of force. In the early 60s Qureishi in order to defend himself and his cadre had emerged as a good organiser of political

wrestlers and would on occasions himself resort in bull fights'

4. A.A. Vakil had suffered for more than two decades as an activist of plebiscite politics. Syed Geelani too was a sufferer, but both were now considered on equal footing as both had sworn faith in the Indian Constitution. But, Vakil was considered a symbol of political fraud and recently recruited member of an Indian agency whereas Geelani was considered ineffective, but a voice of resentment against the Indira-Abdulla Accord.
5. Molvi Iftikhar belonged to a community which was a minority section within the small Shia community. In the older 'Shia-Sunni' distorted history of conflicts he was no match against the mother of the nation (Maadari Meharban), was dubbed as an agent of 'agents of India', but in spite of this kept the great lady and the Sheikh dynasty on tenterhooks.

In Jammu the election was fought as per defined lines. Both the candidates opposing each other Baldev Singh and Balraj Puri had many qualities in common. Though Balraj was a known secular democrat, Baldev Singh inspite of being veteran leader of a communal party had, to his credit, many secular deeds which no Jammu based Hindu Congress leader possessed. Both were perfect gentlemen and neither had capacity to project their own values to the rank and file. Balraj had a disadvantage in that he acted always against undemocratic policies and rule of terror. So, Jammu chauvinist Hindus who usually dubbed his pro-people and humanistic approach as endorsement of pro-plebiscite policy felt annoyed with him. Secondly, the other seven candidates cut a chunk from his vote bank. Thirdly, as National Conference cadres worked for its Congress allies in Anantnag, Udhampur and Ladakh, the Jammu Congress cadre abstained and even supported Baldev Singh openly. The National Conference had yet to create a cadre based unit in various parts of the constituency more so in Jammu city. Finally, the towns of Jammu and Kathua were predominantly pro-Jan Sangh. In spite of all these factors, Balraj Puri was defeated with a margin of about 28,000 votes in an electorate of six lakhs. None claims fairness on either side, but in spite of this the election was considered a healthy sign and a shift in the election process. The new recruited Dogra workers of the National Conference who joined it after 1975 had come to this ruling party for benefits. They considered in Puri a threat towards their vested interests so they worked against him.

Now let us revert to royal fights. Historical treacheries had imposed the dynasty of late Maharaja Gulab Singh as moulder of the destiny of several generations. The tragedy of history created another dynasty—that of Sheikh Abdulla from village Soura near Srinagar. The scion of the Gulab Singh dynasty Dr. Karan Singh fought on the Congress ticket as one of the six candidates from Udhampur Constituency which consists of the districts of Udhampur and Doda. Among Rajputs, Brahmins and even among common Muslīms the concept of divine right of kings had reconsolidated the appreciation for royal dispensation after the experience of the people about misrule, nepotism and corruption. Post-October 1947 circumstances created appreciation for the valued traditions of autocracy. It is in this background that like Kashmiris, the Kashmiri speaking Muslims from this constituency usually quoted the sayings of Sheikh Nooru Din Wali.

> "Then (in the days of decay in human values)
> The street gutters shall overflow like whirlpools.
> The perennial rivers shall dry up,
> And monkeys shall rule the roost."

Five candidates opposed him. The ruling Congress at the centre did all to assure his re-entry into the central cabinet. The National Conference ruling the state held a grudge against Dr. Karan Singh for reasons stated earlier, but Sheikh was consciously aware of the crutches on which he walked to the civil secretariats both in winter capital Jammu and summer capital Srinagar. He had developed the suspicion that even if his ex-Sadr-i-Riyasat, who had illegally dismissed him on 8 August 1953 was rejected by the people by a genuinely democratic verdict, his base would be removed and he would have a fall. With these plus points in his favour the Hindu communal elements also openly supported him. His main rival was a genuine democrat, a socialist and fearless journalist who has inherited political ethics, professional values as a journalist and dedication to the cause from his father Mulk Raj Saraf—rightly called the father of journalism in Jammu and Kashmir. Om Saraf had been critical of the dismissal of Sheikh Abdulla in 1953, had opposed the communal oriented Praja Parishad agitation of the 50s, fought against detention without trial of Sheikh Abdulla and other Kashmiri leaders, headed the state unit of All India Praja Socialist Party and was well known for his principled political ideology and practice. Such politicians hardly percolate their influence in the lower layers of society. It remains superficially rooted among intellectuals only who hardly matter during hustings. More so, they are ineffective in Jammu and Kashmirwhere political charisma lies in deceit, fraud, misleading oratory, philanthropic distribution of largesse amassed from the embezzled assets. Besides, OM Saraf was devoid of an effective party cadre and on the other hand, state and central administrators were actively busy in the campaign against him. The 'heir apparent' of autocracy was made to win by about 59,000 votes. His success was sure, but the margin would have been lesser. Thus a principled scholar and son of the last Dogra ruler had to save his honour with 'unfair means' which amounts to a moral defeat. Politicians, whatever their pretensions, are devoid of such sensibility.

Simultaneously it was the worst defeat for Sheikh Abdulla also who patronised fraud in favour of his enemy and that too against a friend who from 1953 had stood like a rock to work against excesses committed upon the same Sheikh Abdulla and his associates.

This now brings us to another royal battle, though it was no fight but turned into the stature of World War II by the panicky Sheikh dynasty, sycophants of the National Conference and opportunistic civil servants.

It is a fact that by joining power under the Indian Constitution which Sheikh Abdulla had rejected, by accepting the J&K Constitution which he had considered a document of patent fraud and by climbing through the ladder of the Congress Parliamentary party to the pinnacle of power whom he had earlier declared to be 'worms of the gutter', his image shattered. The common people considered this 'action' to be a deviation in his stand and not treachery, but was a 'shift in strategy', so the mass base was not eroded. The new generation, considered the shift to be an act of cowardice and fraud. To them Sheikh Abdulla changed his stance under the persuasive influence of Mirza Afzal Beig and the directions from his wife Begum Akbar Jehan who was the National Conference candidate from Srinagar. Some sections of the people, more so the rural population and women folk considered her an embodiment of sacrifices and so called her "Mader-i-Meharban"—the Loving Mother. It was her image as the loving mother which in 1971 made a khamba-t Shamim Ahmad Shamim to uproot a deep-rooted sprawling chinar Bakshi Ghulam Mohammad.

Threat could be posed by a genuine or formidable candidate of which there was none. The Congress leader Mufti Mohammad Syed and Abdul Qayoom of Charar-i-Sharief both directly worked for independent candidate Molvi Iftikhar against the party whip. However, all put together were not even of nuisance value. To be fair Molvi was proxy candidate of Pradesh Congress Committee headed by Mufti Syed.

Ansari had proved himself an opportunist who in sermons as a Shia preacher had the art to make his audience weep, but in practical life was equated even by his own community as one who represented those traits and treacheries against which Imam Hussain (A.H.S.) sacrificed his life and family. He could criticise the Sheikh dynasty of political inconsistency, but himself had no political morality. He could level charges of amassing wealth against the Sheikh dynasty, but the people knew that within his brief political stint he had acquired such luxuries which Sheikh's family had not seen even during his prime ministership.

He represented a small section of Shia community which had three internal irreconciable divisions. The Sunni majority had deep-rooted enmity with the sect mainly created by Mullas with vested interests of the two sects. But the hatred was ingrained and a century old. In this situation Begum Abdulla had no threat at all, but both the hierarchy of the National Conference and Sheikh's dynasty were crestfallen. One can realise how despots and dictators tremble under the awful fear of public opinion. I had experienced the impact of this psychology in 1962 when the most powerful dictator of Kashmir Bakshi Abdul Rashid had fallen at my feet, but during the campaign in this election I saw another headstrong despot G.M. Shah psychologically shattered. However, Sheikh Abdulla himself was unperturbed as he considered the contest merely a sham. At that time I was sub-judge Shopian, district Pulwama and was invited to make surprise campaign visit of my home district Budgam where I had some pockets of influence. I imposed a condition precedent to seek blessings of Sheikh Abdulla and met him at his residence at Maulana Azad Road. I conveyed the insistence which was being put upon me. Sheikh Abdulla angrily replied:

> "You are a Judicial Officer. In case your participation in campaign is exposed I will not defend you and instead frankly admit your involvement."

This statement could be interpreted in many ways. It can be said that Sheikh Abdulla was a genuine democrat, but this was not borne out by subsequent events. Secondly, perhaps Sheikh considered the contest posed by Molvi Iftikhar as a challenge of no consequence. Thirdly, it can be considered that because of his soft corner for me he never wanted me to get into controversy. My visit to his house did not remain a secret. The complaint was made before Satarawala advisor to Governor L.K. Jha, who requested Ansari the chief justice and I was transferred to Leh.

Out of the three lakh votes polled, the Begum won with a thumping margin of 1,22,641 votes. Ansari polled only 7,431 votes and four others forfeited their security deposits.

Though the people of Jammu and Kashmir were conscious that six M.P.s in a house of 400 members had no say, yet, this participation was a clear indication that negative politics might come to an end if these steps had received positive reaction. It was a prelude to 1977 mid term polls for J&K Assembly and indicated trends too.

Had Indira Gandhi not been humiliated at the hustings and had she again taken over as the Prime Minister the post-election scenario would have frustrated the Sheikh-Indira accord. Sheikh Abdulla would have been either forced to eat humble pie and could have been dethroned mercilessly or forced to accommodate the Congress 'worms of the street gutters.' But, Indira Gandhi's humiliation at hustings, formation of the Janta Party ministry and particularly the election of Morarjee Desai as Prime Minister certain positive steps evolved, which, if consolidated with consistency, would have moulded the political history of Jammu and Kashmir in a manner which could have healed many wounds.

This process ultimately proved that Jammu and Kashmir has no role, not even negligible, to play in the moulding of the political destiny and economic prosperity of the Indian Federation. It convinced the people that the election of six persons from the state can, at best, rehabilitate such politically irrelevant liabilities whom the ruling party here feeds on the largesse of concessions as a sinecure. It is for this reason that within only three years the member from Baramulla A.A. Vakil had apprehended severance of his roots in the politics of his district so his interest again declined. Dr. Karan Singh could not get himself locally rooted as it would have been degrading for a ruler to remain content with the position of a state legislator or even the minister of the state cabinet. Through Begum Abdulla, the Chief Minister Sheikh Abdulla, was interested in keeping the dynasty closer to the seat of power and to have a residential state house in New Delhi besides the houses they occupied in the two capitals of the state. Both the so 'elected' members on the National Conference ticket proved a liability for the party and caused a great reaction in their cadres.

Chapter 28

Mid Term Poll of 1980

The fall of the Congress at the Centre and emergence of the Janta Party gave Sheikh Abdulla a 'windfall' of continuation in power, otherwise the coterie surrounding Indira Gandhi and Sanjay Gandhi would have cut him down and he could not have tolerated such humiliation. His reservations, rather any disapproval of the excesses during the emergency had annoyed the Congress (I) cadre. Had those elements returned to power that would have been considered endorsement of terror and tyranny and many great leaders in India including the family friend of the Indira dynasty, Sheikh Sahib would have been humiliated, but destiny willed otherwise. In the new power equation Sheikh Abdulla through the good offices of Governor L.K. Jha got accommodated.

During the 'Janta Rule' he did not like the policies of vendetta against Indira Gandhi. Appointment of the Shah Commission to probe against misuse of power by Indira Gandhi would in his view have created a wave of sympathy for the rejected lady. Her arrest and detention was openly criticised by Sheikh Abdulla and created around him a halo of elderly statesmanship. Consequently, his criticism of "excesses of emergency was pardoned by Nehru-Gandhi dynasty" and were treated as acts of constructive political maturity.

Within three years the agglomeration of the Janta Party proved a flop. It collapsed under the weight of its own follies. Though by name it was Janta (People's) party, but in reality it was a people-less party of leaders. Every leader had ambition to achieve a position ranking not less than that of Prime Ministership. It was only the Jana Sangh, a constituent with a cadre based party which remained contented with the positions which fell to its lot. It had a definite policy that ambition for short lived Prime Ministership could prove fatal for its survival so it considered it both feasible and practicable to spread its growth like a creeper with the support of great leaders like Jaya Prakash Narayan and Morarji Desai. On the other hand, the immaturity of the kisan leader from U.P. Choudhary Charan Singh was duly exploited by Indira Gandhi and ultimately a members group of ruling Janta Party, under the leadership of Charan Singh defected and formed minority government with the outside support of Congress, which was conveniently withdrawn and so mid-term poll of 1980 was announced.

Before this election vis a vis , the state six parliamentary segments is discussed it is pertinent to sum up the political situation in Jammu and Kashmir in 1980.

1. From February 1975 to June 1977 the people in Jammu and Kashmir expected that the experienced and mass leader Sheikh Mohammad Abdulla would perform miracles and would cure with 'supernatural' acts the deep-rooted ills of corruption and nepotism. Elite and literate sections of the population had no such illusions. They had encouraged Sheikh's renewed contacts with India either to halt through the use of his personal influence any further erosion in the special status of the state or wished that Sheikh Abdulla should commit political suicide lest his ghost rule the national psyche of Kashmiris for decades to come. But both the sections expected that he might cure some diseases in the body polity of Jammu and Kashmir.
2. It was the effect of this psychology that for a period of a year or even for two years an automatic restraint in public life from lower levels to higher became visible without adoption of any preventive measures; the menace of wholesale copying in examination halls stopped; officers became reluctant or cautious to accept bribes and such was the case with the public which restrained themselves from offering bribes and the touts went into oblivion. To be precise, without any positive or negative checks the very installation of a personality—who had preached in mosques and shrines the principles and ideals of honesty and integrity—created an impact. The process of cleaning public life became a voluntary trait. At this stage had Sheikh's family, his cadre and party colleagues contributed to this voluntary process through

their actions, within their respective ambits, notwithstanding the political basic issues, the cleaner public life would have created in Jammu and Kashmir an atmosphere of integrity and honesty.

But to be fair the Indian mechanism had encouraged a bandwagon of concession seekers—rather the pro-Indian limited political groups were created, and sustained by Indian concessions. It was to receive the lion's share as a concession seeker that Molvi Iftikhar Ansari chose Begum Akbar Jehan as his target for the electoral fight. Shortly he found marketability at 1 Asif Ali Road, which upto 1977 was the official residence of the Prime Minister of India. This contagion spread by Congress (I) through its Pradesh ranks of Jammu and Kashmir affected the rank and file of the National Conference, the family members of Sheikh Abdullah and business houses of the pro-Abdulla clique. With the exception of the chairman Molvi Mohd. Syed all members of the state Janata Party unit in Jammu and Kashmir united together to derive maximum concessions, to grab maximum part of the booty, to plunder without sharing with each other the huge sums and funds which the Union of India provides the state not for its economic and industrial development, but to contain and occupy it. Had the Indian government diverted all these funds in constructive and pro-people developmental works, the people of Jammu and Kashmir would not have developed complete aversion against India which resulted in alienation. Analysts here believed that this domination through concessions was specific to the political culture of All India National Congress, but the Janta Party government by its continuation established it as the political policy of Indian governance. It accorded continuation to this policy with immaturity which resulted in terrible contradictions that consequently proved destructive. On the other hand, the Congress party would also keep their local house divided as these groups owed their allegiance and loyalty to one person—either to Nehru or to his daughter Indira or to her son Rajiv. Some of them would occasionally try to get close to the younger son of Indira, Sanjay Gandhi, but such contacts were part of their loyalty to the Nehru-Gandhi dynasty. On the other hand, every leader of the state unit of Janta Party was his own master, the dominant interest to join this bandwagon was to replace the concession-seekers and to loot and plunder the state-resources.

This deep-rooted menace in Kashmir polity along with the inalienable game plan of Indian policy makers could not leave the National Conference leadership and its cadre unaffected. They were not honest political workers even in opposition. They received aid, donations, assistance, charity and all sincere sacrifices from their people. On Idi Qurban the hides of sacrificial animals thousands in number, saffron produce from saffron growers, the Sudqai fitr (charity distributed after observing the month of fasts of Ramdhan) the Zakat fund and one tenth share of the agricultural produce—all these aids and funds were donated by the people generously and collected by these leaders under patronage of Sher-i-Kashmir. Besides, philanthropists across the LOC also usually collected funds and sent them through runners who also deducted their commission; forces and para-military forces guarding borders also took requisite percentage of their commission but, inspite of this huge portions reached these few families scattered from Soura[1], Baghi Magharmal[2], Basant Bagh[3] to Sarnal[4]. What happened to these generously donated funds? To quote an incident from my personal diary in 1958 this author had, as junior defence lawyer of Kashmir conspiracy case, to visit Kud where Nilakanth Hak conducted committal proceedings of that case. Ill health prevented me from going so Sheikh Nazir Ahmad (presently general secretary of the ruling National Conference) and Abdulla Ahad of Shah Mohalla Nawab Bazar worker of the Plebiscite Front left next day in a jeep which met with an accident on the Srinagar-Jammu National Highway near Digdowl. Ahad died on the spot, Sheikh Nazir received minor injuries. The body of the young man was brought to Srinagar and as he had no major male member, I acted as the manager of the family for a full week for which all expenses were borne by the nation by collections. Despite my constant presence and in spite of my protests false accounts of funeral ceremonies were prepared and those big leaders embezzled the lions' share leaving the destitute widow and children unprovided for. It is against this background that as the same hungry leadershp buried the Plebiscite Front, it wore the new gown of the All J&K National Conference and became holders of the national resources.[5]

In this situation the State Assembly was dissolved and the 1977 elections were conducted. Its immediate result was enunciation of the theory that to keep the vote bank intact the concessions for the workers, political sympathisers, cadres and co-travellers were a necessary evil without which the party would get sold in the political auction house. Ministers also felt convinced that the civil servant is the most effective tool to win or lose elections, hence, it was felt necessary to woo them with the same tactics with which late G.M. Bakshi had whetted their appetite. So the revival of corruption became a political tool of post-1977 elections. Corruption got legitimacy under the benign encouragement of the revered great lady, whom the nation had accorded the title of Maadri Meharban (affectionate mother). It grew under her pious prayer sheet (Musala) and around her rosary imported from Mecca. With such encouragement the great national leader Sheikh Abdulla had by 1980 become the symbol of corruption.

After the 1977 Parliamentary Elections and with the installation of the Janta Party government in New Delhi the J&K Jamait-i-Islami again abandoned election politics. It probably went into political hibernation or felt that their political participation was just a futility and so they did not participate in the 1977 Assembly Elections. Up to the defeat of the Congress in India during the 1977 General Elections the state Jamait had developed a tacit understanding with Indira Gandhi which they could not develop with Morarji Desai or after roping Sheikh Abdulla again in the fold, Jamait lost utility for New Delhi and so it went for penance for the previous sins of its leaders. It did not, therefore, opt, to participate in the mid term 1980 poll. During this election only the J&K National Conference was, as a regional party, united under one leader, so despite all inner conflicts it looked like a unified command. Jamait had taken up 'sanyas' and after its worst defeat in the 1977 State Assembly the state Janta Party had experienced a set back and disintegrated. All those whom Nanajee Deshmukh had collected together under the umbrella of elderly Maulana Masoodi, had fallen against one another. Besides, the disintegration of the Janata Party at the center had led to political downfall and bankruptcy at the headquarters of the state Janata Party unit.

The All India Congress Party was also divided into several groups. Visibly there were two factions Congress(U) and Congress(I). The latter too had divided loyalties; the loyalists of the Gandhi-Nehru dynasty and loyalists to the party. Party loyalists were doubted. The other combination in the state remained the successor of Praja Parishad, viz., Jana Sangh which later adopted the nomenclature of Bhartiya Janata Party-BJP or "BAJAPA."

The special feature of this election was that Sheikh Abdulla's National Conference like Bakshi's National Conference fielded candidates from all the six constituencies. As said earlier despots have always felt scared of mass decisions. The despots who claim to have acquired such status by the charisma of their personalities feel more scared and apprehend that even small cracks might erode the myth of their claimed charisma. This is why the Sheikh dynasty exerted pressure to assure the unopposed success of Farooq Abdulla from Srinagar Constituency. In this game all the lessons which Bakshi had taught in 1957 and 1962 which Sadiq had brought home to the Kashmiris in 1967 Mir Qasim had exercised in 1972; the methods initiated by late Sheikh Abdulla in 1950-51 were together put in practice, but with a cunning patchwork behind the screen. Ultimately Farooq Abdulla, heir apparent was deputed to a political training course by his father and was elected MP unopposed from the electoral constituency of Srinagar. Later we will see that by handing over the mantle to the third generation Farooq Abdulla repeated history in 1998-99.

Khwaja Mubarak Shah hailed from an important and respectable family of Kamraz (northern Kashmir). He was one of the earliest law graduates from the area, joined politics after resigning from gazetted state police service and was even a junior cabinet colleague with Sheikh Abdulla up to 8 August 1953 in charge of the finance portfolio. But he was also dubbed as an American agent within one night, dismissed alongwith Sheikh Abdulla and thrown into prison. He was a successful district lawyer and practised before me both with ingenuity and originality though legal profession was not his primary option. He remained devotedly committed to politics and can be considered the leading personality of the second line of Kashmiri leadership. Even Syed Mir Qasim and G.M. Shah were junior in status to him.

I remember an important incident which reveals gentleness. As secretary Legal Defence Committee I attended a meeting with big leaders of J&K Plebiscite Front, presided over by the acting President Sofi Mohammad Akbar. M.L. Qureshi, senior advocate, declined to attend the meeting as it was held in the headoffice of the Front at Tanikpora Srinagar over a sumptious wazwan. During the deliberations Mubarak Shah moved legally sound and practicable suggestions but G.M. Shah, son-in-law of Sheikh Abdulla had no conception of criminal law so did not approve of the suggestions. Mubarak Shah with all humility wished to explain his point of view, but sensed that G.M. Shah disliked insistence so he withdrew his suggestions. The incident, on the one hand caused utter disappointment about Kashmir's political culture (which is not yet changed) and simultaneously lowered the impression of Mubarak Shah in my eyes. During the 70s when I was posted as a judge in Baramulla and Mubarak Shah was a practising lawyer I attempted to seek his explanation about this incident, but he politely avoided doing so.

With his fame as a towering personality of the second line of leadership he was inducted as a powerful minister in the cabinet headed by Syed Mir Qasim on trial basis for 'Indira-Sheikh' accord of 1975 and almost 50 per cent of departments were under his control. The net result was that he proved himself to be a meek and gentle person with no dash and unable to take decisions. Despite these weaknesses his gentle nature, mature political thinking, seniority as a political leader, clean image and known intellectual background ensured that he was the only choice for Sheikh Abdulla. An unknown lawyer, with a stigma of opportunistic political shifts attached to him, with no party base and with no worker cadre challenged Mubarak Shah as an independent from Baramulla constituency and polled 75,256 votes, i.e., 21 per cent of votes polled. These 21 percent votes were consciously polled to protest (a) against the corruption of the Sheikh Government, (b) against the inefficiency of Mubarak Shah during his ministerial tenure, (c) to record disapproval against the new Indo-Kashmir honeymoon in which Mubarak Shah had played an assisting role to Sheikh Abdulla.

Muzzafar Beig bagged hardly 2 per cent votes mainly

from his kith and kin, from the influence he exercised on the Pahari speaking community and from the small pocket of Abdul Gani Lone's People Party vote bank confined to a few villages in district Kupawara.

There are no reasons to suggest any major rigging in the victory of Mubarak Shah, but the voters mainly voted for his personal behaviour and rejected the political novice who within his brief political career changed sides swiftly. However, those who exercised their vote in favour of Mubarak Shah or Muzzafar Beig endorsed the policy to take interest in the elections of Indian Parliament on which they did not pin hopes. The other two candidates in the fray were just purposeless.

The situation in Anantnag was similar where the doyen of an affluent trader family, a successful lawyer with pro-Pak political leanings who had made sacrifices in protest against the Indian occupation of Kashmir had a rival with a similar pro-plebiscite political record. A.M. Naik, the National Conference candidate G.R. Kochak had proved his loyalty to the leader and party whereas A.M.Naik commanded respect as acting President of the Plebiscite Front, but his defection to the camp of pro-Indian politics had lowered his prestige even within his own village, Tehsil, Pargana and district. Here also about 51 per cent voters exercised their right of vote and more than 60 per cent of the polled votes were bagged by the National Conference. Overall participation was a healthy sign for Indian interests, as much as 50 per cent of the population were aware that 4 to 6 members from Jammu and Kashmir would hardly contribute to the evolution of any policy, nonetheless, they registered support to regional aspirations, but within the federation. Had this support been used constructively interest in Indianisation of Jammu and Kashmir politics would have been shaped in phases.

In 1977 Dr. Karan Singh won by a margin of about 59,000 votes, however, this time the National Conference gave him tough fight from Udhampur and the margin of victory was reduced by about 4,000. The number of contestants had increased from 6 to 7. From Jammu the veteran Praja Parishad leader lost. Baldev Singh and Girdhari Lal Dogra had been old adversaries for the assembly constituency of Hira Nagar, which is the home tehsil of both the leaders whose fate was usually decided by the caste factor. Dogra, a Brahmin used to bag votes from his community and even from the scheduled castes whereas Baldev Singh was usually supported by Rajputs.

Leh again projected the Buddhist domination, but by this time instead of regional rivalries (i.e. rivalry between Leh and Kargil regions)) communal rivalry took shape. Had the Indian National Congress been sincere to secular traditions it should have fielded a Ladakhi Muslim this time. The gap was so narrow that in spite of open army support to P. Namgyal he won only with a margin of 6,000 votes.

In J&K Assembly Elections non-state subjects cannot become voters, whereas for parliament elections the voter list is framed according to census figures which records, as voters of Leh and Kargil, the members of the armed forces as well.

The moral from this exercise was that the 1977 Parliamentary elections, 1977 Assembly elections together with 1980 mid term elections initiated a democratic process and process of voluntary involvement in the evolution of Indian democracy.

Notes

1. Ancestral house of Sheikh Abdulla
2. The house of G.M. Shah (son-in-law of Sheikh Abdulla) which originally belonged to a relation of the Maharaja, but was acquired as the first political estate by the Shah family.
3. M/s G.M. Bhat and A.M. Bhat alias 'Reda' resided here. In this house in 1954-55 late Mirza Afzal Beig 'created' the J&K Plebiscite Front.
4. Sarnal the ancestral house of Mirza Afzal Beig at Anantnag.
5. On my piligrimage of "Umra" of holy Keba and holy 'Rowza' of prophet I celebrated Idi-Baqar with my wifes nephew late Irshad Kanth (Buch), a director with a Saudi Construction Corporation in port city of Jedeh. I found volunteers Collecting aid for orphaned Children and widowed women of Kashmir. Witnessed the generous contribution I was shocked after assessment of the lot of martyred Mujahids widows and orphans and the huge largesse collected. It moved the creative writer within me and instantly I created a short story which shook the conscience of all Kashmiri resident Suadis, who heard. Its English translation under the title "Price" published latter in Daily: 'Kashmir Monitor Srinagar, created a stir. The moral is that since 1947 leaders thrived out of the miseries and sufferings of the people.

Chapter 29

1984 Elections

The Hindu Marriage Act, Succession Act and other laws enacted to consolidate the personal laws applicable to other communities except Muslims and Christians contained Sikhs within the ambit of the definition of Hindu. The scheme of the partition of the subcontinent based on the Two Nation Theory also had presumed Sikhs to be an inseparable part rather a Hindu sect. So Hindus, Sikhs, Jains and Buddhists legally and politically constituted one nation, i.e., Hindus. This legal and political conception based on the deeper traditions of Indian history had an emotional background. Even the successful political achievement of All India Muslim League to have a separate nation Pakistan, did not blunt the argument of nationalist Indian Muslims. To them all the communities of the subcontinent form one 'Indian nation' and division has only created two geographical national identities and not any theocratic nationalities. This argument may be debatable, but there can be no dispute that after partition all communities who opted and lived in India accepted themselves as members of one community called 'Indian Nation.' In the same manner the founder of Pakistan Mohammed Ali Jinnah also declared all the communities which stayed back in that country after August 14, 1947 as part of one nation, i.e., the nation of Pakistanis. With this background we can safely argue that though the suspicions were left in the minds of Indian Muslims or created against them, but Sikhs were considered as faithful and sincere Hindus as the Brahmins of Varanasi, Rajputs of Bikaner, Marwarees and were treated as such. This fraternity was to be consolidated constructively after independence in such a manner that no cracks would be allowed or if there were any cracks they would be repaired. But, politicians adopted the same policies of divide and rule with which imperialists had damaged the subcontinent. We have in our earlier discussions asserted that it was the mandarins of South Block

New Delhi who formulated the draft for the memorandum to Cheewan Rigzin in 1949-51 and submitted the same to Jawaharlal Nehru. In 1948 a similar representation was made in the name of Maharaja Hari Singh who then had migrated from the state. Both these memoranda contained neither Ladakhi thought, nor reflected their secular ideals nor does the phraseology used in them convey the sincerity of Ladakhis. The words used were designed to sow seeds of dissension in a place which was by nature a fertile ground, of amity and love.[1] This reference quoted with a purpose to convey that in similar manner the seeds of discontentment were so mischievously sown that the Sikhs had to take recourse to extreme measures so as to convey the argument of their distinct physical and metaphysical identities.

The 1977 election proved to be punishment for the excesses of emergency and it further convinced the political advisors to Indira Gandhi that the family charisma and personality cult could not be transferred through inheritance to the third generation of the Gandhi-Nehru dynasty. The subsequent election of 1980 was not a positive verdict, but again was a punishment inflicted upon those elements who failed to rise above personal vested interests and could not meet the aspirations of the electorate.

It seems that after Indira Gandhi's return to power in 1980 she had not learnt the lessons conveyed by the electorate. Taking no heed of the message conveyed by the masses she worked for the interests of her children and tried to build up the charisma of her son Rajiv in her own life-time by choosing a constituency to feed her family fortune. She started meddling, at higher level with Sikh religious affairs.

In consequence of the sacrilege of the Golden Temple at Amritsar, the pivot of religious activities of Sikhs, Indira Gandhi fell to the bullets. Her only surviving son Rajiv Gandhi was declared as Prime Minister during a communal and sectarian wave of sympathy for the family of the victim leader and vengeance was let loose against the Sikh minority, which till then was considered a facet of Hindu conception. It was now collectively forced to assert itself as a separate nation. This reaction inundated the confidence of the Sikh community, but simultaneously drowned in the waves and tides of the opposition against the heir of the legacy of sacrifices.

The mystery created around the natural death of Sheikh Abdulla on 8 September 1982 aroused some sympathy for his son Farooq Abdulla. Sheikh Abdulla had proved more clever than Indira Gandhi in this matter. He had during his political struggle built an impression that his chief comrade Mirza Afzal Beig would succeed him as the leader. After disowning Beig and deserting him when he was disabled, Sheikh Abdulla tacitly threw feelers to his son-in-law G.M. Shah. These suggestions received a mixed reaction and simultaneously he introduced his son Farooq Abdulla with political manoeuvering, but only as a social worker to whom he had entrusted the establishment of the Institute of Medical Sciences under his name in his own native village Soura. This opportunity given to this non-resident Kashmiri Farooq Abdulla, who had settled, married and become the head of a four member family in London, was not in recognition of his ability as a physician or surgeon; he was a failure as a medical practitioner. People blamed Bakshi that as Prime Minister of Jammu&Kashmir to accord political concessions to the family of Sheikh Abdulla, he had usurped two medical seats from the quota of deserving candidates for the two sons of Sheikh, viz., Farooq Abdulla and Mustafa Kamal. Neither deserved the nomination nor had aptitude for the medical profession. However, as the son of Sheikh Abdulla and with the assistance of his wife, a matron, Farooq Abdulla cultivated extra-professional contacts as the director of this institute. In spite of this, Sheikh Abdulla dismissed suggestions of politicising either of his two doctor sons.

In 1977 Dr. Farooq Abdulla came to Leh where he dined at my official residence along with his family though the stayed in the Leh guest house. Naïve cadres of Ladakhi Muslim National Conference were moved by his approach. They had not remained so close to any Kashmiri National Conference leader for this length of time, hence found in him a sincere, simple and straight person, politically not too ambitious. I conveyed these impressions to Sheikh Abdulla on my return, but he quickly observed (probably to keep me in the dark): "Oh! Farooq? He is a simpleton, an apolitical person with no organisational ability. I will depute the General Secretary of the party." Within a week he sent Mohi-ud-din Shah, General Secretary and late Hisam-Ud-Din Bandey, provincial president to reap the crop sown by Farooq Abdulla.

This incident has been quoted to convey that with subtle manoeuvring he got cultivated in his cadres, a habit of making comparative evaluation for his son and son-in-law. The Sheikh couple engaged family spies to elicit impressions from cadres about the two; they were informed that party workers were very committed to his son-in-law G.M. Shah for his deep affinity with them, organisational capacity and for capability to redress their grievances, but simultaneously they were informed that the workers in general held resentment against the intemperate Shah, but considered Farooq to be a simpleton, a sincere worker above intrigues. Sheikh Abdulla built up the workers assessment with his own tactful contribution and so got him christened as a politician and recruited him as unopposed member of the Indian Parliament continuing the traditions of unopposed political culture which he had imposed wholesale in the 1950 Constituent Assembly Elections. Indira Gandhi had also lent support to the installation of the simple apolitical Farooq Abdulla as against G.M. Shah who was a hard nut to crack. But soon Indira Gandhi realised that Sheikh Abdulla had played his cards carefully; Farooq Abdulla appeared to be neither a simpleton nor apolitical nor so obedient as she had expected he would be. She had a plan to get her favourities like Mufti Syed and Ghulam Nabi Azad installed in Mujahid Manzil—the centre of the J&K Freedom Movement and headquarters of J&K National Conference. For that game G.M. Shah would prove to be a hurdle and in her estimate Farooq Abdulla would concede to any extent, but she failed in her assessment. She found Farooq Abdulla to be not a straightforward simpleton, but an introverted cunning politician and hence a confrontation followed. Its impact and consequences thereof have been discussed in Part - I under sub-heading: 'Communalisation.' The 1983 election to state legislature turned Indira Gandhi into a vindictive revengeful disaster for Indo-Kashmir relationship and Jagmohan brokered this treacherous disaster by creating defections and frustrating the so-called mandate which was not a positive one but a mandate of reaction. Its frustration sharpened the reaction; in this bitter background culminated the process of the division of Hindus and Sikhs as two nations. The assassination of Indira Gandhi made her apolitical son Rajiv Gandhi the symbol of Hindu identity. To reap the harvest, elections were held ahead of schedule.

Political advisors and analysts had foreseen a massive mandate for Rajiv Gandhi so for them six Parliamentary seats from Jammu&Kashmir were not so vital. Hence, they did not allow the party to build pressure for these few seats. Hence, against the background which we have discussed a secret deal for Rajiv-Farooq accord took shape for the joint rule of the two dynasties and so All India Congress virtually left the fight in Jammu&Kashmir to the divided family of Sheikh Abdulla. The Rajiv Government on its part adopted neutrality and watched which way the wind would blow. Jagmohan governor of Jammu&Kashmir had also sensed the developments and was not happy with the chief minister G. M. Shah, who, in his assessment had proved himself to be a 'Mussalman'.

The elected member from Baramulla Kh. Mubarak Shah had died just before Sheikh Abdulla and it was during the lifetime of Sheikh that a non-political, far off relation of the deceased M.P. and ordinary civil servant Prof. Saif Ud Din Soz was elected from Baramulla in a bye-election from this constituency.

Soz, a high school teacher, was not promoted to the lecturers grade in 1960 when G.M. Sadiq, on being reinducted in Bakshi's Cabinet in Jammu&Kashmir as education minister, got 76 non-Muslims promoted/ appointed as college lecturers as against only 17 from the majority Muslim community which created deep resentment and reaction. Bakshi encouraged this reaction and resentment so secretly patronised establishment of Backward Post Graduate Employees Association consisting of representatives from among Kashmiri Muslims, Jammu Dogras and Ladakhi Buddhists. Soz became one of the office bearers of this assocaition which became a ladder for him to rise from school level to college level.

In June 1972 on the initiative of the Chief Minister Syed Mir Qasim a trio of Srinagar based intellectuals Dr. Agha Ashraf Ali an eminent educationist, G.R. Santosh internationally known painter and a distinguished Kashmiri poet G.N. Khayal called a convention of writers, artists and intellectuals who decided to establish a representative organisation. In a close contest this author was elected its president not for any special merit, but probably due to the stiff opposition amongst various schools of literary thought.

At the time the authors literary contribution was confined to one novel and literary popularity hung upon the melody of a 'gazal' which was sung for Radio Kashmir by Raj Begum the Lata Mangeshkar of Kashmir. M. Yousuf Taing was correct in saying that "it appeared not for the poetic eminence of Gauhar but for sweetest voice of Raj Begum that this Gazal attracted popularity." Soz had made virtually no literary contribution whatsoever, but emerged as concensus general secretary of this organisation. The activities of this literary body brought Soz into the limelight and the patron of the organisation, Chief Minister Syed Qasim elevated Soz's position from lecturer to joint registrar of Kashmir University. With his shift to Srinagar the 'Sheikh-New Delhi' parleys were in progress and sensing the inevitability of the situation Soz with his friend M.Y. Taing secretary of state literary academy made it a daily routine to walk around the Maulana Azad Road house of Sheikh Abdulla. Soz's wife was a far-off relation of Mubarak Shah on whose death a bye-election was necessitated for the Lok Sabha. In Kashmir politics the men from town have more formidable say in political parties so the search for a candidate of the local National Conference unit started. It would be safer for the party to nominate one from either of the two bigger towns of the constituency viz Baramulla and Sopore. Baramulla had only two men of stature and such was the case with Sopore. These four, Sheikh Mohammad Maqbool and Ghulam Din Shah from Baramulla and Vakil Abdul Ahad and Hakim Habibullah from Sopore were not ready to merge their identities in a wider sphere and pinned their hopes upon local chances. Mohi-ud-din Wani had acquired political recognition for his proximity with M.A. Beig during Beig-Parthasarthy parleys and was sarcastically nicknamed as 'Parthasarthy' among the cadres. But being close to Mirza Beig group he was not considered for nomination. At this point of time civil servant Soz had become closer to the Sheikh family though in 1975 in private deliberations even in his office, he called Sheikh Abdulla a traitor for his treachery in Kashmir. There were certain reasons favourable for his candidature—he had no political stakes so to the political grouping within the organisational ranks his entry was harmlesss for everyone, besides workers from Sopore considered him a Sopore man as he hailed from that town and was married at Baramulla and had migrated to that town. With these plus and minus points he made his maiden entry into politics as member Indian Parliament. In true civil servants spirit he developed a rapport with various sections of Indian polity including certain media men. On the death of Sheikh Abdulla he remained a faithful mourner and did not dabble in the family succession feud. However, as Farooq Abdulla emerged as chief minister he developed proximity to him, stood by him during his honeymoon with the Indian opposition and played a role for Dr. Abdulla despite his political inexperience after which he was cut to size by Jagmohan (Governor) and defectors of the ruling party. After the assassination of Indira Gandhi, he worked as liaison officer with brokers of power. On the eve of the 1984 parliamentary Elections he had established his indispensability for Farooq Abdulla as his emissary to New Delhi and was also acceptable to the 'access channel' to Prime Minister Rajiv Gandhi.

He got the National Conference mandate from Baramulla. Ghulam Mohi-ud-din Wani who had switched loyalty from late Mirza Afzal Beig to his archrival G.M. Shah, leader of the splinter group of the National Conference contested these elections from All J&K National Conference (Khalida group). Khalida is the sister of Dr. Farooq Abdulla and wife of G.M. Shah, then chief minister. Thus the National Conference was divided into two groups one led by the elder brother and the other by the elder sister. On a similar pattern the five children of Sheikh Abdulla were divided, but the mother threw her weight behind Farooq. Mohi-ud-din Wani had three negative points:

1. He had shifted his loyalty to the same G.M. Shah who had terrorised and humiliated Mirza Baiq who had been a friend and advisor for four decades to Sheikh Abdulla. Mohi-ud-din was accused of treachery along with Mirza Beig. This switch over in the common opinion labelled him as a cheap opportunist. On the other hand, Soz had attracted public appreciation for his loyal and effective support for Farooq. Though Farooq Abdulla was not popular, but he invited general public sympathy as a political martyr wronged by the tactics of Jagmohan.
2. Mohi-ud-din Wani hailed from a remote village, whereas

Soz had a social base in two large towns Sopore and Baramulla.

3. The government of G.M. Shah had initiated the same policies deeply rooted to traditions in Kashmir to win these elections, but Governor Jagmohan through two important civil servants had the impression conveyed that the central policy had undergone drastic change. The causes have been mentioned earlier. This election witnessed large participation of voters in which Soz won with a comfortable majority. It was a vote neither for Farooq Abdulla, nor for Soz nor for the National Conference, but a protest against Jagmohan and against Indira Gandhi.

The grand lady of the Sheikh family, mother of the opposition leader Dr. Farooq Abdulla and mother-in-law of the chief minister was fielded as the National Conference (F) candidate from Anantnag. NC (K) did not field any candidate against her, but the local unit of the Indian National Congress fielded a candidate Peer Hisamud Din. In New Delhi Farooq Abdulla had become very close to Rajiv Gandhi, but the local Congress unit was totally opposed. They had no say as they had no base except among the Nehru-Gandhi dynasty in New Delhi so before completion of an effective deal they would not be restrained by the central leadership, rather they were encouraged to continue the pressure on Farooq Abdulla so that he surrendered with no reservations. Begum Abdullah (Maadar-i-Meharban) won 59 per cent votes, whereas an 'insects of a street gutter' as her husband called Mufti Mohd.Syed and his handful of 'co-agents' like Peer Hisam-ud Din bagged a bit less than 41 per cent. The Begum had further gathered around her the halo of a wronged leader by the faithlessness of her friend Indira Gandhi. It cannot be ruled out that though her son-in-law G.M. Shah was then chief minister the administration was really under the grip of the local Congress leadership and so rigging was a factor which could not be restrained in Anantnag by the interference of Jagmohan; because it was not done in a transparent manner it only narrowed down the margin. In spite of her success, Begum Abdulla was humiliated by a local political worker who had no standing and status among the masses as compared to the 'mother of politial activity' in the state.

In Ladakh constituency a disabled political novice from Muslim dominated Kargil consolidated the Muslim reaction against the propaganda of accorded by Congress to this region as having a completely Buddhist character. Had not the Leh versus Kargil regional politics made Leh Muslims vote for Naimgyal, Qamal Ali would have defeated the central minister. The winning margin was however, reduced to only 8,977 votes. In this election further communalisation was encouraged by both the Congress and National Conference, the two secular stalwarts which once again exposed the immoral pretensions of 'secularists'.

In the two Parliamentary Constituencies of Jammu, viz., Jammu and Udhampur the Bhartiya Janata Party was thrown in the background. The 1983 general elections for state legislature were conducted in such manner by two parties the National Congress and the National Conference that these parties became champions of communal interests of the two communities. The result was, therefore, on the expected basis of population ratio and an incredible political entity Prof. Bhim Singh, representing Panthers Party of the Bhim Singh couple, was trounced by the great political heavyweight of Jammu.

The royal battle was fought in Srinagar where Muzaffar Shah son of the chief minister G. M. Shah had decided to follow his maternal uncle Farooq Abdulla who had fielded Abdul Rashid Kabli. Rashid has so far beaten all records of political opportunism. He was an accused before me when I was judicial magistrate 1st Class Srinagar in 1965 for allegedly committing an affray. Co-accused with him was Bhim Singh, presently president of the Delhi based National Panthers Party and Prof. G.M. Sheikh who has last year completed the punishment awarded to him by a New Delhi designated Court under TADA. Kabli was then dubbed as a pro-Pak agent and is now vice president of the Hindu communal party the Bhartiya Janata Party, now ruling India. In his political evolution he had experienced the leadership of late Molvi Farooq then of Farooq Abdulla and now of Prof. Chaman Lal Gupta. Before him, Mohd. Shefi Qureshi had made a political shift from pro-Pakistan J&K Political Conference to the Indian National Congress though both were ostensibly secular in character. On the other hand, Rashid Kabli has from one communal extreme gone to another. Rashid Kabli's political career was being slaughtered at Tagore Hall Srinagar where his comfortable winning margin of votes was thrown into the dustbin and Muzzaffar Shah the son of the chief minister who was losing was declared elected as M.P. from Srinagar—the game which his first cousin Omar Abdulla successfully repeated in the 1999 Parliamentary Elections. The returning officer showed reluctance to do rigging, but proceeded to allow gangsterism and in that melee of confusion he would declare the elected as defeated and the defeated would emerge as an elected M.P. It is at this juncture that Governor Jagmohan intervened through his confidant Divisional Commissioner Hamidulla Khan and his counterpart in police and the returning officer was warned to conduct the election fairly and G. M.Shah's 'goondas' including one from my own town Charar-i-Sharief were physically thrown away from the counting hall.

While discussing the 1987 elections the author has exposed the claims made by Jagmohan in his book *Kashmir—My Frozen Turbulence* which Indian chauvinists revered as a holy scripture and in which he shifts the whole blame of bungling upon Farooq Abdulla; exonerating himself and Rajiv Gandhi. Can the fans of Jagmohan reply to one question?

"Why did he not intervene as Governor in the Assembly Constituencies of Amirakadal and Haba Kadal in 1987 wherefrom the two losing ministers Mohi-ud-din Shah and Piarey Lal Handoo were declared elected, whereas he had saved Ab. Rashid Kabli in the 1984 Parliamentary elections from Srinagar Constituency of which those two assembly segments form a part?"

A supplementary question arises, "Does it mean that in the fraud which G. M. Shah wished to play in Tagore Hall Rajiv Gandhi was neutral and in the 1987 fraud he joined with Farooq Abdulla and so Jagmohan, the political preacher connived so as to make these two wronged assembly segments fertile nurseries for militancy?

Notes

1. One Sh. Cheewan Rigzin President Buddhist Association submitted a memorandum to the Indian Prime Minister in 1950-51. In this document reference is made to an earlier memorandum submitted to his Highness Maharaja of J&K in 1948 and the demands are repeated in this subsequent

memorandum. The Maharaja was requested: (a) to govern Ladakh Buddhists through his direct legislature and administrative machinery, (b) that the homeland of Ladakh Buddhists should form either a part of Tibet or of a separate region with Hindu majority parts of Jammu, (c) Ladakh Buddhists be permitted to reunite politically with Tibet (d) Ladakh Buddhists be permitted to join with east Punjab alongwith Hindu populated pockets with Jammu.

Why such a proposal? The same memorandum explains :...

"because we have seen more of administrators from Kashmir (Muslims) who have mostly governed us to ruin our cultural kinship with Hindus."

Now let us examine the truth in the claim made in 1948 that a) Ladakh was a Buddhist region and b)it was administered upto 1948 by Kashmiri Muslims.

It will be explained by the table of Constituencies given in the report of Franchise Committee headed by B.J. Glancy in 1933. I quote extracts from para "8"

"Para 8: The identity of the population can best be stated in the following table which shows to the nearest thousand of adult males over 20 year of age in our proposed Constitutencies and in each of the principal Communities:

Constituency	Muslims	Hindus	Sikhs	Buddhists	
Rural Jammu	37	56	2	x	95
Ladakh	41	x	x	x12	52

Thus according to the 1931 census figures Ladakh Muslims deserved 41 out of 52 electoral constituencies, whereas Buddhists according to their ratio of population deserved only 12 representatives. Now in 1948 and 1952 in the memos tutored by South Block Cheewan Rigzin claims the region as Buddhist area exclusively. It was firstly to confuse public opinion and secondly, to create a communal bias.

Secondly, the allegation levelled in 1948 by Cheewan Rigzin that Kashmiri Muslims had ruled Ladakh during Maharaja's time is patently false. It provides only one inference that the tutors in South Block in New Delhi had raised this bogey and convassed to get the idea exploited in future which they did in AD 2000. In June 2000 the same person raised the same plea to counter the impact of autonomy drama played by Dr. Farooq Abdulla and his party in J&K Assembly to move, discuss and approve a resolution on Restoration of Autonomy to J&K with which the people are least concerned. However, it needs a brief mention: that in 1948 my home district Tehsil Budgam was part of Srinagar district then and an elite area had not a single Muslim gazetted officer from it. It had only 54 non-gazetted Muslim teachers, three dozen Muslim Patwaris and thus, was ruled by administrators from the microscopic Pandit community. Will Cheewan Rigzin name only a dozen Kashmiri Muslim officers who had till then formed part of the administration in Ladakh division? It was either ruled by the relatives of His Highness the Maharaja or by imported Kashmiri Pandit officers. The moral of the story is self-explanatory.

NOTES

Chapter 30

A Positive Boycott

Elections to Lok Sabha in 1989 were fought two years after the 'Culmination of Fraud' which the 1987 State Legislative Elections have ultimately proved to be. At this stage both the National Conference and Indian occupation of Kashmir had become intolerable irritants for the people of Jammu and Kashmir.

Under the heading 'Culmination of Fraud' it had been discussed that had the Indian political pandits and institutions of Indian democracy, particularly the Election Commission of India remained loyal to the values enshrined in the Indian Constitution, at the best, two dozen MLAs out of the total strength of 76 would have gone to the Muslim United Front (MUF), an equal number could have gone to BJP and other smaller parties including independents. The National Conference and Congress (I) would have together taken two and a half dozen segments. In all, the National Conference would have remained the majority group and without a coalition there was no alternative. Such a combination of odds would have worked at best for a year or more and a mid term poll was the only inevitability. The process would have consolidated the faith in the viability of democracy and the process would have firstly, isolated the anti-election politics and secondly, made people look deeper into the diversities of the state and to formulate such a political alternative which could, by and large, invite general acceptibility so as to guarantee a durable ministry.

An honest exercise would have created broad-based commitment for democracy which would have convinced even the committed pro-Pak element that it was safer to be part of Hindu majority democratic India rather than to opt for a Muslim majority country where democracy could not take root. But, on the other hand, the 1987 elections consolidated the ranks of uncommitted and even pro-Indian secularists to overthrow the fradulent democracy. They had, in 1987, failed to overcome the fraud imposed by India and so were convinced that the electoral frauds were the cornerstone of Indo-Kashmir relationship' hence, people decided to boycott the 1989 Parliament ary Elections. Even the ruling central party in India namely Congress (I) could not get a candidate in the valley. The defected state Congress stalwart Mufti Mohammad Syed, who was destined to become the first Muslim Home Minister of India after these elections did not dare to contest from his home town, home constituency or home state, but went as a political refugee to U.P. an Indian state.

Though gun culture had received popular approval, but it was yet to take off. It should not be considered or construed that the armed struggle was initiated by the culmination of the electoral fraud in 1987, but it was shaped and popularised by several successive political events which are summarised as:

> (a) Communalisation of 1983 Elections, (b) Engineering of defections at the behest of the representative of India in the state, (c) to frustrate the verdict of the voters by installation of the government of defectors, (d) Rajiv-Farooq accord which had no clause or provision except to restore the status quo and reinstall Farooq Abdulla as chief minister to teach a lesson to the J&K leadership not to care for the electorate, but to be obedient agents of the ruling clique in New Delhi and (e) to play a wholesale fraud in the name of elections so as to distribute the booty of power. The alternative was either to rationalise and accept being colonial subjects of a particular family and to be governed by extra-constitutional frauds or they had to trend the path which was devised in 1947 by late Shiekh Abdul Salam Dalal of J&K Muslim Conference then was carried forward by Dr. Abdul Majeed of Islamabad, Aziz Shago, Haji Jalal-ud-din of Charar (i)- Sharief and hundreds of others. The movement was carried forward by late Maqbool Bhat of Trehgam, then by the warriors of Alfateh group and finally these loose threads were woven into a thousand plied rope by the terrorised election agents of the successful MUF candidates from Amirakadal and Haba Kadal constituencies wherefrom the culmination

of fraud declared the two defeated ministerial colleagues of Farooq Abdulla as elected representatives of that most volatile and conscious electorate.

Till then 'terrorism' had not received popular mandate, but the 1989 boycott of the masses accorded express mandate to forcefully undo the fraud, hence, it was a voluntary revolt. However, the introduction of Kalashnikov, though rare had overawed civil service and police personnel—the two forces which allowed themselves from October 1947 to be used in any manner the ruling clique desired them to act. In the 1950 elections for the Constituent Assembly Prime Minister Sheikh Abdulla, had created such an impact or terror that he required neither help of police nor of civil service to impose an uncontested Constituent Assembly. His draconian laws had created such a situation that no one could dare even to whisper about the consembly or its elections. Similarly overawed, terrorised and frightened Kashmiris could not dream of contesting even a few seats during 1957 and 1962, two general elections to the Legislature. As they saw the fate of Praja Parishad a Jammu based Hindu organisation which advocated for complete integration of Jammu and Kashmir with India, Kashmiris felt that the safety of their person and honour required them to abide by the boycott call of the Plebiscite Front and Political Conference. But, Sadiq had pretended to be a progressive democrat and so a pro-Indian opposition party led by Bakhshi Ghulam Mohammad also was in the field. Hence, notices of appointments of the Returning Officers, Counting Officers, Presiding Officers, Polling Officers, etc., were issued, but to scuttle any democratic exercise, police and civil servants, both were used. Even unscrupulous teachers caught this contagious disease. As discussed earlier all elections were the result of fraud exercised, implemented and perpetuated by government employees. Even if any segment was required to be 'conceded' for opposition such a concession too was implemented through civil servants and police officers.

But in the 1989 Elections both the civil servants and policemen were scared of the gun. It is thus that the gun became the saviour. Had I taken up the gun in 1962 my chief election agent the veteran leader of district Budgam and president of the local bar association late Pandit Damodhar Bhat would not have been forced to strike his head against the door of the returning officer of Budgam constituency only to hear that our papers stood rejected. Those preachers who consider resort to gun as terrorism should ponder upon how in the situation an aspirant to exercise his birthright can act otherwise? I have never handled even a knife, am not able to kill a chicken and am committed to peace and peace only. But at this advanced age, many brazen acts of fraud committed in the name of the Rule of Law force me to learn to handle firearms and to use them so as to restore the rule of law. But had government employees feared not the gun, but the Almighty, had they heard the reprimand of their conscience and had they considered themselves 'Sitas' within the invisible circle drawn around them by the constitution and law the Mahabharata would not have ensued - Lanka would not have been reduced to ashes. The belief with every voter in Srinagar parliamentary constituency that a 100 per cent boycott call would get implemented in letter and spirit and in such situation if any civil servant as returning officer or presiding officer or as poll officer committed some fraud he would be identified and become answerable.

I was then posted as district and sessions judge of district Kupawara, a part of Baramulla constituency. Three segments in this constituency, viz., Uri, Tangdar and Gurez were then also completely (being border tehsils closer to the LOC) under the military where a sort of martial law has been the rule; but particularly in 1989 when the trained militants had started to cross the LOC, these areas were ruled by two guns so the voters were scared. In these areas too abstention from polling was complete, but the officers concerned were forced to mark some votes in favour of the National Conference candidates and in total 5 percent votes were poled. Such forced officials hoodwinked their seniors and marked about 3,000 votes for five unknown independent candidates. Though legally Soz was elected, but had he any political morality he should have accepted the defeat and felt ashamed to occupy a seat in the Parliament. But can a civil servant like Soz or an unsophisticated law graduate like Shafi Bhat prefer morality as compared to the luxurious status of an M.P. ? Both owed their political career and privileges to the kindness of the Sheikh dynasty.

In Anantnag constituency the national Conference candidate was my revered teacher who sometimes lived as a part time lecturer in a private college on a meagre pay, but was committed to democratisation and progressive ideals. In this search for the right path he wandered from the Communist Party to J&K Democratic National Conference, then became an adversary of his fellow progressive friends Sadiq, D.P.Dhar and Qasim and devoted his time to defend the ex-Prime Minister who was subjected to the same vengeance which he himself had been subjected to the same vengeance which he himself had been subjected to in Bakshi's time. But probably Handoo at that stage seemed to have been against the policy of victimisation so defended as a lawyer and political worker the agonies let lose upon the victims. In the process once as DNC leader his full skull got fractured at Wahthora and in spite of a lucrative legal practice he lived precariously. But during Sheikh-Center parleys through Beig and Parthasarthy, handoo threw in his lot with Beig who had created the myth of being the brain behind Sheikh Abdulla. I had assessed at a young age that Beig was just a hoax which was proved true later on. He had no insight about human psychology and failed to understand the men around him. He admitted sometime before his death that he had not understood Sheikh Abdulla. This digression is used to convey that Beig did not understand the moves of Handoo and introduced him to Sheikh Abdulla with high praises for Handoos ability, devotion, sincerity and sacrifices for the cause and did the same for D.D.Thakur.

"Beg Sahib, Handoo feels that we are on the threshold of power and so comes to us with lust for a ministerial berth" reacted the Sheikh.

Beig convinced Sheikh and Handoo also made an assurance that he would not make any such demand particularly during his first term. Once Handoo got a foothold, he became close to the Sheikh Abdulla his son Farooq found in him a political and legal guide. By and large he followed in the footsteps of D.P.Dhar and became the 'mischievous brain' behind Farooq Abdulla with ostensibly guaranteed loyalty, but with roots in South Block.

Handoo enjoyed a considerable amount of goodwill in Anantnag district particularly in the town of Islamabad. But in the 1987 elections he had no chance to get through even by rigging from his home district and so sought a party nominations from the Pandit dominated constituency of Haba Kalal Srinagar. This opportunism exposed him within the local circles in Anantnag as a hypocrite. This constituency has no base for INC (I) , but one cannot deny that Mufti Syed had created a nucleus of a committed cadre which even today stands with him and with his daughter in the recently launched regional party P.D.P. Inspite of this dedicated cadre he did not dare to contest from his constituency nor dared to field any dummy as Janta Dal candidate which he had recently joined. Similarly, Congress (I) left the field. All the parties were aware of the mood of the people against any rigging, so, eight unknown individuals, just to get themselves known filed papers as independent candidates. The nine contestants polled in total 5 percent of the votes and 95 percent boycotted particularly Kashmiri Pandit community remained away from polling booths not only on the ground that they had lost interest in this political force, but had reacted against the faithlessness with which Handoo had alienated his local base. Hence, Kashmir Valley expressed unanimous verdict against the electoral frauds perpetuated against them and it was not only a solid expression of lack of confidence in the Indian Election Commission, but a rejection of Indian model of democracy imposed from the very beginning in this region. Even 5 percent officially shown poll figure was by and large false.

Ladakh Muslims this time asserted themselves and disproved the arithmetic evolved by fraud both by the census department of the Union government and by the field workers of state government who prepared electoral rolls. In spite of registration of armed personnel stationed here as voters from this constituency and in spite of the fact that many of them did cast their vote on communal pattern yet the result proved that Muslim voters outnumbered Buddhists. It is commonly known that this constituency is dominated by Shia sect of Muslims; the women folk of Shias are strictly confined within the four walls of their homes, yet, Hassan Commander won by 4,539 votes. Here neither the Indian political manifestos worked, nor the National Conferences claim of having helped the winning candidate, nor boycott suited their policy. This erstwhile citadel of amity, for reasons totally attributable to Nehru dynasty, Congress rulers, Indian opposition parties and Indian media had fallen prey to the emotional communal divide. So, the Muslim majority Ladakh which had been projected in India and in the world as a completely Buddhist locality in Jammu and Kashmir disproved the falsehood in such propaganda. The communal virus was so contagious here that even the poll staff, law and order machinery and even voters from the army were divided on communal lines. It was thus a fair deal as far as hustings were concerned, but historically proved a disaster for deep-rooted secular traditions of the region which were destroyed completely. Had Jawahar Lal Nehru allowed Budh Vihar in Delhi to develop into a laboratory of traditional Ladakh amity under the name of Ladakh House and had he not christened a secular Buddhist monk who was stationed here as an R.S.S. activist, Ladakh would never had gone this way; the Sheikh dynasty also communalised the situation in Ladakh.

The two Jammu constituencies had also fallen into confusion so no formidable political fight ensued; only the growth of independents gave a show of an election. In Udhampur constituency though the main fight was between the traditional rival parties Congress (I) and Bhartiya Janata Party (BJP) yet 22 other candidates including one from Janta Dal were also in the fray. Turnout of voters was good, but the very pattern of polling demonstrates the mass confusion and thus the 70 percent poll could be treated as a sort of reaction to the call of boycott in the Valley. This reaction was not expressed in a constructive manner, but pivoted around confusion only. The Janta Dal candidate Sheikh Abdur Rehman lost to Dharampaul of Congress (I) by a margin of 30,000 votes.

This voting percentage reveals that Jammu Muslims did not follow the voting pattern of the mainstream in the Valley and did not adhere to boycott for purely `communal' reasons that they had found a chance to vote for a Muslim candidate Sheikh Abdur Rehman of J.D. for the first time in this region. The wave throughout India was for Janta Dal so, Jammu Muslims inferred that this wave might make a tilt in favour of Sheikh Rehman so did not opt for boycott. It invited the inevitable communal reaction in Jammu Hindu vote which went against the general wave not in favour of the Congress party, not for the choice of candidate, not that it was not swayed by the janta Dal wave, but for the sole reason that a Muslim being elected from Jammu in the Lok Sabha might dispel the notion that Jammu is predominantly Hindu. A myth has been created worldwide that Ladakh is a completely Buddhist zone which has since been eroded. Rehman's entry from a constituency of Jammu was stalled so that it does not erode the myth that Jammu is a Hindu region, which is not correct as the psoition is otherwise that it is a composit region.

Similarly, in Jammu constituency the main contest was between Janak Raj Gupta of Congress (I) and Rajinder Singh Chib of Janta Dal who had recently defected to the Dal. The other 19 candidates including the Bahujan Samaj Party, Prof. Chaman Lal Gupta of Bharatiya Janata Party and Ghulam Rasool Asghar of Janta Party could not make a dent. In this constituency the turnout was not attributable to any other factor except for political polarisation and to counter the boycott call in the Valley.

The net result was that whereas the Valley rejected the Indian system of elections, Ladakh provided a chance to Muslims to show their numerical strength after 52 years, Udhampur also had communal strains, but Jammu endorsed positively that Indian system of democracy for their political aspirations or to endorse approval to Indian occupation of Jammu and Kashmir- though guided mainly by communal rather than by political reasons.

NOTES

NOTES

NOTES

Chapter 31

Legislative Cessation

The people of J&K had no direct or even indirect representation in the Indian Constituent Assembly. It has also been stated that the first three Indian parliaments had no representation from Jammu and Kashmir. The un-elected and imposed state legislatures nominated six members to the Lok Sabha. Similar elections, as was the rule for election of J&K Legislative Assembly, would choose six representatives from six constituencies of Jammu and Kashmir from the fourth parliament voted in 1967. Under a complete boycott in the Valley, communal division in Ladakh, reactionary/ process in Udhampur and through a normal election in Jammu constituency six members were sent to the Lok Sabha in the 1989 Elections. With installation of Janata Dal government in New Delhi militancy grew to the extent that the daughter of the Home Minister Mufti M. Syed was taken as hostage and the transfer of detained militants in exchange from the hostage was celebrated as a historic occasion. This surrender by mighty India was celebrated as the first victory after Kashmir was defeated in the mid 16th Century by the treachery of the Mughal emperor Akbar. Since that event Kashmir has witnessed the mass support to militancy becoming simultaneously a commitment and even a compulsion. Against this background the Janta Dal government fizzled out within two years. The Janata Party government was finished off by Choudhry Charan Singh and the Janata Dal government by Chandra Shekhar both having become Prime Ministers by their ambitious adventures. The situation of 1980 got repeated in 1991 and so the dissolution of the Parliament followed.

During this period the whole population had stood by militants and it became an impossible for the Indian government to create an outlet to infiltrate six persons under a sham selection into the Lok Sabha as members from Jammu and Kashmir. Had the state assembly been in existence at that time the Indian process of governance would not hesitate to issue an ordinance restoring the pre-1967 position so it would get six MPs nominated by the imposed assembly which was done for the first three Parliaments. Thus the Eleventh Lok Sabha had no representation from Jammu and Kashmir, even through indirect means.

Chapter 32

Rehearsal of Political Begaar (Corvee)

The Indian government had no qualms whether Jammu and Kashmir was represented in Lok Sabha or not, but faced an awkward situation as it had to amend its concerned constitutional provision to warrant extension of Presidents Rule in J&K which, could not be imposed on Jammu and Kashmir. It is useful to discuss the compromising situation hypotheticated by learned author of *The Constitution of J&K, It's Development and Comments*, Hon'ble Justice A.S. Anand. The author in the third edition of this book states:

> "The Constituent Assembly of the State, as already noticed, was not subordinate of the Constituent Assembly of India. In the present context the 'theory of limited repeal' can be pressed into aid if either the Parliament or the President has the legislative competence to obliterate or repeal any provision of the constitution of Jammu & Kashmir."

In spite of the fact that A.S. Anand has held eminent positions as a judge of J&K High Court, as Chief Justice of two High Courts, as the judge and now as Chief Justice of Supreme Court; but he has left matters in an ambiguous situation. He has not explained whether in case the two Constitutent Assemblies had equal status as sovereign bodies, how could a similar provision in one Constitution have effect of limited repeal upon the other. He has not explained whether the earlier drafted provision of Indian Constitution Article 356 can repeal the spirit of a similar provision contained in J&K Constitution (Sec. 92) passed six years after the Indian Constitution came into force. Framers of J&K Constitution in 1956 modelled it according to the Indian Constitution adopted six years earlier and while drafting and passing Sec. 92, they made full assessment of its implications and consequences in view of Article 356 of the Indian Constitution.

It is pertinent to quote sub Sec (5) of Sec 92 of J&K Constitution:

(5) No proclamation under Sub Sec(1) shall be issued except with the concurrence of the President of India.

Thus assumption of power u/s 92 by the Governor is not an independent act, but is a joint act of both the Governor and President. In passing of this section the constitution makers had sufficient knowledge and understanding of the purport of Article 356,which was in vogue in India for more than half a decade.

A comparative study of Sec. 92 and Article 356 of the two constitutions shows that Sec. 92 provides that if the governor is satisfied that the government cannot be carried under the provisions of the Constitution he may issue a proclamation assuming to himself the functions of the government. Thus, it is the failure of law and order machinery in 1990, which made the governor assume all functions of governance himself. The wording of Article 356 is similar. In 1956 the Constitution makers of Jammu and Kashmir planted the mandate contained in Article 356 in Sec. 92. On the other hand, the Constitution makers of Jammu and Kashmir have not directly or indirectly made any attempt regarding the remedy, which could be put in operation in case of a war, an external agression or an armed revolt. The State Constituent Assembly could not go to that extent as according to the instrument of accession it was the dominion legislature, which could legislate about matters of defence. So the president could have acted under Article[1] 352 if he was satisfied that the situation in Jammu and Kashmir in January 1990 or even July 1990 was one which could be termed as armed revolt. To expose this bungling a separate study is required but suffice it to say that the rule beyond July 1990 was, even under the doctrine of necessity, an illegality as far as the constitutional schemes of India and Jammu and Kashmir are concerned. According to Indian claims J&K Constitution is a sister document of the constitution of the country and according to common belief in Jammu and Kashmir this document too has been drafted in New Delhi by Indian drafters. Men like Sogami, G.M. Satakoji, Mohi-ud-din Khan Yaga Bugh imposed by Sheikh Abdulla in 1950 and purchased by G.M. Bakhshi in 1953, without having any conception of its plus and minus factors voted it as J&K Constitution. Whatever the position, in existence of Sec.92 in J&K Constitution President of India had no mandate to act under Article 356 of Indian Constitution. He could act after 1 July 1990 under Article 352 of Indian Constitution and not under Article 356. Conscious of this situation and position the Home Ministry of India got a decision judicially imposed upon the reluctant Election Commission to hold Parliamentary Elections in Jammu and Kashmir in 1996. As stated earlier the adamant Election Commission had sunk the intense differences amongst its three members and unanimously decided not to include J&K State in their scheme as they correctly held that the Commission was not merely a 'post office' which could deliver the members to Lok Sabha, but had to satisfy itself that such delivery was the result of free and fair elections which, in their view, was impossible in the situation qualified by the Home Minister himself as a 'situation of proxy war.'

In spite of secret parleys between the National Conference and Narasimha Rao's Congress government and in spite of assurances that five out of six seats would be conceded to that party, Farooq Abdulla argued against any elections in J&K, but simultaneously pressed for a two third majority in J&K Assembly, which in his view could be held immediately after Parliament Elections, or simultaneously. Rajesh Pilot, State Minister in the Home Ministry advocated in favour of the condition, but the senior minister S.B. Chavan and his secretary were able to successfully convey that in view of the tight positon of the Congress in the country it would have been full of risks to concede five parliamentary seats to the National Conference and two third majority in State Assembly to that regional party. It was argued that he might even be conceded all the six Parliamentary seats in Jammu and Kashmir, but should share two-third majority in State Legislature equally with Pradesh Congress Unit. The assured support of 5 or 6 MPs could have proved decisive, but 'an opportunist Farooq Abdulla is to be kept within the state under pressures and pulls.' This was the ultimate decision of the PMO and the National Conference ostensibly respected the public sentiment and boycotted elections.

The Pradesh Congress president G.R. Kar had migrated with his family and lived in Lodhi Colony flats in New Delhi. In a small cell like drawing room he would hold mock court sessions in the company of a dozen migrant Kashmiri Pandits settled in Delhi. Other office bearers were similarly migrants either in Delhi or in Jammu. Locally the concession seekers who belonged to the state cadre had either joined with the militants as sympathisers or as activists; or had taken refuge in Tulsi Bagh or Sonwar security zones, where they lived like condemned prisoners, had settled as migrants in the MLA hostel and other government flats in Jammu or wandered in the corridors of 24 Akbar Road, New Delhi to beg largesse and favours from imposed leaders like Ghulam Nabi Azad who had no semblance of a political base either in the Valley or in Jammu or even in his home village Balesa in Badarwah subdivision of Doda district. Similarly, a handful of destitute Congress workers wandered from Patna to Bhopal to seek favours from their ex-leader Qureishi, who during this ordeal enjoyed princely comforts as governor of Bihar and M.P. In these circumstances Congress had no candidates, no proposers, no election agents and no cadre available.

Mufti Syed who had created a group of dependable workers for the Congress, both in Jammu and the Valley had, with his workers, joined the Janata Dal, but after the abduction of his daughter, defeat of the Janata Dal government and total alienation created by forces and paramilitary forces he had fallen in oblivion, had neither courage to contest from Jammu and Kashmir, nor had any cadre which could manage his campaign. So, he sought political asylum from Laloo Prasad Yadav but failed to win an entry for Lok Sabha. An unknown worker Maqbool Dar, who had no political initiation at tehsil level filed nomination papers from his security hideout as a candidate for Anantnag Constituency. His proposers too came from security the same forces who implemented the decisions of the Joint Command consisting of representatives of the regular army, Rashtriya Rifles (RR.), Border Security Force (BSF) and CRPF (Central Reserve Police Force) on the advice and directions of Central Bureau of Intelligence (CBI) and Research Analysis Wing (RAW) fielded another 15 unknown candidates. Among them only Taj Mohi-ud-din the Congress-I candidate was known in some political circles, but within the limits of Batamalo locality in Srinagar. The migrant Kashmiri Pandit community fielded from their refugee camps Sarla Taplo widow of assassinated BJP leader from Srinagar and secret intelligence agencies are believed to have fielded Shuban

Kishan directly through RAW. The other 12 candidates were unknown in political and social circles. It is believed that almost all of them belonged to renegades and so a group of such ex-militants was thrown in the fray only to make show of contest to hoodwink the world.

From Baramulla Congress-I fielded the migrant Pradesh Pradhan G.R. Kar who virtually contested from his hideout at Lodhi colony, New Delhi, his chief election agent, his brother-in-law G.N. Mircha, ex-M.L.A. also operated as migrant from his hideout in New Delhi. With other migrant workers both flew into Srinagar, stayed in Sonawar state guesthouse, arranged meetings with officials of the army deputed in Baramulla constituency under tight security and flew back to Delhi. To make it seem like a contest the 'Unified Command' fielded nine other candidates which included an agent at bus stand Kupawara Din Mohammad Chita. Through Bhim Singh president Panthers Party who has no base in the state particularly in any part of the Valley one Daljit Singh contested on his Panthers Party ticket. Independent candidate Gyani Sant Singh, filed nomination papers and was able to secure 18,331 votes and lost his security deposit. M.N. Kaul, a migrant Kashmiri Pandit candidate sent his papers through post from his refugee camp and received almost all the migrant votes through post. The migrants had and continue to have bitterness against the majority. Their emotional reaction cannot be dismissed summararily nor can extremism in their reaction. They are correct to feel that the majority community was not able to consolidate the traditional spirit of fraternity at the start of the last decade of the previous century. Muslims are also justified to assert in defence that the Pandits were used as a counter by Jagmohan and the armed revolution had come so abruptly that the majority community was lost in confusion. They further claim that the Pandit community suffered proportionately very little whereas the majority community is so sandwiched between the two guns that they apprehend their complete extinction. Neither could the majority community recover from the shock which the abrupt emergence of gun culture caused them nor could the educated Pandit community rationally channelise its reaction. However, their political stand to show their existence as Kashmiris from refugee camps in the plains is justified. Their involvement en masse with Hindu communal forces in India is debatable, but the subsequent happenings delivered dividends to them at the cost of mutual trust they enjoyed with their Muslim brethern. Hence, their enthusiasm in the 1996 Parliamentary elections, which later on fizzled out was a justified circumstance.

Mohd. Sadiq, an unknown personality in district politics of Baramulla was fielded by the Kuka Parray faction of renegades with the patronage of Rashtriya Rifles camps stationed at Baramulla, Hajin and Pattan. Others were thrown in the field by one or the other commanding officers of BSF, CRPF or by the other secret agencies.

Among the whole lot only G.R. Kar was a politician and represented the Prime Minister. Later on even he was sacrificed.

Srinagar constituency had an acute shortage of men. Even the ruling Congress party in the center was not able to get a candidate from this constituency. Though its pradesh unit secretary Taj Mohi-ud-din belonged to the 'active locality' of the city Batamalo, but he and family were so scared of the resentment from their neighbourhood that he migrated from the migration camp in a city security zone to the rural constituency of Anantnag where the machinations by forces behind the screen had decided to crown a defected militant with success.

Due to shortage of men the Congress roped in an ordinary village Shia for the Srinagar Constituency. From 1967 all candidates for this constituency have been fielded from the city of Srinagar because it is Srinagar opinion which moulds political opinion in the whole state. But neither the Congress nor its rival the Janata Dal were able to get even a dummy from the city for this constituency. The Congress had virtually no worker worth the name left in its ranks from Srinagar except Taj Mohi-ud-din and Nazir Ahmad Bhat of Basant Bagh political family. Taj took political refuge in Anantnag and Nazir flatly refused to join.

Magam is a far-off village on Srinagar-Gulmarg road. Shias form hardly 8 percent of the electorate in this constituency. The community has three further divisions; Ghulam Mohd. Mir of Magam was a political novice even for me, who, as one old activist from Budgam district has at least acquaintance with all political activists irrespective of their party affiliations. The Janata Dal had an acute shortage of men. Its Pradesh President Qayoom a prisoner in Tulsi Bagh security zone had openly argued with Sumantra Bannerjee against any electoral exercise in the state in the circumstances which prevailed then. With the support of Governor (retd.) Gen. Krishna Rao he had cleared ground with the National Confrence leader Farooq Abdulla. Both had one thing in common- hatred for Mufti Mohd. Syed otherwise, Qayoom was neither tolerated by the Sheikh dynasty nor by the high command of the National Conference who had assessed that Qayoom was a political creeper who could not stand erect without support. Qayoom was apprehensive of Mufti Syed as he had dared to convey his critical assessment about some acts which Mufti had taken as Union Home Minister vis-à-vis Jammu and Kashmir; Qayoom required support and Farooq Abdulla required to appease Krishna Rao, so the two had come closer. Farooq Abdulla with the patronage of Governor Rao had installed Qayoom as his agent who flatly refused to contest as M.P. from Srinagar though in fact he had the best chances for the party ticket. His other three colleagues in Tulsi Bagh security zone ex-legislators G.M. Bawan, A.G. Namtahali and Peer Gyas-ud-din an ex-Congress minister also refused. Due to this shortage of men an obscene abuse' to politics Farooq Indirabi of Chadora fell in the lot of the Janta Dal. In April 1995 he had taken refuge in a security zone after he concocted a tale that Maj. Mast Gul from Charar-i-Sharief had threatened his life; Mast Gul had not even cared for bigger guns like Qayoom who hailed from Charar-i-Sharief and the question of his advancing threats to Indirabi did not arise.

Though the director hospitality department of J&K government Muzzafar refused to allot him an official hideout, but he begged for mercy lest he might be gunned down. The drama was played in my presence at the Tourist Reception Centre in the office of Director Protocol Mohd. Muzaffar. Farooq Indirabi after leaving studies at middle level joined Mohd. Shafi Simnani editor of the daily *Zamindar* as a hawker. That vernacular paper too depended on change of patronage for its survival. Later, without knowing the Urdu language or journalism he issued his own Urdu paper with a circulation of a few dozen and acted as a volunteer of late Mir Mustafa ex-MLA from Chadora who was gunned down in 1990 by militants. It is said that Indirabi developed contacts with BSF, RR and CRPF commandants. Many such officers of the Indian paramilitary forces minted money in Kashmir by false involvement of innocent people and Indirabi worked as liaison officer. Ultimately he was not able to get many such arrested persons released, could not repay their families, fell under pressure of demands so he took refuge under the pretext of being on the hit list of militants and shifted to a security zone with his second wife, leaving his old pious mother in her house at Chadora. The great Indian party patronised by Mr. Clean, i.e., V.P. Singh regarded him as a popular democrat and he became successor to the spirit of Jai Prakash, Dr. Lohia and Madhulimaye.

Migrant Kashmiri Pandits nominated migrant A.N. Vaishavi and sent a bundle of votes for him through the post. He was accorded the BJP label by the selector in Unified Command. However, progressive migrant Pandits of the city, conscious of the fate of another Pandit candidate marked about 6,000 postal ballot papers from refugee camps in plains for B.N. Dhar, himself a migrant.

Javed Ahmad an ex-militant and leader of renegades was a Rashtriya Rifles candidate with the label of an independent. Rashtriya Rifles officers openly snatched bundles of ballot papers and made his innings to about 39,000 votes. Budgam district had produced a renowned freedom fighter A.R. Rahat who immediately after emergency was declared in November 1947 became a terror for this ex-tehsil (now district) as its emergency officer and soon coined himself epitaph of Sher-i-Budgam. It was considered by Sheikh sycophants as an attempt to create parallels with Sher-i-Kashmir Sheikh Mohammad Abdulla and then he was along with his patron Karra expelled from the National Conference. In the 1953 *coup d'etat* he became block development officer and restarted his tyrannies. Deprived of these privileges after his death, his son Roshan Fayaz Rahat considered it an opportune time to continue with the traditions created by his father, developed contacts with BSF personnel stationed at Shariafabad Budgam, entered the electoral fray as a BSF candidate but with the label of independent, was able to get a few bundles of ballot papers, which, during counting were separated and numbered 17,230 votes cast by only seven BSF officers. Another ex-militant Ghulam Mohammad was a candidate of Kuka Parray, but labelled as independent who got 16,000 less by one vote. Ladies also did not lag behind; Mahboba living in an unknown security zone also bagged about 19,000 votes from the generous voters—the three wings of the paramilitary forces.

Bhim Singh had got elections held under judicial verdict and so was assured one seat for his person, but with the condition that his Panthers Party funded from the secret fund of the Indian Home Ministry would field candidates, from majority of seats so Mohammad Akbar a Panthers Party nominee opened his political score by getting about 37,000 votes. As far as Nazir Ahmad is concerned who fought as an 'independent,' my field work has failed to locate as to who he was! He too got 3,070 votes.

In Ladakh, the contest was triangular and it was not instigated but voluntary, predominantly burdened with communal and regional bias. Muslims were urged to demonstrate their identity and Buddhists were aggressively determined to establish once again that Ladakh is a Buddhist region. The other characteristic was that regional Ladakhis, in spite of superficial division of votes for intense contest between the Congress and BJP were determined to continue with the political domination of the region whereas Kargilites were keen to erode this myth. But several extraneous reasons prevailed and dominated the battle. The APHC call for boycott did not materially alter the local strategy, but Drass and other areas contiguous to the Valley were aware that even if a Muslim Kargilite won as M.P., he would get lost like a drop in the ocean as such elements considered the participation as a 'sin' against the cause. With it the local National Conference cadre also indulged in non-participation. Similarly, the BJP candidate Spalzo Angmo snatched a bunch of 5,000 votes leaving the central minister P. Namgyal in a precarious condition forcing members of the Indian Tibetan Border Force (ITBF) and Indian Tibetan Border Police (ITBP) to come to the rescue of Namgyal. Hence, he defeated his immediate rival Qamar Ali Akhoon, an independent from Kargil by 10,135 votes. Whereas this election too was neither free of boycott influence nor of rigging, but overall more than 50 percent votes polled were genuine. So, boycott did not affect this constituency and fairness was a causalty here also—probably it has become the political culture of Jammu and Kashmir elections.

Right from 1947 there has been an intrigue to divide the three regions of the state by creating a gulf of hatred. Though the state of Jammu and Kashmir was a political entity carved out by the autocratic designs of Maharaja Gulab Singh to widen the domain for exploitation, but in due course the interdependence of these three regions became so vital that no part can exist without the other. The Valley has an independent geographic, linguistic and cultural identity. On the other hand, Jammu and Frontier districts (now Ladakh region) are again federal units of smaller tiny principalities. But as the ex-principality of Basohli in Kathua district in Jammu region can hardly exist economically, administratively and politically without being an integral part of Kathua, similarly Kathua cannot exist as an identity without Jammu, for Jammu economy, the Valley is vitally important, the Valley without Jammu is a body without its lifeline, Kargil cannot survive without the Valley and Leh depends upon Kargil for its access to the world. It was expected that after 1947 Jammu and Kashmir culture would be fostered by constructive synthesis of its sub-cultures. But, unfortunately Indian imperialistic designs apprehensive of the internationalisation of the Kashmir problem and by the fear that majority view might have to prevail, created many divisions. A gulf was created among three units again; Ladakh versus Kargil hatred was created in Kargil district and the Drass, Kargil and Zanskar identities were involved in confrontation. In Jammu Dogri-Punjabi speaking areas dominated Kashmiri-Gujri speaking hill areas. Again Dogris and Punjabis were divided in the plains of Jammu and Gujar versus Kashmiri prejudices were spread.

It is in this background that the situation in Kashmir, districts of Doda, Udhampur, Poonch and Rajouri which made holding of elections an impossibility in the state was taken as a challenge by those Hindus who had right up from 1947 remained committed to complete integration of the state by any means with India. The people who have sown the seeds of alienation in the minds of the majority by raising slogans of 'one constitution', one 'flag' and one 'authority' owe their origin to the reaction which the Maharani (wife of Maharaja Hari Singh) demonstrated on the occasion of the abdication of family rule. To quote from the autobiography of Sheikh Abdulla, *Atish Chinar,* p.214:

"As this carvan (caravan of fleeing Maharaja) reached Udhumpur the Maharani Tara Devi disheveled her hair in such a manner of agony which flooded the emotions (of Hindu population) and the image of royal goddess which she exposed in her agonised lap created a havoc of revenge against local Muslims."

Since that day the R.S.S. cadres consolidated into Praja Parishad which became the J&K unit of Jansangh that merged with Janta Party with its definite independent identity and became a formidable communal force known as Bhartiya Janata Party. It had a formidable cadre and declared commitment for complete integration with India so, it always participated in elections to have psychological integration. Though from the first election held in 1950 for the Constitutional Assembly it had always dubbed electioneering in Jammu and Kashmir as a game of fraud, but for larger interests of their ideology the party compromised with all the fraud. Though they did not have even a token presence in the Valley or Ladakh, but did not exclude the Valley and Ladakh from their electioneering politics. Why? It was to boost their ideology, hence their active participation in Jammu and Udhampur constituencies. Congress(I) had also a base and tradition to fight from these constituencies. The Janta Dal leader Mufti Syed, "did not possess guts to face electorate from any Constituency in J&K and ran to Bihar," yet his party, sensed the winning chances of the party in India, was justified to participate. Bhim Singh the 'broker' who had made holding of elections a direction given by judicial verdict was assured by the Home Secretary Padmanabhia a berth from one constituency of the region, so, his involvement with the elections had an ulterior aim. To achieve the goal he had even 'invested' three candidates in three parliamentary segments of the Valley only to get his personal seat conceded from Udhampur. Another splinter group of Congress headed by Tiwari as Cong-(T) also had some stakes—at least to introduce the party. Bahujan Samaj Party too had links among lower caste Hindus; hence, all these parties and some Independents were expected to take part. As a reaction members of the 'unified command' had a plan to show that the people were totally committed to elections so, threw 40 persons into the field. The record number of candidates was an 'irrational reaction' to the boycott policy in the Valley. As this boycott policy was not a consciously evolved political process, but based on armed threats, so the reaction was similar; instead of declaring participation in elections as an act of treachery, the political leadership of APHC should have managed the movement in a manner in which the abstention from voting would become the inevitable decision of the voter. Instead of imposing the decision with threat the voter should have been left free to choose between election and no election. The mass verdict was for boycott, but the threats issued justified forces to impose an election by similar force. The threat of force caused a communal reaction both in Udhampur and Jammu constituencies, but the home secretary and home minister who were committed to Panthers Party could not prevail upon the members of the 'unified command'. From New Delhi he would on occasions criticise the forces for misuse of their force, so was persona non grata with the 'unified command'. Hence, the commitment of Chavan and Padmanabhaia was dashed to the ground and safe return of Prof. C.L. Gupta was facilitated. Bhim Singh who had played the role of a petitioner to get the election judicially imposed was forced to expose the fraud of this election in his press conference.

In Jammu constituency too, though these extra-constitutional agencies-paramilitary forces manning unified command were committed to the BJP, but the interference from P.M.O. directly through the Cabinet Secretary and the role which Mangat Ram Sharma Congress candidate had played as defender of the excesses of the forces the senior officers of BSF, CRPF and RR did not allow their juniors to destroy Sharma and so this running mate of G.R. Kar opened the score for his party from Jammu.

It was not an election to choose representatives nor it was an election between 'an election' and 'no-election' but it was an open game of "impositions." Militants had a game plan to impose a boycott and defence forces and paramilitary forces had a game plan to impose the elections. Had not militants threatened with imposition of boycott, people would still not have participated as they had neither faith in the elections nor any choice. But, the moral was derived by Harkrishen Singh Surjeet for educating Farooq Abdulla who was made to understand that if he did not participate similarly, an assembly would be imposed even without him. India had a preference for Farooq Abdulla for two reasons: a) He had some social and political base in Srinagar which moulds the political destiny of the state. Mufti, the other choice had, in his view, no base in the city; b) He inherited goodwill of being the son of Sheikh Abdulla who had been projected both by India and by Pakistan, as the symbol of Kashmir.

It is a democratic right of every citizen to cast his vote or to seek vote albeit with some reasonable restrictions. It is, therefore, in exercise of this inherent right that considerably large number of criminals have become law-givers in various state legislatures in India and such people have even sneaked into Parliament. 'Criminal' is not one who commits robbery, dacoity or murders, but one who is convicted for any crime by the Court of Law and if such conviction stands the scrutiny of appellate courts then alone do such persons come within the definition of criminals. However, notorious persons in various parts of India, maybe even unscrupulous criminals, have some values and it is their commitment to such values that they have some sort of charisma for some sections of the downtrodden. In this background we will examine whether these renegades had, before being christened as militants, any pro-poor role; had they as social workers then served their localities or what has been their role with their people when they were within the discipline of so-called 'Jehad'; what role they played after their defection and the manner in which they defected. It is the reputation which they had acquired from pre-militancy days till the announcement of the 1996 Parliament elections which could have nourished a political aspiration in their hearts.

It is one of the blunders of Indian analysts that they consider the emergence of militancy as an abrupt phenomenon, which, in their assessment was the reaction of the 'culmination of fraud' 1987 general elections. It is a fact that this fraud pushed the process of revolution into an armed revolt though the process had started with landing of the Indian army in Jammu and Kashmir, but it was limited and could be nipped in the bud had the Indian government allowed the institutions of democracy to grow in Jammu and Kashmir. On the other hand, instead of taking corrective measures, the rulers in New Delhi encouraged coercive measures. The process of revolution was enunciated and carried forward by dedicated cadres who believed that if they died in the process they would achieve martyrdom and if they lived they would survive as Gazis (warriors of the Holy War). The flood of resentment after 1987 and the encouragement which this resentment received from the public in Bohri Kadal Chowk when the Indian government surrendered on the issue of the release of the Home Minister's daughter Rubia Syed made militancy an attraction for many. Kashmir has developed a culture of imitation in each matter and, therefore, Kalhana qualifies Kashmir character as 'Fond of Novices'. It is in this background that cricket culture was swiftly swayed by the Kalashnikov culture. A good number took to arms for fashion, another group resorted to this culture for the sake of competition or to defend itself against local rivalry. In this melee the frightened workers of the ruling National Conference and their rival Congress workers also took refuge under the gun.

The two distinct elements remained distinguishable by their mannerisms and work culture even under the umbrella of a single militant organisation. The devoted militant conscious to his cause, would behave like a soldier of God, who, in spite of his finger on the trigger, would tremble in His fear. His close comrades who had taken up the gun either as a matter of fashion or as a reaction or with other motives would demonstrate by his behaviour, the arrogance which is the natural trait akin to criminality. During 1990 August-September a group of militants entered my house at 2 pm, sat in my drawing room, kept their arms conspicuously on the table so as to display the arms in an exhibition.

"Our one boy is ill, we require some money to treat him."

I expressed truthfully that due to continued strikes I was not able to cash any cheque from the bank, but in the meantime my children came with their pocket money, about 1,100 rupees; the group leader took only four hundred rupees notes, and returning the balance said: "only three or four hundred will suffice for his treatment, we would have realised this small sum even from the village of our hideout with no difficulty but we don't want to beg money from such people who might misunderstand us, that will harm our mission."

A few days later a group of 17 militants came to my residence to spend the night there. My wife served them like young obedient servants, but there was only one who resented this and felt ashamed for asking us to serve them. The others rebuked him. "Let these judges and scholars who have ruined this nation be given a lesson". But the sophisticated group revolted and voluntarily served their colleagues on our behalf. In 1993 when as a Trustee of Muslim Auqa Trust I returned from New Delhi after briefing our lawyers to move an SLP in the Supreme Court regarding inmates in Hazratbal shrine, a group of 'militants' perforce removed my Maruti car from my garage and fired targetting my wife and daughters when they defended the plunder. Later in 1995 the same group were pioneers of the renegades in our locality.

Who then became a renegade? Such groups had no ambition other than to loot and plunder. Political ambition was cultivated in them only on the eve of this election by different agencies of forces and paramilitary forces. Otherwise they had defected to channelise the ingrained criminality in themselves.

In nourishing political ambitions with this refuse of society which had itself no such idea or even awareness; various agencies of the paramilitary forces, even many officers of the regular army and emissaries of RAW and I B played a vital role. The renegades themselves had no capacity even to be dummies in this game. They had turned to militancy to exploit avenues for job opportunities; they defected from those ranks with the same swiftness and after defection had to work either as runners or as informers or as special police constables or as human cover for regular and paramilitary forces while on action during combing operations. In comparison to all such assignments the politicisation by their masters enhanced their position to the limited sphere of their families at least in nourishing ambition to occupy berths in the parliament; they were divided even and made to oppose each other to do or die in the new situation. The northern leader of defectors Kuka Parray was assured that his ideologue Tiku, who tied his destiny with a New Delhi agency, would be crowned as M.P. from southern Anantnag Constituency; his southern counterpart Naba Azad was assured by local commanders that only his nominee would be seated in the Lok Sabha; similar contradictions were created in Baramulla.

In this confusion and with transparent 'defence' strategy the two stalwarts of the ruling party at the centre, viz., Pardesh President of Congress(I), Kar and his secretary Taj Mohi-ud-din, from Baramulla and Anantnag respectively levelled charges in joint and separate statements, specifically accusing forces and paramilitary forces of stage managing the success of two renegade candidates from these two constituencies. The prime minister had to intervene directly and followed the issue persistently through his cabinet secretary. In the rest of the country the wave was in favour of Janata Dal its candidate from Anantnag an unknown migrant from Shaangas area of Anantnag district also openly accused Rashtriya Rifles for clear bungling to hoist an ex-militant as M.P. The writ of the PMO however, left no impact, but various agencies in the field like BSF, CRPF, RR and behind-the-screen agencies like RAW and IB were all working in different directions. The Rashtriya Rifles was adamantly in favour of BJP; RAW and IB were openly committed in favour of Capt. Tiku; the regular army commanders were openly working for Ikhwan (renegade militant) candidate.

The position was similar in Baramulla and ultimately the command in charge decided to distribute these two seats in 50:50 ratio to the party in power (Congress-I) and party expected to come to power viz Janata Dal. Finally, Kar of the Congress party bagged Baramulla seat and Dar of J.D. won the Anantnag seat. Both shamelessly did not lose a second to highlight the role of renegades who according to their claim, frustrated the boycott call and 'saved the democracy.' Only two days earlier—on the day of polling, both of them had accused forces, paramilitary forces and renegades of butchering democracy in separate statements circulated to the local and Indian press. Even BBC carried these statements in its news bulletins.

In this election the microscopic community of Pandits

once again actively joined with elements that have always hurt the collective ego of Kashmiris. The so called journalists and pseudo-intellectuals of this community like Sham Kaul and M.L. Charagi and others came from Delhi to ridicule the sentiment of Kashmiris and the democratic system of India while they used the electronic media to spread blatant lies however, the video camera could not hide their guilty conscience transparent from their long faces. Though Jammu region stood communally divided during these elections too, but there was no enthusiasm among the rational sections of the Hindu population as they were convinced that the atmosphere for elections was an impossibility in the soil which had become the field for an unprincipled war. From the facts and circumstances narrated above, we can safely sum up that the parliament elections were a rehearsal for political corvee (Begaar) so as to subject Kashmiris to the condemned old system of begaar—but in deceptive and different manner. In the old days it was the downtrodden common Kashmiri individual made to undergo forced labour, but in these elections Indian rulers tried a system under which Kashmiris, irrespective of any distinction could be ruled under a system of political begaar; hence, the method was sharpened to be applied for general elections, which otherwise could not be imagined in the near future.

It is reliably learnt that after obliging the union home minister and his ministry, Bhim Singh was assured that his Panthers Party—a party without any cadre or following—would be conceded one seat each from the Valley and Jammu division. It was also decided to concede one constituency to renegades (Anantnag) and one to Janta Dal from the Valley, whereas Leh was decided to be given to Congress, BJP would get only one seat from Jammu. Later on during hustings a mess was created in which the Pradesh Congress leadership—'Kar Mangat Ram' combine put pressure and these two were conceded two constituencies from Baramulla (Kashmir) and Jammu. It disturbed the joint plan of the IB, RAW and army officers who resisted damage to assured interests of the BJP. On the other hand, Janata Dal leadership also exercised pressure to concede either Srinagar or Anantnag seat in favour of the party. Between the two unknown and insignificant candidates of the party Farooq Indirabi and Maqbool Dar the latter overshadowed the former and Dar found place in the central cabinet too. Bhim Singh who was deceived and disappointed lodged protests and exposed the farce of these elections. To quote from the *Indian Express* 9 June 1996 'Changing mood of parties in Kashmir,'

> "On the other hand, Panthers Party chief Bhim Singh and his associates, who put up a fight in all the three constituencies in Kashmir valley, are angry. They were on the forefront of demanding elections in the state. Now they are threatening to boycott the Assembly polls as and when these are held".

Bhim Singh met Prime Minister Deve Gowda and urged him to institute an enquiry under a sitting Supreme Court judge to probe poll frauds in the state. A memorandum was submitted on his behalf to President Shankar Dayal Sharma. In a joint meeting Bhim Singh and his three defeated candidates accused the government of stifling democracy once again not only in Kashmir, but in Jammu also. Summing up the opportunistic traits of these state manufactured candidates, the *Express* news service, in the same article writes:

> "The mood and loyalties of political parties in Jammu and Kashmir have changed after the election in the state—depending whether these have won or lost."

In Srinagar constituency there was neither any such ex-militant as candidate in the field who would have been introduced to the rank and file of the army, nor to any other paramilitary organisations; nor were the candidates of Congress and J.D. known in any quarters. Farooq Indirabi was thrown in the field by local JD chief Qayoom just to ridicule the idea of holding elections evident from his statement which he had issued on the eve of roping in this man from his own village Chadora who was not able to get the vote even of his widowed mother as she too considered him a slur on the Peer family. The Congress Pradesh President and secretary, both were fighting for their own survival so had no interest in the third rate unknown villager Mir Magami. The unified command could not decide up to the end as to whom to crown with success. The BSF commandant Chadora, RR captain at Gopal Pora and CRPF unit posted at Radar Station Charar-i-Sharief were in favour of Farooq Indirabi, the forces stationed at district headquarter Budgam and BSF cadres posted at Sharifabad had taken decision for Mir Magami. In this conflicting situation the forces did cast the bulk of votes in Chadora and Charar-i-Sharief constituencies in favour of Farooq Indirabi; these very agencies cast bundles of ballots in favour of Mir Magami in Beerwa, Budgam and Khan Sahib assembly segments. In Srinagar city the minimum number of ballots (5 percent) used were recklessly and aimlessly marked in favour of various candidates. From Gandarbal tehsil due to the influence of the local Gujar leader the army worked for Mir Magami, the Congress candidate. In the final result unknown Magami defeated by 1,599 votes the equally unknown Farooq Indirabi.

It will remain a mystery as who defeated whom and who was whose creation during the 1996 Parliament elections.

Chapter 33

Accord a Title

The Congress(I) made the U.D.F. government dance to its tune and in a dramatic way Sitaram Kesri withdrew support to the Deve Gowda government which created the situation for another mid-term poll for which Congress(I) was not prepared. Attempts to avert the situation were made; compromise arrived at the choice of a politically rootless and cadreless leader I.K. Gujral. This arrangement too did not last long to carry the 10th Parliament even from May 1996 upto May 1998 and a mid term poll was necessitated by March 1998.

Immediately after installation of Deve Gowda government, in September 1996 legislature in Jammu and Kashmir was proposed. Now according to political lexicon a 'popular' government was ruling the state it was the government of All J&K National Conference which had to play a role in these parliamentary elections. It did not enter into electoral alliance with any party as it had fully assessed that the centre or the occupying forces would not deviate from the policy of keeping this ruling Junta in Srinagar fully satisfied. Farooq too had with his political clout impressed upon all the forces in India and the 'Unified Command' in Jammu and Kashmir (the real rulers of J&K) that the National Conference, in every circumstances was committed to support whichever party was elected by the people of India to occupy the seat of power in South and North Blocks of New Delhi Secretariat. With such assured commitment, though almost all political parties of India, which had units in Jammu and Kashmir or had only individual contacts did join the fray in this state, but, without any stakes. However, in the Valley Congress(I) candidate Mufti Mohammad Syed, whom the loyalists of the Gandhi-Nehru dynasty considered an enemy within, fought the National Conference in Anantnag constituency with his personal contacts cadres and skill, rather with the prevailing mandate from the Indian Secret Services. Mufti Mohammed Syed has given to the new generation a political heir, his daughter Mehbooba, who has proved an asset for him. Whereas the successors of Sher-i-Kashmir Sheikh Abdulla proved a liability for him and ultimately distorted the history he had created.

The National Conference had virtually conceded this seat and the unified command too was committed to their ex-home minister, therefore, both borrowed a civil servant from the security zone who had nothing but aversion against him among the ranks of the National Conference cadres. The B.J.P. had also purchased Showkat Hussain, an unknown figure. The junior minister in Ministry of Home Affairs, New Delhi, M.M. Dar was the Janta Dal candidate. Rashtriya Janta Dal is only a regional party confined to Bihar and has no state units in any other state, but could secure a candidate from Anantnag through a Bihar 'Rifles' officer posted in Kukar Nag, Anantnag District. All India Indira Congress (secular) an unknown party even in Arjun Singh's Madhya Pradesh also found a candidate Mohammad Akbar from this constituency through the efforts of Bakshi a deputy commandant in the BSF. Bhim Singh usually manufactures candidates, one such candidate being Mohd. Yousuf Ganai; this job has proved immensely profitable for him. Affixing these curious labels on the surrendered militants the constituents of the Unified Command did not feel content and so different groups fielded six other candidates. According to this evolved scheme, Farooq Abdulla despite his reluctance, had to yield. The Cong-I candidate Mufti Syed was declared successful defeating a writer civil servant M.Y. Taing, a recent entrant into politics who is considered the creation of late Shamim Ahmad Shamim whose family accuse that Taing was behind the reasons which made Shamim die in a dejected manner. The National Conference cadre considered him a favourite of the Sheikh dynasty, who had, in their view polluted the story of the struggle. Later Mufti confessed that "he was thrown in the fray to accord the husting a colour of an election."

In Baramulla the central minister of Forests and Environment Soz was challenged by 28 other candidates. It is a wonder of Kashmiri politics that the ruling Janta Dal could not get a candidate from this constituency, but the BJP which never had an opening in Kashmir could get a candidate in Din Mohd. Chichi. The renegade Kuka Parray turned politician under the active patronage of Rashtriya Rifles and then under the umbrella of RAW formed a political party consisting of ex-militants and some migrant Pandits. Kuka Parray's J&K Awami League fielded an ex-militant Majeed Ganai responsible for devastation of huge willow forests around Wular Lake. I was sitting in the office room of Baramulla district Bar Association to represent an appeal before learned District Judge Baramulla when a person came under direct escort from Srinagar airport with a mandate from the Bhartiya Kisan Kamgar Party. This man Mohd. Yousuf Qureshi approached me to represent him before the returning officer to fill in his nomination papers and to plead his case.

It is curious that the said party is not even known in Kisan Sections of U.P. (India) so how was Qureshi roped in? Why? And by whom? The reply to all these questions is clear. Bhim Singh was provided with a candidate in Qadir Dar by the same agencies. Another party based somewhere in India 'Lok Shakti' was made to paste its label upon the forehead of another ex-militant Nazir Zergar by whom?

No one in Jammu and Kashmir has even heard or understood the meaning of 'Akhil Bhartiya Manav Seva Dal', but a unit of this party was also created by the 'unified command'. Hence, an ex-militant, who in the recent past held responsible for heinous criminal acts by the same agencies, was fielded as the nominee of this party for the Lok Sabha.

A Supreme Court senior lawyer, Muzzafar Hussain Baig also fought as an independent. On that day, 16 February 1998 I was in Baramulla Bar Association when Baig ex-member of this association also entered to interact with his ex-colleagues. Just before his arrival the majority of lawyers had expressed themselves against these 'imposed,' elections, advocate Mohammad Maqbool Mir being the most vocal in his expressions. When Muzzafar Baig entered within minutes the same Mir Sahib joined him and started canvassing in his favour. The other members having seen the comparison between Baig and Soz preferred the latter but overall, the lawyers community was committed to boycott not for only negative reasons, but for certain positive political grounds.

Abdul Gani Vakil, a member of the same fraternity and a committed Congress worker was fielded by that party, but was ditched during the campaign which led the Congress leaders to openly demonstrate against the immorality inherent in its Kashmir policy. At the party level they fielded Gani, who risked his life and did not let down the party, but the party in the field propagated Baig with whom there existed, some behind the screen arrangement—even at central level.

To lend credence to the argument that like other constituencies in India, the Baramulla Constituency also witnessed a close contest, the stage managers were not satisfied with candidates from 8 parties and with one formidable candidature of Supreme Court lawyer as an 'independent' they recruited a gang of 20 other ex-militants as independent candidates. The real contest was confined between the central minister Soz and the Supreme Court Lawyer Baig.

In 1980 Sheikh Abdulla imposed his son Farooq Abdulla upon Jammu and Kashmir politics by selecting him as member parliament (unopposed) from Srinagar and Farooq Abdulla passed on the banner to the third generation in a similar manner. The Congress again failed to get a candidate from the city not because Congress members of the city living in security zones were reluctant to cash one lakh rupees which was provided for each 'contestant' from the secret fund, but the party high command had given clear indications that it was committed to concede Srinagar seat for the Sheikh dynasty. It was under the 'Central intervention' that Omar Farooq was persuaded to return from a Gulf country, but the local Congress leadership was reluctant to deliver this seat on a silver platter to Omar and discovered a dummy—Syed Mehdi a Shia from a religious clerk's family of Budgam. It needs a mention that no rural candidate can cut any ice in this urban constituency, that too a representative of a community which constitutes only 8 percent of the electorate; this community too is both vertically and horizontally divided into several sections. Molvi Abbas Ansari and Syed Hussain (brother of Syed Mehdi) both belonging to A.P.H.C. were protagonists of boycott, whereas Molvi Iftikhar (MLA on Congress ticket) was at that time Farooq Abdulla's cabinet minister. So, Mehdi rationally had no base. A.R. Kabli joined the fray as a BJP candidate. The custodians of the security zone affixed the BSP label upon Mohi-ud-din Akhoon an inmate of the zone otherwise the Bahujan Samaj party, an organisation of backwards has no base in Srinagar because it has neither scheduled castes nor OBCs. Similarly, three independents were created and fielded from a similar zone.

But the whole set up of candidates convinced the electorate that it was the common decision of all Indian political parties and on their guidance it was being implemented by the agencies of forces and paramilitary forces to hand over the mantle to the third generation of the Sheikh dynasty. In whisper campaign voters dubbed the A.P.H.C. the exponents of boycott policy also as lackeys of this game. In their view imposition of boycott was to facilitate a cakewalk for Farooq Abdulla's apolitical son, hence a section not guided by the faith in the system, but in their hatred for the Sheikh dynasty and as a reaction against dynastic rule defied boycott. But the majority who were committed to boycott had no option but to stay back from the polling booths, they had assessed what the final result would be.

One section voted to inflict defeat upon Sheikh Abdulla's grandson whose birth had been celebrated as a festival by these very people in the 70s. The candidates who were against him were mere pygmies in comparison even to the volunteers of Sheikh Abdulia. Kabli the only candidate worth the name was himself saved and protected by Farooq Abdulla from political emasculation at the hands of Muzzaffer Shah. A small number participated willingly, many were forcibly dragged to booths and the bulk of votes was cast by ministers of the Farooq Abdulla cabinet and MLAs like Shafi Bhat and an ex-intellectual (now an MLA) G.M. Bawan. Syed Mehdi a Shia had no chance to get support from even half of 8 percent voters in the Shia community. In spite of these circumstances the people decided:

> "In case if we are forced to go to booths we will prefer Shia, congressite, rural Mehdi upon the attempt to replace Gulab Singh's family rule by Sheikh dynasty rule."

This was the individual decision of every voter. My birth place Charar-i-Sharief, a cent per cent Sunni town had so many anecdotes to convey about the Ichgam and Budgam Shias that in 1959 when I joined the Bar at Budgam and started living there my mother and other womenfolk were apprehensive about my safety. I dispelled such impressions in my own family, but otherwise the town population carried tales of prejudices. Even from that town the majority of such voters who were forced to booths marked ballot papers in favour of Syed Mehdi. It is after 2 pm that Ab. Qayoom the education minister and his gang members themselves cast bundles of votes marked in favour of Umar.

In Srinagar, Gandarbal, Kangan the same practice was forced upon the staff and opposition polling agents; it was practised by ministers Ali Mohd. Sagar MLAs Shafi Bhat and Mubarak Gul and other known 'goondas' of the National Conference. In this constituency firstly, voters were forced by paramilitary agencies to go to polls— they had no choice at the booths so they voted for Syed Mehdi who won, but clearly success of the chief minister's son was managed by force and by fraud. This was no success, but a defeat for Sheikh Abdulla after 18 years of his death.

In Baramulla the voters brought to booths by force voted for the lesser evil Muzaffar Baig an independent though he too was the subject of controversy. Ultimately Soz won because town people in Baramulla, Sopore, Hundware, Kupawara, Bandipra and Patan inspite of the terror let loose, abstained from polling and these unused ballot papers were used by the ministers who hailed from this constituency. They are A.A. Wakil, A.R. Choudhry, Molvi Iftikhar, Mushtaq Lone, Mohd. Sahfi who used those in favour of the National Conference candidate, Soz.

The bungling in this constituency has no far reaching consequences since Soz was a new entrant in politics and the political creation of such bungling, but to commit rigging for Sher-i-Kashmir's grandson is a tragedy which has become the theme of a political elegy composed by an old traditional poet—a fan of Shiekh Abdulla.

In Srinagar constituency out of about nine lakh voters only about 2 and a half lakh votes were shown to have been polled. Personal verifications and cross-checking showed that 15 to 20 percent votes were polled which included the votes of migrants sent through post whereas the percentage was brought to 30 percent only. Out of those 15 percent to 20 percent votes actually polled, the grandson of the Lion of Kashmir polled not more than 5 percent, yet was sent to Lok Sabha. In spite of destruction, devastation and complete alienation either Indian leaders refuse to learn and so continue to perpetuate political frauds upon the people of Jammu and Kashmir, otherwise they have no alternative except to justify their earlier blunders. In this affair the Sheikh dynasty got the image of Sheikh Abdulla destroyed.

In Baramulla the percentage of polled votes was shown to be 40 percent, whereas it did not actually go beyond 25 percent in spite of terror, force, fraud and farce.

However, the number of votes 93,000 which Baig polled provided material for Indian agencies, media, government propaganda machinery and opposition leaders to cause a great confusion in some world capitals. Even a team of American based Kashmir Study Group, which visited India including Jammu and Kashmir were made to receive an impression that the people of Jammu and Kashmir want to take part in elections, but after one year these quarters got satisfied that the votes polled by Baig were not voluntarily cast.

Ladakh witnessed a straight contest this time based on communal and regional divisions. Kargil proved its majority and an independent Muslim candidate won against a famous Ladakhi Buddhist politician and ex-central minister.

The Congress once again proved that Jammu Hindus preferred their party to the BJP to represent its interests as the saviour of their communal aspirations. It can be deduced that the two provinces of the state stand divided on vitally important political issues and so require separate treatment.

From the very beginning there has been a deliberate attempt on the part of both the countries with neo-colonist interests in Jammu and Kashmir, viz., India and Pakistan to create a void between these regions and between the two communities of Frontier viz. Ladakh. Pakistan's attempts in 1947 and 1965 to concentrate only upon the Valley and to sway and win only Kashmiri leadership to its side created the impression in Jammu that the Kashmir imbroglio in Pakistani perception means dispute about the Valley only. This situation disheartened those elements in Jammu who had genuinely believed that the destiny of the state, on the whole, was to be determined by its people. Such sections had with the lapse of time rationalised and come to terms with the status quo and were cowed down by the pro-occupation enthusiasm. The Muslims in Jammu province were shattered for quarter of a century under the fatal impact which the brutal killings in November 1947 of lakhs of Muslims had left upon their minds. Hence, they could not consolidate their shattered being for all these decades. The rulers, for their vested interest and to exploit them, divided them in several fragments and arrayed Gojars against Kashmiris, Punjabi Muslims were set in confrontation with Gojars and so on. After 1989 as militancy took the Valley in its grip, Jammu people could not channelise their reaction in any direction and cohesion could not be evolved in the two regions. Similarly, the Ladakh region had its peculiar problem for three decades, in spite of being in near about majority, the Muslims of this frontier area had to lie low and were not able to repudiate the wide scale propaganda that their area was only a Buddhist populated region. To counter this propaganda they had to react communally, even though communalism was alien to this region. Such propaganda could be countered only by participation in elections. Kashmir is recognised as a laboratory of mutual amity, tolerance and harmony, but Ladakh was in the forefront of it. It is only in Ladakh where inter community marriage existed from earlier times.

There was a single solid community of Ladakhis with no divisions, but through Cheewan Rigzin the communal virus was imported from India. Had it been done by Pakistan it would have been pardonable as that country exists on communal division, but Pakistan had no such access in either of the regions of Ladakh. Even Pakistan was not able to create communal pockets in Kargil where

Muslims are in majority, here also communalisation grew as a reaction to the communal twist with which New Delhi moulded some Buddhist monks. To be fair to common Ladakhis—both in Leh and Kargil they retained and protected their age-old communal harmony. But it is with the active abetment of the Congress that the Buddhist majority in Leh introduced violence to impose a communal strain on Jammu and Kashmir politics. The National Conference did not lag behind; it consolidated Muslim reaction of Leh minority and Kargil majority. The main actor has been the Congress and particularly the Nehru-Gandhi family. A chain of instances which if put together and discussed shall establish, beyond any doubt, that late Jawahar Lal Nehru sowed the seeds of communal dissension in Leh and his daughter Indira Gandhi developed it on a wider scale. Sheikh Abdulla and his son Farooq consolidated the reaction in Kargil into regional bias and Muslim communal reaction.

I do not mean that Nehru was communal, but as the very 'secular' conception is devoid of any moral sanctions so this idea is used to suit vested interests. Where such interests could be fed with the very blood of 'amity' such secularists do not hesitate to do so.

This communal divide was nourished by the two secular parties viz. the Congress and the National Conference as is manifest from the recent elections held to Ladakh Autonomo· Hill Council in November 2000 and from its results.

It is evident that in all the three regions Valley of Kashmir, Frontier (Leh & Kargil) and Jammu, communalism has eaten into the vitals of politics. Adherence of the Valley to the boycott cause conveys its rejection of India. Hindu dominated two and a half districts of Jammu region (viz., Jammu and Kathua district and sub-district of Udhampur, i.e., Udhampur district minus Reasi sub division) are enthusiastically involved in elections not for their faith in democracy, but for their commitment to the occupation of Jammu and Kashmir as part of Hindu majority India, by any means. Similarly, in case of Muslim majority districts of Jammu (Poonch, Rajouri, Doda and Reasi subdivision of Udhampur district) the conflict between 'boycott' and 'participation' is the psychological game played upon the people of these areas by the chauvinism of both the Valley based leadership and Jammu based politics. In the same manner Leh communalism owes its origin not in communal hatred, but in political, cultural, racial and linguistic subjugation imposed by Dogra rule during the mid- 19th Century upto mid-20th Century. Had not policies of India provided it a communal and anti Kashmiri channel it would have been moulded into a different course. Precisely it would have sought secession from imposed unity and would have looked towards its cultural mainstream, but the situation in Tibet confused their minds. In this confusion New Delhi, earlier opened a channel through 'illogical' and 'unreasonable' tutoring of Cheewan Rigzin and Lama Lobzang; later on providing political asylum to Dalai Lama, which made Ladakh Buddhists see a ray of hope in New Delhi. Now Ladakhi youth is fed up with that unnatural alignment. Likewise Kargelites would never take to confrontation with Ladakhites, but for the reason that the Ladakh hegemony created communal frenzy in Leh which surpassed the limits and went beyond the controlling ambit of the founders of that policy too. Ultimately they alienated Kargil which is the lifeline for Leh.

The real picture of the thinking of the people of Jammu and Kashmir can be gauged only as the disintegrated units of Jammu and Kashmir are integrated in the pre-1947 administrative pattern and then alone a free election is held which should not only be free from extraneous meddling, but must also be free from expansionist manoeuvring of Kashmir's two neighbours—India and Pakistan.

Chapter 34

Ninety Nine Confirms Eighty Nine

In the introduction to this book it has been pointed out that the main sources are personal diaries, personal enquiries and investigations which have been checked and cross-checked with such democrats who have lived through these ups and downs in the political process in Jammu and Kashmir; who from 1947 or even before that have actively involved themselves with the movement for democratisation. We could have to some extent relied on print media of the two countries and papers published in very small numbers in Jammu and Kashmir, but these newspapers for aggressive national interests imposed a sort of self-censorship about reporting events in the two parts of the occupied territories or whatever they conveyed was based on concoction for propaganda purposes or was distorted to an extent that such reporting not only annoyed Kashmiri readers, but ultimately eroded faith in the Indian press. Pakistani media also has remained burdened with designs to propagate an anti-India tirade. In this tirade of propaganda on both sides truth and constructive reporting were mercilessly butchered. A personal incident is quoted to convey the pressures on the Indian press about its handling of Kashmir affairs. This author was a student of Aligarh Muslim University from 1955-57. Those days any person who came to India or an Indian who entered into Jammu and Kashmir had to obtain permits (a sort of visa). On the completion of our two-year course we approached the Trade Commission of J&K Government at 5, Prithvi Raj Road New Delhi, but among a batch of 65 Jammu and Kashmir students, 17 were refused entry including this author. Others were Hamidulla Khan who in the early 90s was Advisor to Governor Jagmohan, Abdul Gani Mir who later became a junior minister in the Sadiq ministry and also included A.G. Lone who also became minister in the Mir Qasim government and is now the All Party Hurriat Conference leader. This batch of students sat down in protest in the office of the Trade Commissioner from where they were physically dragged out at 6 pm to the lawns. A group of MPs lead by N.G. Gorey and Mir Mushtaq Ahmad, Socialist leaders of India called on us, correspondents of various Delhi based newspapers also interviewed us, took photographs depicting our miserable situation and probed the causes of the virtual externment of about one and a half dozen youths. Next day we expected the news in all national papers and also expected that pictures published in those papers might invite public sympathy. But not a single paper had given even the briefest coverage. We called at offices of the *Statesman, Hindustan Times, Times of India, Indian Express, Milap, Al-Jamiat* and other English and Urdu dailies, but were not allowed access to any member of the editorial staff of any paper. We forced a brief standing meeting with Frank Moraes in the corridor of his office who directed us to see his assistant in news section, a soft spoken and straightforward South Indian. He expressed the inability of his paper to give coverage as in his view late in the evening they had received a 'warning' from South Block, New Delhi which conveyed:

"Pakistan Foreign Minister Sir Feroz Khan Noon is in New York. Any news about A.M. Kashmiri students shall prejudice Indian case so avoid publication". However, the warning even conveyed that the Home Minister G.B. Pant had taken up the matter with the Prime Minister of Jammu and Kashmir G.M. Bakshi. In this game that truth might jeopardise the falsehood in the respective cases of India and Pakistan before world fora that the truth about Kashmir became a casualty.

Upto 1972 the local press remained guided by the special staff headed by Ghulam Qadir Gandabali; then was subjected to the guidance and governance of the state information department; then remained dependent on the distribution of favours of state advertisements (which is the only source to sustain a paper) later it remained under strict vigilance of the state and was subjected to draconian laws. After 1989 it remained sandwiched inbetween the two guns—the Kalashnikov of the militant and 303 guns of the state. The state had not so far created a network for collective reporting and so remained fed by state press notes or the press notes of militant organisations, or by the statements of their above ground leadership. The national press right from 1947 onwards remained represented and dominated by Kashmiri Pandits either directly or indirectly.

Elections held to the 13th Lok Sabha on 5, 11 and 18 September 1999 were held during the period I was working on this book. As the 12th Parliament stood dissolved on the suggestions of my publishers I immediately started collection of material for this chapter.

On 9 August 1999 Sudhanshu Pandey I.A.S.[1] (non-state subject imported Indian officer) Director Information J&K Government issued a brochure entitled 'Jammu & Kashmir Lok Sabha 1999' expecting that the "people with same enthusiasm will welcome the elections to be held next month as they have welcomed and participated previously." To quote from the foreword of this booklet:

> "Due to turmoil in the State people were denied this precious right for some time but when they got chance to vote both for previous two Lok Sabhas and one for the State Assembly they came out in large numbers to choose their representatives."

It is this absurd falsehood which common people dub as shameless misinformation of this successor organisation to the great I.C.S. (i.e., I.A.S. cadres). Instead of becoming ambassadors of goodwill from the people of India to the people of Jammu and Kashmir it stands condemned as one of the worst agencies which became a vital cause for alienation of people of Jammu and Kashmir. The narration of this anecdote will illustrate the point. It is a historical fact that Praja Parishad agitation in Jammu launched in the early 50s was meant for complete integration with three slogans 'one flag', 'one constitution' and 'one head of the state'. In 1969-70, I was posted as Chief Judicial Magistrate of Kathua district in Jammu (south). Khosla an I.A.S. officer (an imported officer from India) was posted as District Magistrate in place of Ram Nath Wazir from Baderwah. On his posting the cadres of Praja Parishad celebrated a festival as they considered this posting as a step towards complete integration, but meanwhile, this member of the prestigious service fixed green and red bulbs outside his office room. The applicants and litigants and even lawyers could never dare to enter except when the green signal was on. Even the president Bar Association, the veteran respected politician,

'Lion of Dogra Desh, Th. Baldev Singh could not, nor Lala Chanan Shah Assistant Commissioner and A.D.M. enter the Collector's office room. It was ironical that from 10 AM to 4 PM only the red light was used to light the corridor. On this welcome posting we (myself, my sessions Judge Hakim Mohd. Sadiq and Ab. Hamid Khan S.P.) were considered as officers from 'expansionist valley.' Thakur Sahib one of the few clean politicians of this state expressed his views about this regrettable situation. Annoyed about facing this continued contempt one day Thakur Baldev Singh with other lawyers of the Praja Parishad forced his way into the out of bounds chamber of the Collector. What he 'saw therein' his friend guide and leader Atal Behari Vajpayee may directly enquire and learn from him. Sudanshu Pandey acted with the same contemptuous behaviour towards his subjects in his ruled colony, but deceived his own people beyond Lakhanpur.

The same mouthpiece of falsehood claims:

"People are gearing themselves for ensuing elections"

The same booklet provides the number of voters for the 1999 elections. In the previous one issued on 12 February 1998 the same department provides 1998 figures. The two tables are:

S. No.	Constituency	Voters in 1998	Voters in 1999
1	Srinagar	853183	853183
2	Ladakh	143492	143492
3	Udhampur	1015540	1009868
4	Jammu	1448366	1424328
5	Anantnag	799778	804983
6	Baramulla	757255	762237

On comparison this table shows:

1. There was no change either in Srinagar or in Ladakh constituencies. In other words either no revision, review or recheck of electoral rolls had taken place in these two constituencies or if taken the death had eliminated as many voters as had obtained the age of franchise during this year which is not possible. The angel of death does not act with rational calculation, but such acts can be expected only from the government agencies working in

Jammu and Kashmir. The logical inference is that no preparation, review or revision of electoral rolls for these two constituencies had taken place. The presumption fully supports the boycott of the people and of the officers deputed for roll preparation. The electoral rolls prepared for 12th Lok Sabha were made the basis for the voting to the 13th Lok Sabha. It, in other words provides another serious inference that the youth who obtained franchise during this year were denied the right to vote, whereas the dead who had left this world during these 19 months came out from their graves to cast their votes.

2. In Udhampur constituency the number of voters within 19 months had decreased by 5,672 instead of increasing. There was no epidemic nor did this area undergo any natural calamity. Why should we confine the decrease to only 5,672 voters, but we should also hold that more than 20,000 people who had acquired age of franchise during this year were either not registered as voters or their equal number had perished due to some natural or human onslaught. There is no such evidence that more than 20,000 voters were killed during this year, hence, the only presumption is that either the electoral rolls prepared for 12th Lok Sabha were a fraud or the recent one is bogus. The reality is that voters neither for 12th Lok Sabha nor for the 13th Lok Sabha elections took any interest to involve themselves with the electoral process. It reveals the mood of non- participation in Jammu region too.
3. The case with Jammu constituency which is similar in 1999 shows decrease of voters compared 1998 figure by 24,000 voters. Inferences are the same as drawn in para(2) above.
4. Only in Anantnag and Baramulla an increase of upto 5,000 votes in each is recorded. But personal investigations from the staff in charge for revision of polls in these two constituencies showed that neither the field staff participated to circulate previous rolls by pasting its copies on conspicuous places, nor was there any question decided for correction of any entry. Hence, the nominal change brought was a mutilation of the record made in a haphazard manner. This is logically also not believable because the increase within about two years

is recorded at the rate of decimal one five per cent (.15%).

In this background the boycott as in 1989 was a popular reaction. Yet the Election Commission under the dual patronage of its Chairman M.S. Gill and its active member G.V. Krishnamurthy considered this mass apathy a challenge to the Commission, so connived with the State Government to consolidate the process of fraud in the name of elections in Jammu and Kashmir. Though earlier Gill had opined that boycott also amounts to expression of an opinion 'which also is a democratic right.' Why then did the military, paramilitary forces, members of special task force and officers deputed on election duty prosecute this policy of fraud and force with vigour? It is presumed that in the internal and external situations to which India stands exposed about Jammu and Kashmir, its political, civil and military ideologues find only one mask to cover that is to compound the fraud by piling up their deliberate common blunders. All agencies act in a patently neo-colonialistic manner, but with immaturity which exposes them to ridicule.

Let us first introduce J&K Peoples Democratic Party to our readers who have known Mufti Mohammad Syed, an active character of Kashmir politics. He had not struggled nor made any sacrifice whatsoever as he was an entrant to post-1947 political scene. Even as a college student during the mid 50s he was known as an ordinary worker of the ruling clique which had no roots among the masses, rather after 1953 were dubbed as traitors by the people. In 1957 a splinter group of the ruling National Conference formed DNC. As a student Mufti was its sympathiser, returned from Aligarh Muslim University after passing Law graduation in 1959. He had just joined the lower ranks of the pro-Indian opposition party DNC which again merged into the parent party the National Conference. The president of the ruling party Prime Minister Bakshi Ghulam Mohammad conceded some constituencies for the merged group and showed inclination for one or two persons including Syed Mir Qasim from district Anantnag. Qasim put forward the claim of his brother Syed Hussain, but his leader Sadiq considered it as an exposure to nepotism which Bakshi's men would exploit, hence a second name emerged of the fresher Mufti. Bakshi had a gameplan behind this proposal, that if Qasim and his leader insisted on Syed Hussain or any senior politician he would accuse that group of nepotism and would simultaneously attract to his ranks literate pro-Indian youth. Thus, a dramatic opening was made for Mufti by the prevailing situation. Within a brief period Bakshi got axed under the Kamraj plan, Shamsud Din took over as Prime Minister, Sadiq group parted company without forming a separate party and Mufti remained loyal to this group. The Moi Muqqadas agitation forced replacement, Shamsud Din was replaced by G.M. Sadiq, his group was limited and thus a chance offered entry for Mufti who was elevated to the rank of a junior minister. He became known in political circles and acquired some value in the corridors of power in New Delhi. In the late 60s his association with Mir Qasim against the Chief Minister G.M. Sadiq cultivated an interest for him in the minds of occupants of the official residence of Prime Minister Indira Gandhi.

Congress leaders never desired the emergence of popular political personalities. They feared that such mass based politicians would resist the policies of erosion in the constitutional guarantees for Jammu and Kashmir. Hence, Sheikh Abdulla whom Indian rulers themselves introduced worldwide as a 'popular leader' was axed by the sharp-edged deceit of Nehru. Though he was not the voice and symbol of popularity in Jammu and Kashmir as India projected him, but among all the leaders in both parts of Kashmir he mustered the support of an organised cadre. In spite of his adamant posture about special status of the state he would have proved a viable link within constitutional limits, but Jawahar Lal Nehru himself broke this bridge. Bakshi who showed some reluctance for certain measures, met a similar end. Sadiq who succeeded Bakshi died a broken man. In this process the colonial policies had eliminated the first line of the National Conference leadership and the mantle was received by Mir Qasim who stood in the second line of leadership much below the ranks of D.P. Dhar, Mubarak Shah, Sofi Mohd. Akbar and others. D.P. Dhar ruled behind the screens as a superpower in Jammu and Kashmir. Men like R.P. Saraf and K.D. Sethi were thrown away. Sofi, Mubarak Shah, Mohi-ud-din Hamdani and others had joined the Plebiscite Front. Therefore, a question racked the minds of men around Indira Gandhi as whom to build as a counterweight to Mir Qasim to keep him under constant threat. Hence, Mufti from third or fourth rung was encouraged to play that role. Meanwhile, Qasim was used to trap Sheikh Abdulla and destroy him politically and Mufti was briefed to humiliate him. Had not Indira Gandhi crumbled under the weight of the excesses of the emergency, Mufti would have been made to emerge as a super Sher-i-Kashmir by cutting the image of Sheikh Abdulla into pieces. He had sufficiently trained two of his proteges late Mustafa Mir and A.M. Naik for the job. In 1999 A.M. Naik was used by Farroq Abdulla son of the Sher-i-Kashmir to humiliate the same Mufti.

Mufti posed a political challenge to the Sheikh family through the source of power—the Nehru-Gandhi family in New Delhi and it is under the pressure of this 'insect of the street gutter (as Sheikh Abdulla had specifically named him) that the great leader of Kashmir remained in constant danger and to keep his chair intact for his progeny he surrendered his ego completely, which was his only quality. After Sheikh Abdulla's death it is Mufti who arranged the installation of Jagmohan and divided the Sheikh family. He did not like the rapprochement between the Nehru and Sheikh dynasties and as in 1986 Rajiv Gandhi and Farooq Abdulla came closer, Mufti distanced himself from Rajiv. He could not be subordinated by Farooq Abdulla, but Mufti did not like to work with him and so parted company from the Congress, joined V.P. Singh, became Home Minister of India, reinstalled Jagmohan who made Dr. Farooq Abdulla to opt for political wilderness. In 1998 he bagged the Anantnag seat for Congress. It is a historical reality that from 1962 to 1972, Mufti was returned to state assembly merely by fraud and in 1998 it was again an agreed arrangement under which he got elected to the Indian parliament. But he found the strong lobby of Congress closer to Farooq Abdulla. Farooq corrupted that lobby by accommodation of G.N. Azad and Karan Singh as Rajya Sabha members at the cost of his party interests. The dominant tactic was to strengthen the anti-Mufti lobby in that party, so, Mufti had to part ways. Where to go? It is the tragedy of events that the sons and daughters of Sheikh Abdulla by their actions devastated whatever positive image Sheikh Abdulla had left in history. On the other hand, Mehbooba, the eldest daughter of Mufti became his political protégé and elevated Mufti Mohd. Syed into a politician with 'some formidable public base.' The role of his daughter encouraged him to form a regional party, i.e., Peoples Democratic Party (PDP), but it also suffered immediately due to a limited cadre base in the city. Consequently, in 1999 the party also projected itself as a group of the 'daughter, father' duo and a non-resident Kashmiri Muzzafar Hassan Baig became the third in this trio. So, the electoral battle of this party remained, like initial programme of family planning, confined to a red triangle. This triangle exerted itself to convince people to take part in elections, but the positive abstention of people made them suffer. People believed that PDP was a proxy creation of central secret agencies to motivate a section of the people to erode the boycott call. The assumption that Mufti could stand against the popular call of APHC proved fallacious. It is clearly evident from the statement of Mufti which he made after elections in Jammu that he was cheated by the centre to take 'part' but was 'ditched'. They had assessed correctly that not for any positive contribution of PDP, but for utter resentment against the treachery of the Sheikh dynasty, the people, in case of participation in elections would prefer a lesser evil, but the boycott changed this whole strategy. The official machinery filled in the ballot boxes in Kashmir division with ballot papers marked in favour of the National Conference (the ruling party in the state) and in Jammu division with the papers marked for the BJP (the ruling party in the center). In 1975 the protege of Mufti Mr. Naik defeated the same Mufti. Umar, the son of the Chief Minister made a fraudulent entry into the Lok Sabha; A.R. Shaheen who had defected several times from the National Conference and had just returned was made to win over Muzzafar Baig of PDP and the erstwhile close confidant of Farooq Abdulla, Saifud Din Soz, an independent candidate was trounced; a retired police officer from Kargil was made to slow down a reputed politician of Ladakh; BJP candidates Prof. C.L. Gupta and Vishnu Dut benefitted in similar manner from the Jammu region.

At this juncture M.S. Gill and the Election Commission acted in the larger interests of democracy and confined the declaration of the results on actually polled votes. Such a cautious and transparent approach would have not posed any threat either to the National Conference or to the BJP or to the coming together of these two parties, but would have consolidated belief in democracy. Indian rulers are not only causing erosion among the masses of Jammu and Kashmir against India, but creating disillusionment about the very viability of democracy. Had they strictly shown the real percentage which actually participated, it would not amount to a no-confidence decision against India, but would establish, at best that the people had not accepted the manifesto of any political party in the field or were not attracted by any party or any of the contesting candidates.

In the first general elections in 1952, the Congress candidate won from Taran Taaran Constituency in east Punjab by polling only 20 percent votes. The elected MP represented all the four lakh voters, for full term of five years. In the fair arrangements too no ISI agent would become an M.P. Either of those candidates who represented pro-Indian leanings in their policies and conscience would enter the Peoples' House of India. Particularly in Jammu, in our assessment only BJP nominees would get elected even by fair means for many reasons, which are as follows:

1. The Congress had suffered a great setback due to the fact that Mufti took away to his new party a solid group of its workers.
2. The party was so divided by its internal conflicts that no Promethean heat would infuse energy in its ashes.
3. Muslims of both the constituencies in that region had boycotted, so the vote base of both the Congress and the National Conference had completely shattered. Thus, the Hindu vote had to go to BJP.

In these circumstances there were good chances for BJP from both these constituencies. But the forces received encouragement to politicise their ranks and so became instrumental to impose a political order. They behaved least intelligently. Force is their culture so the forces eroded otherwise the legitimacy in the decision. Jagmohan has rightly observed that in 1983 in state Assembly elections, the Zadibal constituency would have gone to the National Conference, but to increase the margin for the nephew of Sheikh Abdulla bungling was done. Jagmohan will hardly accept it, but the same practices were repeated in two Jammu constituencies to 'assure' the victory of the BJP. As far as Ladakh is concerned this time the genesis of boycott swayed Kargil; the post-Kargil situation had not only disturbed the electorate, but caused complete alienation there also. Circumstances demanded that in Ladakh constituency the polling should be postponed till the Kargilites were rehabilitated, but the center left the decision to the mercy of the state government. As BJP had no base in this constituency and had assessed that in case of a contest the real fight would be confined to the Congress and National Conference and so avoided the postponement and conceded the seat in favour of its expected ally. So, ultimately in the war torn constituency the National Conference nominee was imposed by same methods.

Srinagar constituency saw a tough fight between the son of the chief minister, the daughter of the ex-home minister of India (sister of Rubia Syed who became the first VIP hostage to Kashmiri militants) and a Congress nominee.. No ripples were created and people remained positively indifferent though the press qualified it as a 'battle of titans. The official record showed about 11 percent votes polled, whereas the facts are alarming. My home constituency Charar-i-Sharief has about 55,000 voters out of whom only 2,200 were polled upto 2 pm. Then two ministerial colleagues of Farooq Abdulla, Abdul Qayoom and Ab Rahim, both voters of this constituency raided the polling booths at Charar-i-Sharief, Nagam, Bade Para, Pukharpara, Goggi Pathri and a few other places and fraudulently increased the 2,200 votes into 24,000 ballot papers. The polling agents of PDP lodged protests and at certain booths the staff in charge with the active interference of paramilitary forces made distribution of unused ballot papers and a few bundles were given to the PDP and Congress candidate agents also, but the bulk went to the National Conference candidate. At a specific polling booth in the town of Charar-i-Sharief when the polling agent of Mehbooba Mufti protested against this practice the officer in charge also felt convinced and tried to restrain the men of Qayoom. The security officer in charge threatened:

"You are all agents of Hurriyat. We are not interested in the success of one or in the defeat of the other, we are interested in the defeat of boycott call, so, you also bring your men and they also shall be allowed to mark as many votes as they like."

As many came whom Qayoom could arrange and to silence the other polling agent they too were allowed to mark a given number in favour of their respective candidates. Three days before polling Umar Farooq, in an election rally held at Charar-i-Sharief which was mainly attended by school children threatened "both Qayoom and Rather are employees of our family, if they fail to arrange votes for me in this Constituency, they will lose their jobs." The two met the challenge well. One of such agents (a distant relative of mine) claimed to have marked 155 ballot papers. The game was similar in Kangan and Ganderbal assembly segments. In Hazratbal constituency with an electorate of 115,000 inspite of fraud, only 4,269 votes have been shown as polled though in reality this figure is also false. Thus the percentage was only between 5 percent to 6 percent. *Kashmir Monitor* dated October 7, 1999 has published details of the fraud played in this Constituancy and so was done by other dailies. However after cross-check of these details I sum up the gist as under.

The National Conference activists with the active connivance of the state police especially its Special Operation Group (SOG) polled bogus votes in various assembly segments. In Srinagar city only, they polled around 20,000 bogus votes. Clashes took place in counting halls among counting agents at the International Convention Complex. The clashes took place as the Congress objected to the presence of ministers who guided employees on election duty to act to their advantage. Other clashes ensued about 1636 unsigned votes found in Ganderbal lot, all in favour of NC. The returning officer over-ruled the objection and allowed those unsigned ballot papers. The law requires that the presiding officer should sign the ballot paper after the voter is properly identified and given the chance to exercise the right. But maximum number of the ballot papers did not bear the signatures of such officers. It will require a full chapter if we discuss only this Constituency.

In Anantnag out of eight lakh voters about 92,000 in total have been shown as polled ie. about 12 percent. But what was actual position.

All Opposition Candidates including M.Y. Tarigami (CPM) Mufti Mohammad Syed (PDP) Peerzada Mohd. Syed (Congress), Mohd. Altaf Paddar (Awami League) and Showkat Hussain Wani (BJP) raised objections alleging that SPOs without uniform were functioning as counting agents for the ruling National Conference Candidate...

This news was published in all the papers and even relayed from electronic media. Hundreds of ballot papers were unsigned, packed in bundles, majority of ballot boxes did not bear proper seals. After investigations and even after examining many of my old friends now in ruling National Conference, I have come to the conclusion that only 5 percent votes were actually polled.

About Baramulla the following chart will explain the tally:

Total	NC	Soz	PDP	Awami
Polled	(A.R. Shaheen)	(Independent)		Leauge
167567	84252 votes	11330	47630	24355

The ex-militant Awami Leauge Candidate supported actively by Rashtriya Rifles bagged this whole number of 24355 votes only from Sonawari and Bandipora assembly segments. All the newspapers exposed that Kuka Parray, ex-militant turned legislator raided booths in these two segments alongwith groups of militants, threatened election staff and in bulk polled votes which were almost all unsigned. A few officers deputed on the duty narrated their woeful tales that had they resisted they would have lost their lives.

In Karnah, Hundawara and Lolab the Forest Minister, behaved more violently than Kuka Parray did. Inspite of protests from their subordinates in State Forest Department who were posted on election duty on the insistence of Choudhry, the two ministers did cast bogus votes which the unscrupulous returning officer could not reject but were counted as valid votes. It is thus that the actual poll in this Constituency too did not exceed 7 percent to 8 percent.

This election exposed the previous victories of Prof. S.D.

Soz who always claimed popular mandate from this very constituency. This time he had emerged as a hero on all India level, by his single vote he had overthrown BJP government in the center and for the first time, he became known as a politician among the people; with enhanced clout. During these elections he bagged a genuine lot of votes. In 1988 and 1989 he had not even bagged half of the number of the votes which he polled this time, but then the huge numbers shown in his favour were similarly bogus as this time Shaheen and Muzaffar Beig or Kuka Parray's nominee did bag some.

Some comments are recorded here:

"Scores of ballot papers contained slogans in favour of Azadi"—All News Agencies and official record.

Ajay Chrangoo chairman Panun Kashmiris Political Affairs Committee (an organisation of migrated Kashmiri Pandits) asserted in Jammu on 25 September 1999 that fraud was perpetuated through postal voting also.

"Existing procedure of casting postal ballots has been devised in such a way so as to allow adequate space for manipulation by powers that may be."

M.K. Teng, another leader of migrants and an author, urged the EC "to assess the implications of ensuring the right to vote of the Kashmiri migrants."

It is necessary to state that migrant Pandits sent postal ballots from their refugee camps in Jammu or New Delhi and other cities from India, but those papers were changed in favour of the National Conference candidates. Inspite of transparent proof the Election Commission did not enquire.

This table will reveal the 'magic' performed by our election authorities. The polling in almost all the assembly segments was over by 2 pm. Thereafter, a curfew like situation prevailed. Whoever chose to cast their vote or was forced to the polling booth performed his voluntary duty or begaar by 2 pm. But with the magic wand which the Indian Election Commission has provided to the officers on election duty they can make or mar the situation. The voting pattern in Baramulla constituency is given below:[1]

S. No.	Name of	Percentage of votes	Percentage after

	Electoral Segment	8 am to 3 pm (Five Hours)	3 pm to 4 pm (One Hour)	
1	Karnah	24%	43%	Excess 19%
2	Kupwara	18%	25.35%	Excess 7.35%
3	Lolab	20.57%	37%	Excess 17%
4	Hundwara	18%	30%	Excess 22%
5	Langate	35%	50%	Excess 15%
6	Sopore	1.4%	5%	Excess 3.6%
7	Sangrana	1%	2.5%	Excess 1.5%
8	Baramulla	14.1%	17.78%	Excess 3.77%
9	Pattan	15%	20%	Excess 5%

In village Shilwat in Sonawari Assembly segments villagers were forced by jawans of Rashtriya Rifles (an army wing trained to counter the insurgency) to come out from their houses, and form a waiting queue near the polling booth so that video cameras of various media agencies particularly of Door Darshan (Indian TV) could take their pictures to misinform Indian viewers and the rest of the world. Villagers protested, the forces fired upon them indiscriminately killing Hilal Ahmad, Gulzar Ahmad and Abdul Gani on the spot and injuring a dozen or more.

In 1998 Kashmiri Pandits showed committed enthusiasm for elections but this time Panun Kashmir, an association of migrant Pandits also appealed for boycott.

Soz Sahib who has been himself imposed on the political scene of Kashmir by electoral frauds has in a detailed statement issued on 20 September 1999 asserted that the "Election Commission of India has by active connivance deepened the alienation of J&K people." He has in detail highlighted such frauds for which he placed sufficient and convincing proof before the Election Commission, but was told to agitate the matter in an election petition. It is widely known that such petitions will hang for a decade in the judicial system.

The judicial system? Soz knows the calibre of people who man that since he has also contributed in selection of some men. Mufti Mohd. Syed who owes his political origin to similar electoral frauds, has acted right from 1962 as a staunch activist of political suppression and activised process of erosion of democratic institutions including judiciary. But he too, at the end of his career, was taught a similar lesson for his fault of being too committed to the occupation. On September 14, 1999 Mufti declared that the state administration and BJP government at the center were in a nexus to perpetuate electoral fraud on the state. He accused the two governments and Election Commission to have repeated 1987 (the election which we have qualified as 'Culmination of Fraud' and in which Mufti was himself, a conniving party). Explaining the charges he said the 'State Task Force' and 'SPOs' were used in rigging elections, official machinery was brazenly and openly misused, the National Conference legislators and ministers captured booths and indulged in bogus polling. He accused the Election Commission of 'open connivance.'

The Pradesh Congress Committee also exposed the violence with which the National Conference rigged the elections despite the connivance of the central leadership of this party with Farooq Abdulla due to the relationship between the Sheikh dynasty and the Nehru Gandhi family.

Tarigami who under the arrangement worked out by an ideologue of CPM. Harkrishen Singh Surjeet shared a berth in the Legislative Assembly elections with the National Conference and entered into the state house under that arrangement which imposed the 'Election by Begaar' in 1996 upon the people of Jammu and Kashmir also reacted against the 1999 fraud. On October 1, 1999 in his statement he repeated the charges which Mufti also had levelled against the central and state governments and the Election Commission. Harkrishen Singh Surjeet too suggested that a nexus existed between the center and state governments for bogus votes, fraudulent elections and rigging. On 1 September 1999 the Secretary state unit of CPI (M) who in 1996 shared the platform of fraud with the National Conference asserted that "National Conference manipulated elections, from beginning, the drama of 1987 was replayed, it is 1987 which brought death and destruction and changed the whole complexion of the situation." He warned that "neither Farooq Abdulla and nor the Central Government learnt lessons from its past blunders."

On October 10, 1999 the *Indian Express* published a story researched by two of its correspondents Vikramjeet Singh and Mir Ehsan entitled 'Dragged to Booths they put

Fingers Down.' The subheading is 'Record number of voters in Kashmir got fingers inked, left ballots blank. The story reveals that 'in Baramulla Constituency the number of invalid votes exceeded the number of votes which the sitting MP (Soz) got'. Hitting out with sarcasm the reporters summed up "This ghost candidate who got all invalid votes ranked fourth in the list of more than a dozen contenders." In Pattan segment 23 percent votes polled reflected this trend as it saw the worst coercion. The reporters reported that the Chief Election Officer S.V. Bhave said "If some one is forced to vote, then he can deliberately reject the vote, so, he cannot rule out the possibility of coercion."

In another statement to *Daily Kashmir Times* Jammu, Mufti Syed could not restrain himself from exposing the secret that "in future the center cannot be trusted as they had assured me but duped me ultimately." This confession makes it clear that Mufti had jumped to 'erode' the boycott only with an assurance that his seat would be conceded, but ultimately as he was not able to create cracks in the determination of the masses to boycott the elections then all assurances melted. It again indicates that these elections from 1996 to 1999 (both for Parliament and State Assembly) are in reality a contest between two options: Elections v/s No Elections. The Indian government is determined to impose an election and voters are determined to frustrate such an imposition.

Reputed Indian journalist and an outstanding lawyer A.G. Noorani exposes 'Rigged Elections for Legitimacy' in *Daily Kashmir Monitor* Srinagar September 28, 1999, "If 1998 elections were forced by renegade militants this time it was National Conference Government which imposed the fraud."

Rekha Choudhry and Ashitosh Kumar summed up the details of this fraud in *Daily Kashmir Times* 5 November 1999 under the heading 'Travesty of Elections in Kashmir.' They sum up:

> "There were reports carried out by the local press about the active role played by the army, BSF, Rashtriya Rifles and the special operation group all through the electoral process. In the language of the army, it was merely a process of 'education and explanation' to ensure a good voter turn out."

Quoting a minister (name not given)[2] these two reporters say:

> "If Pakistan can use force to get the polls boycotted here why can't we counter it by using our security forces to forcibly make people come out and vote."

A delegation of the All India People's Resistance Forum (AIPRF) consisting of journalists, advocates, intellectuals and trade unionists from Andhra Pradesh, Bihar, Punjab and Delhi visited Kashmir, toured various parts of the state and issued a Joint Statement demanding a probe into atrocities, withdrawal of military forces and urged for cancellation of polls. The factual report of the delegation reveals the atrocities committed upon the people in the name of elections and that if such is the manner in which people shall have to exercise franchise then democracy should be banned and autocracy restored worldwide.

"Ram Teri Ganga Maili"

Bollywood produced a famous movie with this title and since then this phrase is used as a proverb which has even been used in relation to Indian elections. It is admitted that the electoral process in India has not remained unpolluted just as the sacred waters of Ganga have not remained all pure. However, Hindus take 'Ganga Jal' (water from this sacred river as a token of reverence). On the fraudulent return of Umar Farooq to parliament this time in the same manner in which he made maiden entry into politics as member of the Lok Sabha in 1998 even the state BJP qualified his election as 'the result of naked bungling.' Even the senior vice president of the All India Bhartiya Janata Party the late Mr. Sharma joined with the state unit of his party to demand the cancellation of the fraudulent success of Umar from Srinagar and to get a fresh election conducted in this constituency. But soon central BJP admitted all the four National Conference members of parliament fraudulently elected into the NDA coalition and inducted the same Umar as a junior minister in the central government headed by the same BJP which had declared his election as an act of fraud, force and farce. The principled vice president of BJP was told at his Ferozeshah Road residence by a Jammu based BJP leader: *"Aap Logon ney*

Ganga Jal Key Saath Muter Milaayaa". (You people have mixed impure urine with the sacred pure water of Ganges)

"I also reacted with the same phrase", said Mr. Sharma but was told by a senior party leader (a minister) that *"cow urine when mixed with Gangajal also becomes sacred"*.

The Autonomy proposal passed by two-third majority in June 2000 by the so elected J&K Assembly in 1996 and the summary treatment of rejection accorded to it by the Central Government necessitated a comparative study with the impact of the Hizb-ul-Mujahidin offer of unilateral cease-fire. This study will also elucidate that how the creators of fraud dismiss the decisions of such created legislature.

Notes

1. In my next book "J&K—Part or Colony" under an appropriate heading "Administrative Colony", I am establishing with statstics and data that this state is ruled as a colony by the Indian bureaucracy, police officers and technocrats. Upto 1964-65 mainly Indian Muslims were posted in Jammu and Kashmir on these important assignments, but now without any reservations the key posts in administration and police are filled by Hindu officers imported from India. Now even from the rank of Deputy Superintendent J&K Police to its Director General 80 percent to 90 percent officers are Indian Hindus.The same is the case with land revenue department from Additional Collector (A.C.) to Financial Commissioner, in the civil secretariat from Deputy Secretary to Chief Secretary etc. the ratio is almost the same.

   India builds world opinion by the argument that the Muslim majority state of Jammu and Kashmir is the symbol of Indian secularism, but is that character represented through its main institutions? For the past 54 years has any Kashmiri Muslim been elevated to Supreme Court? Has any eminent Kashmiri scholar ever been inducted as member Union Public Service Commission? Planning Commission of India? Law Commission? Press Commission of India? Or even as member, Vice Chairman or Chairman of CAT (Central Administrative Tribunal)? Has any Indian State, so far, allowed any Kashmiri Muslim to function as its Chief Secretary/ Director General Police/ Financial Commissioner/Chief Justice or even additional Chief Secretary or Inspector General of Police. From 1947 we have seen about 2 dozen Chief Secretaries, but so far out of them only four or five were Kashmiris. Similarly I.G.Ps and DGPs have all come from outside except for three locals. At present among Secretaries to Government and in J&K Police all are Indian Hindus. The Chief Secretary, Governor, D.G.P., Chief Justice, Accountant General—all are Indian Hindus. What does this one-way traffic mean? Does it reflect anything other than that Jammu and Kashmir is a colony administered by the Indian Home Ministry or is it demonstration of secular identity. Besides, the real rulers are the army and paramilitary forces.

2. My enquiries have shown that the minister who made this 'straight forward' statement is Mr. A.M. Sagar.

Chapter 35

Drama of Autonomy

The Sheikh-Indira Accord of 1975 had no attraction except that the further erosion in the special status 'shall' be arrested and the erosion already made might, to a great extent, be reversed. Sheikh Abdulla repeatedly assured his cadres that the pre-August 1953 political position would be restored. People were conscious that on the borrowed legislative support he could not do much, but the 1977 elections, which gave him two-thirds majority created genuine expectations that he would initiate a comprehensive constitutional amendment which would annul all post-1953 constitutional amendments particularly the most controversial sixth Constitutional Amendment Act of 10 April 1965. Instead, taking a cue from the 42nd Amendment to Indian Constitution, through sixteenth Amendment Act of 17 February 1977 Sheikh Abdulla amended Sec. 52 of J&K Constitution raising the life term of J&K Assembly from 5 to 6 years. The Janata Party government greatly did undo the 42nd amendment to Indian Constitution, but Sheikh Abdulla or his successor son did not undo the mischief perpetuated under the 16th Amendment Act. Had Sheikh Abdulla or his son taken such a step it would have dispelled the common impression that the Sheikh dynasty was interested in safeguarding its rule rather than in the restoration of the states special status. So after 1975 till his death in September 1982 Sheikh did not consider it worthwhile even to nominate an expert committee (even on organisational level) which could have examined all such constitutional amendments made after August 1953 under Sec.147 of J&K Constitution which could be annulled, modified, amended or retained. Instead five constitutional amendments have been made during the second term of power of Dr. Farooq Abdulla from July 1987 to November 10, 1989. The present Assembly has also passed two bills of amendment; all such amendments were meant to erode special status of the state which provides sufficient evidences that from 1975 till 1997 there has been no abatement in this erosion. It is only during the first term of Farooq Abdulla's Chief Ministership (1982-84) that no constitutional amendment was introduced or passed nor any significant presidential (constitutional) order was applied. Similarly, the period of G.M. Shah ministry remains free from such an 'achievement'. The reasons are clear. During the first term of Farooq Abulla the relationship between the Sheikh dynasty and Indira's family was under great strain. G.M. Shah's Congress supported ministry had a bare majority so could not take risk of defeat on a constitutional amendment.

The election manifesto of the National Conference issued for 1996 Elections was either just to confuse its own cadre or to have a distinctive character against other All-India parties in the fray so, it stressed for restoration of regional autonomy. People had since dismissed this political gimmick of the Sheikh dynasty as they had been disappointed by their duplicity when both the father and the son enjoyed two-third majority, but instead of reversing the process of erosion in internal autonomy they accelerated it. Besides, the people had no charm in phraseology, but in the real exercise of power by the institutions fairly and fearlessly. They found no attraction in words Wazir-i-Azam, nor had any aversion for the phrase 'Chief Minister. To them you might call head of the state executive or head of the state by any name, but in their view, they would always remain sandwiched in the Indian power game.

However, as a gimmick immediately on his reinstallation as chief minister under the auspices of all the 'national parties of India' Dr. Farooq Abdulla appointed two committees for suggestion of measures to have autonomy within the Indian federation and to accord autonomy to three units of the state. In June 2000 after four years, the House discussed in detail, in an emotionally surcharged atmosphere and passed a resolution with voice vote almost with unanimity. Certain relevant questions do emerge. The important one is 'Why did the assembly by-pass Section 147 of J&K Constitution?'

Why the House did not choose to reverse the erosion it had itself made of the State Autonomy and why did it go with a begging bowl to patrons in New Delhi who bluntly refused. It is a fact that certain erosions were made through presidential orders applying provisions of the Indian Constitution to Jammu and Kashmir. Such applications cannot be undone by the State Assembly, but had it completed the part which it had to perform then the question about abrogation of such provisions would arise. An explanation of this background is necessary to convince the readers that the Autonomy proposal passed by the J&K Assembly in June 2000 and immediately rejected summararily by the Indian Cabinet was just an eyewash.

Firstly, it is argued that the Farooq government having failed on all fronts tried to cover its failures by diverting the public mind through the unnecessary discussions on autonomy. This argument is not tenable, but even fallacious because that issue does not involve any public interest so the question of covering failures under this cover does not arise. Even if that had been the purpose behind the discusssions it should be treated again as a failure in understanding the public mind who had no interest in autonomy.

Secondly, it is averred that after India and Pakistan the two neighbours with a strained relationship became nuclear powers the issue of Jammu and Kashmir has become a potential nuclear threat. Therefore, the world exerted pressure to avoid a holocaust in South Asia with the USA getting much too involved. To lessen the intensity of such pressure Farooq Abdulla was advised to play an emotional drama in the form of a marathon discussion in the House attracting world attention so that New Delhi also gets involved and in the so agreed heated involvement in Srinagar and New Delhi some concessions to restore the eroded 'autonomy' would be declared. It was argued that with such superficial concessions the pressure exerted by world powers would for some time get eased and diverted. Contenders of this theory believe that as the marathon deliberations on the issue did not divert the mind of influential world lobbies from the gravity of the core issue of resolving the Kashmir issue hence, the behind the scene initiators of the discussions, political pandits in New Delhi withdrew this ineffective card they had played. With such withdrawal and ostensibly by rejection of any measures about autonomy the BJP government at the Center has for the time being, pacified its ideological mentors in Rashtriya Sewak Sangh (RSS).

Thirdly, it is stated that as the Central government initiated parleys with the leadership of APHC, Farooq and his National Conference by these lengthy discussions tried to convey that even if the Sheikh dynasty and its main organisation the National Conference have both become ineffective in the changed political scenario, yet both do possess a nuisance value. As the heat of the discussions did not cut any ice even within the Amargarh Palace (the Assembly Hall in Srinagar) so this ineffective resolution was shelved by the Center and the lesson learnt was that the dynasty and the organisation had both lost even nuisance value and could not now, even play the role of an effective colonial agent in Jammu and Kashmir.

The inevitable emerged in the form of contemptuous treatment of the decision of the 'House of the people of J&K.' Had this House in any real sense reflected the aspirations of the people and had it the mandate of the people no dictatorial autocracy ruling in New Delhi would dare to dismiss this decision so contemptuously.

The discussions in the Assembly Hall were echoing in its corridors and comments were being made on the treatment the proposal met from New Delhi when a supremo of a militant outfit Abdul Majeed Dar issued a statement from his hideout, some unknown and unspecified place, regarding unilateral cease-fire; the issues discussed and passed by a formidable majority in the legislature evaporated in the atmosphere. The outfit by the admission of the Union Government and media sources commanded recruitment of only about 800 militants. Thus the moral from these two successive developments is, that the single militant's voice commands more respect and sanctity than the two-third majority of the J&K Assembly could command. Why? Not because these 800 militants are armed with 800 guns. How those 800 Kalashnikov guns stand against a disciplined army of six lakh soldiers with sophisticated arms. But it is because they possess the mandate from the people who provide emotional and material support to them. On the other hand, the decision of two-third majority of legislators receives a contemptuous rejection and not even a minute's discussion. Why? Because the party to which the resolution was submitted for consideration knew that this assembly had no mandate, but was a house imposed by their own fraud and force. Such comments were made openly even by central ministers like Arun Jaitly and others.

The moral of the story provides a great lesson that the situation in which Jammu and Kashmir is occupied by two powers, the legislatures of the occupied territory or its judiciary cannot influence the decisions imposed by New Delhi or Islamabad. The decision conveyed through this proposal passed by the two third majority of the imposed house met with the same contemptuous treatment by New Delhi with which Islamabad frustrated the thought provoking lucid judgment of Azad Kashmir Supreme Court passed by it regarding the transfer of northern areas of Jammu and Kashmir to Azad Kashmir. Even the lone voice of a legislator or an order of a subordinate judge would carry weight if the system had the mandate of the people behind it.

Self styled analysts of Kashmiriology who consider the boycott of elections a negative step on the part of the people of Jammu and Kashmir should have a rethink. People are correct in their decision that unless they, the people of Jammu and Kashmir are restored the territorial unity which they possessed on August 15, 1947 and unless they are given a chance to express their opinion fearlessly to draft its Constitution without any external pressures and influences; their participation otherwise under imposed systems is bound to get the genuine aspirations stifled by the imported moulders of their destiny. These imported moulders of destiny in this part of Jammu and Kashmir include the governor, the Chief Justice, Chief Secretary, Director General of Police, other Judges of High Court, Secretaries to Government, Inspectors General of Police, District Magistrates, District Superintendents of Police, rather all organs of officialdom who are imported from India. Similarly, such imported masters in Azad Kashmir are masked differently, but have veto power even over the decision of the President of Azad Kashmir.

Chapter 36

Pertinent Question

Why did the world's largest democracy which withstood varied challenges, which had evolved properly and is growing in the way its constitution makers moulded it; allow so brazenly a suffocation of human aspirations in Jammu and Kashmir? Why did the great leaders of India who guided Afro-Asian countries to nourish aspirations for building value based democratic institutions in these two backward continents should have openly destroyed those very values in Jammu and Kashmir? The answer is simple for all such questions—all this has been done for and under Article 370 of the Indian Constitution. This article which was neither demanded nor accepted by the people of Jammu and Kashmir, but was a unilateral act of Indian Constitution-makers assured special status strictly in accordance with the terms and specifications of the Instrument of Accession supposed to have been executed by the Jammu and Kashmir monarch in exercise of the sovereignty attributed to him. The relevant clause, for our discussions, is part (b) of Article 370 which reads:

> "(b) Power of the Parliament to make laws for the said state shall be limited to:
>
> (ii) Such other matters in the aid list as, *with the concurrence of the State* the President may by order specify.

The article strictly confined the Indian Parliament to pass laws within the specifications stipulated in the appendix to the instrument of accession. Thus, there was a clear demarcation which, in accordance to Mahabharata symbolism was a defined and visible *Laxman Rekha*. Withdrawal from this Rekha (line), was simultaneously conveyed by devising the provision for Presidential Orders which could be passed and issued only 'with concurrence of the state.' While issuing a constitutional application order the President of India could not seek concurrence through referendum so, the word state used in clause (ii), (b) Article 370 meant the 'representative State government.' Two years before adoption of this constitution the term 'popular leadership' was devised and used in the proclamation purported to have been issued by His Highness the Maharaja appointing so-called 'popular leader' Sheikh Abdulla as Prime Minister of Jammu and Kashmir. We have earlier unravelled the myth and mystery of this popularity of leadership, but it will amount to defying history if we say that Sheikh abdulla was devoid of public support. He had a mass base, he had charisma, commitment and was aware of his role and position in history. He therefore remained 'aggressively' committed to the terms and conditions which his life-long enemy Hari Singh had imposed in the accession document. In reality it was a bilaterally agreed arrangement between the two friends Jawahar Lal Nehru and Sheikh Abdulla. Hari Singh was either forced by circumstances to sign, or he had not signed at all or situation emerged in a manner which made him a superficial signatory to an arrangement between his adversaries. Whatever the case, Sheikh Abdulla remained strictly within the ambit of Laxman Rekha, but Jawahar Lal Nehru had intentionally devised the invisible erosion of this Rekha by enforcing the Delhi Agreement in 1952. Jawahar Lal Nehru had made Sheikh Abdulla realise that the popularity attributed to him was purely a myth devised by him; this realistion was made when in 1950 Sheikh Abdulla was compelled to go for elections of the Constituent Assembly. Sheikh Abdulla apprehended dangers in holding an electoral battle so he sought the green signal for 'Selection without Discretion' which exposed him totally. Jawahar Lal Nehru wished to exploit this weakness of Abdulla, but the latter had some tricks up his sleeve to regain his eroded position as a mass leader, hence, became reluctant to surrender his 'prerogative' of concurrence causing a break in their relationship. Jawahar Lal Nehru was conscious of the corrupt practices of Bakshi, but knew that at least he had a social base in Srinagar and so installed him in place of Sheikh Abdulla. In spite of being politically without a base Bakshi too could not be so generous in the matter of 'concurrence' as Nehru expected. Therefore, a 'baseless' agent G.M. Sadiq kept the concurrence letter 'signed' and 'sealed' before it was sought.

All the democratic institutions were scuttled beyond Lakhanpur—the border town between Kashmir and East Punjab. It was done only with the purpose which in clear terms falls within the ambit of political fraud. It is unfortunate that the nations which were subjected to colonial subjugation through fraud and farce should develop similar ambitions much earlier than they had attained freedom from such domination.

There was no harm in nourishing ambitions to make Jammu and Kashmir, 'a paradise on earth' a part of one or the other country of the subcontinent; that position might even prove beneficial in the larger interests of people of Jammu and Kashmir. But the way in which both the bigger neighbours planned to integrate and assimilate Kashmir's being with their aggressive ego had *ab initio*, neo-colonist designs. This intention has been dominant while providing sub clause (b) (ii) to Article 370 of Indian Constitution. It was the mature and tactful exercise of the same intention which Pakistan exercised with immaturity and tactlessness while owning or disowning the tribals. Pakistan's contention was that the tribals had come to Jammu and Kashmir to liberate it from the autocracy, but according to Indian perception they were raiders and according to the nationalist Kashmiris their dominant design was to deprive Kashmir nation of its national ego and to the oppressed majority they were saviours. The moral of this discussion is that, to get free concurrence from state governments of Jammu and Kashmir, India through electoral frauds imposed legislatures and governments in Jammu and Kashmir. Thus the Indian Government has a constitutional mandate contained in Article 370 (b) (ii) to impose administrations by unabated frauds bungling and rigging in Jammu and Kashmir. This is why that in spite of terrible lessons taught by history, Indian rulers and its Election Commission did not hesitate to impose the same two rejected ministers Mohi-ud-Din Shah and P.L. Handoo again in 1996 from Amirakadal and Haba Kadal Constituencies, wherefrom their imposed success in 1987 caused wholesale destruction to Kashmir people, its economy, its culture and which created an unbridgeable gulf between Jammu and Kashmir and India.

It has been meaningfully conveyed that the electoral frauds perpetuated upon J&K are meant to over come the difficulties and barriers imposed by Article 370(b)(ii) upon Indian rulers so that a process is completed under which the Soverignity which the erstwhile ruler HariSing had exclusively reserved for himself and which in 1950 (according to the imposed view and per JK peoples' view it had vested from 15, August 47 in them (the people of J&K) totally transferred to his subjects; is gradully surped by the occupying government under a deceptive democratic package. In this context readers are requested to grasp the every clause of Instrument of Accession (Though the people dispute its existence as well as binding value) and particularly read with stress Article 7. It is contained some where else but to stress the repition is excused:

"PARA 7: Nothing in this instrument shall be deemed to commit me in any way to acceptance of any future constitution of India or to detter my discretion to enter into arrangements with the Govt of India under any such future Constitution".

Now please read Appendics (EPIII)_. It is an extract from White Paper issued by Govt. of India on 25, Nov. 1948. It claims that the Regent Karan Singh" had earlier bound himself to the "Consitiution shortly to be adopted" i.e. the Constitution of India. Now peruse Procalamation of the ruler (Note 6 Chapter 6). It shows appointment of Karan Singh as Regent but mischiviously does neither containe the date of issue and nor indicates as from which date it was to take effect. However it was published in Extra Ordinary State Gazett of June 9, 1949. This received effect from that date and so Karan Singh was not Regent on 25, Nov. 1948. Hence there is no 'bondage' binding JK to Indian Constitution.

Chapter 37

Epilogue

While preparing this book for the press, I find the situation ripe for an Indo-Pak conference on Jammu and Kashmir which indirectly means for restoration and reestablishment of peace and democracy in the subcontinent. No one except an agent of disruption, an enemy of progress and only a destructive mind can expressly or tacitly, sabotage the process of peace. But the process needs to be initiated with genuineness involving the representatives of the aspirations of the concerned people.

I have started discussions on elections while making a reference to a folk anecdote common in the Valley. In similar manner a shawl weaver of down-town, Srinagar, commenting on the process quoted a common Kashmiri proverb:

"*Shaayad Thawan Hoon Keerisey Manz*" (Probably they will keep the corpse of the dead dog lying in the well.) The proverb was coined on the basis of a true anecdote. It is said that a Muslim locality had, for drinking water facility, dug out a well into which a dog jumped and died. The water became contaminated and polluted. The inhabitants approached the Muslim jurist of the locality, who opined that after bringing out hundred buckets of water from the well the people could use the water. After some time the people again approached the Mufti, "Sir we have removed hundred buckets of water from the well but it yet smells foul."

"Have you removed the dead dog before removing the required quantity of water?" asked the Mufti. The locals were astonished and rushed to remove the dead dog.

'Tripartite' deliberations connote the involvement of the three parties to the dispute; India, Pakistan and the people of Jammu and Kashmir. India and Pakistan are both represented by their two governments established by law. On the other hand, there is tacit recognition given to All

Parties Hurriyat Conference(APHC) by the two governments of India and Pakistan to represent Jammu and Kashmir in such deliberations. This 'tacit' recognition by the Indian Government has invited different types of comments in Jammu and Kashmir. The Indian Home Minister,L.K. Advani has also tacitly conceded this argument and has expressed that before granting permission to APHC leaders to go to Pakistan, the state government and other leaders would also be consulted and 'involved'. The terms 'State Govt.' and 'other leaders' are so wide that the use of such terms keeps options open to 'hawks' to jump upon the doves.

Dr. Farooq Abdulla and his 'irrelevantly talkative' minister both have prima facie made claim of representation basing it upon the 1996 'political corvee - the election imposed by Begaar upon the people. But till this election is declared null and void and its nature is exposed officially by the Government of India, these so elected members of the Legislature shall have a claim to hoodwink the democratic world. Neither these so elected members, nor their patrons in Delhi, nor the agencies which imposed them have so far honestly made a statement that even if they represent people their representation is confined to the mandate given under J&K Constitution under which this state is an irrevocable part of India. Nowhere does the Constitution make admission directly or indirectly of the dispute about the future of the state. So, even if we consider that the 1996 Election was genuine that too gives a mandate to Farooq Abdulla and his colleagues to rule this state as part of India. Neither did their manifesto seek a broader representation, nor could they do so, nor did the voters envisage giving them a representative character so as to empower them to represent the destiny of the people of Jammu and Kashmir at an international forum. Under the scheme of the Indian and J&K Constitutions under which Dr. Farooq Abdulla's J&K National Conference or C.L. Gupta's J&K Pradesh Bhartiya Janata Party or Tarigami's Marxist Party, or any other 'national' or 'regional' party fought elections or won it have all surrendered international relationship to the Central Government at New Delhi. Thus, Farooq Abdulla, Prof. Gupta or any other person who participated in these elections as 'national' party or 'regional' party have no say in the framework under which the Government of India works or acts.

Such arguments provide a solid pretext to hawks to sabotage or reverse the process of reconciliation.

Equally the term 'other leaders' is a phrase which can be exploited in any manner, even to reverse the constructive steps taken. These 'other leaders' include various parties, fractions and groupings of Kashmiri Pandits, Jammu Dogras, Kargilites, Ladakhis, Zaskaris, Kashmiri speaking minorities in Poonch Rajouri, Pogli, Siraji, Pahari and Keshtawari speaking linguistic minorities and more so the dominant Kashmiri speaking majority of Doda district and the bulk of the Gojar population.

We create history, but cannot afford to unlearn from it—our own creation. In 1964 the subcontinent covered some ground when, as an emissary of Jawahar Lal Nehru, Sheikh Abdulla met F.M. Ayub Khan in Pakistan. But, Jawahar Lal Nehru's death reversed the whole process, otherwise the enthusiasm with which Sheikh Abdulla and his party were given send off from New Delhi was unparalleled in the history of the two nations. Dr. Farooq Ashai who had witnessed receptions accorded to President Eisenhower, Premier Chou En Lai, King Ibni Saud and Queen Elizabeth in Lahore remarked "The reception accorded to Sheikh Abdulla in Lahore and Rawalpindi was unparalleled and excelled all those which I have witnessed there." But with the death[1] of Jawahar Lal Nehru, hawks in both the countries played a role and within nine months a second war broke out in the agonised subcontinent.

Therefore, before cleaning the polluted well let us in the idiom of the semiliterate shawl weaver remove the corpse from the well. How?

Readers might attribute motives of partiality to us on the grounds that while criticising the 'elected' men I recognise the representative character of APHC. But such is not the case.

While discussing the phrase 'popular leader' used in the title' Maharaja's Proclamation' appointing Sheikh Abdulla as Prime Minister we have qualified this as a clever device to impose a person who at the party level, had run away from the elections held only two years before. None can deny that Sheikh Abdulla would attract thousands of people to congregations and hold them spell bound as is the quality of a mass leader. It was with his arrest that the Quit Kashmir movement, in spite of the fact that it was rejected unanimously by the Executive Committee of J&K National Confence, caused an upheaval in the state then. But such support, such charisma, such popularity was related to existing circumstances. People had hatred against autocracy, so, Sheikh Abdulla's challenge of autocratic rule amounted to the expression of the suppressed aspirations of the people. Hence, it was a sort of negative support emerging from negation of autocracy. The same negative support would have qualified as a positive mandate from the people had such mandate been obtained through known democratic measures; had Sheikh Abdulla's party taken part in elections and won a majority, history could have justified his claim of popularity as a real verdict.

The manner in which the 1996 elections were imposed and the system under which they were conducted could not attract the participation of the APHC in those elections, but that too does not absolve it from seeking a positive mandate for representation of the people. The popularity it commands bears a relationship with the prevalent situation; people are against imposed occupation and the APHC channelises that 'negation' in a disciplined movement. So, it is an equally negative type of popularity which could be confirmed into positive character only by known democratic means. Besides, this agglomeration strictly represents the Valley and its Muslim population; no group, party, organisation of Kashmiri Pandits, Jammu Dogras, Jammu Muslims, Gojars, Buddhists and Paharis are connected with it. Even the exponent of right of self-determination Shabir Shah and his party is not covered under this umbrella. Even if it had involvement with it of all sections of Jammu and Kashmir population, from all regions and districts, that too cannot be a substitute for popular representation.

It does not mean that we would like the process for which the initiation has begun to be reversed and a referendum to elect the representatives should proceed all the stages of this initiated process.

The parties to the dispute are committed to the right of self-determination for the people of Jammu and Kashmir. Its form has also been decided and agreed upon, but if that form i.e. plebiscite is considered not practicable the right can well be exercised by involving the chosen representatives of the people of Jammu and Kashmir state with the Governments of India and Pakistan. The APHC leadership if allowed to meet Indian and Pakistani representatives must stress that the genuine and democratically elected representatives should be associated with other two groups in this behalf. They should honestly confess that they have no democratic mandate though that agglomeration claims popularity among the masses.

Such an election can neither be held under the constitutional schemes of India and Indian occupied J&K, nor under similar schemes of Pakistan and Pakistan occupied J&K. The matter cannot be left to ambiguous and obscure interpretations. It is in the light of discussions made in this book and as a conscious student of Kashmir affairs from 1945 till date that this author must put forth his views as how to obtain the verdict about the genuine democratic representation of the people of Jammu and Kashmir.

The formula constructively thought over and discussed with other aware people is evolved in the following paragraphs. It is not necessary that this formula should be accepted with or without modifications it can become a basis to understand the psyche of the people of this state on both sides of the LAC. The leadership of the APHC committed to the right of self-determination should ponder upon and persuade the two governments to have solid shifts in their respective policies with preference for evolving a democratic method to choose the representatives, who, could genuinely assimilate the aspirations of the people of Jammu and Kashmir for permanent peace and prosperity of the subcontinent including Jammu and Kashmir. As part of the destiny of the subcontinent the J&K imbroglio will have an automatic solution in accordance with universally acclaimed right of self-determination.

The formula is succinctly presented below:

1. Both the parts of Jammu and Kashmir be demilitarised. Only such forces of the two countries should be stationed in the barracks as are required to meet any threat from third parties.
2. New Delhi and Islamabad may nominate two governors for the two parts under their respective control and assemblies and the ministries established under the two

constitutions be dissolved and constitutions of the two parts will remain suspended.

3. Within a stipulated time the two governments should nominate an Election Commission of three distinguished democrats, tested and known for their integrity. Preferably Seshan may be the man from India and Moin Qureshi from Pakistan. The two governments may either, on their own, or through the U.N. Secretary General get an Afro-Asian who is a reputed democrat appointed as the chairman of this J&K Election Commission.
4. Such an Election Commission needs to be empowered to get electoral rolls prepared, reviewed and revised under their directions through such official machinery which will be answerable to ommissions, irregularities or acts of ommission to none, but to the J&K Election Commission and its verdict shall be not only final but binding.
5. The J&K Election Commission may appoint a delimitation committee under it, constituted by reputed honest persons and men of integrity. The commission may or may not involve men from Jammu and Kashmir as the members of such committee.
6. The Committee may be invested with the power to have electoral segments on the basis of the regional contiguity as was the administrative set up till 15 August 1947. The Committee might guide itself by the following principles:
   a. It will see racial, topographic, geographical, linguistic and cultural affinities while devising these electoral segments.
   b. Each segment should include 40,000 voters. If the situation demands lesser number of voters or larger, it can constitute an electoral segment, but the member representing a segment upto 40,000 will in the House of Representatives have value of 'one digit' to his/her vote. The value of the segment representing more than 50,000 upto 80,000 and even one lakh shall be two in the final count. In no case can any segment tie up more than one lakh voters.
   c. The Committee shall divide Jammu and Kashmir in 250 electoral segments.
   d. While devising electoral segments it might also, if the need arises, devise segments for permanent state subjects of Jammu and Kashmir residing in (i)various parts of India, (ii)in various parts of Pakistan and (iii)in various parts of the world.

7. The so constituted house of 250 members representing various parts on this side of LAC or on that side and residing outside the state segments shall be allowed to meet in Srinagar/Jammu/Muzaffarabad as the weather and situation at that time demand.
8. The so constituted House shall evolve its procedure, conduct rules and ancillary powers itself.
9. It will constitute a Committee of Representatives representing according to population all the regions as they existed on 15 August 1947.
10. The said Committee of Representatives shall finally involve themselves with the Governments of India and Pakistan to get the problem finally decided.
11. In Constituting the Committee of Representatives every region (as it existed on 15 August 1947) should get involved positively. However, no region will have veto nor the more populated region/regions can be allowed to frustrate genuine aspirations of the minority region. To have safeguards against such frustration the election to the committee of representatives should positively involve at least one third of each region in the election of every member to the committee of representatives.
12. It would be worthwhile to make the involvement of the people a positive reality so that the two divided parts under the two powers need to be administratively supervised by one and the same person.
13. It can also be worth consideration if India and Pakistan both appoint the heir of the ex-ruler ie. Dr. Karan Singh as 'governor from India in Srinagar/Jammu and governor from Pakistan in Muzzaffarabad. Like U.N. observers presently, the so appointed governor alongwith his office can be allowed to move freely'.
14. The so appointed governor may form a cabinet from able administrators, intellectuals and reputed men of integrity which may assist him to run the administration.
15. The governor would have no superintending authority upon J&K Election Commission which shall be free to its conscience to create a history of peace and prosperity.
16. The Supreme Courts of India and Pakistan in consultation with respective governments and J&K Election Commission may spare eminent retired/working judges for hearing of election dispute, if any, when required by the J&K Election Commission.

These outlines can be further expanded, but the dominant interest should be to remove the corpse from which the foul smell is emanating from the contaminated water in the well.

In AD 1556 Akbar imposed a 'convenient representation' upon us and 'obliged' by having liberated us from 'misrule, sectarian governance and permanent disorder'. But Kashmiris never accepted any such representation and consequently Akbar and his successors had to rule us as a misruled colony. These agonies darkened our fate permanently and it culminated in our sale in 1846. In 1947 India claimed the involvement of popular leadership and Pakistan also did the same. The result is that for the last 54 years the earth of Kashmir has became a graveyard for youth from Jammu and Kashmir, from India and from Pakistan.

Now if in 2001 or even during 2002 or 2003 both India and Pakistan for their own vested interests—for their peace and prosperity to avert an atomic holocaust in the subcontinent, jointly impose upon us 'representatives' who may suit them—the Kashmir tangle between India and Pakistan might come to an end, but it will positively become a hot bed of international intrigues. The question may be posed as to who will allow it? The reply is, 'the same Kashmiris who invited Afghan liberators in 1947, welcomed India with slogans of "Azad Hindustan, Zindabad" to flush out the same tribal who was adamant about imposing his power and then slogans "let these Indian dogs clear this soil" echoed as India continued with the age old process of imposition. We Kashmiris are hospitable and entertain our guests, but once the guest tries to impose his presence they have been known to react violently and dangerously too.

It has not specifically been stated as what will be referred to the electorate upon which they will have to exercise their franchise. It is not that they will be asked to elect a legislature which will pass laws, give the reins of power to the majority party and accord the status of the opposition to the second party having arithmetical preference. On the other hand, the people, the erstwhile subjects of the Maharaja of Kashmir will be asked to 'elect' their representatives, who will with the governments of India and Pakistan enter into parleys to finally decide the dispute of Jammu and Kashmir with two dominant considerations that the decision so evolved becomes an outcome of the collective will of the people of Jammu and Kashmir and such collective will considers constructively the building of permanent peace and prosperity for the subcontinent.

The J&K Election Commission constituted in accordance with the norms stated above shall with the consultation of the two governments involve eminent judges, rights activists, authors of repute, scientists of great recognition, outstanding intellectuals, famous academicians and respected journalists from the world at large, particularly from non-aligned countries, SAARC, Commonwealth countries and European Parliamentarians as permanent observers who shall observe all stages of the election including preparations of electoral rolls, delimitation of constituencies, revision and circulation and approval of rolls, canvassing, unarming of all armed groups, polling, carriage of ballot boxes, counting of votes and final announcement of results. Under such constant vigil people in Jammu and Kashmir will be sufficiently powerful to protect their precious vote.

Finally, after the decision, the so elected House of the people of Jammu and Kashmir may by a two-third vote convert itself into a Constituent Assembly for Jammu and Kashmir to draft a constitution, if the state accedes with any country then within the framework of that country's constitution or otherwise one which the evolved decision demands to be given as code of conduct to this nation.

These suggestions are just to start a concrete work plan. It is not required that they should become the basis, but these suggestions can provide a direction subject to sincerity from all quarters. Sincerity is the *sine qua non* for resolution of such disputes which have become an incurable malignancy. These suggestions are only an outline for churning of varied viewpoints which will provide us with a formula.

Before concluding I would like to accord a different interpretation to a famous saying of prophet Mohammad (PBUH) than the one given by eminent Sufi saints—Muslim mystics. It is reported that while returning from a holy war the Prophet (PBUH) said to His companions:

> "We are reverting back to bigger Holy War (Jehaad-i-Akbar) from the smaller Holy War (Jehaadi-Asghar)." Mystics interpret the term Jehaadi Akbar (great Holy War) as 'war with inner evil self' whereas in their view the war on the battlefront is smaller Jehad. I beg to differ with their interpretation about Jehaad-i-

Akbar. The history of wars fought by the Prophet in His time will show that even during their engagement with pagans on the war front the 'servant of God' has to remain simultaneously engaged in war with inner evil designs. It is for deviation from this engagement that the companions of the Prophet had to experience the initial reverses in the war field of 'Uhad'. Hence, the mystic interpretation, in my view, does not hold good. Even from later events which swiftly shaped thereafter, we find that Prophet Mohammad (PBUH) addresses letters to various world leaders conveying to them His message of Tawheed (monotheism). With this precise discussion I submit that by 'Jehaad-i-Akbar' (Great Holy War) the great Prophet meant the diplomatic war on the Peace Front. In this context, the need of the hour is to engage with the greater holy war 'Jehaad-i-Akbar'. The followers of this Great Leader of Peace (PBUH) are to initiate the process.[1]

An unnecessary but relevant controversy has been introduced which some have dubbed as a tacit support to the intrigue of trifurcation of the state of Jammu and Kashmir on communal grounds. The controversy is merely technical and artificial; it revolves around the theme whether the Kashmir problem is rooted in religion or in politics. Considering its history and background of freedom movement in Jammu and Kashmir both these views are based on genuine material and so are its two facets.

For two centuries this state was ruthlessly ruled; the target of those miseries and tyrannies mainly remained the downtrodden, agriculturist, artisan, manual labourer, petty trader and even the lower middle class. These sections of the society belonged to majority community i.e. the Muslims who constituted 80 percent of the population. The civil servant – even petty officials, landlords, the agents of big landed estate holders, even petty land revenue basic official patwari or a police constable formed the backbone of exploiters. They mainly hailed from the minority community. Though low caste Hindus too were victimised sections, but they were insignificant in number. Hence, the majority i.e. the Musalman had to rise and rise against centuries old terror. It was the incident of sacrilege of the Holy Book of Muslims (Quran), which made the volcano of resentment to burst. Qadeer broke the news of this sacrilege in a religious congregation in the main center of Muslim religious activity

Khanquahi Moula. So, Qadeer became the pioneer of revolution and religion played an all-important role. In the process, the revolution form did undergo some changes in its exterior, but its interior remained burdened with a religious core. This agitation pioneered by religious causes was modelled and organised by a party manned only by Muslims under the nomenclature of all J&K Muslim Conference. The agitators under the banner of this outfit launched an agitation for establishment of *Zimadar Nizami Hakoomat*—Rule of Law, but this agitation for 'rule of law' was nourished with religious slogans like *"Narai Takbeer?Allaho Akbar;" "Narai Risala? Yaa Rasoolalah;" "Narai Hyderi? "Yaa Ali Yaa Ali" and "Islam? Zindabad"*.

After defection of a formidable section of leadership and cadre from it and after they formed All J&K National Conference the interior remained strictly the same though on its exterior some additions were seen. They included the inclusion of some Hindus in its ranks and with the constant use of Muslim religious slogans another slogan formed in secular phraseology and designed for cult orientation was also introduced

Sher-i-Kashmir Kaa Kiya Irshaad
Hindu Muslim Sikh Itihaad.
(The dictat of Sher-i-Kashmir is to preserve Hindu, Muslim and Sikh unity)

The Indian National Congress had engineered this split to use its allies in Jammu and Kashmir through whom they could counter the influence of two-nation theory in Jammu and Kashmir. But, the propounder of that theory Jinnah had himself provided exception clause to his theory as far as Jammu and Kashmir was concerned. On July 24, 1944, he advised the Muslim Conference to carry local minorities along. The Indian National Congress through Sir Gopala Swamy Ayyangar, who was inducted as Prime Minister of Jammu and Kashmir, created a hostile division between the two organisations, the Muslim Conference and National Conference which were both mainly Muslim organisations for all practical purposes. The National Conference remained more committed to Muslim centres of religious activity like Hazratbal, Shahi Mosque, etc. Its leader Shiekh Abdullah would start his public speeches with the recitation of the verses of Quran which Mr. Jinnah dubbed as "Singing of Quran." With such recitation he will spel bound audience and would criticise Jinnahs theory.

Even after moulding his destiny under Indian political patronage, Sheikh Abdulla and his National Conference remained committed to religious politics of Muslims by taking under his grip the Muslim Waqf properties. This pro-religious strain on his politics was even transparent from his 'promise' speech from the religious pulpit of Hazratbal in 1948 which the poet laureate of Kashmir versified under the title: *Ahad Namai Hazratbal* (See *Kuliyati Mehjoor* Pub: J&K Academy). After Signing Delhi Agreement in 1952 he on his arrival from Delhi straight by drove to Hazratbal where he addressed a ready made gathering of two lakhs of devotees and explained the philsphy of Ascendence "Meraj-un-Nabi." Concluding his speech and swearing in the names of God and his Prophet (P.B.U.H.) he assured to carry ahead the mission of the martyrs of July 1931. Addmittly their mission was pure religious or Islamic. It is probably this trait too which became one of the immediate causes of his dismissal and arrest on 9 August 1953. From 1953 to 1975, the secular leader Sheikh Abdulla, the Plebiscite Front which he patronised and J&K Political Conference though active with a political agenda yet remained under the influence of religious emotions. The epithets accorded to the character of 'assassinated' freedom fighters as martyr (shaheed) and to the warrior (Gazi) owed its origin to the verses of the holy Quran which were recited from these political stages. The compromise of non-Muslims with the politics of repression let loose by Indian rulers, their adjustment with massacre of democratic institutions by India in Jammu and Kashmir and connivance with corruption and nepotism of Indian installed agencies in Kashmir—were all facets of 'religious politics'. Hindus adjusted with all that because it came from Hindu India and their reaction against such policies would, in their view, loosen India's (Hindu) grip upon Jammu and Kashmir. Policies on both the sides remained what can be termed either communal or religious politics. To a Hindu India is the abode of the Hindu religion and to a Muslim Pakistan is the cradle of Islam, so, the strains on the politics of both the communities has been religious. Only a microscopic minority existed from both the communities which was guided by political, geographical, cultural, secular or democratic considerations. There is a limited number of Muslims, who, out of their commitment to democracy and secularism are committed to India though deploring its undemocratic policies in Jammu and Kashmir. The majority in pro-Indian sections is of concession seekers. Similarly a smaller number of Hindus, which can be counted on ones fingertips, 'consider', for geographical and other reasons Kashmir's destiny safer with Pakistan. Otherwise the division is but communally guided rather devised by political reasons or is evolved by psychologies of action and reaction.

After 1989 when the form of the struggle evolved into militancy the concept of martyrdom became completely puritan, strictly Quranic and mainly religious. The reaction of Kashmiri Pandits was against the slogan *"Ham Kiya Chahtein Hain? Nizami Mustafa"*—We want strictly Muslim rule to be implemented.

The cemeteries of martyrs throughout Jammu and Kashmir show that it is a religious struggle. From 1931 till date all the martyrs numbering a lakh were mainly Muslims. On the other hand, the en masse exodus of Pandits is another facet of religious action and reaction to the Kashmir question. But it is a fallacious theory to dub the struggle or reaction to it as purely communal though it has definite religious strains upon various phases and dimensions. It is as political as was the liberation movement of India or as was the movement for creation of Pakistan.

The liberation movement of India was mainly considered as reconsolidation of Indian heritage which means revival of Hindu culture. These facets are evident from the day to day programmes of government owned media. Similarly, the movement for creation of Pakistan was not for establishment of a theocratic state, but to have a separate homeland for Indian Muslims where they are not ruled by the Brahmin in place of a White Britisher.

Against this background it is evident that the problem of Jammu and Kashmir is purely political, but with religious strains. Both facets of this problem are so closely interlinked that denial of either factor is pure hypocrisy. It is hypocrisy to qualify it as merely a religious problem and likewise it is self-deceit to say that the problem is merely one of politics.

Before this book goes to the press, two very important

developments have taken place which can be considered as a solid leap towards three party involvements The Indian government nominated K.C. Pant as its interlocutor to negotiate with Jammu and Kashmir political parties on the Kashmir dispute. The very personality of K.C. Pant hardly attracted sensitivity of Kashmiris with the mission and from the moment it was named people here felt that it was one more calculated bluff. In 1974 Indira Gandhi nominated G. Parthasarthy as her emissary who could formidably engage Sheikh Abdullah's emissary Beig without giving rise to any controversies before or during the deliberations. He was, besides being the son of a great man, himself also a known diplomat and had the reputation of being a successful negotiator. On the other hand, K.C. Pant had only the reputation of being the son of a freedom fighter—one time Home Minister of India. The drastic changes in his political morality had already exposed him to the sensitivities of Kashmiris as a man interested to retain a 'posh bungalow' in posh colony of Civil Lines in Delhi. Secondly, he talked irrelevantly which exposed him to utter partisan attitude and so could not invite any confidence.

Arjun Singh acted as reconciliator in Punjab during Rajiv Gandhi's rule, but had a mandate as governor of that state which made his task easier and people of that state also considered that the New Delhi was serious to evolve some solutions. The Punjab problem had a limited sphere, whereas the Kashmir imbroglio has wider implications. Besides, Arjun Singh had two distinguishable facets in his personality. He was a committed loyalist of the Nehru Gandhi family and had a known base in the politics of his state, which with all limitations provides confidence to a politican to deal and act with courage. On the other hand, neither could K.C. Pant be treated as a loyalist of the Sangh Parivar, nor does he exist anywhere in the odd conglomeration of the N.D.A., nor does he have any base in his state or even in Delhi where he is now officially entrenched. Hence, he spoke too irrelevantly to woo the hawks and doves in New Delhi and thus, nipped in bud his own mission which could yield no result but would at the least, keep political analysts engaged and would thereby, diminish the strains created by unabated repression in Jammu and Kashmir. His abortive mission once again established that India is interested more in bluffs than to make sincere efforts even confined to its own national interests.

The second bluff was the unilateral ceasefire announced by the Indian prime minister and its unilateral withdrawal in the month of April 2001. The very call for ceasefire between the militants and forces was merely a misnomer. If we go deeper into the causes of the malaise, it is due to indefinite and unabated ceasefire imposed upon Jammu and Kashmir in 1949 by the two warring nations that the locals were sandwiched in an imposed division caused by this ceasefire convenient to Indian and Pakistani interests with the result that people in Jammu and Kashmir attributed all ills to this unnatural and unrealistic ceasefire which divided Kashmir. Consequently, the gun culture dawned in 1989 autumn to undo with artificial line of division. In other words, the gun culture swept into the inhabited areas—villages, towns and city localities to undo this ceasefire. The ceasefire imposed in 1949 was a cessation of hostilities that could be guaranteed only by the resolution of the Kashmir dispute. But, inspite of bilateral talks between the two hostile nations and between New Delhi and Srinagar this malignancy remained. Consequently, across this line in both the parts, misrule, denial of basic human rights and further opening of respective agencies to perpetuate this unnatural division became the policy of India; and Pakistan connived with that situation. Pakistan on the other hand, perpetuated a policy of hatred and retaliation. The weaker side logically has the option in hypocritical manipulation only. The sandwiched Kashmiri was forced to undo the very cause of those ills, i.e., the ceasefire imposed in 1949. By the end of the millennium every village of Kashmir, every 'mohalla' of the city of Srinagar, every town situated in the plains of Jammu became an active war field between Indian forces and militants. Take the example of my native place: if my outer house is situated in close contiguity to a military/ paramilitary bunker my own inner house could have been, in the dead of night, occupied by other gun-wielders. Where, in this situation does A.B.Vajpayee wish to draw the ceasefire line? Will it be drawn dividing the compound of my house, or does it amount to dividing my own family? Hence, neither did this unilateral ceasefire have any logic behind it, nor could it work, nor did it make any difference in the situation on the ground level. It added to the misery of the civil population with much more severity. It is during this so-called ceasefire that a locality only one kilometre ahead of my house on Srinagar-Charar Road 'Batapora' (Wahthora) was reduced to ashes. One house, in the interior of that village, was occupied by militants. The army received the message of their presence and laid siege to the village; the other side resorted to firing, killing a dozen soldiers. Consequently, the military reduced the whole locality to rubble even killed a few civilians and only two militants. On June 16, 2001 in the same Wahthora village in Gopalpara colony a similar tragedy occurred. The moral is that any declaration of ceasefire should be bilateral which is possible only with the simultaneous initiation of deliberations armed at undoing the –'1949 Imposed Ceasefire'.

On the eve of 14–16 July Indo-Pak summit the leadership of APHC has started canvassing to get a berth reserved for itself in these deliberations. It provides strong inference that this agglomeration has since resiled from its known and declared stand of holding a plebiscite in Jammu and Kashmir under U.N. auspices as agreed by the parties. It further provides a tacit basis for the view that before coming to the table Pakistan might have 'surrendered' claim for plebiscite because its agency in APHC cannot insist for its placement without such direction from their principal mentors. Thus, a basis is created for pondering that there exists a search to find out an alternative solution beyond the agreed one, which cannot be imposed by India and Pakistan nor can the involvement of their agencies accord to the formula thus evolved, a semblance of popular support from the people of Jammu and Kashmir.

Last year in July, after proof reading this chapter was added but for the tight schedule of publishers the manuscript could not go to press. Events have seen swift turns. It has been tragedy with people of Jammu and Kashmir that all these turns compounded the strains of uncertainty. The common theme of speeches of Sheikh Abdullah was that "our boat is badly caugtht in torrents". Though his dynasty sailed safe to the shore but, even after 1975, he would continue with this oft beaten theme. Our position; in-spite of drastic turns remained the same. Every turn which events have taken did complicate our destiny. Inspite of the failure of Agra Summit there was hope that tension in Sub-Continent might ease, that might facilitate the solution of our problem which has deprived us of human dignity.

For last one year we have witnessed terrific intensity in the intrigues, conspiracies, conflicts, obscurities and unscrupulous polity on local level, in the Sub-Continent and on international level. These events are shrouded in ambiguities that the logic and reason fails locate responsibilities upon persons and places.

September 11, 2001 events in USA gave rise to world solidarity against terrorism. But similar acts of terrorism followed immediately thearafter here in Srinagar Legislative Assembly on 1st October and on 13 December on Indian Parliament. Both were ostensibly attacks on democracy at the time when such forces in the world have joined together to have coordinated protection of the institutions of the democracy. Under the pressure of world coalition to safeguard and consolidate the organs and traditions of democracy, choice to target Assembly Hall and Parliament House for acts of terrorism provided logical and reasonable argument for Indian Government that the armed struggle in Jammu and Kashmir is part of terrorism and against the democracy. But the slip shod haste and perfunctory manner, with which within moments, Government of India fixed the responsibilities upon persons and organizations provided equally logical and reasonable arguments to the struggling Kashmiris and Pakistan Government. Both qualify those as self inflicted injuries.

As far as the incident of 1st October 2001 in Jammu and Kashmir Amargarh Palace (Assembly Hall) is concerned manner looked ambiguous. From the adjoining office Verandah of Director Jammu and Kashmir Archives Srinagar an Inspector General of CRPF (an Indian officer) who has come to collect an information saw the gunmen who had entered the Assembly Hall were rushing towards the CRPF. The I.G. had visited this office to collect an information. As he saw the gunmen who had entered the Assembly Hall were rushing towards the CRPF posted on duty, the officer, for love of his jawans, anxiously cried "Oh! They will kill my men". But instead they fired upon the employees of the legislature who were unarmed and were lying beneath the office tables. The jawans of CRPF guard were spared.

An officer of the Assembly Secretariat was fired at in presence of his own daughter whom he had appointed on daily wage basis. She narrated that the assailant militants attacked specifically ordinary employees and in-spite of haveing chance to kill he members of paramilitary force and lawgivers they did not touch them.

Other allied arguments also exposed a mysterious situation. Similarly certain circumstances which are closely relevant to 13th December occurrence in Parliament House are also taxing the mind. Situation in which both these occurrences have matured provide more than one hypothesis and unless strong corroborating circumstances do not come on limelight till then ambiguous confusion is to prevail. It is difficult to hold any one responsible on doubtful circumstantial evidence. But the manner in which both the occurrences were exploited on diplomatic front and the dividend this exploitation provided to one party has a relevance for assessment.

It is also clear that since the visit of Mr. Clinton to the Sub-Continent which concided with Chatti Singh Pora massacre of Sikhs and with the butchering of 14 villagers of Azad Kashmir situated close to LAC, we have noticed that these acts of mayhem have usually coincided with the visit of some US official authorities or British Ministers or other dignitaries who have brief from their governments to persuade the two belligerent neighbours: India and Pakistan to initiate peace process. It seems that to stall such initiation these acts of madness have become "necessary". The very recent tragedy of Kaluchak Jammu where even suckling babies were not spared also coincided with the visit of a dignitary to India.

Leaving it to Almighy and future inquisitive but honest research to unravel these mysteries I confine this concluding chapter relevantly to the impact it left upon the future course of elections in Jammu and Kashmir.

The devastation let loose from 1989 particularly did convey no lesson to the authorities in New Delhi. We have discussed how they remained prisoners of the status quo under discussions on 1996, 1998 and 1999 Parliamentary elections and 1996 Assembly elections. We have also bailed out Indian authorities that the situation was imposed upon them to impose an election in 1996. However it has also been argued that for imposition of an election in that situation history might exonerate them of their treacheries with democracy but imposition of a person, group of persons or a family makes their culpability unpardonable. The last six years should have opened their eyes and they should have evolved a policy to initiate a process of building of confidence in democracy and for creating commitment to Indian democracy which would ipso facto have re-orientation of Indo-Kashmir relationship. We cannot avoid repetition so have to stress that all factors relevant linked Kashmir with Pakistan except one factor, ie urge for democracy. It was probably only this aspect and not the charisma of any person which made initially Kashmiri Muslim to reject Two Nation Theory. I must correct the impression that like Muslim minority in India, the Hindu minority in Jammu and Kashmir both expressly and tacitly contributed and is contributing to Jinnah's theory. But, as said, in early 50's the 'selection without discretion' shattered these hopes and process to reject India started. Indian authorities and their imposed agents remained accelerating this process. Though India directly ruled through its Unified Command, forces and paramilitary forces, the imported services (civil, police, judicial etc), yet, the imposed civil authorities in Farooq government remained greatly sandwiched. So, their all black deeds remain attributed as sins of India in Jammu and Kashmir. With whatever colour Indian government, media, political parties and leadership paint it but the imposition of the present government in 1996 established that it was merely continuation of occupation rather to initiate a process of confidence building. The present NDA government is also keen to continue with the same policy. Had Indian leadership taken any lesson from the devastation of post-1989 era they should have since started measures to lay foundation of democratic institution with immediate demolition of vested interests.

Present leadership in New Delhi is repeating the blunder which Mrs. Indra Gandhi committed immediately after fall of East Pakistan in 1971. We have earlier stated that Sheikh Abdulla sought through his two emissaries nothing more than a guarantee (already enshrined in the constitution and the national conduct evolved by Indian people) of a free and fair elections.

But, instead he was offered to take reigns of power in Jammu and Kashmir directly but the "fairness in polls" without a pre-arranged accord was not conceded. In the result, the accord of 1975 widened the gulf and consolidated the belief that "luxury of democracy"is not in our destiny. Even in democratic package Kashmir has to get the receive "humiliation".

The strains on NDA policy regarding 'JK Elections' continue to be the same. 'Fairness' can be 'allowed' (not guaranteed) but with pre-condition if APHC fights elections. In other words 'fairness' is pre-conditioned. Does it mean that presently the pro-Indian opposition parties, including the one in power in centre BJP, are not entitled to the luxury of fairness. Even if 'luxury' is pre-conditioned with the condition that voters of Jammu and Kashmir should persuade leaders and ranks of APHC to participate in coming elections in October 2002, they are justified to be assured and satisfied that assurance is not merely a trap but a calculated shift in the perceptions of Indian leadership.

"Prime Minister has assured from special Pandal of Lal Qila in his independence day message to his nation about transparent fairness in Jammu and kashmir elections and has reiterated assurance on March 19, 2002 on the floor of Lok Sabha, what more do you want" canvasses too optimistic apporach of this author.

"But in between these two assurances Mr. Vajpayee got exposed in the last week on February (just before twenty six days of the reiteration of his assurance made on the floor of house)" replied, the realistic analyst within this author.

On February 21, 2002 in Jammu-Poonch Parliamentary Constituency bye-election caused due to the death of sitting member was held. What happened will require additon of a chapter, which second edition of this book will positively contain. But a few hints will suffice:

As polling started in the morning of 21, February 2002, voters were yet to gather, that several grenades were hurled in Rajouri and Darhal assembly segments. Blame usually goes to militants and they too are in haste to brow-beat us by owning every act whether done by them or by some other vested interests. But, what happened. National Conference candidate Mr. Talib Hussain on 22, February 2002 held a press conference and claimed that "the polling staff" in both the segment ran away and did not return to resume their work. The returning officer asserted that the staff returned to duty and polling took place which looks absurd as no civil servant can throw his life in the trap of death. The opposition candidates Congress I, PDP, and Panthers Party all confirmed this assertion of Mr. Talib. But BJP state unit on its part and on the part of their candidate supported the contention of R.O.

Election Commission intervened on the request and stayed the counting. On resumption of counting the BJP candidate who was leading till then in whole of the constituency was thrown to second number and Congress-I which was second trailed third and the third Mr. Talib Hussain by the margin of the votes from those two electoral segments trounced all.

Now BJP claimed this whole a magical fraud of the ruling National Conference and justified openly the policy of boycott of elections. Talib Hussain who was certain that no polling took place in those two segments is himself puzzled how those bundles of votes came out of the ballot boxes marked in his favour. Why on 22nd February 2002 BJP, supported the assertion of concerned R.O.? They were given to understand that the 'agency' concerned has marked bundles of votes in their favour but the 'hired' agency immediately, before it could perform the job, was used by immediate boss, the ruling clique in the state.

In such circumstances will the US emissaries, British diplomats and western democrats define how to assure with transparency a fair lection. They cannot. Their insistence to accept mere assurances devoid of certainty exposes their own compulsions. The USA and Britain both possess two perceptions about democracy and the both views are in conflict with each other. They as "superior nations" believe and consider that real democracy is only for their citizens, their countrymen and even their domestic servants have right for honoured dignity as voters. On the other hand they with contempt believe that people living in 3rd world should remain obediently contended under despots, kings, dictators or psudo-democrats, whom Britishers and Americans patronize.

European democrats are probably themselves failures as

true democracies so, are, unable to appreciate the tragedies of the people of Jammu and Kashmir though they understand that this region has been continuously deprived of fair and free elections.

Let us understand as how the voter of Jammu and Kashmir can get assured in this behalf. We have given our suggestion here in before. However, avoiding repetion in details, the points are again summed up. Before such summing up it is to be impressed that no attempt has been made to cultivate faith. Ten percent voters have not this time volunteered to file review or revision petitions against the lopsided, incomplete, ineffective and obsolete electoral rolls originally prepared in 1983. Notices have been issued, proclamations made and relayed daily from electronic media and print media that the voters should collect their identity cards in urban areas from the offices of municipalities and in rural areas from the offices of tehsildars. In the prevalent situation when I am allowed in my own locality to walk only if I possess I-card and show identity on demand, many a times to non-State Subject (who can not under law get class four job in Jammu and Kashmir or own a moiety of immovable property). BSF or CRPF constable, who hardly is able to read, looks at my photograph and allows this reputed writer, advocate and ex-judge to enter into his residence. In such a situation an I-card authenticated under the authority of India Election Commission is a boon for me. No militant organization has prohibited to collect the said card. On the other hand the People's Election Commission Co-Chairman Mr. Tapan Bose, a renowned human rights activist of international fame visited various district head quarters in company of Mr. Ashok Aggarwal a Supreme Court Lawyer of repute and both have impressed the voters to collect their I-cards from the notified places. The dead line expired on July 15, 2002. But to our ground work hardly 10% of urban voters have availed of this opportunity. In tehsil offices of Chadora and Budgam the satistics shown is not better rather it is worse. Why this apathy? Mere assurances do not create confidence which never existed here in Jammu and kashmir, which was once put to experiment in 1977 but eroded with much severity and venom. The assurance of Atal Bihari Jee made on 15, August 2001 from Lal Qila was nipped nude in Jammu-

Poonch bye-election in February 2002. How then, with this record of incredibility the seeds of faith can be sown and nourished to grow.

Our suggestions are:

1. Persuade the present government of state to opt for dissolution of assembly and recommend assumption of power by governor under Sec. 92 of Jammu and Kashmir Constitution. Be cautions that Farooq government is not dismissed except on the charges of corruption. Otherwise sensitive voter will be justified to hold that undemocratically atmosphere of democracy is tried to be created. The foundation of virtue laid on vice must fall.

2. Before such drastic change, a dynamic politician of repute, a known democrat neither police officer, nor a military man and nor a retired bureaucrat should be given the occupation of Raj Bhavan.

3. Cultivate discipline among the ranks and files of paramilitary forces from a jawan up to highest official impressing upon them to work as ambassadors of goodwill from the people of India and from its democracy to the people of Jammu and Kashmir. Hence, they should be impressed to confine their duties within their Rekha. They must be made conscious of the contribution they have to make in building such confidence which in the situation prevalent they can do by protecting the safety of voter and not by involving themselves in the campaign to 'undo' the boycott call. It is impressed that the state police should not be deputed on election duty as the recruitment during six years has badly infused the intolerant blood in the veins of Jammu and Kashmir police. They can, at the spur of moment, be purchased by any 'contradiction' and used to sabotage the faith.

4. Extend time after governor rule for review and, revision of rolls and for collection of I-cards.

5. Encourage frequent visits from groups of rights activists, ex-diplomats, known democrats, intellectuals, eminent lawyers, reputed writers from various states of India and eminent members of the 4th estate. They should not remain based in posh localities of city but should nourish the democratic aspiration in rural areas and should move frequently in remote villages and localities.

6. As Election Commission has completely lost its face in Jammu and Kashmir so one of its members should greatly remain based in Srinagar/Jammu. His presence will on the one side boost the too humiliated morale of the voters and shall on the other side confine the staff on duty strictly within their 'Seema' (prescribed limits) as they have developed a culture to go astray.

7 The Election commission should strictly adhere to show and record the correct ratio of the turn over the voters. No world forum can pass an ex-party decree against india if only 10% of votes polled is correctly recorded and shown. Even if any quarter exploits the less turn over, reasons to counter are convincingly available. The non-turn over is related to rejection of manifestoes, parties or candidates. The counting should follow under the constant observations of distinguished observers.

Less turn over and non-participation of major political alignments might provide an argument but it can neither invalidate the elections nor can make the legislature lopsided. The best it might return a hotchpotch and so a hung assembly. subsequent exercises are bound to consolidate the faith in the system and boycott policy will within three trials became redundant. That does not mean kashmir imbroglio will get solved by that process but as Mr. M.J.Akbar has put it: ". . . .the epicenter of Kashmir problem is within Kashmir itself and that is where it has to be addressed first and foremost".

The Indian kashmir policy has been burdened with erroneous assumption from its very start. It has never tried to allow an accord between the peoples of India and Jammu and Kashmir. That accord can be achieved only through the assimilation of the democratic aspirations of people of Jammu and Kashmir with those of the aspirations of Indian people.

In 1954 November late Shri Ashok Mehta (a great Indian socialist leader) while addressing a mammoth public gathering in Parade Ground Jammu had said, "Nehru acceded with Sheikh Abdullah in 1947 it ended in fiasco in August 1953, the accession with Bakshi might live for a decade and I might enter into similar 'accession' with Khawaja Umar Bhat but all such personal rapports are short lived. There should be accession of the people of Jammu and

Kashmir with the people of India".

The great democrat had vision and his visionary advice is more relevant today. Though his disciples Chandar Shekhar and George Fernandes have unlearnt his lessons.

Let me now sum-up other some developments which are becoming a prelude for a book on 2002 elections.

APHC nominated sometimes back a People's Election Commission which can monitor and supervise elections to elect representatives from the both divided parts of Jammu and Kashmir so as to sit with Governments of India and Pakistan to finally decide "Jammu and Kashmir dispute". Though I can very well claim that this agglomeration has put in black and white which this epilogue had suggested last year but I will not accuse them of plagiraism as the book is yet unpublished and their decision is not strictly a copy of our suggestions . On is my view it is but a counter bluff to blunt the Indian bluff contained in their empty assurances for free and fair elections. APHC could have got the dividends of this counter-bluff had this Peoples Commission hired offices in Srinagar/Jammu/Muzzaffarabad, had it initiated to convince people to co-operate with the formation, review, revision of rolls and had it persuaded them to obtain I-cards. It is on this basic material they could, at the least, arrange an opinion poll, such functioning would have made blunt the Indian diplomatic offensive, they would have been forced to evolve a defensive posture and locally they would have consolidated the morale of the masses.

There were gossips of emergence of third front and much noise was heard about defection of a group of Hizb-ul-mujahideen. But, except the assassination of Mr. Ghani Lone nothing has come on surface. Only yesterday the propfounders of the 3rd Front politics unequivocally declared that election cannot provide solution for this "imbroglio". I think the conception is erroneous. The elections to be held under the Indian and Jammu and Kashmir Constitutions have nothing to do with the Kashmir problem though confidence building in the institutions of democracy can by itself provide avenues for facilitation of easing the tension in between India and the people of Jammu and Kashmir. Restoration of such normalcy is bound to reflect upon the policy of Pakistan and finally will provide a meeting ground for the contenders.

Many recent activities and statements have put the Kashmiri voter under a dilemma. On 18th June Mr. Lyngdoh CEC India has in Jammu stated, "the elections here assume international importance — given the situation in the state, eye at the international level are focused on the exercise". In 1996 the international gaze deeply penetrated into the frauds which were perpetuated in ballot booths in Jammu and Kashmir, but the Election Commission of India least bothered. In February 2002 you (Mr. Lyngdoh) overruled the genuine objections raised about conduct of elections in Rajouri and Darhal electoral segments of Jammu Parliamentary Constituency during the bye-election held. "You even eroded the assurances which Prime Minister had given to the nation on independence day".

Mr. Armitage US Deputy Secretary of State, said on June 24th, "It is very important to have a free and fair elections in Kashmir that is free of violence and one that is judged to be free and fair by the international community". But Mr. Armitage has not evolved a scheme under which international observation can supervise these elections to keep it free from violence of the two guns and cheating, deceit and fraud which has become sine qua non of elections in Jammu and Kashmir.

On June 28th honourable PM has declared, "the imposition of Presidents Rule is being discussed as a means to ensure free and fair polls in the state". Mr. Prime Minister! most humbly I submit that it is inner neo-colonial ruler within you who talks about Presidents rule because Article 356 has no application to Jammu and Kashmir. Earlier discussed the 1964 Constitution Application Amendment Order is null and void because we have in our Constitution similar provision in section 92 and Delhi Agreement of 1952 has ruled out application of Articles 356 and 360 to Jammu and Kashmir. Besides can Governor rule exercise any magic. Dr. Farooq has very rightly asked you that in 1996 the elections were held under Presidents rule. It is Governor who imposed this government by fraud. The basic principle is to adhere to positive measures which can lay base of democratic traditions.

To come out of the mess the Indian Government is suggested to have a shift in its Jammu and Kashmir policy and instead of thinking and acting as a occupying nation it should start to think and act as a big brother and as a country of which Jammu and Kashmir is considered to be part of their life-line. Indian life-line runs through democracy and until Kashmir is treated a part of Indian democracy all the experiments of New Delhi will fade in futility.

The strains on Indian policy have become too transparent. It has evolved a policy to have another; 'Imposed hustings'. Second scene of "Political Begaar" is goint to be played. In 1996 immediately after parliament elections which Dr. Farooq boycotted he was tacitly warned to rule Jammu and Kashmir under a farce of elections lest be ready to face criminal charges of proved cases of corruption. He was made to peruse coolly the charge-sheet exposing his corrupt deeds of amassing wealth as Chief Minister.

This time at the first the known secular link in APHC. Mr Muhammad Yaseen Malik was persuaded to jump in elections alongwith other leaders of APHC. He was even got persuaded through an American lobby also. But he flatly refused. Hence persecution. A pair of lovers was arrested en route from Jammu and dollars were recovered from the girl who claimed that the sum was brought by the couple from Kathmandu where it was given to them by one PAK based militant leader for Yaseen to be spend for subversive activities. It was dubbed and qualified a "Hawala Transaction". Such courses are used for illegal conversion of currencies otherwise easily horse loads of dollars can be imported safely from Pakistan by the known routes wherefrom huge quantities of ammunition are, according to Indian Defense Ministry views, imported in Jammu and Kashmir and where from thousands of militants safely enter and go for acquisition of training. Such bags of dollars so smuggled are not to be thrown in Dal Lake but used for assigned purpose which use is not possible at all without Hawala. Such agencies are not based in Jammu and kashmir. Hence had these seized dollars been delivered in Kathmandu the concerned Hawala agency would have given its exchange in Indian currency. This factor exposes this story as fiction but the plot is too loose and devoid of any suspense.

On June 8, 2002 the collection of my five poetry compilations: "Sehra Te Saraab" was released in Tagore Hall Srinagar in an impressive distinguished gathering held under the auspices of Jammu and Kashmir Academy of Art, Culture and Languages. Almost all the intellectuals from all walks of life were invited. But among politicians of many colours only Syed Ali Shah Geelani, a prolific Urdu prose writer in Jammu and Kashmir attended. Within twelve hours he was arrested alongwith his two sons-in-law and he his lodged in Jharkhand Jail. This persecution is meant to force him to desist from opposition to participate in coming elections. People in the circumstances feel that imposition is the only game plan. The person Mr. Imtiaz Bazaz, on whose alleged statement, Mr. Geelani was arrested has been released. On 16th July 2002 the APHC in a statement issued qualified the arrest and acquisition of receiving money as a hoax and asserted that the arrest of Geelani was to defame the leadership in which government has failed.

The struggling organizations who are known as secessionists in Indian media have real difficulties in participation of elections and to opt for power means for them to bury with their past their future as well. It is a misnomer to say that winning of elections will provide them a democratic basis as representatives of people. No! not at all. The representative character which the peoples mandate can provide to a winning party under prevalent Indo-Kashmir, constitutional scheme is to act within the limited purview of those constitutional limitations. Such party/parties have, as a ruling junta or as opposition in legislature a binding to deal with subjects falling within the state list. The very basis of formulation of Indo-Kashmir relationship are provided in the contents of Accession Document. Provisions contained in Indian Constitution reflect the terms of this Document. Delhi Agreement formulated a corrigendum to this deed to explain the conditions of Accession, to define the ambit of the would be Jammu and Kashmir Constitution which was at that time in process and was latter on promulgated in 1956. The deed of Accession has surrendered only three domains of state activity exclusively to center. Foreign affairs is conspicuous among the three. Any party taking part in elections held under the prevalent constitutional schemes immediately looses claim to qualify Jammu and Kashmir as a 'disputed state'. Even if such party may continue to possess such notions has to leave those exclusively to the care of central government, particularly foreign affairs department. They cannot even claim to be consulted in this behalf. Statements are issued by office bearers of National Conference (ruling party in Jammu and Kashmir) like its General Secretary Sheikh Nazir that Jammu and Kashmir is disputed and should be solved internationally. But its Presidents, father and son duo–Farooq and Umar having positions in ruling clique are committed to the self deceiving theory of "integral part". In this background to ask such parties to fight elections under the prevalent constitutional scheme is to force them to become political converts by persecution and by persuasion of pseudo democrats of the world, may it be Mr. Armtage or Mr. Straw representing great world democracies, USA and Great Britain.

However, if given a chance to elect representatives of JK people (who will represent people of Jammu and Kashmir in tripartite conference) our earlier suggestion provide a key.

Note

1. In his historic address to his nation in January 2002 President Parvez Musharaf also made reference of this Hadis (saying of Prophet) and gave the same interpretation. Which I have accorded I but he has remained too precise. Had my book published earlier I would infar too much but now I can only with pride claim that my interpretation has evineed formidable support, so we must adhare to Jihad-i-Akbar (the greater holy war) to be fought on peace front with sincere, truthful and reasonable convassing.

Appendix (EP)–I

Breakdown of Constitutional Machienary

92. 1. If at any time the Sadar-i-Riyasat is satisfied that a situation has arisen in which the Government of the State cannot be carried on in accordance with the provisions of this Constitution, the Sadar-i-Riyasat may be

Proclamation

(a) assume to himself all or any of the functions of the Government of the State and all or any of the powers vested in or exercisable by anybody or authority in the State:

(b) make such incidental and consequential provisions as appear to the Sadar-i-Riyasat to be necessary or desirable for giving effect to the objects of the Proclamation, including provisions for suspending in whole or in part the operation of any provision of this Constitution relating to any body or authority in the State:

Provided that nothing in this section shall authorise the Sadar-i-Riyasat to assume to himself any of the powers vested in or exercisable by the High Court or to suspend in whole or in part the operation of any provision of this Constitution relating to the high Court.

2. Any such Proclamation may be revoked or varied by a subsequent Proclamation.
3. Any such Proclamation whether varied under sub-section (2) or not, shall, except where it is a Proclamation revoking a previous Proclamation, cease to operate on the expiration of six months from the date on which it was first issued.
4. If the Sadar-i-Riyasat by a Proclamation under this section assumes to himself any of the powers of the Legislature to make laws, any law made by him in the

exercise of that power shall, subject to the terms thereof, continue to have effect until two years have elapsed from the date on which the Proclamation ceases to have effect, unless sooner repealed or re-enacted by an Act of the Legislature, and any reference in this Constitution to any Acts of or laws made by the Legislature shall be construed as including a reference to such law.

5. No Proclamation under sub-section (1) shall be issued except with the concurrence of the President of India.
6. Every Proclamation under this section shall, except where it is a Proclamation revoking a previous Proclamation, be laid before each house of the Legislature as soon as it is convened.

Appendix (EP)-II

356. Provisions in case of failure of constitutional machinery in State.—(1) If the President, on receipt of a report from the Governor[1][***] of a State or otherwise, is satisfied that a situation has arisen in which the Governement of the State cannot be carried on in accordance with the provisions of this Constitution, the President may be Proclamation—

(a) assume to himself all or any of the functions of the Government of the State and all or any of the powers vested in or exercisable by the Governor[2][***] or any body or authority in the State other than the Legislature of the State;
(b) declare that the powers of the Legislature of the State shall be exercisable by or under the authority of Parliament;
(c) make such incidental and consequential provisions as appear to the President to be necessary or desirable for giving effect to the objects of the Proclamation, including provisions for suspending in whole or in part the operation of any provisions of this Constitution relating to any body or authority in the State:

Provided that nothing in this clause shall authorise the President to assume to himself any of the powers vested in or exercisable by a High-Court, or to suspend in whole or in part the operation of any provision of this Constitution relating to High Courts.

2. Any such Proclamation may be revoked or varied by a subsequent Proclamation.
3. Every Proclamation under this article shall be laid before each House of Parliament and shall, except where it is a Proclamation revoking a previous Proclamation cease to operate at the expiration of two months unless before the expiration of that period unless it has been approved by resolutions of both Houses of Parliament:

Provided that if any such Proclamation (not being a Proclamation revoking a previous Proclamation) is issued at a time when the House of the People is dissolved or the dissolution of the Hourse of the People takes place during the period of two months referred to in this clause, and if a resolution approving the Proclamation has been passed by the Council of States, but no resolution with respect to such Proclamation has been passed by the House of the People before the expiration of that period, the Proclamation shall cease to operate at the expiration of thirty days from the date on which the House of the People first sits after its reconstitution unless before the expiration of the said period of thirty days a resolution approving the Proclamation has been also passed by the House of the People.

4. A Proclamation so approved shall, unless revoked, cease to operate on the expiration of a period of [1][six months from the date of issue of the Procalamtion]:

Provided that if and so often as a resolution approving the continuance in force of such a Proclamation is passed by both Houses of Parliament, the Proclamation shall, unless revoked, continue in force for a further period of [2][six months] from the date on which under this clause it would otherwise have ceased to operate, but no such Proclamation shalkl in any case reamain in force for more than three years:

Provided further that if the dissolution of the House of the People takes place during any such period of [2][six months] and a resolution approving the continuance in force of such Proclamation has been passed by the Council of States, but no resolution with respect to the continuance in force of such Proclamation has been passed by the House of the People during the said period, the Proclamation shall cease to operate at the expiration of thirty days from the date on which the House of the People first sits after its reconstitution unless before the expiration of the said period of thirty days a resolution approving the continuance in force of the Proclamation has been also passed by the House of the People:

[3][Provided also that in the case of the Proclamation issued under clause (1) on the 11th day of May, 1987 with respect to the State of Pubjab the reference in the first

proviso to this clause to "three years" shall be construed as a reference to 1[Five years.]

[2][(5) Notwithstanding anything contained in clause (4), a resolution with respect to the continuance in force of a Proclamation approved under clause (3) for any period beyond the expiration of one year from the date of issue of such Proclamation shall not be passed by either House of Parliament unless—

(a) a Proclamation of Emergency is in operation, in the whole of India or, as the case may be, in the whole or any part of State, at the time of the passing of such resolution, and

(b) the Election Commission certifies that the continuance in force of the Proclamation approved under clause (3) during the period specified in such resolution is necessary on account of difficulties in holding general elections to the Legislative Assembly of the State concerned:]

[4][Provided that nothing in this clause shall apply to the Proclamation issued under clause (1) on the 11th May, 1987 with respect to the State of Pubnjab.]

Chapter 38

Transparent Tradition

(2002-Elections J&K Assembly)

Elections to 9th J&K Legislative Assembly held in four phases in September-October, 2002, are quadrangling in electoral muse. It is the first ever electoral exercise which in real sense can be deemed transparent one. This book in chapter 12 deals with general elections of 1977. It was discussed under an appropriate heading, "An Election or Democracy by Intimidation". I considered it as first exercise in J&K which can be termed as Election but the great historian and political analyst of J&K, Pandit Prem Nath Bazaz, qualified it as democracy by intimidation. Such contradictory assessments were due to the fact that information about that process was suppressed by muscle power.

A second characteristic of the present election is also unique. It is the first ever electoral process which resulted into the overthrow of deeply entrenched family rule of Sheikh dynasty. Such a result was, before the elections, considered an impossibility. Before the polling dates were declared, it was reported by media (not baselessly) that the only politically-based PDP leader, who had much acceptability in his Tangmarg constituency, was apprehensive and he was reported to have made efforts to get NC mandate which was considered a visa for entrance into the State legislature.

The third characteristic of these present hustings lie in its fragmented verdict which uniquely provided a chance to a microscopic minority (PDP with 7% of total vote) to dictate to its bigger partner in coalition.

Fourthly, the coalition was imposed which might retard the initiation of the process of faith building in the institutions of democracy because the verdict is not for marriage of inconvenience of old parties but to seek a fresh mandate as early as possible.

A hundred days trial given to Mufti Syed ministry has convinced the elite (which makes and mars the public opinion) that whatever the intentions and designs of the ruling clique, the results will be frustrating due to the chauvinistic bossism of the Central Government and super constitutional role of the unified command which in reality rules the state. In these circumstances it has become a distant goal to establish a civil society in J&K. The failure of this ministry to disband Special Operation Groups and Police Task Force, which it had conspicuously highlighted in its manifesto, again consolidates the belief that any government in J&K, even popular one, cannot deliver goods. All such governance has to remain sandwiched in the constitutional contradictions and due to the neo-colonial obstinacy of Delhi rulers. Its administrative impotency has been demonstrated through the transfer and posting orders of civil servants and police officers issued by this Government during its tenure of three months. These orders have convinced even an illiterate villager that in the imposed set up of administrative rules, business conduct rules and the imposition of Indian cadre services–all factors constitute only one impact—that the elected party/parties have to play ancillary role whereas the real power lies somewhere else. The height of indecision is so alarming that on 12th October, 2002, the Advocate General (A.G.) and his colleagues, Law Officers, in the two wings of the state High Court submitted, as tradition goes, their resignations. But it was relayed from electronic media on February 15, 2003, that Mr. Altaf Naik was appointed as A.G after the Law Minister Mr. Baig hurled a threat of resignation. It took four months to take this vital decision which should have been carried out just after the swearing in ceremonv of the state cabinet.

These failures have been mentioned here to bring home the point to our readers that any government, even elected, one has to function as an elected, responsible and accountable rulers.

The vital question is whether this election in real sense was transparent and if so what it conveyed to conscious voters of J&K, their successors—yet to be enrolled as voters, to observers from Indian Election Commission, to the NGOs and to the media. This achievement of transparency of 2002 elections is an admitted fact. On Independence Day in

2001, the Hon'ble Prime Minister had assured this transparency, and that public commitment got fulfilled. But as every facet of Kashmir politics is shrouded in mystery or like a modern art piece deserves more than one interpretation, sometimes contradictory in nature, the transparency of these elections has made the inherent ambiguities dominant upon our political behavior clearer. This transparency reveals the obscurities with which Kashmir political process has evolved since 1947. The contradictions in the transparency of these elections can be gauged by contradictory interpretations which its results have received. Pakistan President, his ministers, the official spokesman of his Government, all hailed people of J&K for their valour and courage to have implemented boycott inspite of terror let loose upon them to participate in the elections. Mr. Vajpai, the Prime Minister, his Deputy Mr. L.K. Advani, and even US Ambassador in India congratulated voters of J&K to have ignored threats to their life and come to booths to exercise their democratic right. Mr. Advani in his momentary enthusiasm forgot that challenging the virus of previously held elections would tarnish the fabric of Indo-Kashmir relationship. He did not hesitate to say in a speech telecast live from the Doordarshan on 12 October, 2002, as :

"This is the first free and fair elections I have witnessed for the last 52 years."

Thus this verdict justifies the assessments made in this book about all the elections from the one held for J&K Constituent Assembly in 1950-51, and challenges as unfair and tainted the elections held to the 2nd Legislative Assembly in 1962, which, under a centrally orchestrated mechanism, installed Sadiq Government in 1964. It was that Government which concurred with the imposition of President of India (Constitutional Application) Orders upon J&K and eroded the guarantees given under the "disputed" instrument of accession and Delhi Agreement.

This chapter will assess whether Parvez Mushraf and his government are correct or Mr. Advani and his ministerial colleagues or none of them.

In chapter 15 we have dealt with various stages which during the process of elections are to be covered.

The basis of fairness lies in the cardinal faith which a participant in election bears with the system under which such voters demonstrate their commitment with that particular soil. None can doubt that Kashmiris have deep-rooted commitment with their soil. Sacrifices offered by them so far overshadow the struggles for freedom fought in other parts of the world. The first stage to express that commitment with the soil bears testimony in the participation of the people with the specific statecraft of that soil. People of that soil must consciously feel either by the practices of their predecessors or by their own or by voluntary usages, customs, practices etc., they or their predecessors have evolved a code of conduct to choose their rulers. Such conduct is either inherited through blood or evolved or bears both the qualities for installation of governance that suits to the aspirations of the inhabitants of that soil. It is such voluntarily inherited or evolved system of governance to which the subject remains committed to offer even sacrifices of any kind. In this very vital matter the people of J&K feel alienated from those systems imposed upon under an international intrigue, under the conceived and delivered fraudulent devices of two ruling nations. The Kashmiri in both the divided parts has developed a belief that he has been sandwiched by the imposition of four constitutions. All these imposed constitutions contain those guarantees and privileges which have been enshrined in U.N. charter but the people are dead opposed to those documents. Why? Because in evolving either of the four systems or the synthesised system of those four codes of conduct, the citizen of J&K has, at no stage, been involved, directly or indirectly.

To grasp our contention please once again read chapters 6, 7,19, 20, 23 and 24 and even epilogue to this book.

Pakistan Government and its chief agencies in J&K harp upon the single tune that the elections cannot substitute for plebiscite. Who argues so? Even such chauvinistic interpretation accorded by India to electoral exercises in J&K has resulted in a deadly reaction against elections. Even the tested agent of India, Mr Omar Abdulla, the N.C. President, has in his election speeches, more than once, argued that the elections in J&K bear no effect upon the disputed nature of J.K. The same has been the strain of the statements and speeches of P.D.P. leaders—"Papa" Mr. Syed and daughter

Mehbooba. Thus instead of harping upon this off beaten irrelevant theme they should explain to the powers, about imposed nature of systems upon the people of J&K. Can Pakistan or its patronised APHC leadership bear courage to argue on such lines. Because, Pakistan has itself imposed contradictory systems upon PAK and directly ruled Northern districts of J&K. To be precisely relevant at the onset of 2002 general elections the psychology of the people sandwiched in contradictions of imposed systems proved the main factor for their abstention.

To be fair, Indian Election Commission could not help to liberate the Kashmir psyche from such impact. The second stage after evolving a voluntary national code of conduct is to involve voters' aspirations with the defining of electoral segments. Discussed earlier both the exercises in this direction held in 1950 and 1990 had wilfully jeopardised voluntary involvement of the people. The Election Commission this time on the eve of elections could not undo this wrong. So, the voters whose genuine interests were subjected to geremandering were asked to remain content with the imposed definition of electoral constituencies.

The third most vital stage but the first in the process of election to be repeated on the eve of every electoral exercise relates to preparation, review, revision, amendment and final preparations of electoral rolls possibly free from errors. In this connection I quote, the statement of Mr Pramod Jain I.A.S., the Chief Electoral officer of the state, as follows:

"There was no master copy of electoral rolls, no intensive revision had been done, electoral rolls were not even in proper serial number."

We share our assessment and analysis of the following table with our readers:

TABLE: ELECTIONS IN J&K

Total Electorate

Year	Kashmir	Jammu	Ladakh
1987	1878310	1539269	95101
1996	2381949	22407691	138467
1999	2422631	2463744	143719
2002	2546913	2892290	172945
	2809578	**3015173**	**174083**

According to this table the total electorate in Jammu division in 1987 has risen almost the double on the eve of 2002 elections and has even exceeded by two lakhs the number of voters in Kashmir valley. According to the rate of the growth as shown in Jammu and Ladakh the number of voters in 2002 in Kashmir valley should have been at least thirty-eight lakhs. No epidemic has caused mass death of one million of Kashmiris. More than one reason is accorded for this unreasonable statistics shown in election records. Firstly, some argue that the Government of India has an evil design to project the majority area of the valley as a minority region. In my view such contention is fallacious. No Government whatsoever its nature, can share such mischievous secrets with ordinary field staff like census and electoral roll enumerators. Second argument attributes this false statistics to the threats of militants. Such contention provides the inferences that either the militant is so popular that his charisma is accepted as heavenly gospel or the state administration has become impotent enough and inspite of the web of military cantonments established in the heart and lungs of localities the Indian might has failed to contain it. But I must depose before the world court that just during these hustings I faced a group of militants in my locality and found them totally indifferent to the process of election. Their leader said in clear terms: "We have left it to the overground leadership. Our involvement with such "Biddats" (innovations) derails us from our real "tract."

If one is committed to a system he can manage to register his name in rolls as he does to register himself as a ration holder or to register his cow for artificial insemination. But the reality is somewhat else. It is voluntary, desired and manifest non-involvement of the people with the imposed political system. This non-involvement with roll preparations is their commitment for boycott.

The tempered record in Kashmir too does not reflect the partial involvement. It is the field staff member of Land Revenue department charged with the duty of preparation of rolls who copies previous prepared rolls of 1983, deletes as far as his memory or ration card holders list helps him. He deletes the dead or includes young ration holders of the families. It is, therefore, in this list of 2002, about 25 to 27 percent enrolled as voters are children below 18 years of age, and on an average 7 to 9 percent are such voters who are since dead. To be fair, out of six million voters registered in the state 32 to 36 percent are either under age or dead.

In Jammu and Ladakh too the people nowhere have participated with this process of registration of voters. There also it is the subordinate employee of Land Revenue department, like his counterpart in the valley, who acts both as a voter and as the registrar of voter list. The difference lies in perception. In Kashmir while discharging the two duties this field official cares for the sentiment of his people and distorts the record in one manner. In the other two parts of the state this employee is guided by the psychology to show these two regions more populated than the valley. Central or State Governments are mute spectators incapable to provide any direction in this situation.

The very important stages in the process are the stages of nomination, scrutiny of papers, campaigning, the polling, carrying of ballot boxes and other election material to and fro the booths, the counting of votes and final declaration. Our contemporary history which this book has highlighted shows that frauds have been rampant during the carriage of election material, counting of votes and even during the declaration of results. But commonly the polling process only is considered as the elections and thus we find that reports of observer teams or media cover the supervision of this stage only. During the elections various agencies observed strictly this stage of polling only, and let us now go to those reports.

The observers observed only the four phases of the polling in a summary manner. Such casual visits detect the conditions prevailing in and around the polling booth at that particular point of time. In a hurry to visit another booth the team stops for a while and then leaves. This summary view can reveal some strains upon the systems and not the lapses and irregularities which have been so particular and distinguishable in J&K that even hawkish detective eye will fail to detect. Such visits can at best be surprise visits only. It is only for the immaturity of the otherside that such surprise visit can detect the actions of army, para-military forces,

SOGs, renegades and militants. Otherwise such surprise visits leave very less impact. Any act of terror in militancy infested State is ordinarily attributed to "militants" but deeper understanding and indepth probes proved otherwise. Bear in mind the massacre of Sikhs at Chati Singhpora on the eve of Bill Clinton's visit and thereafter the happening at Patherbal. Later events showed the massacre was to hoodwink U.S.A. President and the objective was achieved. Hence when during the process of polling militancy related act is performed summarily the responsibility can be attributed to the militant but in confused situation of J&K such act needs sufficient probing and then alone it can be determined whether it was handiwork of militants or of other agency or agencies.

Now let us have a general study of the nature of observation. Election Commission of India appoints some members of Indian Administrative Service posted outside J&K to observe the polling. They are usually ignorant of the topography of areas under their observation. On their arrival by air they enjoy entertainment as State guests from the Hospitality and Protocol department. They are provided cars from the state motor garages and those very drivers are usually tutored to narrate to their passenger the overawing tales of militancy, and thus he observes enjoyment in and around Lal Chowk. The reports of observors are consigned in the Election Commission office in New Delhi and might see the light of the day if some result is disputed and an election petition is filled before J&K High Court. During 1983 and 1987 elections the E.C. appointed District and Sessions Judges of J&K as observers but their reports annoyed Government and E.C. So the practice was stopped. In 1987, as E.C. observer I had the privilege to supervise some constituencies in central Kashmir and as such I found that the Returning Officers and Deputy Commissioner successfully hoodwinked even me who remained shuttling constantly from District Court Complex (where counting of Khansahib constituency was underway) to the Town Hall (where votes of other constituencies were being counted). The distance was 1/2 kilometer. As the crafty civil servant has acquired expertise in election frauds even the supervision of one constituency by one E.C. supervisor will hardly detect such frauds.

This background in mind, we shall now discuss the reports of NGOs (India-based) who observed the polling process for their deeprooted commitment to democracy. I have also kept a cautiously vigil myself as far as possible and deputed, within my sources, my own group to some adjacent constituencies. That observation will get synthesised with the discussion on those three published reports. I will also refer to the information I received from media. Three types of media reportings were found. A section, as usual, behaved as mouthpiece of fraud and did not only connive with fraud but encouraged it. "Aaj Tak" news channel was, in this field on the forefront. At many places their cameramen asked the forces to force out from homes groups of people—both men and women—and make them to stand in front of the booth. As the forces did the same, Aaj Tak camera showed to the Indian people the 'voluntary' participation of masses. On 1 November, 1951, in its editorial *Hindu* hailed the imposition of 75-unopposed-member Constituent Assembly as 'ratification of accession by every single voter'. This time the duty to disinform and mislead Indian listeners was discharged by Doordarshan, Akashwani (India T.V. and Radio) Aaj Tak and Zee News. On the other hand, the print media had repented for their previous lapses and excesses with Indo-Kashmir amity. By now they have, to a great extent, been constructive in reporting.

The third type was the publication by media or the relays from B.B.C. and other radio and TV channels of the accusations and counter-accusations of the Government backed candidates, opposition parties or the facts and figures of fraud and force exercised by the Government agencies as released to media by APHC and other organisations for boycott. Similarly, the state and central governments and even Pakistan Government spokespersons on occasions released press notes which were all fairly carried by respected organs of media. In such reporting the media agencies least aligned themselves with the allegations or counter-allegations.

New Delhi-based Center for Study of Developing Societies (CSDS) has published the gist of the details of its study in *Indian Express*, New Delhi, Wednesday, October 9, 2002. The study is entitled J&K polls 2002, "The Fairest of them all".

Besides going into the manner in which polling in four phases (not the full process of Elections) was conducted the CSDS has made a comparative study of 2002 Elections with its earlier elections and has unambiguously qualified the present exercise comparatively an improvement. This comparative study makes a bold admission about the frauds which were *sine qua non* for all previous exercises in the name of elections. The report of CSDS has neither been challenged directly by the State or Central Government nor its correctness is disputed by the leaders and parties who advocated boycott.

CSDS on the basis of their limited observation with their limited resources in manning and financing their activities have qualified within one sentence the character of present elections as "substantially fair it was not free." This report has summed up malpractices as :

- There were allegations of a systematic exclusion or deliberate inclusion of bogus names in the rolls, some of the allegations were true. But there were only three cases where the electoral rolls were possibly tempered...........
- Of the 76 booths observed there were four booths where polling agent of only one party was present ....
- We got seven reports all from the valley of the polling party playing a partisan role..........
- The practice of a person being allowed to vote again and again was recorded in substantial numbers.
- There was only one case where supporters of the opposition were systematically turned back as their votes were already cast.

A precise discussion on each point

As far as the first point is concerned, on my enquiry, I disagree with the contention that there was a systematic exclusion or deliberate inclusion in the voter lists for the interest of any political outfit. It was purely on the basis that voter had boycotted with preparation, revision and review of voter rolls. At places such non-cooperation appeared helpful to one political alignment so the malafides attributed are least fortified. Another pertinent question also arises.

Was this boycott in response to APHC call or under the threat of militants or for lack of faith in the Elections and in the dark side of Indian democracy imposed in J&K. I am of the view that it is for the latter reason and it is therefore that even the voter lists in Jammu and Ladakh regions are lopsided. In those regions too the faith is since eroded in the institutions of Indian democracy.

Jammu or Ladakh Muslim does not participate in the final phase of elections i.e. the polling phase for his commitment to democracy but to demonstrate his decisive presence in these areas. Similarly the Jammu Dogra or Ladakh Buddhist does not participate for his commitment to democracy but to emphasise that the two regions of Jammu and Ladakh are not composite regions but predominantly Hindu and Buddhist areas respectively. Being interested in such superficial design they, the voters of Jammu and Ladakh, also involve themselves with the process at the latter stage of polling only and till then even during preparation of Electoral Rolls they adopt negative approach of non-cooperation. This behaviour provides both types of inferences. Pro-boycott parties infer to their advantage that the electorate is lured by their slogans, and the last hour participation in this process during the polling is exploited by the other side. They claim that the people have endorsed faith in the system. It is therefore highly necessary for our NGOs who are outsiders to assess the freedom or otherwise in the elections to observe with particular stress the pre-polling stages of electioneering.

Second point relates to the presence of polling agents. Here it must be borne in mind that it is from 1996 that Indian policy makers evolved schemes to provide a colour of contest to elections so the men are thrown with different labels by the Indian agencies in the electoral arena. Such men have no base or cadre. Hence they are usually paid to cash as interest the fame of defeated candidates and so they least need polling agents. Besides, some alignments or outfits are created at the spur of moment who do not need the services of polling agents. This time even the present ruling PDP jumped in the field without a nucleus of a widespread organisation and hijacked some independent candidates and affixed PDP labels upon their collars. They could manage to get less than 1/5th of the total number of legislators, that too only from the rural areas of the valley due to the negative role of National Conference particularly, during these hustings. In J&K a political culture has evolved right from 1949, when Zaudar elections were held, and true to that culture polling staff on duty cannot suppress its political opportunism. The members of C.S.D.S have cited seven such cases but had they supervised only my home constituency of Charar-i-sharief they would have found, to their dismay, that ruling party candidate, Mr. A.R. Rather, had through the good offices of the district development commissioner, Mr. Bassar Khan, got appointed his relatives as polling officers and presiding officers. Though at the intervention of Election Commission of India some were changed. But the self appointed polling staff at polling booths of Nagam, Badipora, Hafro Batapohru, Narpora, Watakul, Gogjipathri, Wangwas, Derwan Nowgam, Pakharpora and the whole of Kandi area facilitated the re-entry of ex-Finance Minister in the State Legislature.

The team of CSDS has pin-pointed that at seven booths a group of persons did cast their votes more than once. Though, it is badly insufficient reporting but is greatly revealing. Had they posted only two "mute spectators" at two places of my native place, Charar-i-sharief, and my present place of residence they could have found that two groups had exercised proxy franchise for a good number of voters. I can even give their names but discussion will be too lengthy. At Charar-i-sharief, the relatives of Mr. Abdul Qayoom, the then revenue minister (a local guy) and henchman of the N.C. candidate Mr. Rather, did this job for him during the second half day of polling, and in Kalapora a group of close relatives of Chadora P.D.P. candidate Mr. Javed Mir did it for him.

Systematic casting of votes of the 'respectables' in their absence is an old practice, and it was exercised this time with more vigour as the very authors of this fraudulent electioneering, the Pradesh Congress cadres were on fore-front either under their party label or under the ex-Congress stalwart, Mufti Mohammed Syed. The 'boycott' has been total in towns and in cities not only for the cause that urban elite stands committed to APHC or has deeprooted commitment to militancy. It is mainly because a more consciously aware elite does not endorse such a system where only the heads are counted. The majority is of such elite which has seen elections in Indian States and have, after comparative study, got satisfied that Indian democracy has contradictory two standards—one for the Indians and the other for the occupied Kashmir. It is in rural areas too that such elite remains in-doors during the actual hustings. But professional proxy agents do cast votes in their absence and I declare on oath that since I became a voter in 1959 till date I have never cast my vote nor my late parents did so and nor my wife. Please check the record, you will find that I have this time exercised franchise from two places of my two residences. Hence for the particular information of C.S.D.S. the votes of such 'voters' are shown duly exercised who hardly go to polls or even if they go before conclusion of polling they, to their dismay and surprise, find that their ghosts have already done the job for them.

Details of this report cannot be enumerated here but those interested might peruse the full report of this center.

The very important document on these elections is the 77-page report published by J&K Coalition of Civil Society, Srinagar, and Civil Society Initiatives, B-14, IInd Floor, Gulmohar Park, New Delhi. (For brevity we will refer it as Initiatives).

Just after the first phase of these elections held on September 16, 2002, a report by J&K coalition of Civil Society was published in an English daily from Srinagar, *Greater Kashmir*, and immediately the official spokesman of the State Government refuting the charges leveled therein dubbed this organisation as "hitherto unknown". Thus the very status, stature, credentials and bona fides of this coalition were challenged. The tune and tone of the spokesperson revealed that the Government considered this body as a sham organisation floated by some agency / agencies or power or party just to discredit the electoral process. If I close my eyes to this vital aspect and take benefit from the report with which such an "hitherto unknown" organisation is connected, I will be inviting serious doubts for the credibility of my work.

The Delhi-based Civil Society Initiatives is affiliated with the famous "Other Media" and is manned, run, organised and administered by the talented independent and impartial

Indians who are deeply committed to the values in Indian democracy for establishment of a civil society throughout the country and take care for such neglected pockets in India where human dignity is subordinated to the expansionist designs. J&K and states in the East India are the scars on the face of Indian democracy. So this Civil Society Initiatives lay particular stress upon the supervision of organs of democracy in these states. But the J&K Government has singled out the 'Coalition' and dubbed it an 'hitherto unknown'. This places a burden upon me to explain the socio-political geography of this organisation and in case its character is shrouded in mystery or doubt I will have to examine whether the association of the "Initiatives" with the "Coalition" discredits the former.

The human dignity fell under terrible strains during the first ministry of late Sheikh Mohd. Abdulla (October 1947 to 8 August, 1953) and even a defense lawyer was not available to the victims of State persecution. The successor Government of Bakhshi Ghulam Mohammed followed this inherited statecraft with vigour and added values in nepotism and corruption to this state terror. Mr. G.M. Sadiq, the third veteran leader of our freedom struggle, a known progressive, added new devices to rationalise the political fraud created and established by his predecessors with all primitive measures. In spite of this unabated terror and humiliation of human dignity no forum of Human Rights activists could emerge. Even Bar Associations could not generate a sensibility in their own cadres about their own honor and professional integrity. Other honorable professionals like doctors, teachers and engineers opted for the safety of their vested interests in a society dominated by misrule. It is a unique coincidence in our history that as the "coward", "timmed" and "weak" Kashmiri did undergo a new culture of courage, valour and strength by taking gun to vindicate his humiliated honour, simultaneously a reasonable campaign to highlight these violations also emerged. Whereas HAJY Group (Hameed Sheikh, Ashfaq Majeed, Javid Mir and Yasin Malik) promoted a culture of valour, a trade union leader and a known communist party activist from Kashmir, Pandit Hardey Nath Wancho, became the pioneer Human Rights activist. His junior comrade in State CPI unit, Mr. Parvez Imroz, Advocate, joined him. But

Wancho was gunned down. The State prosecuted a group of Jamiatul Mujahideen outfit alleging them to have killed him. The State TADA court acquitted them. However, the Indian Supreme Court set aside the acquittal, convicted them and sentenced them to undergo life imprisonment. Both the courts acted upon the same evidence. The highest Court of the people has, since convicted the Government for silencing, forever, a reliable, independent and impartial voice, and so have accorded the title of a 'martyr' to him. Mr. Imroz remained committed to his legacy and played some role during the 1994-95 Charar-i-sharief siege and destruction of town and shrine situated there. A militant fired at him near his home at Kralapora but he survived. This brought him in limelight as successor of 'Wancho' and as such he acquired recognition, and was invited to Human Rights conferences within the country and outside. This halo around him created an interest. He enjoyed monopoly for worldwide tours but he did never dare to tour the terrorism infested and far flung districts of Doda (in Jammu) and Kupwara (in Kashmir). As soon as the world attention was focused on Human Rights violations in Kashmir, an all India conference of Pakistan-India Forum for Peace and Prosperity was held at Srinagar (Welcome Hotel). This author presided its inaugural session attended by dignitaries from India who included Admiral Ram Das, Tapan Bose, Ved Bhasin, Balraj Puri, Deen Dayalam, Gautam Navalakha, Dr. Syed Syedien and others.

The conference concluded with passing a resolution to establish J&K Federation of Civil Societies and the founders unanimously evolved a twelve-clause M.O.U which was adopted as its constitution and each of the fifteen founding fathers of the Federation signed this document. Mr. Parvez Imroz was nominated its ad hoc chairperson (convenor) who was provided with the services of two young lawyers, Mr. A.R. Hanjora and Mr Shahwar Gauhar. He neither utilised their services nor collected the accounts and minutes earlier handed over by him to his trusted man Mr. Ashraf, nor as per mandate he made efforts to expand the society nor did he allow to prepare rolls so that elections of a chairman, three vice-chairmen from three regions, general secretary, three regional secretaries, controller of finances, one press secretary and nine executive members could be held within six months i.e. by October 2001. He imposed a stalemate for one year with the only ulterior design to get the Federation disintegrated lest a democratic set up is evolved which shall subject his functioning to a democratic discipline. He could not convince his own friends, the two founding members, of his fiscal relationship with a N.G.O. known as OXFAM. While remaining constantly on move from Geneva to New York to Sweden to Jakarta he did not associate or organise local visits to go deeper in the worst pockets of Human Rights violations in Doda (Jammu) and Kupwara (Kashmir), the two remote districts, so as to see how the innocent villagers are used as human cover to moving army conveys. As he sensed that the democratic culture might subject him to a discipline he disassociated, disintegrated the democratically established JK Federation of Civil Societies. To keep his "interests" unchallenged, he with a group of pseudo activists, hoisted a banner of J&K Coalition of Civil Society upon his chamber.

It looks really alarming that a man who belongs to an autocratic culture with dictatorial strains upon his functions and who runs away from inner party democracy, who has no code of conduct (registered) of his society which is not even a group but claims himself to lead a coalition is just deceiving the cause. Should such a man or his associates supervise function of democratic process in the State. But logic lies in sifting of chaff from grain and not to throw away the full bag of grain because it contains chaff.

The Civil Society Initiatives is widely recognised Delhi-based democratic organisation associated with famous "Other Media" which include men of reputation like Kalpora Sharma, Prabhu Ghate, Gautam Navalakha, Vijan M.J. Indu Prakash, Dr. Prakash Louis, Javed Naqvi, E. Deendayalan, Lata Jishnu, Ram Rattan Chatterjee and others.

Now let us examine the association of the Civil Society with this coalition. On page 67, the 77-page brochure issued by the Initiatives and Coalition jointly under the title "Independent Election observers team report"mentions that for lack of local response in Jammu it could not cover Jammu except Doda district. This lack of support should not be taken as a negative blanket statement that Jammu has lacked in democratic commitments. No, in recent times it has shown exemplary awareness and tolerance. But a section of reactionaries led by BJP, Bajrang Dal and Shiv Sena have evolved violence and intolerance; their culture endorses the excesses let loose on J&K people and work for the Keeping of territory of J&K within Indian geography. These very intolerant people have been patted by Mr. Vajpai on 10-02-2003, as protectors of the country against militancy. Hence Jammu democrats have been scared by their aggressive postures and therefore could not co-ordinate supervision of elections. On the other hand, Initiatives got support, guidance association from one-man coalition of Mr. Parvez which they required. Parvez to them was the successor of Wancho; they have not examined him as a democrat. But they should have seen whether he has a democratic organisation with an adopted code of conduct registered under state laws and with an elected body. The association of Initiatives with Coalition does, in no case, discredit this lucidly prepared report.

The "Initiatives" evolved reasonably convenient modus operandi so as to perform result-oriented task. Four teams were formed, each team was assigned different areas. During the first phase (16-9-02), Team-I observed district Kupwara, Team-2 observed some constituencies in district Baramula and similarly Teams-3 and 4 monitored Sonawari, Bandipora, Rafiabad, Baramulla and Sangrama constituencies. The similar procedure was adopted for the subsequent phases. Each team, after observation, prepared a joint report and all the four reports of the four teams were collated, sifted and edited. Such exhaustive report of four phases is covered in this brochure.

Summing up study report analyses:

"...these elections were held in the presence of heavy deployment of security forces. It was counter productive. Common people in J&K live amidst the constant presence of forces... In their perception they are living under the siege of Indian troops....."

This report analyses the polling held in four phases in its three sections. The first deals with coercion, the second highlights malpractices and the third deals with popular perceptions. As the popular perception is concerned sufficient are the above lines quoted from the report. From my childhood when I was studying in 7th class (October 1947) upto 1989 (when I was a senior sessions judge) I always felt living as a prisoner in wider jail. After 1989, I feel I am under an execution of a death warrant confined in solitary confinement.

Even exercise of democratic process has subjected JK people to untold process of coercion. On page 170, I have quoted what I faced during 1996 elections.

This time, jawans of Rashtrya Rifles, Border Security Force and CRPF did not terrorize the state people to vote for a particular candidate or party but in rural areas particularly terrorised the villagers to cast votes, "may be to invalidate the ballot " and forced them to get their fingers marked positively. General threat was hurled that absence of inkmark on fingers would justify any persecution and even might cause the "custodial death". Scared people adopted devices to dye their fingers. One such device caused arrest of a group. The Initiatives report on page 43 mentions that during the third phase team-1 visited "Wachi" electoral segment and as they reached in village Sugam in Shopian Tehsil (Distt. Pulwama) all villagers were holding demonstration, and it transpired that Rashtrya Rifles had taken four persons, Mehrajud Din Lone s/o Ghulam Mohammad, Zahoor Ahmad Ganai s/o Mohammad Afzal Ganai, Mohammed Iqbal Wani s/o Mohidin and Bashir Ahmad Bhat s/o Ghulam Mohammed, all residents of the same village and all aged 18, in custody, and villagers apprehended any risk to the four detained boys. The allegation against them was that at 4.10 p.m. after polling, the army had arrested them on the charge that they had stolen indelible inkpot from the polling staff. The detained persons admitted that they secretly used the election staff ink to dye their fingers so as to escape the wrath of army.

Though in my constituency Chadora, where I presently live, there was no such pressure detected and even the militants or cadres of APHC did not impose the boycott. But in my home constituency of Charar-i-sharief the force was used by army and paramilitary forces in the adjoining rural area of the town. The town was free of any pressure from anyside, so a voluntary boycott prevailed. However malpractices showed enhanced figures of the votes cast. That fraud has generally annoyed the town people.

This type of coercion, threats and warnings of militants to abstain were not so clear and generally complained in areas closer to L.A.C in Jammu. In some constituencies some candidates "paid" good *nazrana* to army or BSF officers to drag people to the booths. It was particularly done by Mr. M.R. Choudhry, ex-Forest Minister, at Handwara but the forcibly dragged people out of anger did cast their votes to his independent rival candidate. On the other hand, his ministerial colleague, Mr. Mohiud Din Shah, showed more practical wisdom. His constituency Batamalo is the backbone of the present movement so committed to boycott. Yet Mr. Tariq Kara, scion of the great Kara dynasty which had produced freedom fighters like Mohiud Din Kara and G.M. Sadiq could convince a small section to go to booths, that could undo the fate of Mr. Shah. But he hired the services of one-time co-travelers of militants called locally Soyath, who went with guns covered under masks and threatened such families to remain in doors.

Generally the army committed sacrilege of mosques, herded the Imams of the mosques like POWs and forced them to announce from pulpits through public announcement systems for participation lest they might have to face dire consequences. At Drugmula (Kupwara) Brigade H.Q., Imams of the mosques were herded in and made to issue threats from mosques to the villagers. This report gives such details and quotes an eminent member of Kupwara Bar Association, Mr. Khurshid Iqbal Shah.

The members of forces forcibly dragged people in many constituencies to the booths. The observers of Team-4 during the 4th phase reached "Uchar" in Banihal constituency and caught jawans of 24-RR and Renegades dragging people out from their houses and herding them in and around polling booths. On being caught they ran and one did hide himself in a rice husker. In Pattan, Baramulla, Sonawari, Sangrama, Charar-i-Sharief, Pulwama etc., similar acts were found in vogue.

In the Wachi constituency, the ladies in presence of army personnel leveled charges against the "Security" forces. The gravest charge was of indecency. The army jawans stripped themselves naked in presence of village women hurling the immediate threat of 'Sex assault' upon them if they abstained from polling.

Malpractices have become the distinguishable trait of J&K elections. Through this and all other reports these malpractices are transparent even to the blind eye. Transparency is the only achievement of 2002 Elections. The previous frauds would remain a close breast secret or an ambiguous mystery. Discussing the malpractices, which were made transparent with 'pride and pleasure' this time one of my Delhi-based South Indian friends was right to observe, "Indian democracy is so transparent in J&K that no mask shall cover its nudity." Let me here quote a few instances contained in this report, summing up of C.S.D.S. and the "Independent observers Report" compiled by Rural Litigation and Entitlement Kendra (RLEK).

Many of such malpractices have erupted in the electoral system throughout the sub-continent. These include casting of bogus votes, role of money and muscle power, ouster of of genuine voters from booths forcibly, use of defective ballot machines (EVM), kidnapping of opposition sympathizers and attacks on polling booths. These malpractices have become inalienable traits of the electoral process in the sub-continent. Its intensity may vary in degree or proportion.

The Kendra Report on page 22 describes that its observers satisfied themselves that the outgoing minister (N.C. candidate) was given EVMs for misuse in Handwara constituency.

Now a question arises how and why these malpractices in J&K have eroded the very credibility of elections. The answer is clear. In other parts of the country, and even in other countries of the sub-continent, the "malpractices" are exceptions, these have become a rule in J&K. In other states of India malpractices are carried out by the corrupt candidates, aggressive political parties or by some overactive members of state administration. But in J&K, these malpractices are authorized and implemented under the patronage of the state. This time the security forces, charged with the duty to protect the sanctity of elections, imposed these malpractices as a 'security measure'. In Pakistan, elections to National Assembly and Provincial Assemblies were held during the same period when we in India-occupied J&K were required to elect the Legislative Assembly. In Pakistan too malpractices were alleged but with specific allegations attributing to some blue-eyed boys of the army. In Gujarat (India) malpractices of serious communal dimensions were alleged. But these malpractices (in J&K) this time were not put in to help some blue-eyed boys or to eliminate some naughty boys but 'to impose an election' upon the reluctant people, dead opposed to participate. Here it must be taken note that the masters, behind the screen, were sure that even the smallest participation would result in the change of the occupation agencies.

The third team of sincere, non-political, non-aligned and non-inclined (to any state politics) group which observed the four phases of September-October 2002 polling in J&K belonged to Dehra Doon (India) based NGO, "Rural Litigation and Entitlement Kendra" (R.L.E.K.). This Kendra is headed by Mr. Avdesh Kaushal, who has been awarded the national honour of Padamshri for his contribution to the cause of environment and for the rights of marginalised communities. He utilised the services of devoted volunteers including lawyers, media men, students, workers of community development, technocrats, human rights activists, environmentalists, social workers and devotees of democratic values. These two dozens of young boys and girls came from various parts of India including the three regions of J&K state. Its 90-page brochure entitled "Jammu & Kashmir Elections 2002 How Free And Fair" sums up the observation of these free and energetic budding activists. Half of the brochure carries general information about J&K state gathered from various published sources of Government of India and J&K State Government; hence many mistakes have crept in. It shows 'Urdu' as spoken language in District Srinagar and Gojri as the language of District Kupwara. Kashmiri is the majority language in both these districts.

The members of "Initiatives" are more experienced and seasoned workers in various fields of human rights whereas the team members of RLEK are freshers. The likings, dislikings or particular bent of mind may be attributed to the teams of "Initiatives". They might have, during many years, since they have remained involved with this activity, developed one or the other viewpoint about the national psyche of Kashmiris and about the behaviour of institutions of Indian democracy in J&K. On the other hand, these boys and girls of RLEK as freshers, entered upon this august task with a clean mind. With this description of the background let us share the observations of these sincere youngsters.

About election management the report sums up, "The election body made every effort to 'try' and maintain impartial and satisfactory conduct. However, at times, it could not deliver the desired effect." In our assessment of the ground realities the 'efforts' of Election Commission though (this time) were bonafide but were totally eroded by the security forces in their attempt to "impose" an election. Had Mr. Lyngdoh, CEC, succeeded to contain the "insecurity" created by the security forces the Indian Election Commission would have, to a great extent, bailed out itself honorably.

As far security arrangements were concerned the report mentions that the160 additional companies and 237 existing companies of CRPF were neutral as they were outsiders. There has been no allegation about their liking or disliking of any particular candidate or party but the members of RLEK have not bothered to discuss in this report about the 'force' used by forces in imposing these Elections. They confined their probe only to district Rajouri in Jammu division which in February 2002, had witnessed biased attitude of the forces when they were called to maintain law and order. We have already discussed that the state forces then openly worked for National Conference candidate in that parliamentary bye-election whereas the CRPF cadres forced people to vote for BJP. Such a strain was absent this time. Particularly in the districts of Poonch and Rajouri the militants imposed boycott and the CRPF imposed elections. Neither the non-participation nor the participation in these two areas can be deemed, treated or even considered as voluntary exercise.

This report has confined the allegations leveled against the impartiality of poll staff only to Handwara constituency where the Independent candidate Mohud Din Sofi, Forest Minister in the ruling coalition, had declared his withdrawal from elections on 15th September 2002, twenty-four hours before the poll, unless 43 "proved partisan" poll staffers were not changed. In this constituency allegations leveled created some positive result but in Charar-i-sharief where the ex-Finance Minister, Mr. A. R. Rather, had got his own relatives or of his local ministerial colleague, Mr. Abdul Qayoom, appointed as polling officers and presiding officers who consolidated the tradition of fraud were not changed. Thus the tradition established in 1957 bye-election was consolidated openly.

About the postal ballots this report quotes the statement of Mehbooba Mufti, Vice President of the present ruling PDP, saying "this is another trick of the ruling party to sabotage the process." We have discussed earlier as how this device has been adopted with the connivance of the commission. Campaigning is the *sine quo non* for fair and free elections. The report of RLEK has gone a bit lengthy in the superficial nature of this aspect. If I delve deeper it will add to the volume. Hence I hold that in a war-torn state ruled under draconian laws and subjected to the intrigues of various overground and underground agencies financed by India and Pakistan a fair campaigning in the state is an impossibility. It is relevant here to state that this region, besides being subjected to the ordinary preventive and 'criminal' legislation is being grinded under very dangerous pieces of legislation which include: Enemy Agents Ordinance, Armed Forces Special Powers Act 1958, J&K Prevention of Terrorism Act 2002, J&K Public Safety Act 1978, J&K Egress and Internal Movement Act and the J&K Prevention of Suppression of Sabotage Act. To expose the shortcomings of the ministry in office the opposition candidate has to challenge its record on human rights front that too in this state which has, so far in history, never witnessed even a brief spell of human dignity. Such exposure requires to highlight the custodial deaths, illegal confinements, acts of torture in J.I.Cs (Joint Interrogation Centers manned by Army, BSF, CRPF and J&K Police) and the acts of molestation of women. Such exposures require the references about the acts of army and paramilitary forces. Can such criticism be allowed in a locality where two army bunkers are located within every small locality? Can such references be made under the threat to be prosecuted for treason because the neo-colonist laws referred to above bring such criticism within the purview of "treason". In such background a "Tamasha" of campaigning was strictly allowed to criticise "persons" and not policies. Such "Tamasha" was discussed even by children in street. In my nearby locality in village Gopalpora I was getting my beard trimmed by a barber in his saloon that a paid group of ten boys approached their colleagues to earn hundred chips for the day by accompaning them in a bus in which they had to roam around the constituency.

"No we did not enjoy it yesterday, though we were entertained at lunch, provided with tea and biscuits twice and given 150 chips in the evening."

Candidates hired buses, matadors, taxis and other small and heavy vehicles, even the carriers of brick kiln owners, and hired services of some unemployed boys, carried them in those vehicles fitted with loud speakers playing tape recordings of Indian film songs. The only sign indicating the allegiance of the propaganda vehicle was the banner of the candidate and party. The campaigning throughout India is similar but there is a considerable difference. In India/ Pakistan such hired political labourers at least, through slogans and at street addresses, explain shortcomings or achievements of the party in power or ruling party. Though militants did not impose boycott this time as in 1999, yet we witnessed violent attacks upon election parties, candidates or upon their sympathisers. In Noorabad constituency, four attacks were made on N.C candidate Sakina Yatoo. Aashya Nishat and Mushtaq Lone, the NC candidates from Wachi and Lolab respectively were gunned down. Such attacks though attributed to militants can be explained in the light of later similar attack made on the elected PDP member of Pampore constituency which has been prima facie proved to be the result of internal feud. Hence in our view "Mujahideen" had left the game to the conscience of the people as they had observed during 1999 Parliamentary elections that the masses are committed to boycott. Similarly this time APHC leadership also left the matter to the people or the left-over leadership felt scared as the veteran fighters like Syed Ali Geelani, Mohd. Yasin Malik, Haji Ghulam Nabi Sumji, Qazi Abdul Ahad, Sheikh Aziz, Musrat Alam, Dr. G.M. Habbi and others were thrown behind bars. Thus the campaign for "Boycott" was terrorised, which as a reaction, consolidated the mass support to abstain from voting.

Another facet of these elections observed by all the observing agencies including media was the "Children participation". It is the juvenile psyche that a child enjoys anything new. Unmindful of the burden of the book load the child has to carry on his delicate and feeble shoulders, he feels enthusiastically allured with a new jeanbag. Similarly rows of children were caught by media camera waiting to cast votes by proxy almost in every segment. This itself speaks volumes about the general apathy of masses. It is unfortunate that people in India or Pakistan or even in Washington and London see the happenings through prejudiced lenses of their spectacles. Indian chauvinistic psyche is determined to believe and convince others that non-participation of elections in J&K is an act of sabotage of democracy masterminded by Pakistan and implemented by militants. Pakistan on the other hand forgets that the J&K people too have, like any other community in the world, to act sometimes (even against their conscience) to eliminate an immediate danger in situation. It has to overthrow some most unwarranted elements and in special circumstances in special pockets to demonstrate its existence. But unmindful of such realities Pakistan and its allies in J&K attribute even genuine participation, at places, as a result of invisible coercion. Both these views are jaundiced.

To shorten these discussions a mention is relevant that the official figures of Election Commission show that only 822567 voters out of 2809500 have exercised their right to vote. Only 29% have participated in Kashmir division which include the "children" and other proxy voters, votes cast through intimidation and fraud. Our personal assessment makes it clear that in the city of Srinagar including posh areas of Bagati Barzula, Rawalpora, Hyderpora, Peerbagh, Chanapora, Natipora, and Rambagh in district Budgam and town of Charar-i-sharief the boycott was 93 percent successful. On the other hand in rural areas there was a partial participation. In remote areas the "terrorised" population had no alternative but to oblige the CRPF, BSF and regular armed forces. These villagers had no option but to be docile and silent. However, at certain places participation was voluntary. Closer to my house, in village Gopalpora, is situated a big contingent of CRPF in "Solar House" - a hired private building. They did not overawe anyone to cast their vote or get their fingers marked. Probably they saw from morning a normal number of locals ready to cast votes. This was the situation even at Kralapora and even in the small village of Mauchawa which was the fortress of militancy during nineties and has three conspicuous martyrs cemeteries. Similarly at Tehsil headquarter of Chadora a good number of people waited to exercise the right of the vote without any threat hurled either from militants present around or from Rashtrya Rifles posted in the locality. This 'voluntary' participation in certain parts was transparent but strictly in rural areas. In the same Chadora constituency the urban area within Srinagar Municipal limits demonstrated a complete boycott. In Nowgam, where Mufti M. Syed resides, the Team-3 of the 'Initiatives' found that upto 9.15 am, only 26 votes out of 1425 were polled. At 3.15 pm when my deputed person visited the booth the number had swelled to 103. Here in Chadora the ruling party sitting MLA had become a political malignancy which needed to be removed by painful surgery.

In Budgam, the rural area situated on Indira Gandhi Road, observed a civil curfew. Only Shias of Budgam, Ichgam, Palar villages participated and Sunnis remained confined to their homes. It should not be considered that Shias are pro-elections. They have been more vocal against India since October 1947, but the present election was trial of strength between the fans of divided Agha family of Budgam. The uncle of child candidate Roohula, Syed Agha Hussain, is the vice-president of APHC. He secretly threw his weight in favour of his nephew.

This brings us to conclude that the valley consciously boycotted not only for their commitment to Pakistan but for many more reasons. The valley people are aware of the sandwiched character of institutions created by the constitutional scheme. They have found that the "Lion of Kashmir" was made the "fox" of Kashmir by these contradictions inherent in this scheme. In Jammu, Hindu reaction consolidated a counter strain. Irrespective of their faith in the functioning of democracy in J&K, the Hindu sentiment is guided by the strains to demonstrate that J&K is an integral part of Indian geography. These strains have made a section of youth intolerant. There can be no denial of the fact that overall Jammu has proved its inherent tolerance but exceptions are also visible. It is therefore that NGO observers could not get even a small group of locals to align with them. It should not be construed that the successors of Ved Bhasin, Balraj Puri, Om Saraf, Krishen Dev Sethi and others have all joined the forces of reaction. No, they are more committed to the inherited values but they have been over-awed by the hooliganism of Shiv Sena, Yuva Janta Morcha, Bajrang Dal, VHP and others. These intolerant sections have given birth to similar tendencies among Jammu Muslims, Gojars, Kashmiris and even among Sikhs. So to show their existence they have demonstrated their existence irrespective of their faith in the system.

The strains on Ladakh region have already been discussed.

Lastly a very important factor which leaves an impact of many inferences on the fairness in polls and faith in the process is the Judicial review of disputed results. The J&K Representation of Peoples Act like the similar law of India provides forum to challenge such disputes. The forum created under such law does not act *suo moto* but chariot of justice is to be set in motion by the aggrieved. In these elections almost every result is subjected to various and serious flaws which are prima facie sufficient to warrant quashing of such declared results.

The first case I take is of Budgam where Election Commission has bungled and played with intricacies of procedural ambiguities. It has not only connived but encouraged the demolition of faith in its fair play. The ruling party NC fielded one minor scion of Budgam Shia cleric (Agha) family. The opposition proved that the said ruling candidate Roohula had passed Matriculation examination from Tyndal Biscoe School Srinagar in 1999 at the age of 16 years under Roll No. 808211. It was established that he was born in 1983 and he was only plus 18 years of age in 2002, hence, unqualified to become a Legislator under Law. The returning officer rejected this authentic record and declared him major on the fake record. His classmates and co-players are yet to get themselves enrolled as voters but he has been made a legislator. Election Commission did not disturb the finding of the "fact" recorded by RO. None of the aggrieved has opted for petition nor even his main rival Agha Mehmood, now a leader of ruling PDP. Why?

In the same district, in Charar-i-sharief constituency PDP defeated candidate Mr. Lone has unearthed the frauds played by A.R. Rather particulary in Kandi areas. Such facts could greatly undo the result. Mr. Lone is in the high command of PDP. Why didn't he opt for a petition?

In Srinagar city all the constituencies witnessed a total boycott with fake and proxy polling of four to seven percent. Mr. Tariq Kara, general secretary of PDP and the defeated candidate, could easily within two or three hearings before Tribunal, get undone the thin margin with which his rival has won. Similar is the case of Sonawar, Habbakadal, Idgah and Khanyar constituencies but why Tariq Kara, Mrs. Wakhloo (Cong-I), Mr. Vaishnavi (secretary PDP) and Abdul Gani Khan (Cong-I) did not opt for legal remedy? In Jammu division many returned candidates of N.C., Cong-I and BJP sufferred total infirmities but why the aggrieved parties compelled their cadres not to agitate against the electoral frauds. In Bandipora two ex-militants had a straight fight which was confined to their ex-militant cadres as people abstained. But Javed Shah of NC. did not choose to highlight judicially the excess committed by his rival militant. In Sonawari in the 1996 election Mr. M.A. Lone of N.C. highlighted before media the bungling with which Kuka Parray (renegade politician) trounced him but the former did not challenge the result. This book has earlier discussed such inferences derived therefrom. In this election with those very methods Mr. M.A. Lone paid Kuka Parray in the same coin. Mr. Parray exposed that game but has not sought legal remedy. Why?

It is clear that almost all results of the present elections had sufficient reasons for action but the persons who were affected did not utilise them. There are three reasons for this voluntary deprivation. Firstly, there is no hope and faith in the lengthy system of election petitions nor the judicial system has, overall, come to the expectations. Secondly, the parties which have snatched some score for them in this battle have no faith in themselves to get similar number of legislators in bye-elections after quashing of the results of present election. They have clear understanding that it was not people's will which gave to each party some legislators but was a mere chance created by the boycott. Third is the most important factor which has deterred the defeated candidates and their parties to go to Tribunals because they were all fielded by one agency i.e. Government of India. The purpose of their fight with each other in electoral battle was a mock show to undo the impact created by boycott of the people. The forces behind these parties, from Cong-I, PDP, N.C., BJP, N.P.P, Marxists to independents, would never allow their agents in court cases where they would have to expose rampant bungling, rigging, malpractices, proxy votes and other irregularities.

The exhaustive study of ISS in detail corroborates our own study, the studies of Coalition and Initiatives, the observations of C.D.S.D and L.R.E.K discussed above. However, this study points out the coercion elements to which the citizens of this unfortunate region have been subjected. ".....Security forces only brought the voters to the booth and did not tell them whom to vote...."(Mr. Manoranjan Mohanty, one of the distinguished observers from this Institute). We have sufficiently emphasised in this chapter that unlike 1996 the forces of occupying country were not interested to impose any party or group of parties but to impose an election. This exhaustive report with details corroborate our contention. Mr. Ajit Bhattacharjee and Manika Chopra, the other dedicated fellows of this Institute, have "heard many complaints about co-ercion by security forces but we did not personally witness any". These distinguished persons ought to have involved themselves widely and should have shared the experiences of the observers of Team-3 from Initiatives.

This report also describes the threats hurled by militants. It does not, with fairness, state whether they could attribute all such awe and threats to the ranks of militants or whether that was the handiwork of party politics or the result of both these factors particular to the situation in Kashmir

At page 18 this report dabbles with utter ambiguities and makes misleading surmises to probe into this mandate of compulsion. It has tried to find the strain on this "choice" whether it was for India or Pakistan. All the study groups and observers are unanimous that the people of J&K are sandwiched in between the coercion from security forces and terrorists. Hence to derive such far-reaching conclusions from such forced exercise is not closer to logic. Such an activity can be compared with a would be mother on who has conceived of collective rape and is only interested to be relieved of the burden of foetus, least disturbed whether it is male or female.

The democrats in India and in western countries, without grasping this psychology of sandwiched Kashmiri, tie him with the club of democracy and force him to assimilate with imposed systems. Hence all these agencies equate a Kashmiri voter with an Indian/Pakistani or a Swedish voter. All of them have voluntarily evolved disciplines of their governance. On the other hand, I am forced to rationalise the imposed discipline in the same manner in which M/s Bush and Blair are adamant to impose their perceptions upon the world community.

The Pakistan game is also equally ridiculous. They are conscious that it is Sheikh Abdulla and his political outfit N.C. which has landed this State in this unfortunate state of "eternal" uncertainty and exposed its people to the dangers of humiliation and annihilation. It is not only political treacheries of the Sheikh dynasty which are widely resented but the continued sacrilege with which this dynasty has usurped the religious properties of Muslims, and misuses continuously this sacred trust. Inspite of this Pakistan and its agents here in J&K persuade the people to allow this imposed dynasty to exploit this state as its family fiefdom continuously.

It is within these two ambits that the results of September-October 2002 Elections are to be studied. It has strains of utter lack of faith in the imposed democracy but it derives immediate dividends under the imposed system to demolish these feeble bridges of imposition.